DIGITAL TECHNOLOGY AND CHANGING ROLES IN MANAGERIAL AND FINANCIAL ACCOUNTING

STUDIES IN MANAGERIAL AND FINANCIAL ACCOUNTING

Series Editor: Anne M. Farrell

Recent Volumes:

Volume 1:	Setting the Standard for the New Auditors Report: An Analysis of Attempts to Influence the Auditing Standards Board
Volume 2:	The Shareholders Use of Corporate Annual Reports
Volume 3:	Applications of Fuzzy Logic and the Theory of Evidence to Accounting
Volume 4:	The Usefulness of Corporate Annual reports to Shareholders in Australia, New Zealand, and the United States: An International Comparison
Volume 5:	A Power Control Exchange Framework of Accounting Applications to Management Control Systems
Volume 6:	Throughout Modeling: Financial Information Used by Decision Makers
Volume 7:	Applications of Fuzzy Sets and the Theory of Evidence to Accounting II
Volume 8:	Corporate Governance, Accountability, and Pressures to Perform: An International Study
Volume 9:	The January Effect and Other Seasonal Anomalies: A Common Theoretical Framework
Volume 10:	Organizational Change and Development in Management Control Systems: Process Innovation for Internal Auditing and Management Accounting
Volume 11:	US Individual Federal Income Taxation: Historical, Contemporary and Prospective Policy Issues
Volume 12:	Performance Measurement and Management Control: A Compendium of Research
Volume 13:	Information Asymmetry: A Unifying Concept for Financial and Managerial Accounting Theories
Volume 14:	Performance Measurement and Management Control: Superior Organization Performance
Volume 15:	A Comparative Study of Professional Accountants' Judgements
Volume 16:	Performance Measurement and Management Control: Improving Organizations and Society
Volume 17:	Non-Financial Performance Measurement and Management Practices in Manufacturing Firms: A Comparative International Analysis
Volume 18:	Performance Measurement and Management Control: Measuring and Rewarding Performance
Volume 19:	Managerial Attitudes Toward a Stakeholder Prominence within a Southeast Asia Context
Volume 20:	Performance Measurement and Management Control: Innovative Concepts and Practices
Volume 21:	Reputation Building, Website Disclosure and the Case of Intellectual Capital
Volume 22:	Achieving Global Convergence of Financial Reporting Standards: Implications From the South Pacific Region
Volume 23:	Globalization and Contextual Factors in Accounting: The Case of Germany
Volume 24:	An Organizational Learning Approach to Process Innovations: The Extent and Scope of Diffusion and Adoption in Management Accounting Systems
Volume 25:	Performance Measurement and Management Control: Global Issues
Volume 26:	Accounting and Control for Sustainability
Volume 27:	Intellectual Capital and Public Sector Performance
Volume 28:	Performance Measurement and Management Control – Behavioral Implications and Human Actions
Volume 29:	Adoption of Anglo-American Models of Corporate Governance and Financial Reporting in China
Volume 30:	Sustainability Disclosure: State of the Art and New Directions
Volume 31:	Performance Measurement and Management Control
Volume 32:	Servitization Strategy and Managerial Control Volume
Volume 33:	Performance Measurement and Management Control: The Relevance of Performance Measurement and Management Control Research
Volume 34:	Non-financial Disclosure and Integrated Reporting: Practices and Critical Issues
Volume 35:	Perspectives on International Financial Reporting and Auditing in the Airline Industry

STUDIES IN MANAGERIAL AND FINANCIAL ACCOUNTING VOLUME 36

DIGITAL TECHNOLOGY AND CHANGING ROLES IN MANAGERIAL AND FINANCIAL ACCOUNTING: THEORETICAL KNOWLEDGE AND PRACTICAL APPLICATION

EDITED BY

ALLAM HAMDAN
Ahlia University, Bahrain

BAHAAEDDIN ALAREENI
Middle East Technical University, Turkey

AND

REEM KHAMIS
University College of Bahrain, Bahrain

emerald PUBLISHING

United Kingdom – North America – Japan
India – Malaysia – China

Emerald Publishing Limited
Emerald Publishing, Floor 5, Northspring, 21-23 Wellington Street, Leeds LS1 4DL.

First edition 2024

British Library Cataloguing in Publication Data
A catalogue record for this book is available from the British Library

ISBN: 978-1-80455-973-4 (Print)
ISBN: 978-1-80455-972-7 (Online)
ISBN: 978-1-80455-974-1 (Epub)

ISSN: 1479-3512 (Series)

Printed and bound by CPI Group (UK) Ltd, Croydon, CR0 4YY

CONTENTS

PREFACE

In today's rapidly evolving digital landscape, technology has permeated every aspect of our lives, revolutionizing the way we communicate, work, and interact with the world around us. The field of accounting is no exception to this digital transformation, as new technologies continue to reshape the roles and responsibilities of professionals in both managerial and financial accounting.

The book you hold in your hands, titled "Digital Technology and Changing Roles in Managerial and Financial Accounting," explores the profound impact of digital technology on the accounting profession. It delves into the dynamic changes occurring within the realm of accounting, shedding light on the emerging trends, challenges, and opportunities that lie ahead.

Traditionally, managerial accounting focused on internal decision-making processes, while financial accounting centered on reporting financial information to external stakeholders. However, with the advent of digital technology, the boundaries between these two branches have become increasingly blurred. Organizations now have access to vast amounts of data, enabling them to make more informed decisions, optimize performance, and drive strategic initiatives.

This book serves as a comprehensive guide for professionals, academics, and students seeking to understand how digital technology is reshaping the roles of managers and accountants. Through a multidimensional approach, we explore the myriad ways in which technology is transforming accounting practices, including automation, artificial intelligence, blockchain, cloud computing, data analytics, and more.

Each chapter provides a deep dive into specific aspects of digital technology and its impact on managerial and financial accounting. We examine case studies, real-world examples, and empirical research to illustrate the practical implications of these technological advancements. Additionally, we discuss the challenges and risks associated with the integration of digital technology, such as data security, privacy concerns, and ethical considerations.

We hope that this book inspires readers to embrace the opportunities brought about by digital technology and equips them with the knowledge and insights needed to navigate the evolving landscape of managerial and financial accounting. Our aim is to foster a deeper understanding of the profound changes occurring in the accounting profession and to empower individuals to thrive in this digital era.

We would like to express our gratitude to the contributors who have shared their expertise and knowledge, making this book a comprehensive and valuable resource. We also extend our thanks to the readers for their interest in this important subject matter.

Prof. Allam Hamdan
Dean, Full Professor of Accounting, College of Business and Finance, Ahlia University, Manama, Bahrain
Dr. Bahaaeddin Alareeni
Assistant Professor of Accounting, Middle East Technical University, Turkey
Dr. Reem Khamis
Assistant Professor of Finance, University College of Bahrain, Manama, Bahrain

ACKNOWLEDGMENTS

We would like to express our sincere gratitude to Prof. Abdulla Y. Al Hawaj, the Founding President and the Chair of the Board of Trustees of Ahlia University, Bahrain for his unwavering support and dedication to the advancement of scientific research. His invaluable guidance and expertise have been instrumental in the success of our research efforts. We would like to express our special thanks to the book series editor, Dr. Anne M. Farrell, for her encouragement, guidance, and support throughout the entire process. Also, we would like to thank all the authors who contributed their time, knowledge, and expertise to make this book a reality. Lastly. I would like to thank the referee of our book for their insightful comments and constructive feedback, which have helped us to improve the quality of the book.

PART I

TECH-MANAGERIAL, FINTECH AND FINANCIAL INNOVATION

CHAPTER 1

UTILIZING BIG DATA ANALYTICS LIFECYCLE FOR EARLY DETECTION OF SUSPICIOUS FINANCIAL OPERATIONS: A PROPOSED MODEL FOR MONEY LAUNDERING DETECTION

Mohammed Elastal[a], Mohammad H Allaymoun[b] and Tasnim Khaled Elbastawisy[c]

[a]*Mass Communication and Public Relations, College of Communication and Media Technologies, Gulf University, Sanad, Kingdom of Bahrain*
[b]*Administrative Science Department, College of Administrative and Financial Science, Gulf University, Sanad, Kingdom of Bahrain*
[c]*Accounting & Financial Science, College of Administrative and Financial Science, Gulf University, Sanad, Kingdom of Bahrain*

ABSTRACT

This chapter proposes a model for discovering suspicious financial operations such as money laundering. To achieve this, the authors reviewed research papers on money laundering and financial institutions' cases and problems, especially those related to financial transfers. They also collected primary data through face-to-face semi-structured interviews with financial companies' owners and experts in financial transfers to identify hypotheses that help discover suspicious transfers. The chapter discusses the six big data analysis cycle phases from problem discovery to model deployment to identify suspicious transfers.

Digital Technology and Changing Roles in Managerial and Financial Accounting: Theoretical Knowledge and Practical Application
Studies in Managerial and Financial Accounting, Volume 36, 3–14

ISSN: 1479-3512/doi:10.1108/S1479-351220240000036001

The chapter uses hypothetical data and models to discuss the results and focuses on exchange companies willing to analyze financial operations. The chapter proposes tools that exchange companies can use to monitor and prevent suspicious transfers including data visualization and machine learning algorithms.

Keywords: Big data; big data analysis lifecycle; money laundering; financial transactions; decision making; fraud

1. INTRODUCTION

The focus on information technology has significantly increased in the last few years to the extent that it has become one of the essential features of the modern era. Parallel with this increase, the volume of data has increased steadily (Mathew, Brintha, & Jappes, 2023). As a result, the term big data has emerged, and the necessity for analytical tools to extract knowledge quickly and accurately has arisen – such knowledge critical to developing information and communication systems. Analyzing, storing, processing, and distributing big data (big in volume and complex in terms of structure) require non-traditional tools (Patra & Roy, 2023).

One of the essential features of the non-traditional tools used in analyzing big data is its ability to quickly analyze enormous volumes of data collected from different sources such as websites, sensors, and social networks (Parashar, Sharma, Rana, & Balaji, 2023). Analyzing such data allows for creating correlations between and among variables to help decision makers identify opportunities, threats, and challenges, including predicting the commercial trends of companies, combating crime in the security field, and many others (Wang, Gunasekaran, Ngai, & Papadopoulos, 2016). Such predictions make decision makers better understand their companies' situations and thus make the decision that achieves their companies' desired goals (Feldman & Ingram, 2009).

Big data analysis helps financial institutions mitigate (if it does not prevent) operational risks and combat suspicious transactions and fraud (Tabesh, Mousavidin, & Hasani, 2019). Moreover, big data analysis helps financial institutions observe their customers' behavior and thus develop informed strategies to improve their service and gain much profit. Banks, for example, make appropriate decisions quickly and accurately with the help of big data analysis (Ravi & Kamaruddin, 2017).

Billions of dollars move through global markets every day. With the help of big data analytical tools, financial institutions can monitor data quickly and accurately, make predictions, detect patterns, and develop predictive strategies (Darvazeh, Vanani, & Musolu, 2020). Unlike traditional tools that cannot analyze unstructured data, non-traditional means can process unstructured data (convert it into readable format) and then store and interpret it to help financial institutions identify opportunities, assess risks and threats, and thus make informed decisions such as improving the service or preventing fraud (Agrawal et al., 2011). Worth mentioning here that data analysis relies mainly on creating default patterns for suspicious transactions and applying them to financial transactions. This enables banks to freeze card transactions and immediately notify customers of security threats. This also allows banks to identify suspicious transactions and fraud signs by analyzing massive user behavior data using machine learning (Leo, Sharma, & Maddulety, 2019).

Nowadays, there are many challenges facing electronic financial transactions, including the ease of money transfer and the lack of tools and techniques that help detect suspicious transactions and reduce financial crimes such as money laundering and fraud (Nicholls, Kuppa, & Le-Khac, 2021).

Even though information technology, which has become a feature of this era, has made conducting financial operations so easy, there is a darker side to using such technology, namely in money laundering. Vienna's 1988 Convention describes money laundering as a punishable crime, defining it in Article 3.1 as the concealment of the sources of illegally gained money. The said convention criminalizes anyone who does so or helps another escape legal consequences (Booth, Farrell, Bastable, & Yeo, 2011).

Employing the life cycle of big data analysis, this chapter proposes a methodological framework for discovering suspicious financial transfers such as money laundering. The proposed framework seeks to achieve that end by establishing several hypotheses and applying them to suspicious financial operations. All the stages of the life cycle of big data analysis will be displayed and discussed in the coming pages.

This chapter explores the big data analytics lifecycle and its impact on organizations. The chapter includes an introduction that explains the importance of understanding the lifecycle and a literature review that examines existing research on the topic. Section 3 outlines the research methodology, while the Section 4 describes each lifecycle stage and examines its role in achieving organizational goals. The section also identifies challenges and best practices related to implementing the lifecycle. The chapter concludes with a summary of key findings and implications for practice and future research.

2. LITERATURE REVIEW

Big data can be defined as huge (in volume) or complex data to be quickly analyzed and processed by non-traditional relational data-processing application software – data that traditional methods cannot analyze and process (Casado & Younas, 2015). Big data's essential characteristics include volume, velocity, and variety; its forms include structured, semi-structured, and unstructured data; its sources are social media, portable devices, and the Internet of things (IoT) (Mohammed, Humbe, & Chowhan, 2016). Organizations use big data analytics in machine learning projects, predictive modeling, and other advanced analytics applications. Many organizations today use big data analytics to improve operations and competitive advantages, make appropriate decisions, provide better customer service, customize marketing campaigns, increase profits, and reduce costs (Stephenson, 2018).

The benefits of big data analytics include making appropriate decisions fast. Companies can access different data sources to gain insights and act accordingly, discover patterns that help them determine their performance, and frame patterns for suspicious operations so they can identify potential risks and neutralize them (Balachandran & Prasad, 2017).

The data analytics lifecycles are usually designed to solve the problems of organizations that use big data. The big data analytics lifecycle is a six-stage methodology meant to reach practical results with the help of which analysts set priorities, define requirements, identify needs, and give a general perception of the expected outcomes. This step-by-step methodology helps companies redefine their purposes and organize activities and tasks, such as obtaining, processing, and analyzing data. The big data analytics lifecycle is a circular process that consists of investigating the problem, developing appropriate hypotheses to solve the problem, planning a model, building the model, communicating the results, and finally operationalizing the results (Allaymoun, Khaled, Saleh, & Merza, 2022).

Emphasizing the importance of employing the data analytics lifecycle, Allaymoun (2022) employed the six-stage methodology to monitor the performance of a group of Islamic banks in 2019 and 2020 (Allaymoun, Qaradh, Salman, & Hasan, 2023). In addition, the author used this methodology to determine the extent to which Covid-19 affected the banking sector. For his study, Allaymoun used Google Data Studio (GDS) to analyze the data, considering the problem framed and the hypotheses developed in the discovery phase.

Allaymoun, Al Saad, Majed, and Hashem (2023) also used the data analytics lifecycle to help the virtual Mega Start Company explore the problems that cannot be discovered by employing traditional methods and make the right decision to solve those problems. Highlighting the importance of applying all stages, the author indicated that dealing with such problems requires building effective patterns commensurate with the situation and the hypotheses developed. In another paper, Allaymoun et al. (2023) clarified, employing graphics generated by GDS, that the data analytics lifecycle benefits companies as it helps them build predictive models for improving customer services, tracking sales operations, exploring risks, and predicting the future (Allaymoun et al., 2022).

3. RESEARCH METHODOLOGY

Besides identifying the appropriate procedures for developing a preliminary model for the big data analytics lifecycle stages, several research papers on money laundering were reviewed and meta-analyzed to understand better how to apply the big data analytics lifecycle effectively. The articles reviewed for this study included papers on the modern tools, mechanisms, and techniques organizations employ to discover and limit money laundering. In addition, financial institutions' cases and problems were reviewed and analyzed, especially those related to financial transfers.

For this study, primary data was also collected through face-to-face semi-structured interviews with financial companies' owners and experts in financial transfers – the semi-structured interviews allow researchers to ask questions whenever a question comes to mind. The interviews helped the authors identify the hypotheses that help discover suspicious transfers. The point is to review the big data analytics lifecycle stages to discover suspicious transfers.

4. BIG DATA ANALYTICS LIFECYCLE

In this part, the big data analysis cycle phases will be explained. Fig. 1.1 shows the six phases, and the explanation later shows how a clear methodology capable of detecting money laundering was reached.

It is worth mentioning here that the paper used hypothetical data and models to discuss the results and applied them to exchange companies to analyze financial operations and thus discover suspicious transactions.

4.1. Phase 1: Discovery

The first phase of the big data analytics lifecycle is discovering the problem that exchange company's face. The company's data science team will identify and explore the problem, create context and knowledge, and identify the projects required and available data sources during this phase. Additionally, the team develops hypotheses that can be tested with the data later.

4.1.1. Learning the Business Domain

It is crucial to comprehend the problem's domain. When exchanging money, exchange companies must discover suspicious operations, money laundering, and fraud to enhance financial procedures, implement the law, and monitor

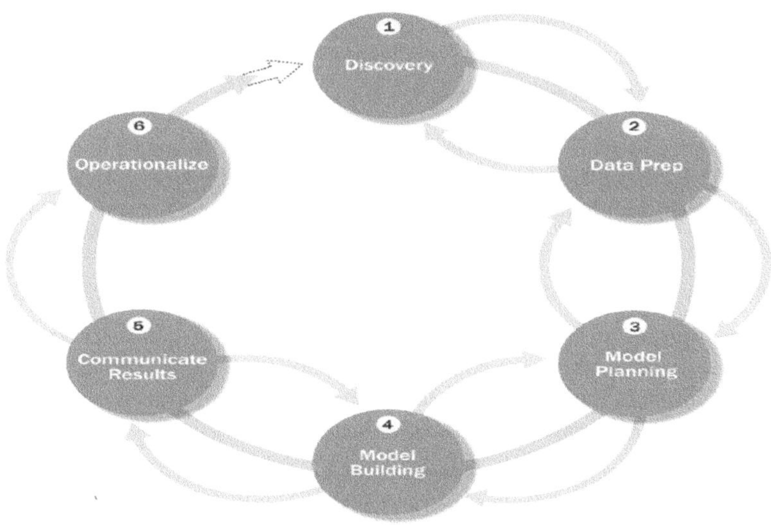

Fig. 1.1. Overview of Data Analytics Lifecycle (Dietrich, Heller, & Yang, 2015).

operations to stop suspicious activities. This issue needs to be recognized because of its seriousness and pervasive effects. It may have a regional and local impact on enterprises, economies, and society. Money laundering has a variety of detrimental repercussions on the economy. Financial institutions that unintentionally participate in money laundering are exposed to the danger of seeing sudden changes in their assets and liabilities. The public authority is alerted by the news of money laundering at certain banking institutions. In this scenario, there will be more pressure on these institutions' audits, which will harm the institution's reputation.

4.1.2. Resources

The exchange company must ensure the availability of resources such as technology, tools, systems, data, and people. Additionally, there must be proof of every previous exchange transaction from the preceding year to proceed to the next stage. The team can advance to the following level if these characteristics are available. The following specifics must be included in transactions:

1. Information about the customer, including name, ID card or passport number, birthdate, address, phone number, and bank account number.
2. Information on suspicious financial transactions.
3. The purpose of the exchange or transfer.

4.1.3. Framing the Problem

A suspicious transaction may involve several elements that individually may not appear noteworthy but, when taken together, raise concerns that the transaction may be connected to the conduct of a serious crime such as money laundering, terrorism financing, or both.

Transactions must be assessed in light of what is reasonable and consistent with the norms of a specific exchange company line. The determination of whether there is a ground for suspicion must be made after properly evaluating all pertinent information, including knowledge of the customer's line of work, whether the transactions are consistent with the accepted industry standards, and financial background, history, and behavior.

4.1.4. Developing Initial Hypotheses

Creating a group of IHs is one of the crucial elements of the discovery phase. After investigating the issue under investigation, it was discovered that the exchange company had many suspicious transactions. The parameters that would be used to spot questionable transfers are listed below:

IH1: Customers receiving payments from different addresses or sources (Dietrich et al., 2015).

IH2: Individuals with debits or credits in excess of BD 50,000 over 24 hours at any location (Dietrich et al., 2015).

4.2. Phase 2: Data Preparation

Data preparation, which involves gathering, processing, and purifying data before modeling, is the second stage of the data analytics lifecycle. The team must now provide a reliable environment to investigate data outside the production environment. The team must be introduced to big data and projects to start working with the IT and accounting departments and create an analytical sandbox. The team must extract, transform, and upload the data to ETLT to be transferred to the sandbox. Access to clean data is made more accessible with this method. The team should additionally have access to all kinds of data. To develop an analytics sandbox, this step necessitates tight coordination with the IT and accounting departments.

The team will be able to evaluate the quality of the accessible data through the earlier phases. The team's ability to complete the following stages of the lifecycle process will depend on the accuracy of the information available. In addition, the team must fix any data issues to accomplish its objectives. The exchange company must also consult a data scientist to adapt the data, clean the data, standardize the data sets, and carry out the transformation.

4.3. Phase 3: Model Planning

The exchange company will now offer tools to spot suspicious transactions and money laundering. The theories will be assessed using the resources available to determine whether the clients are involved in money laundering or questionable transactions. At this point, team members will essentially evaluate and examine each client's transactions to see if any of them meet the premise – the case in which they will be flagged as suspicious transactions. Each transaction must contain information about the customer, a justified reason for the transfer, and an explanation of why the transaction seems suspicious.

IH1: Customers receiving payments from many sources.

Table 1.1 shows some transactions of a customer who received payments from different addresses in a short period. The exchange company must collect information about the customers who receive payments from different sources (different addresses) because that might lead to fraud or money laundering.

IH2: Individuals with debits or credits in excess of BD 50,000 over 24 hours at any location.

Table 1.1. Transactions of a Customer.

Date	ID	Bank Account	Amount	Address
10/09	85012xxxx	BBK5435xxxxx	↓ BHD 1,000	Riffa 912
13/10	85012xxxx	BBK5435xxxxx	↓ BHD 2,500	Muharraq 214
13/10	85012xxxx	BBK5435xxxxx	↓ BHD 1,590	Isa Town 318
13/10	85012xxxx	BBK5435xxxxx	↓ BHD 2,950	Hamad Town 492
14/10	85012xxxx	BBK5435xxxxx	↓ BHD 1,620	Sanad 384

Table 1.2. Some Suspicious Transactions of a Customer.

Date	ID	Bank Account	Amount	Address
27/09	94920xxxx	ABC2376xxxxx	↑ BHD 52,000	Riffa 912
11/10	85012xxxx	BBK5825xxxxx	↓ BHD 64,000	Muharraq 453
15/10	85012xxxx	BBK5575xxxxx	↓ BHD 59,000	Zinj 983
20/10	85012xxxx	BBK5435xxxxx	↓ BHD 70,462	Hamad Town 782
23/10	63352xxxx	KFH5392xxxxx	↑ BHD 61,000	Saar 324

Table 1.2 shows some suspicious transactions of customers with debts and credits of more than BHD 50,000 over 24 hours at any location. Therefore, the exchange company has to search behind the customers who receive or transfer payments over BHD 50,000 as it is a suspicious transaction that might lead to fraud or money laundering.

4.4. Phase 4: Model Building

In the fourth step, the team employed various analytical techniques. This included the data scientist's work, which improved the company's financial operation, law enforcement, and process control, which aimed to reduce the number of suspicious transactions. Additionally, Fig. 1.2 shows the difference in the results of suspicious operations before and after using the big data analysis life cycle on money transfers. It demonstrates how the number of suspicious transactions declined after the investigation.

4.5. Phase 5: Communicate Result

The team devised several methods in the fifth stage to derive meaning from the study and pinpoint the most significant and pertinent findings. It has been determined that this project successfully identified dubious transactions and clients engaged in money laundering. The team must now compare the parameters to the objectives based on the activities of the earlier stages. This phase is carried out in collaboration with several parties, including stakeholders. The team will also need to decide how successful the outcomes will be. The group must also evaluate the analysis' primary results and business value and describe the findings to key stakeholders.

The project has produced several results, including the capacity to spot suspicious activities by identifying clients who receive payments from several sources or addresses as well as people with debts or credits totaling more than BHD 50,000 over 24 hours. The team will be able to summarize significant findings from the project and document initial findings by the end of this phase. Additionally, the team should get input from other parties to assess its performance against the set objectives. Results from the big data analytics lifecycle are disseminated internally through conferences and presentations and publicized via social media and blogs for awareness.

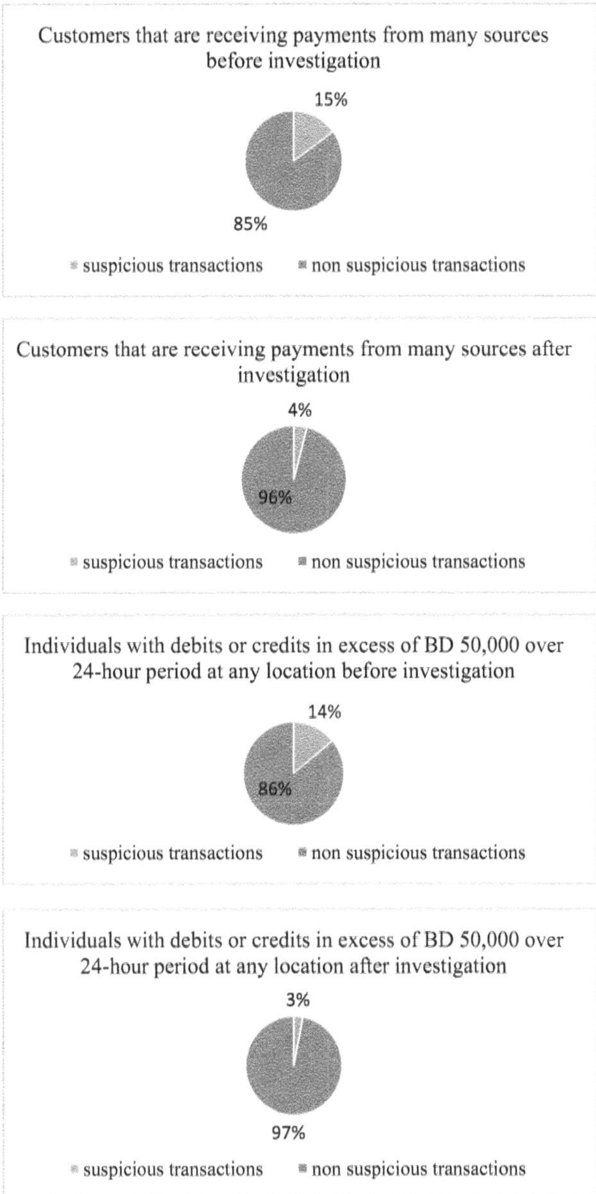

Fig. 1.2. Compares Suspicious Transactions and Non-suspicious Transactions.

4.6. Phase 6: Operationalize

The final phase of the cycle, called operationalize, pertains to reaching conclusions by producing a thorough report highlighting the preliminary findings, coding, briefings, and presenting results to stakeholders. The data is now observed the same way in the sandbox and can be compared to the intended targets. The team can return to any stage and change the input if the outcome deviates from the previous intent – this will result in new outputs.

In the case of the exchange company, the team will be able to determine the advantages of their project from a bigger picture and publish the work in a controlled manner. The analytics team at this stage approaches deploying the new analytics methods or models for the first time in a production environment. It is essential to mention here that deploying the analytics methods on a small-scale rather than a wide-scale basis reduces the risk and allows the team to manage it effectively.

It is also essential that an adequate system (to prevent money laundering) should identify suspicious transactions based on the customer's history, indicating whether the customer was a political person, whether there had been an unusual change in the customer's account name, or whether s/he had an account in Frontier buildings. This was discovered after implementing the big data analytics lifecycle. The compliance officer must thoroughly examine the customer's data after a warning was given to prove suspicion of money laundering. Documents, procedures, and data will be compared to the data in the system as part of the analysis. The information gathered throughout the know-your-customers procedure can be used.

5. CONCLUSION AND FUTURE WORK

The primary purpose of this chapter is to explain how to employ big data analytics lifecycle in applying laws, monitoring financial operations, and reducing financial crimes. In other words, this chapter utilized the big data analytics lifecycle methodology to propose a model, based on several hypotheses obtained from literature, for discovering suspicious financial operations such as money laundering at an early stage. The big data analytics lifecycle is a circular process that consists of the following steps: discovery, data preparation, model planning, model building, communicating results, and operationalization. The proposed model was built on these two hypotheses: (a) to identify customers who receive payments from different sources or addresses; and (b) to identify customers who receive more than 50,000 BD over 24 hours.

Worthy of mentioning here that, besides the graphical and analytical results this chapter provides for detecting suspicious operations, it paves the way for building a more comprehensive model in the future employing a more considerable number of hypotheses. This complete model is expected to provide financial institutions with an integrated solution to help decision makers discover and address suspicious operations promptly and early.

REFERENCES

Agrawal, D., Bernstein, P., Bertino, E., Davidson, S., Dayal, U., Franklin, M., … Widom, J. (2011). *Challenges and opportunities with big data 2011-1*. West Lafayette, IN: Purdue University.

Allaymoun, M. H., Al Saad, L. H., Majed, Z. M., & Hashem, S. M. A. (2023). Big data analysis and data visualization to facilitate decision-making-mega start case study. In *International conference on business and technology* (pp. 370–379). Cham: Springer.

Allaymoun, M. H., Khaled, M., Saleh, F., & Merza, F. (2022, April). Data visualization and statistical graphics in big data analysis by Google Data studio–sales case study. In *2022 IEEE technology and engineering management conference (TEMSCON EUROPE)* (pp. 228–234). Piscataway, NJ: IEEE. https://doi.org/10.1109/TEMSCONEUROPE54743.2022.9801964

Allaymoun, M. H., Qaradh, S., Salman, M., & Hasan, M. (2023). Big data analysis and data visualization to help make a decision – Islamic banks case study. In *International conference on business and technology* (pp. 54–63). Cham: Springer.

Balachandran, B. M., & Prasad, S. (2017). Challenges and benefits of deploying big data analytics in the cloud for business intelligence. *Procedia Computer Science*, *112*, 1112–1122.

Booth, R., & Farral, Q. C. S., Bastable, G., & Yeo, N. (2011). *Money laundering law and regulation: a practical guide*. Oxford: Oxford University Press.

Casado, R., & Younas, M. (2015). Emerging trends and technologies in big data processing. *Concurrency and Computation: Practice and Experience*, *27*(8), 2078–2091.

Darvazeh, S. S., Vanani, I. R., & Musolu, F. M. (2020). Big data analytics and its applications in supply chain management. In L. R. Martínez, R. A. O. Rios & M. D. Prieto (Eds.), *New trends in the use of artificial intelligence for the Industry* 4.0 (pp. 175–200). London: IntechOpen.

Dietrich, D., Heller, B., & Yang, B. (2015). *Data science & big data analytics: Discovering, analyzing, visualizing, and presenting data*. New York, NY: Wiley.

Feldman, D. L., & Ingram, H. M. (2009). Making science useful to decision makers: Climate forecasts, water management, and knowledge networks. *Weather, Climate, and Society*, *1*(1), 9–21.

Gilmour, P. M. (2022). Reexamining the anti-money-laundering framework: A legal critique and new approach to combating money laundering. *Journal of Financial Crime*, *30*(1), 35–47.

Leo, M., Sharma, S., & Maddulety, K. (2019). Machine learning in banking risk management: A literature review. *Risks*, *7*(1), 29.

Mathew, D., Brintha, N. C., & Jappes, J. T. W. (2023). Artificial intelligence powered automation for Industry 4.0. In A. Nayyar, M. Naved, & R. Rameshwar (Eds.), *New horizons for Industry 4.0 in modern business. Contributions to environmental sciences & innovative business technology*. Cham: Springer. https://doi.org/10.1007/978-3-031-20443-2_1

Mohammed, A. F., Humbe, V. T., & Chowhan, S. S. (2016, February). A review of big data environment and its related technologies. In *2016 international conference on information communication and embedded systems (ICICES)* (pp. 1–5). Piscataway, NJ: IEEE.

Nicholls, J., Kuppa, A., & Le-Khac, N. A. (2021). *Financial cybercrime: A comprehensive survey of deep learning approaches to tackle the evolving financial crime landscape*. Piscataway, NJ: IEEE.

Parashar, B., Sharma, R., Rana, G., & Balaji, R. D. (2023). Foundation concepts for Industry 4.0. In A. Nayyar, M. Naved, & R. Rameshwar (Eds.), *New horizons for Industry 4.0 in modern business. Contributions to environmental sciences & innovative business technology*. Cham: Springer. https://doi.org/10.1007/978-3-031-20443-2_3

Patra, G., & Roy, R. K. (2023). Business sustainability and growth in journey of industry 4.0 – A case study. In A. Nayyar, M. Naved, & R. Rameshwar (Eds.), *New horizons for Industry 4.0 in modern business. Contributions to environmental sciences & innovative business technology*. Cham: Springer. https://doi.org/10.1007/978-3-031-20443-2_2

Ravi, V., & Kamaruddin, S. (2017). Big data analytics enabled smart financial services: Opportunities and challenges. In P. Reddy, A. Sureka, S. Chakravarthy & S. Bhalla (Eds.), *International conference on big data analytics* (pp. 15–39). Cham: Springer International Publishing AG. https://doi.org/10.1007/978-3-319-72413-3_2

Stephenson, D. (2018). *Big data demystified: How to use big data, data science and AI to make better business decisions and gain competitive advantage*. London: Pearson.

Tabesh, P., Mousavidin, E., & Hasani, S. (2019). Implementing big data strategies: A managerial perspective. *Business Horizons*, *62*(3), 347–358.

Wang, G., Gunasekaran, A., Ngai, E. W., & Papadopoulos, T. (2016). Big data analytics in logistics and supply chain management: Certain investigations for research and applications. *International Journal of Production Economics*, *176*, 98–110.

CHAPTER 2

THE BEHAVIORAL INTENTION OF FINTECH USAGE: APPLYING THEORY OF PLANNED BEHAVIOR IN JORDAN

Mohammad Ali Al-Afeef[a], Ayman Abdalmajeed Alsmadi[b] and Najed Alrawashdeh[c]

[a]*School of Business, Finance and Banking Department, Al-Bayt University, Mafraq, Jordan*
[b]*Al Zaytoonah University of Jordan, Amman, Jordan*
[c]*Isra University, Amman, Jordan*

ABSTRACT

The main objective of this study is to examine the impact of the Theory of Planned Behavior (TPB) on the behavioral intentions of Fintech usage. The model incorporates perceived behavioral control, attitude, and subjective norms, and the researcher has also included perceived risk and perceived trust. This study involved 192 respondents who were Jordanian citizens. An online questionnaire was used as the survey instrument for data collection. The proposed hypotheses were statistically tested using SmartPLS and SPSS software after examining the data based on initial assumptions. The outcome of the data analysis supports several published hypotheses, with all hypotheses being supported. The significant value of this research lies in its examination of the TPB in the Jordanian context, incorporating perceived

Digital Technology and Changing Roles in Managerial and Financial Accounting: Theoretical Knowledge and Practical Application
Studies in Managerial and Financial Accounting, Volume 36, 15–25

Published under exclusive licence by Emerald Publishing Limited
ISSN: 1479-3512/doi:10.1108/S1479-351220240000036002

risk and perceived trust. To the best of the authors' knowledge, no previous study has tested the TPB in the Jordanian setting by including perceived risk and trust to understand the behavioral expectations of Jordanian citizens regarding Fintech usage.

Keywords: Perceived risk; Theory of Planned Behavior; Fintech usage; perceived trust; perceived behavioral; subjective norm

1. INTRODUCTION

The prosperity of countries and ensuring their stability and growth depends on the effectiveness of their economic system, which depends mainly on the financial sector. The effectiveness of their economy is the main point on which any economy depends to increase its ability to achieve economic development by providing the necessary funding for various institutions. The financial sector is a mixture of markets and institutions which direct investable funds from parties with a surplus to those with a deficit. Latter is regarded as a mirror of any nation's economic situation, depending on the economic situation, which is impacted negatively by financial sector weakness and vice versa. However, recent developments in all sectors were reflected in the financial sector, mainly revolving around technological developments. Recent developments mean completing many financial transactions and services efficiently through simple steps on computers or mobile phones after it took time and effort to achieve them.

Modern technologies enabled the activation and spread of financial innovations in an unprecedented manner, which led to the emergence of a new term known as financial technology. FinTech, or financial innovation, is a rising field that can be portrayed as imaginative monetary items and administrations empowered by Ajzen (1985). It additionally alludes to the utilization of innovation to convey monetary arrangements. The term's starting point can be followed to the mid-1990s and alluded to the "Financial Services Technology Consortium," started by Citigroup is an undertaking to work with mechanical collaboration endeavors (Al Bataienh & Alafeef, 2018). FinTech applications have recently extended to remember advancements for monetary proficiency and instruction (Alafeef & Malkawi, 2016). The main objective of this study is to find the impact of TPB on behavioral intentions of Fintech usage. In addition, this chapter intends to answer the research question:

RQ1. What is the impact of TPB on behavioral intentions of Fintech usage?

The remainder of this chapter is organized as follows: Section 2 provides a brief overview of the research background and related literature. Section 3 develops the research, Method. Section 4 describes the results. Section 5 presents the research and discusses the findings. Section 6 discusses the findings and key research implications. Finally, Section 7 concludes the chapter with research limitations and recommendations for future research.

2. LITERATURE REVIEW

2.1. Planned Behavior (TPB) Theory

Ajzen developed the hypothesis of contemplated activity (TRA) in 1985 to make the hypothesis of arranged conduct. According to Alafeef, Singh, and Ahmad (2011) the theory was developed to defeat a restriction in the hypothesis of contemplated activity (Azjen, 1980). Subjective norm (SN), perceived behavioral control (PBC), and attitude toward the way of behaving are parts of the hypothesis of arranged conduct.

According to TPB, an individual's intention to act in a certain way is influenced by their Attitude toward behavior, PBC and subjective norms. The TPB is still being applied to various studies in various sectors to study consumer behavior, such as COVID-19 vaccination uptake, Solar PV Adoption, additionally and in predicting the adoption intention of electric vehicles to Predicting Intention of Using Fintech (Alafeef, Singh, & Ahmad, 2011; Al-Ajlouni 2021; Alghusin, Abdalmajeed Alsmadi, Alkhatib, & Mohammad Alqtish, 2020; Alsmadi, Alrawashdeh, Al-Gasaymeh, Al-Malahmeh, & Moh'd Al_hazimeh, 2023; Alsmadi et al., 2023). Various cross-cultural studies have shown that TPB can be applied to explain behavior intentions in both Western and Eastern cultures. However, some researchers adopted this TPB model to study the use of M-Banking, predictors for E-Government adoption of SANAD App services in the Jordan context (AlHadid et al., 2022), and predicting entrepreneurial intentions among postgraduate students (Alrawashdeh, Alsmadi, & Anwar, 2022). The researcher also has used other theories, such as TAM and UTAUT, in many previous articles in different contexts (Alsmadi, Aalrawashdeh, Al-Gasaymeh, Al_hazimeh, & Alhawamdeh, 2023; Bae & Chang, 2021; Barnidge & De Zúñiga, 2017; Chen & Aklikokou, 2020; Fishbein & Ajzen, 1977; Kim, Ferrin, & Rao, 2008).

2.2. Behavioral Intention

The motivational factors that affect behavior are the subject of this. The likelihood that the behavior will be carried out increases with the severity of the intention to do so. It demonstrates one's expectations of a particular machine's behavior and may be interpreted as acting (Ajzen, 1985). According to Alafeef et al. (2011), the most impressive medium of an individual's activity in the TPB is Behavioral Intention, which also reflects an individual's eagerness to carry out the actions (Fishbein, Jaccard, Davidson, Ajzen, & Loken, 1980).

2.2.1. Subjective Norms

The assumption that most individuals support or oppose the way of behaving is the subject of this. It concerns a person's beliefs about whether their peers and other important people think they should do the behavior. In addition, the social influence that energizes or beats specific conduct down is reflected in subjective norms (Hansen, Jensen, & Solgaard, 2004). Several studies (Jerene & Sharma, 2020; Lam & Hsu, 2006; Puschmann, 2017) have demonstrated that behavioral intention has been positively influenced by subjective norms (Reisinger & Mavondo, 2005; Rivis, Sheeran, & Armitage, 2009).

2.2.2. Perceived Behavioral Control

Alludes to an individual's perception of how easy or difficult it is to carry out the ideal way of behaving. An individual's view of social control changes depending upon the circumstance and the moves they initiate. Thus, an individual's view of conduct control fluctuates depending upon the circumstance. The hypothesis' progress from the hypothesis of contemplated activity to the hypothesis of arranged behavior was caused by adding this later construct (Tanveer, Zeng, Irfan, & Peng, 2021).

2.2.3. Perceived Risk

Venkatesh, Ramesh, and Massey (2003) allude to individuals' conviction that there are vulnerability and unfavorable impacts in buying an item or participating in the way of behaving, and Perceived Risk is estimated by people in a specific circumstance (Yaseen & Qirem, 2018). Using financial services always comes with high risk (Al-Salahat, 2022). Perceived Risk related to FinTech use is viewed as an essential obstruction for innovation adopters. Also, we can define Perceived Risk as "users' perception of the uncertainty and the possible negative consequences regarding the FinTech use (Patra & Roy, 2023). Perceived risks associated with FinTech applications can be classified into operational, financial, security, and privacy concerns" (Barnidge & De Zúñiga, 2017).

> Trust is the willingness of a party [trustor] to be vulnerable to the actions of another party [trustee] based on the Expectation that the other party will perform a particular action necessary to the trustor, irrespective of the ability to monitor or control that other party. Making oneself vulnerable is taking a risk. Trust is not taking a risk per se, but rather it is a willingness to take the risk. (Barnidge & De Zúñiga, 2017)

2.2.4. Perceived Trust

Trust has always been essential in influencing e-commerce in general (Puschmann, 2017; Reisinger & Mavondo, 2005). Jarvenpaa and Tractinsky argue that an absence of Trust keeps customers from participating in web-based exchanges (Fishbein et al., 1980).

2.2.5. Hypotheses

H1. Intention toward Fintech usage affects adopting Fintech usage.

H2. Subjective norms influence individual's Behavioral Intention to adopt Fintech usage.

H3. PBC influences individual's Behavioral Intention to adopt Fintech usage.

H4. Perceived risk influences individual's Behavioral Intention to adopt Fintech usage.

H5. Perceived trust influences individual's Behavioral Intention to adopt Fintech usage.

3. METHOD

This research employs an online survey and 158 respondents were involved to examine the determining factors of Jordanian consumers' behavioral desire to use FinTech. The Jordanian survey questions were measured using a 1 to 5 Likert scale going from 1 addressing emphatically differing and 5 addressing firmly concurring. The operationalization of the research parameters guided survey questions development. The first part of the questionnaire entailed collecting information about the respondent's gender, education, income, occupation, religion, age, bank account, and marital status. The respondent's interest in Fintech usage was questioned in the second section.

The second section is intended to function as a measurement instrument adapted from previous research on the TPB and its development in predicting Jordanian citizens' and general behavioral intentions. The conceptual model includes 19 questions about five constructs: Attitude, Perceived Risk, PBC, subjective norms, and perceived Trust. Using the Likert scale from 1 to 5, each item is evaluated.

For the analysis of covariance structure models, the IBM SPSS Statistics module SmartPLS (Analysis of Moment Structures) was made like structural equation modeling (SEM), confirmatory factor analysis (CFA), path analysis, and used to carry out the analysis. (Barnidge & De Ziga, 2017). It is frequently contrasted with other factual applications intended for comparison purposes. Fig. 2.1 shows the proposed hypotheses of the study and conceptual model.

3.1. Measurement

The multivariate regression technique estimates the structural and measurement models simultaneously. Indicators' reliability, construct reliability or internal consistency, and discriminant validity and convergent should be established to assess reflective constructs. To establish indicator reliability, the external loadings should be higher than 0.70. However, if the measurement model meets the internal consistency and convergent validity thresholds, loading greater than 0.5 is acceptable (Alsmadi et al., 2023). To establish Cronbach's α, internal consistency and composite reliability (CR) values should be greater than 0.7. In addition, establishing convergent validity needs a greater than 0.5 average variance extracted (AVE).

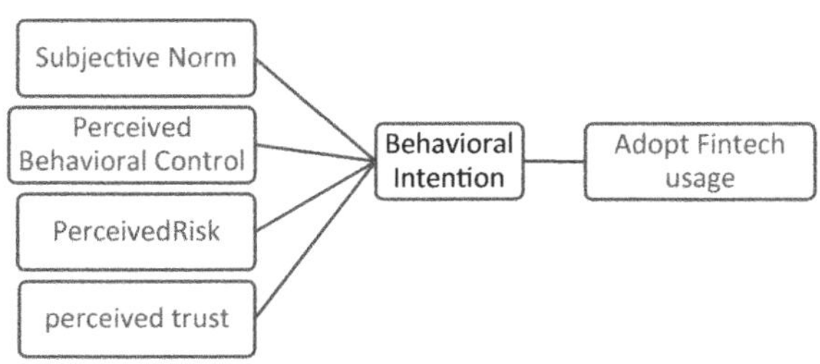

Fig. 2.1. Conceptual Model and Hypotheses.

4. RESULTS

As per Table 2.1, all speculations show united legitimacy on the grounds that Cronbach's α, CR, NFL, and AVE for every speculation are more massive than the suggested level.

Table 2.2 shows the discoveries of the AVEs square root as well as the relationship coefficient grid. The strong message on the inclining addresses the square base of AVE for every variable. Contrasted with their tantamount relationship coefficient framework with the Likert-scale build, the AVE for every variable worth has more critical than the connection coefficients. This result prompted the revelation that the scales had significant discriminant legitimacy. In addition, Fig. 2.2 shows the research model as an output of PLS.

Structural relationships between the variables as hypothesized, namely (SN, Perceived Risk, Perceived Behavioral, Perceived Trust, Behavioral Intention, and Adopt Fintech Usage). From the analysis, Table 2.3 shows that all factors affect behavioral intention positively.

After substantial external model assessments were laid out, we progressed to the second step of the PLS way model to assess the effect of autonomous factors on the reliant variable. The underlying model tried connections between Conduct Aim (subordinate variable) and emotional standard, Perceived Behavioral, Perceived Risk, and Perceived Trust (independent variables). In addition, relationships between Adopt Fintech Usage (dependent variable) and Behavioral Intention (independent variables) were tested.

To gauge the measurable meaning of the way coefficients, we utilize the way coefficient of the underlying model. In light of the outcomes, Behavioral Intention significantly and positively affects Adopt Fintech Usage (*H1*) with $\beta = 0.629$. SN and Perceived Behavioral significantly and positively affect Behavioral Intention

Table 2.1. Validity and Reliability Test Results.

	Cronbach's α	CR	AVE
Adopt Fintech _Usage	0.803	0.884	0.717
Behavioral _Intention	0.866	0.909	0.713
Perceived Behavioral _Control	0.702	0.832	0.623
Perceived_Risk	0.809	0.893	0.743
Perceived_Trust	0.718	0.839	0.638
Subjective _Norm	0.702	0.785	0.549

Table 2.2. AVEs Square Root and Correlation-Coefficient Matrix.

		1	2	3	4	5	6
1	Adopt Fintech Usage	0.846					
2	Behavioral Intention	0.748	0.844				
3	Perceived Behavioral Control	0.778	0.738	0.789			
4	Perceived Risk	0.738	0.754	0.659	0.861		
5	Perceived Trust	0.659	0.668	0.64	0.712	0.798	
6	Subjective Norm	0.698	0.72	0.708	0.52	0.681	0.74

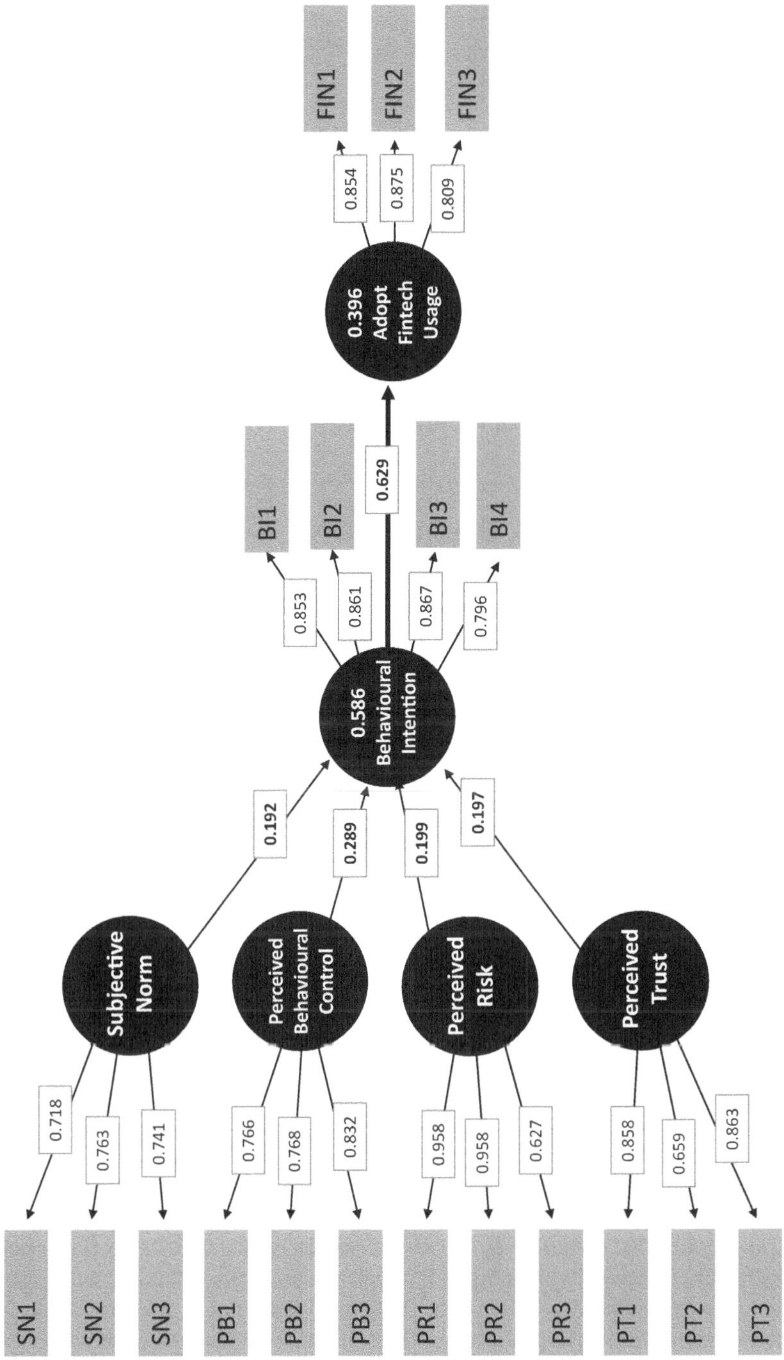

Fig. 2.2. Measurement Model.

Table 2.3. Direct Effects of Independent Variables on Dependent Variables.

	Hypothesized Path	*T*-statistics	*P*-values	Result
1	Behavioral Intention → Adopt Fintech Usage	17.435	0	Significant
2	Subjective Norm → Behavioral Intention	2.762	0.006	Significant
3	Perceived Behavioral → Behavioral Intention	3.925	0	Significant
4	Perceived Risk → Behavioral Intention	3.278	0.001	Significant
5	Perceived Trust → Behavioral Intention	2.864	0.004	Significant

(*H2*) with $\beta = 0.192$ and (*H3*) with $\beta = 0.289$. Perceived Risk significantly and positively affects Behavioral Intention (*H4*) with $\beta = 0.199$. Perceived Trust positive effect has a significant and positive effect on Behavioral Intention (*H5*) with $\beta = 0.197$. From the results, one can conclude that all the hypotheses are supported.

Cronbach's α, standard factor loadings (NFL), and AVE were utilized to assess the internal consistency and dependability.

5. DISCUSSION

This study means to experimentally research utilizing the PLS-SEM strategy factors that influence clients' Conduct Aim to embrace FinTech. Emotional Standards, Saw Social, Saw Chance, and Trust is the variables. As displayed in Table 2.3, the factual examination uncovers the satisfactory exploration model. On the side of *H1*, the outcome uncovered that Conduct Aim applies a positive and massive effect on Take on Fintech. Concerning emotional standards, the discoveries uncover a positive and massive effect on the Expectation to embrace FinTech in Jordan, supporting *H2*. These discoveries substantiate the past consequences of comparative examinations, where emotional standards have been featured positively, affecting bank clients' expectations to take on FinTech. Moreover, social impact prompts utilizing specific installment-type administrations and clients' Conduct Expectations to take on new advancements [1 + 12 – 14]. This outcome suggests that in this advanced period, many bank clients will acknowledge FinTech for their exchanges because their family members or partners use and underwrite it.

Also, when built up by close partners, popular assessment could impact the choice to utilize computerized methods for dealing with monetary exchanges. In this manner, as they experience FinTech administrations, clients could present Trust in others to utilize them. Moreover, on the side of *H3*, this study insists that Apparent Social affects Jordanian financial clients' Goal to embrace FinTech. The review's outcomes likewise affirm that Apparent Gamble has a positive critical relationship with the Expectation to take on FinTech. In this way, supporting *H4* in these discoveries confirms the past aftereffects of comparative examinations (Al-Ajlouni, 2021; Alafeef et al., 2011; Alsmadi et al., 2023). They have seen Chance firmly connected with people's FinTech reception goal. The consequences of the concentrate likewise affirm that Apparent Trust has a substantial positive relationship with the Expectation to take on FinTech; these discoveries verify the past consequences of comparable investigations (Alsmadi et al., 2023); the solid positive and critical connection between Trust and Goal to embrace Islamic Fintech. Jerene and Sharma (2020) saw Trust impacting actual m-banking reception and portable financial utilization.

6. CONCLUSION

The aftereffects of this study contribute particularly to the Fintech reception and TPB hypothesis writing. According to a theoretical perspective, this examination has widened the comprehension of the variables impacting Fintech reception in Jordan according to the viewpoints of current clients and possibilities who are not current clients. The super hypothetical commitment of this exploration was broadening the essential model TPB and testing regarding Fintech in Jordan.

The discoveries of this examination will help monetary establishments and policy makers as a device to decide the progress of taking on Fintech administrations in Jordan. The discoveries of this study recommend that to draw in the utilization of Fintech administrations in Jordan, the monetary foundations and specialist co-ops should think in credits other than the fundamental ones examined earlier. On the other hand, Jordan is viewed as a Muslim country with firm Islamic convictions, which sets out a high freedom to take on Islamic money overall. The review covers Fintech benefits and decides no Islamic monetary administrations. As the nations with the more significant part are Muslims, Monetary consideration and the job of Islamic money should be seen distinctively in Muslim and non-Muslim nations (Puschmann, 2017).

In hypothetical ramifications, the review discoveries fill the information hole in Fintech and innovation reception. The consequences of this study are expected to animate the collaboration of scholastics and the business to equip the utilization of the computerized economy with Fintech and Islamic Fintech creations. This will be accomplished by further developing the Fintech reception rate and administration strategy.

This study explores innovation reception among shoppers in Fintech; accordingly, it helps the Fintech business fire up to comprehend the purchasers' interest in tolerating Fintech. Besides, organizations can likewise gather customer conduct in financial innovation. Worried about approach suggestions. Policy makers ought to foster a system incorporating lawfully withstanding client agreements and security guidelines to increase client trust. Similarly, it is an overall peculiarity that a singular looks for a peaceful and solid installment instrument, which builds their advantages and diminishes misrepresentation and security-related gambles. The client feels less undermined and more secure in this situation, improving confidence in the Fintech administration.

6.1. Implications

- The study sheds light on the elements that influence the behavioral intention of Jordanians to use fintech.
- The study's findings may be utilized by policy makers and financial institutions to develop strategies and initiatives to encourage the adoption of fintech in Jordan.

- The study emphasizes the significance of subjective norms in affecting fintech usage intentions in Jordan, implying that social influence is a crucial component to consider when boosting fintech adoption.

6.2. Limitations

- Because the research was carried out in Jordan, the findings may not be applicable to other situations with diverse cultural, economic, and regulatory circumstances.
- The study relied on self-reported data, which might be biased by social desirability and may not fully reflect actual fintech usage behavior.
- The study did not look into real usage of fintech services, and future research should look into actual adoption and usage of fintech services in Jordan.

6.3. Future Research Directions

- Future study should look at the aspects that impact real adoption of fintech services in Jordan, such as usability and user experience.
- Future study should look at the influence of demographic parameters including age, gender, and income in determining fintech uptake and usage in Jordan.

REFERENCES

Ajzen, I. (1985). From intentions to actions: A theory of planned behavior. In *Action control: From cognition to behavior* (pp. 11–39). Berlin, Heidelberg: Springer.

Al-Ajlouni, M. I. (2021). Predicting entrepreneurial intentions among postgraduate students using the theory of planned behavior: Jordan case. *International Journal of Entrepreneurship and Small Business*, *44*(3), 235–255.

Al Bataienh, M., & Alafeef, M. (2018). Online shopping: Perspective the unified theory of acceptance and use of technology (UTAUT): Case study on consumers in governorates (Irbid, Jerash, Ajlon and Mafraq). *An-Najah University Journal for Research-B (Humanities)*, *32*(12), 2327–2356.

Al-Salahat. (2022). محمد سامي. Endowment and blockchain technology: Investment and finance from the sharia perspective. *Journal of College of Sharia & Islamic Studies*, *41*(1), 11–26. doi:10.29117/jcsis.2023.0349.

Alafeef, M. A., & Malkawi, A. F. (2016). An investigation into the adoption of mobile banking application in Jordan research article. Journal of Informatics and Mathematical Sciences, *8*(4), 287–294.

Alafeef, M., Singh, D., & Ahmad, K. (2011). Influence of demographic factors on the adoption level of mobile banking applications in Jordan. *Research Journal of Applied Sciences*, *6*(6), 373–377.

Alghusin, N., Abdalmajeed Alsmadi, A., Alkhatib, E., & Mohammad Alqtish, A. (2020). The impact of financial policy on economic growth in Jordan (2000–2017): An Ardl approach. *Ekonomski Pregled*, *71*(2), 97–108.

AlHadid, I., Abu-Taieh, E., Alkhawaldeh, R. S., Khwaldeh, S., Masa'deh, R. E., Kaabneh, K., & Alrowwad, A. A. (2022). Predictors for E-government adoption of SANAD App services integrating UTAUT, TPB, TAM, Trust, and perceived risk. *International Journal of Environmental Research and Public Health*, *19*(14), 8281.

Alrawashdeh, N., Alsmadi, A. A., & Anwar, A. L. (2022). FinTech: A bibliometric analysis for the period of 2014–2021. *Quality – Access to Success*, *23*, 176–188.

Alsmadi, A. A., Aalrawashdeh, N., Al-Gasaymeh, A., Al_hazimeh, A. M. D., & Alhawamdeh, L. (2023). Adoption of Islamic Fintech in lending services through prediction of behavioural intention. *Kybernetes*, 1–23. https://doi.org/10.1108/K-10-2022-1362.

Alsmadi, A. A., Alrawashdeh, N., Al-Gasaymeh, A., Al-Malahmeh, H., & Moh'd Al_hazimeh, A. (2023). Impact of business enablers on banking performance: A moderating role of Fintech. Banks and Bank Systems, *18*(1), 14–25.

Alsmadi, A. A., Moh'd Al_hazimeh, A., Al-Afeef, M. A., Al-Smadi, A. W., Rifai, F., & Al-Okaily, M. (2023). Banking services transformation and financial technology role. *Information Sciences Letters*, *12*(1).

Bae, S. Y., & Chang, P. J. (2021). The effect of coronavirus disease-19 (COVID-19) risk perception on behavioral intention towards 'untact' tourism in South Korea during the first pandemic wave (March 2020). *Current Issues in Tourism*, *24*(7), 1017–1035.

Barnidge, M., & De Zúñiga, H. G. (2017). Amos (software). In *The international encyclopedia of communication research methods* (pp. 1–3). Hoboken, NJ: Wiley Blackwell.

Chen, L., & Aklikokou, A. K. (2020). Determinants of E-government adoption: Testing the mediating effects of perceived usefulness and ease of use. *International Journal of Public Administration*, *43*(10), 850–865.

Fishbein, M., & Ajzen, I. (1977). *Belief, attitude, intention, and behavior: An introduction to theory and research*. Reading, MA: Addison-Wesley.

Fishbein, M., Jaccard, J., Davidson, A. R., Ajzen, I., & Loken, B. (1980). Predicting and understanding family planning behaviors. In I. Ajzen & M. Fishbein (Eds.), *Understanding attitudes and predicting social behavior*. Englewood Cliffs, NJ: Prentice Hall.

Hansen, T., Jensen, J. M., & Solgaard, H. S. (2004). Predicting online grocery buying intention: A comparison of the theory of reasoned action and the theory of planned behavior. *International Journal of Information Management*, *24*(6), 539–550.

Jerene, W., & Sharma, D. (2020). The effect of e-finance service quality on bank customers' fintech e-loyalty: Evidence from Ethiopia. *International Journal of E-Business Research*, *16*(2), 69–83.

Kim, D. J., Ferrin, D. L., & Rao, R. (2008). A trust-based consumer decision-making model in electronic commerce: The role of trust, perceived risk, and their antecedents. *Decision Support Systems*, *44*(2), 544–564.

Lam, T., & Hsu, C. H. (2006). Predicting behavioral Intention of choosing a travel destination. *Tourism Management*, *27*(4), 589–599.

Patra, G., & Roy, R. K. (2023). Business sustainability and growth in journey of industry 4.0 – A case study. In A. Nayyar, M. Naved, & R. Rameshwar (Eds.), *New horizons for Industry 4.0 in modern business. Contributions to environmental sciences & innovative business technology*. Cham: Springer. doi:10.1007/978-3-031-20443-2_2

Puschmann, T. (2017). Fintech. *Business and Information Systems Engineering*, *59*(1), 69–76.

Reisinger, Y., & Mavondo, F. (2005). Travel anxiety and intentions to travel internationally: Implications of travel risk perception. *Journal of Travel Research*, *43*(3), 212–225.

Rivis, A., Sheeran, P., & Armitage, C. J. (2009). Expanding the affective and normative components of the theory of planned behavior: A meta-analysis of anticipated affect and moral norms. *Journal of Applied Social Psychology*, *39*(12), 2985–3019.

Tanveer, A., Zeng, S., Irfan, M., & Peng, R. (2021). Do perceptions of risk, self-efficacy, and openness to technology matter for solar PV adoption? An application of the extended theory of planned behavior. *Energies*, *14*(16), 5008.

Venkatesh, V., Ramesh, V., & Massey, A. P. (2003). Understanding usability in mobile commerce. *Communications of the ACM*, *46*(12), 53–56.

Yaseen, S. G., & Qirem, I. A. (2018). Intention to use e-banking services in the Jordanian commercial banks. *International Journal of Bank Marketing*, *36*, 557–571.

CHAPTER 3

THE ROLE OF ARTIFICIAL INTELLIGENCE IN STOCK FORECASTING IN INDONESIAN STOCK EXCHANGE FIRM

Ariq Idris Annaufal[a], April Lia Dina Mariyana[b] and Ratna Roostika[c]

[a]*Magister Program, Management Department, Universitas Islam Indonesia, Yogyakarta, Indonesia*
[b]*Magister Program, Management Department, Universitas Islam Indonesia, Yogyakarta, Indonesia*
[c]*Lecturer, Management Department, Universitas Islam Indonesia, Yogyakarta, Indonesia*

ABSTRACT

The financial sector's growing interest in leveraging artificial intelligence (AI) for forecasting has been noted in recent years. In this chapter, we delve into the application of AI in financial forecasting within Indonesia's stock market. Our primary focus is to assess how AI's prediction potential can impact investors and financial regulators in this context. Our review spans existing literature on AI and financial forecasting, recent developments in the Indonesian stock market, and ethical and regulatory concerns that surround AI in finance. Our analysis indicates that AI can enhance forecast accuracy in Indonesia's stock exchange; however, we must also consider limitations and challenges.

Keywords: Artificial intelligence; stock forecasting; Indonesian stock exchange; investors; financial regulators; finance; Indonesia

Digital Technology and Changing Roles in Managerial and Financial Accounting: Theoretical Knowledge and Practical Application
Studies in Managerial and Financial Accounting, Volume 36, 27–35

Published under exclusive licence by Emerald Publishing Limited
ISSN: 1479-3512/doi:10.1108/S1479-351220240000036003

1. INTRODUCTION

As the global financial market continues to increase in complexity, traditional investment analysis methods may not be sufficient anymore. This underscores the need for more efficient and effective investment analysis and decision making. AI-powered solutions can provide more comprehensive and real-time analysis of market trends and risk factors, thus enabling investors to make better-informed decisions. Furthermore, in a rapidly evolving market, staying competitive demands the integration of AI-powered solutions. Both investors and brokerage firms are increasingly adopting AI solutions to improve investment analysis and decision making. Therefore, for Indonesian stock market players, the adoption of AI-powered solutions is essential to attract more investors and stay ahead in the game.

Indonesia's stock market has grown significantly in recent times, with the Jakarta Composite Index reaching its all-time high in 2021. This has piqued the interest of financial analysts and investors alike in accurately predicting the stock trends of the Indonesian stock exchange (IDX). One promising method to achieve this is through the use of AI in financial forecasting, which has gained significant traction due to its potential to enhance precision and efficiency in financial analysis. Research conducted by Ma et al. (2021) suggests that AI-powered machine learning techniques outperform traditional methods in financial forecasting. They concluded that the use of AI-based models leads to higher levels of predictive accuracy in anticipating stock prices and portfolio returns.

In the IDX, AI plays a vital role in financial forecasting due to the intricate and unpredictable nature of the market. AI methodologies, like machine learning and natural language processing, can analyze a vast amount of data from multiple sources, such as economic indicators, social media, and financial news, to detect patterns and make reliable stock trend predictions. Nonetheless, while AI in financial analysis has exhibited promising outcomes, certain obstacles require addressing. As per recent research by Mhlanga (2020), the major hurdles in using AI in finance are the dependence on data, the indispensable technological infrastructure, and the softness and transparency of AI models.

Despite its potential benefits, the use of AI in financial forecasting also raises ethical and regulatory considerations. For instance, there are concerns about algorithmic bias, data privacy, and transparency in AI-driven financial analysis. Furthermore, financial regulators need to ensure that the use of AI in finance does not create systemic risks or undermine market integrity. The use of AI in financial analysis also has significant potential implications. According to research conducted by Broussard et al. (2019), the use of AI technology can help improve the efficiency and accuracy of decision making in portfolio management, as well as help identify new risks and investment opportunities.

This chapter aims to examine the role of AI in stock forecasting in the IDX, with a focus on the effectiveness, challenges, and potential implications of using AI in financial analysis. This chapter will review existing literature on AI and financial forecasting, as well as recent developments in the Indonesian stock market. It will also discuss the ethical and regulatory considerations surrounding the use of AI in finance. The findings of this chapter are expected to contribute to the growing body of research on the use of AI in financial analysis and provide insights for investors, financial regulators, and policy makers in Indonesia.

The IDX, also known as Bursa Efek Indonesia, is the primary stock exchange in Indonesia. It was established in 1912 and is headquartered in Jakarta, Indonesia. The IDX facilitates trading of equities, bonds, mutual funds, and other securities.

The IDX is supervised by the Indonesia Financial Services Authority (OJK), which ensures that the exchange operates transparently and in accordance with applicable laws and regulations. The exchange is open for trading from Monday to Friday, with the exception of national holidays and other days that have been designated as non-trading days.

There are a number of firms that are listed on the IDX, including large corporations, small and medium-sized enterprises, and state-owned enterprises. Some of the largest companies listed on the exchange include Bank Central Asia, Astra International, and Bank Mandiri. The IDX is an important source of capital for Indonesian businesses, and it provides investors with opportunities to participate in the growth of the country's economy.

Investing in the IDX can be an important way to build wealth over time, as the Indonesian economy has shown a strong potential for growth. By investing in a range of stocks listed on the IDX, investors can diversify their portfolios and reduce risk. Additionally, the IDX provides investors with access to a wide range of local companies, which can be important for those interested in supporting local businesses and understanding the local market. Finally, the IDX is a well-regulated exchange, which means that investors can typically buy or sell shares at any time without affecting the market price.

Overall, investing in the IDX can be an important way to participate in the growth of the Indonesian economy and build wealth over time. However, it is important to carefully consider the risks involved and seek professional advice before making any investment decisions. It also raises a question about what are the benefits and limitations of using AI in financial forecasting within Indonesia's stock market, and what are the ethical and regulatory considerations that need to be addressed for its effective implementation?

This chapter consists of five subsections with introduction as the first section explaining theoretical questions and emerging phenomena on the use of AI in predicting the stock market. The second section is methodology describing the theoretical framework on how to conduct the research. The next section describes the conceptual framework where it references past study on the same fields of studies as a base in conducting the research. The fourth section is a discussion where the conceptual framework and theory that have been done by reviewing other researches is discussed. The last section concludes all the components and findings from the conceptual framework that have been discussed in this chapter.

1.1. Research Objectives

The research objectives of this study on the role of AI in financial forecasting in the IDX are twofold. First, the study aims to assess the effectiveness of AI techniques in financial forecasting and compare their performance with traditional methods. This will involve a comprehensive analysis of the related articles of AI-based predictions in different market conditions. Second, the study will investigate the challenges and potential implications of using AI in financial analysis, including ethical and regulatory issues. By addressing these objectives, the study seeks to provide valuable insights for investors on the benefits and limitations of AI in financial forecasting and its implications for the IDX.

2. METHODOLOGY

To examine the impact of AI on stock forecasting, a quantitative approach via mini-review can be employed to substantiate previously formulated propositions or hypotheses (refer to Fig. 3.1). This research topic carries significant weight when placed within the context of financial market operations that rest on individual investors' decisions. Its aim is to gauge the extent of AI's involvement in predicting financial performance, stock prices, and enhancing investor experience. Surveying investors of the Indonesian stock exchange through direct interviews can provide precise and reliable data, making it the most fitting research method to explore the realm of AI.

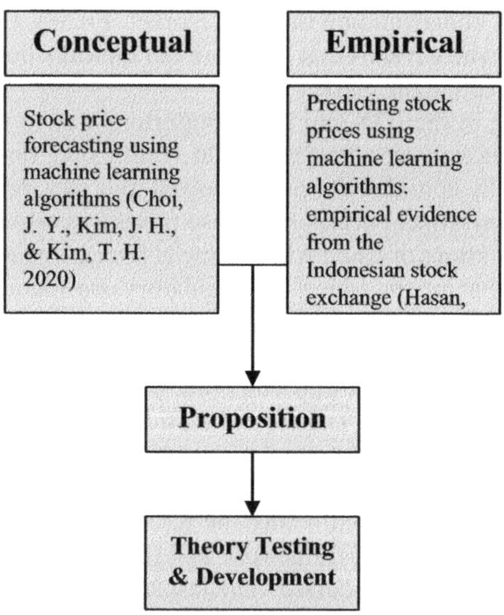

Fig. 3.1. The Conceptual Framework (Developed by the Authors).

3. CONCEPTUAL FRAMEWORK

3.1. Effectiveness of Artificial Intelligence on Stock Forecasting

In the fundamental analysis, the SVM model can predict public sentiment with an accuracy of 76% (Mokhtari, Yen, & Liu, 2021). Neural and hybrid-neuro approaches are ideal for stock market forecasting since they provide more accurate outcomes than the traditional models used in the majority of studies (Chopra & Sharma, 2021). The most appropriate method for stock market prediction is to use multiple algorithms such as ANN, Random Forest, SVM, LSTM and combine their results for predictions, and also considering all the factors affecting the stock market price such as news sentiment, currency, commodity prices and other international stock exchange market data (Patel, Patel, & Yadav, 2021). It was determined that SVM, DNN and LSTM are the most often used approaches for stock market prediction (Weng, Lu, Wang, Megahed, & Martinez, 2018). In summary, these studies suggest that artificial intelligence can significantly improve the effectiveness of stock forecasting, with AI-based models demonstrating superior performance compared to traditional methods. These findings support the increasing trend of adopting AI in financial analysis and forecasting.

3.2. Challenges of Artificial Intelligence on Stock Forecasting

While AI has demonstrated great potential in improving stock forecasting, there are also several challenges associated with its use in this context. Although AI can predict the stock price trends or public sentiment about the stock markets, its accuracy is not good enough. Furthermore, while the linear regression can predict the closing price with a sensible range of error, it cannot precisely predict the same value for the next business day (Mokhtari, Yen, & Liu, 2021). There are no established techniques for designing the optimal ANN model or network, and the right model (with high prediction accuracy) is highly dependent on the complexity of the data and implementation (Göçken, Özçalıcı, Boru, & Dosdoğru, 2016). The accuracy of classification algorithms in predicting buying, selling, or holding a stock is not satisfying enough and can result in loss of capital (Mokhtari, Yen, & Liu, 2021). In summary, while AI has the potential to revolutionize stock forecasting, there are several challenges that need to be addressed.

3.3. Implication of Artificial Intelligence on Stock Forecasting

Experimental results showed that event embeddings-based document representations are better than discrete events-based methods, and deep convolutional neural networks can capture longer-term influence of news events than standard feedforward neural networks. In market simulation, a simple greedy strategy allowed our model to yield more profit compared with previous work (Ding, Zhang, Liu, & Duan, 2015). Investment banks and financial institutions as well as brokerage firms who are investing and trading in financial markets can use specialized market-trend analysis and prediction systems that are developed using the insights gained in such targeted text mining research efforts as this work. The existence of such intelligent systems for those institutions assists with making better financial decisions which lead to considerable financial returns on their investments and avoidance of severe losses (Nassirtoussi, Aghabozorgi, Wah, & Ngo, 2014). Forecasting accuracy of CGFS outperforms the rest of approaches regarding MAPE evaluation, and CGFS can be used as a suitable forecasting tool to deal with stock price forecasting problems (Hadavandi, Shavandi, & Ghanbari, 2010). AI's expert systems are developed to tackle intricate issues and make informed decisions. These systems were some of the earliest successful AI technologies (Kumar, Srivastava, & Prakash, 2023).

4. DISCUSSION

The IDX has also joined the global trend of utilizing AI for financial forecasting. This study delved into the effectiveness, challenges, and potential implications of AI in predicting stock prices of IDX firms. The findings revealed that AI techniques, such as machine learning, deep learning, and natural language processing, can provide trustworthy and precise predictions. Compared to traditional forecasting methods, AI-based models exhibited higher accuracy rates, faster processing speeds, and greater flexibility in adapting to market complexities.

Despite the potential benefits, employing AI in financial analysis presents several challenges and ramifications. Transparency and interpretability of AI models remain a primary obstacle, as it hinders analysts and investors' ability to comprehend how the predictions are generated. Additionally, the ethical and regulatory considerations regarding AI adoption pose challenges such as data privacy, security, and bias.

Overcoming its obstacles, a study has concluded that utilizing AI in financial forecasting on the IDX brings more advantages than drawbacks. Employing AI-based models assists with enhanced decision making for investors and analysts, allowing for better identification of risks and opportunities, and ultimately, strengthening the overall efficiency of financial markets.

Therefore, this study highlights the importance of adopting AI in financial forecasting in the IDX, while also recognizing the challenges and potential implications that must be addressed. The study's recommendations include enhancing transparency and interpretability of AI models, ensuring compliance with ethical and regulatory standards, and promoting further research and development in the field of AI-based financial analysis.

Investing in the Indonesian stock exchange (IDX) can be a smart decision for those looking to diversify their portfolio and participate in the growth of the Indonesian economy. The IDX is the primary stock exchange in Indonesia, and it provides investors with access to a wide range of local companies from small- and medium-sized enterprises to large corporations.

One of the benefits of investing in the IDX is the potential for long-term growth. Historically, the Indonesian economy has shown a strong potential for growth, and as a result, many companies listed on the IDX have experienced growth in their share prices over time. By investing in a range of stocks, investors can diversify their portfolios and reduce risk.

In addition to potential long-term growth, the IDX also provides investors with access to local companies. This can be important for investors who are interested in supporting local businesses and understanding the local market. Investing in the IDX can also provide investors with liquidity, as the exchange is well-regulated and offers a liquid market for buying and selling shares.

However, as with any investment, it is important to carefully consider the risks involved and seek professional advice before making any investment decisions. Investing in the IDX carries some risks, such as market volatility, political instability, and currency exchange rate fluctuations. It is important to have a clear investment strategy and to diversify across different stocks and asset classes.

Overall, investing in the IDX can be a good option for those looking to participate in the growth of the Indonesian economy and build wealth over time. It is important to do thorough research, assess the risks involved, and seek professional advice before making any investment.

5. CONCLUSION

The potential benefits of leveraging AI for financial forecasting in the IDX cannot be overemphasized. Experts in finance and AI attest to the superiority of AI-based models over traditional forecasting methods, leading to significantly higher returns. Despite the benefits, AI-based stock forecasting comes with its fair share of challenges, such as data quality, interpretability, transparency, and ethical and regulatory concerns. Overcoming these challenges is crucial to realizing the full potential of AI in financial forecasting. The adoption of AI in IDX firms and other financial institutions can boost investment decisions and aid in better managing financial risks.

Investing in the IDX can be a wise decision for those looking to diversify their portfolio and participate in the growth of the Indonesian economy. The IDX provides investors with access to a wide range of local companies, which can be important for those interested in supporting local businesses and understanding the local market.

Investing in the IDX also offers potential for long-term growth, as the Indonesian economy has shown a strong potential for growth. Additionally, the IDX is a well-regulated exchange, which means that investors can typically buy or sell shares at any time without affecting the market.

However, as with any investment, it is important to carefully consider the risks involved and seek professional advice before making any investment decisions. Investing in the IDX may not be suitable for everyone and it is important to understand the potential risks and rewards involved. Therefore AI can help investors in deciding what to invest and when to invest.

5.1. Implications

There are several promising avenues for future research in the field of stock forecasting in the IDX that warrant investigation. One such area is the potential for integrating disparate AI solutions to enhance forecasting accuracy. For instance, researchers may explore the viability of leveraging natural language processing and machine learning algorithms to analyze media coverage and social media activity for insights that could inform stock predictions. Additionally, there is an opportunity to examine how AI can facilitate more responsible and sustainable investment practices in the IDX. By investigating the effectiveness of AI in pinpointing and analyzing environmental, social, and governance factors that impact investment decisions, researchers may shed light on how AI can support sustainable investment strategies in the Indonesian context.

Incorporating AI-powered solutions in stock market predictions may have practical benefits for investors. AI algorithms can sift through extensive data, detect trends and patterns, and make forecasts based on relevant factors such as past data and market trends. This approach may mitigate the effects of human biases and emotions and lead to more consistent, objective investment decisions. The use of AI in stock analysis also offers real-time insights, which can help investors respond promptly to any market changes and make informed investment choices. Furthermore, integrating AI in stock forecasting can keep IDX firms competitive in a rapidly changing market by equipping them with advanced tools and technologies for investment analysis and decision making.

REFERENCES

Broussard, M., Diakopoulos, N., Guzman, A. L., Abebe, R., Dupagne, M., & Chuan, C.-H. (2019). Artificial intelligence and journalism. Journalism & Mass Communication Quarterly, *96*(3), 673–695.

Chopra, R., & Sharma, G. D. (2021) Application of artificial intelligence in stock market forecasting: A critique, review, and research agenda. *Journal of Risk and Finance Management*, *14*(11), 526. doi:10.3390/jrfm14110526

Ding, X., Zhang, Y., Liu, T., & Duan, J. (2015, July 25–31). Deep learning for event-driven stock prediction. In *Proceedings of the twenty-fourth international joint conference on artificial intelligence*, Buenos Aires.

Göçken, M., Özçalıcı, M., Boru, A., & Dosdoğru, A. T. (2016). Integrating metaheuristics and artificial neural networks for improved stock price prediction. *Expert System with Applications*, *44*, 320–331. doi:10.1016/j.eswa.2015.09.029

Hadavandi, E., Shavandi, H., & Ghanbari, A. (2010). Integration of genetic fuzzy systems and artificial neural networks for stock price forecasting. *Knowledge-Based Systems*, *23*(8), 800–808. doi:10.1016/j.knosys.2010.05.004.

Khadjeh Nassirtoussi, A., Aghabozorgi, S., Ying Wah, T., & Ngo, D. C. L. (2014). Text mining for market prediction: A systematic review. *Expert Systems With Applications*, *41*(16), 7653–7670. doi:10.1016/j.eswa.2014.06.009.

Kumar, S., Srivastava, M., & Prakash, V. (2023). Challenges and opportunities for mutual fund investment and the role of industry 4.0 to recommend the individual for speculation. In A. Nayyar, M. Naved, & R. Rameshwar (Eds.), *New horizons for Industry 4.0 in modern business. Contributions to environmental sciences & innovative business technology* (pp. 69–98). Cham: Springer International Publishing. doi:10.1007/978-3-031-20443-2_4.

Ma, J., Wang, Y., An, X., Ge, C., Yu, Z., Chen, J., …Yang, X. (2021). Toward data-efficient learning: A benchmark for COVID-19 CT lung and infection segmentation. *Medical Physics*, *48*(3), 1197–1210. doi:10.1002/mp.14676.

Mhlanga, D. (2020). Industry 4.0 in finance: The impact of artificial intelligence (AI) on digital financial inclusion. *International Journal of Financial Studies*, *8*(3), 45. doi:10.3390/ijfs8030045.

Mokhtari, S., Yen, K. K., & Liu, J. (2021). Effectiveness of artificial intelligence in stock market prediction based on machine learning. *International Journal of Computer Applications*, *183*(7), 1–8. doi:10.5120/ijca2021921347.

Patel, A., Patel, D., & Yadav, S. (2021, August 27–29). Prediction of stock market using artificial intelligence. In *Proceedings of the 4th international conference on advances in science & technology (ICAST2021)*, Bahir Dar.

Weng, B., Lu, L., Wang, X., Megahed, F. M., & Martinez, W. (2018). Predicting short-term stock prices using ensemble methods and online data sources. *Expert System With Applications*, *112*, 258–273. doi:10.1016/j.eswa.2018.06.016

CHAPTER 4

THE FACTORING 2.0 IN THE ERA OF THE FINTECH REVOLUTION CONTEXT

Wissem Ajili Ben Youssef[a] and Nadia Mansour[b,c,d]

[a]*EM Normandie Business School, Métis Lab, Le Havre, Paris-France*
[b]*University of Sousse, Sousse, Tunisia*
[c]*University of Salamanca, Salamanca, Spain*
[d]*LARIME Laboratory, ESSEC, Tunisia*

ABSTRACT

The health crisis linked to COVID-19 has made digitization a significant issue for companies regardless of their form or geographical location. Our research focuses on the financial technology (Fintech) revolution in the context of international development. Its theoretical framework lies in both the fields of Fintech and factoring. As innovative start-ups that combine finance with new technologies, Fintechs have been able to disrupt the banking world in a few years by challenging its traditional practices. We use the case method to analyze two Fintech in-depth, and our results highlight the upheaval of Fintechs in the factoring sector. The supply of the analyzed Fintech is a limited working capital requirement. Furthermore, Fintechs may threaten classical banks due to the innovation of their offers and business models. However, the Fintech revolution focused on corporate finance is still in its infancy.

Keywords: Working capital requirement; Fintech; factoring; small and medium enterprises (SME); business model; France

JEL classifications: G21; O30

Digital Technology and Changing Roles in Managerial and Financial Accounting: Theoretical Knowledge and Practical Application
Studies in Managerial and Financial Accounting, Volume 36, 37–51

Published under exclusive licence by Emerald Publishing Limited
ISSN: 1479-3512/doi:10.1108/S1479-351220240000036004

1. INTRODUCTION

The financial industry has experienced an accelerating pace of technological innovation in recent years. In the medium to long term, the landscape of financial products and services is expected to change dramatically, driven by new trends such as blockchain and crypto assets. The transformation affects financial products, services, and the various operators' value chains and business models (Fischer, 2021).

The financial intermediation function, traditionally performed by banks, is no longer the primary source of profit for banks. Indeed, the technological transformation has led to the emergence of new players, pure players whose business model is based on technology as their main value-generating activity. According to the Global Findex database, between 2014 and 2017, beyond 500 million adults worldwide opened an account with a financial institution or via a mobile phone operator.

Fintechs are now present in all six segments of the financial services market, namely: (1) payments, (2) insurance, (3) deposits and loans, (4) fundraising through crowdfunding and online platforms, (5) investment management for retail investors and SMEs looking for complex investments tailored to their needs, and (6) market provisioning driven by automation and the blockchain. Indeed, Fintech is presenting itself as a solution for VSEs and SMEs that need help accessing the traditional factoring market (Tricaud, 2018).

The expansion of Fintech is relatively recent and has accelerated recently. These companies benefit from a favorable international technological and regulatory environment and follow new customer practices. Indeed, at the technological level, many innovations have contributed to lowering the cost of entry of Fintech in the banking market. These innovations include mobile and cloud technologies, algorithms, automated tools, artificial intelligence, big data, and blockchain. At the same time, the change in consumer behavior, which makes their mobile phone a preferred means of contact with their bank, has encouraged the development of Fintechs. In 2020, global investments in Fintech recorded $105.3 billion, with 2,861 deals (KPMG, 2021).

On the other hand, many companies are experiencing a global context characterized by resource scarcity. While large companies can turn to the capital markets and go public, SMEs remain more dependent on bank financing. There need to be more resources to finance the operating cycle to ensure the existence of some businesses, exposing them to liquidity and even solvency risks. At the heart of this threat to companies are frequent problems related to cash flow, especially the management of working capital requirements (WCR).

Our research is in line with existing literature on the financial sectors' transformation into the digital age, mainly the works of Youssef and Rakotondratsimba (2022), Kumar, Srivastava, and Prakash (2023), Mathew, Brintha, and Jappes (2023), Parashar, Sharma, Rana, and Balaji (2023), and Srivastava (2023).

This article presents traditional factoring and SMEs' management of working capital through a literature review. In the third section, we discuss factoring 2.0 and the disruption brought about by Fintechs. Finally, we conduct a case study of BNP Paribas Factor, the European leader in factoring, trade receivables, and payables management solutions. A comparative analysis between BNP Paribas Factor and the French start-up Finexkap completes the case study.

2. TRADITIONAL FACTORING AND MANAGEMENT OF SME'S WCR

Within a company, optimization of the WCR and rigorous and regular cash flow management is essential for the smooth running and development of the business, whatever its size.

2.1. The Management of the WCR in the Case of SMES and TPE

In the literature, WCR management is analyzed from three different perspectives: (1) the influence of an optimal inventory policy (Bougheas, Mateut, & Mizen, 2009; Gariglia & Mateut, 2010); (2) the management of customer credits (Molina & Preve, 2009, 2012); (3) and the management of supplier debts (Cunat, 2007). Nevertheless, in examining the relationship between WCR and performance, Autukaite and Molay's (2014) study considers the operating cycle's different elements (inventories, customer credits, and supplier debts). Many studies argue that WCR impacts profitability and firm performance (Enqvist et al., 2014; Gill et al., 2010; Haq et al., 2011; Mosa et al., 2012). Peel, Nicholas, and Carole (2000) focus on the specific case of SMEs and argue that they depend on short-term debt and have a high level of WCR. Garcia-Teruel and Solano (2007) highlight that a high WCR can reduce the company's profitability. Therefore, there would be an optimal level of WCR, allowing SMEs to maximize their profitability. Aktas, Croci, and Petmezas (2015) also support a policy of optimizing WCR. According to them, companies that converge toward an optimal level by increasing or decreasing their WCR improve their inventories, operational performance, and, ultimately, their profitability.

WCR represents the cash needed to finance the operating cycle, that is, the company's activity. It is thus a vital indicator of the company's short-term financial health in that it measures its ability to finance its operating cycle from internal resources. Many authors have tried to demonstrate the link between WCR management and a company's profitability. Raheman and Nasr (2007) concluded that companies invest large amounts of money in their WCR, expecting to achieve profitability, but that the level of profitability will depend on how well the WCR is managed. The authors agree that optimizing working capital is essential for growing companies; it ensures success and sustainability if profitability and liquidity are combined (Peel et al., 2000). In this context, the quality of the customer portfolio and the receivables managed by the company are determining factors for the effectiveness of factoring in financing working capital.

2.2. Traditional Factoring

In contrast to medium- and long-term financing, which is intended for investments, various short-term financing methods allow the company to finance its operating cycle. Among these methods is factoring, a "financial management operation or technique whereby [...] a specialized organization manages the accounts receivable of companies by acquiring their debts, collecting them on its behalf and bearing any losses on insolvent debtors" (Effosse, 2014). This method allows companies to improve their cash flow and reduce the costs of managing their accounts receivable. It is, therefore, a global offer, justifying an often-high price.

It is also important to note that factoring is carried out within the framework of an agreement between the parties. This formula generally includes financing, credit insurance, and the collection of unpaid receivables. It is a simple and flexible method in which the assigned receivables are also subject to the financial institution's approval. Once the invoices have been assigned, the company receives a drawing right on the financing line made available to it. This contract is open-ended but can be terminated at any time by both parties. When a company assigns a customer's invoice, it must assign all invoices related to that customer. Financial institutions will finance the entire turnover of that customer (with some exceptions), not allowing companies to keep the "good" invoices for themselves.

For a long time, perceived as being reserved for companies in difficulty, factoring is now experiencing a new rebound, making it an even more competitive sector. New offers have emerged: "confidential" factoring, in which clients are not informed of the purchase of their receivables by a factor; "delegated management" factoring, in which companies retain management of their client relations and collection; and "balance" factoring, in which only the balance of the company's receivables is financed. The different models of factoring contracts are shown in Fig. 4.1:

The factoring contract stands out from other financing solutions because of its simplicity (total assignment of the balance of the receivable) and modular aspect (Bonin, 2016). Factoring (Klapper, 2006; Vasilescu, 2010) is the only procedure

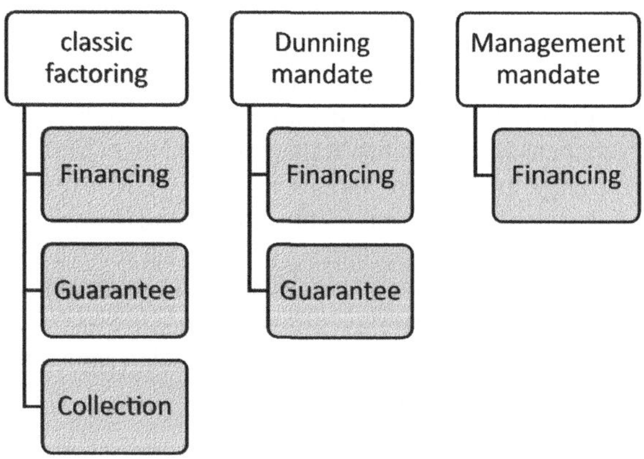

Fig. 4.1. Modules of the Different Factoring Contracts.

offering a complete receivables management formula, including uncapped financing, a guarantee, and debt collection.

As in the hotel and transport sectors, the finance industry is now facing the entry of new players into the market, the Fintechs. They reflect the digital revolution in the financial sectors by combining the words "finance" and "technology." Small entities can then compete with or complement the offers of the traditional players in their sector.

3. FACTORING 2.0. AND THE DISRUPTION BROUGHT ABOUT BY FINTECH

The specificity of Fintechs is the integration of technology into financial solutions. The way companies operate is affected by payment delays. However, traditional factoring could be more suited to SMEs and VSEs. Hence, the importance of factoring as a new form of financing. Many start-ups have also developed several online offers, which facilitate financing management by making it faster.

3.1. The Fintech Revolution: Genesis, Characteristics, and Key Facts

The development of Fintech is based on innovative technologies, new business models, and changing customer behavior. According to Bouyala (2016), these new technologies would enable customers to be offered more decadent and generally less expensive products and services than traditional offerings. Thus, this lower cost can be explained by the structural size of Fintech (Milian, Spinola, & Carvalho, 2019) and the smaller number of employees they employ, resulting in lower fixed costs than traditional players. Furthermore, the arrival of these new companies on the market would also be facilitated by regulators and public authorities to boost competition in closed-sector sectors.

Through technological tools, Fintechs have succeeded in penetrating the banking business and have specialized in their sectors: payment services, retail banking, data collection and analysis, management solutions, and finally, investment and financing services (Llorca, 2017). The operating principle of these Fintechs is to offer innovative solutions for specific services in line with new customer practices (Philippon, 2017). The combination of new digital technologies and innovative financial services allows start-ups to boost the world of finance (Weichert, 2017). Indeed, with attractive prices, simplified administrative management, and flexible financial services, start-ups are disrupting the business model of traditional financial players.

3.2. The Role of Fintechs in the Transformation of Factoring

The Fintech revolution is bringing many benefits to businesses and is boosting the factoring market. For many business leaders, this remarkable financial sector transformation is just beginning. However, the main difficulty faced by factoring

Fintech is undoubtedly getting in touch with customers. Indeed, assigning receivables through a fully digitalized process requires high trust between the customer and Fintech. A lack of trust could be a natural brake in the development of Fintechs (Salerno, Sampagnaro, & Verdoliva, 2021).

In the case of factoring Fintechs, it must be stressed that while financing and invoice transfer are done exclusively digitally, the study of invoices requires human intervention. Moreover, Fintech can consult the analyses previously carried out by the insurers' teams and the scores they have given to the various companies. Furthermore, while the credit insurer's teams analyze debtor and member risks, the factoring 2.0 companies' teams assess the quality of the invoices, which are the only tangible proof of the debt. This analysis of invoices is decisive for the pricing of the Fintechs' offer. Thus, the human presence in analyzing the three main risk factors positions these start-ups as serious, solid, and trustworthy companies (Avenier & Thomas, 2015). In addition, the Fintechs' teams are present to monitor the entire factoring process.

Regulators have facilitated the arrival of Fintech in the financial sector, notably by improving the legal and regulatory framework. Nevertheless, factoring Fintech often needs help to make itself known and to be recognized as offering reliable financing solutions. By neither being a bank nor a credit institution and proposing offers that disrupt the entire sector, these "start-ups," as journalists call them, are obliged to create partnerships.

To simplify this digital transformation, many people are thinking of a future alliance between Fintech and traditional players (Llorca, 2017). According to PWC's Global Fintech Report 2017, about 40% of banks are considering investing directly in Fintech-developing services that improve their own, and about 20% are considering possible buyouts. Indeed, by acquiring these young start-ups, banks ensure their rapid adaptation to the new needs of customers. Thus, the sector's future could be created through the cooperation of all players.

Authors such as Hornuf, Klus, Lohwasser, and Schwienbacher (2020) and Allayanis, Yemen, and Lane (2018) have focused on the different forms of strategic alliances that can take place between traditional banks and Fintech. Hornuf et al. (2020) argue that banks favor alliances with Fintechs when they have a well-defined digitalization strategy and rely on dedicated structures (Torriero, Montera, & Cucari, 2022). On the other hand, traditional banks are investing more frequently in acquiring small Fintechs and developing partnerships with larger ones. Today, a new challenge for regulators is to develop rules that favor innovation and the creation of Fintech while preserving financial stability and consumer safety.

4. FACTORING 2.0: A CASE STUDY

Our case study aligns with the work of Stake (1995) and Merriam (2009). It is based on a socio-constructive or interpretive approach insofar as one of the authors was in personal interaction with the Fintech under analysis. Thus, the data was collected in the field during 2018 and then updated as we went along. We aim to describe, explain, and explore the Fintech phenomenon in its real-life context

(Yin, 2003, 2009). According to Yin's typology (2009), our case is revealing and representative. It is revealing because it allows us to analyze a new phenomenon that was previously inaccessible, namely Fintechs. The case is representative and typical in that it can be informative about the behavior of Fintechs specializing in factoring and SME financing.

Furthermore, we exclude from the framework of this study the post-positivist approach developed by authors such as Yin (2003, 2009) or Eisenhardt (1989, 2021), which implies the development of a conceptual framework and a study protocol aimed at consolidating the validity of its results.

4.1. Presentation of the BNP Paribas Factor

Factoring is an efficient solution adapted to each type of company. However, new factoring companies have emerged recently, offering innovative financing solutions that meet a real need for VSEs and SMEs. Unlike traditional factoring companies, Fintech has an innovative business model.

According to the Bank of France, France is the leading European country in financing Fintech, with investments rising from 19 million euros in 2014 to 611 million euros in 2020. We are therefore witnessing a real revolution in the financial system due to the emergence of Fintech, filling the inability of traditional players to keep up with the changing needs of consumers.

BNP Paribas Factor is Europe's leading network of factors and is present in more than 60 countries, ensuring a solid reputation for the group. The factor offers "tailor-made" factoring solutions: fixed price, à la carte, or balance transfer solutions in France or abroad. As a traditional factoring player, BNP Paribas Factor offers credit insurance and debt collection services, with or without the factoring contract. The financing solutions offered by the BNP Paribas subsidiary are based on a complete diagnosis of the client's receivables, enabling it to meet the client's needs as closely as possible. The company places great emphasis on customer relations. Each member is assigned a dedicated customer relations officer and sales manager team with legal, accounting, and operational skills.

Created in response to the arrival of Fintech on the factoring market, BNP Paribas Factor has launched three types of fixed-price contracts:

- Impulsion First: for financing up to €40,000, that is, 15 invoices assigned per month. No application fees, no deposit, and no commitment.
- Impulsion Situation: for financing up to €120,000, that is, 15 invoices assigned per month. No file fees and no commitment, but with a personal guarantee from the manager of €30,000.
- Impulsion Premium: financing up to €180,000, that is, 30 financeable monthly invoices – no file fees and no commitment, but with a possible guarantee.

The management of these contracts is done in a dematerialized manner. Once the need has been identified with the factor's teams, the client can sign the contract electronically, monitor its financing in real time and submit its invoices online. These offers are very similar to those proposed by Fintechs but do not have the same advantages.

For SMEs and large accounts, the factor offers a range of products, classic or international, with invoice financing in 48 hours. This offer includes various factoring solutions: balance assignment (complete assignment of the customer's outstanding balance), line-by-line financing (invoice-by-invoice financing), or reverse factoring (supplier financing), with or without confidential management, delegated or not. It is also possible for companies to benefit solely from a management and dunning service for trade receivables. BNP Paribas Factor provides its clients with online services to simplify the management of these offers. These services allow them to access the contract in real time, declare their new debtors online, and obtain an instant response regarding their acceptance by the factor. Financing applications can also be online but only for "Impulsion" contracts.

However, it should be noted that the time required to validate files remains long for BNP Paribas Factor, which must submit each file to a credit committee and must also carry out audits. The Factor's watchwords are "fluidity" (tailor-made offers), "simplicity" (a dedicated expert assists the company in setting up the contract), "speed" (financing between 8 and 48 hours – excluding file validation), and "performance."

Mainly aimed at small businesses, business creators, and entrepreneurs, the package offers up to €180,000 in financing from €240 per month.

Thus, BNP Paribas Factor's strategy focuses on the client relationship and experience. This situation justifies the group's imposing structure and the staff it employs. In addition, the group's international presence facilitates the development of its client's businesses. Based on an in-depth analysis of the client's position, BNP Paribas offers products and services that are increasingly adapted to the client's situation. Its recent digital transformation allows it to compete with Fintechs, but more is needed to match the quality of its offers. The leading financial indicators for BNP Paribas are presented in Table 4.1.

The leading financial indicators allow us to confirm that the financial structure of traditional factors is more stable than that of Fintech start-ups, notably thanks to interbank support. BNP Paribas Factor needs to be financially stable as a bank subsidiary.

4.2. The New Factoring Business Value Chain

Faced with the arrival of Fintechs on the market and the evolution of corporate demand, traditional factors have begun their digital transformation. However,

Table 4.1. Leading Financial Indicators of BNP Paribas Factor Between 2016 and 2018.

	31/12/2018 (Eur)	31/12/2017 (Eur)	31/12/2016 (Eur)
ROE from net income (%)	25.07	43.91	29.72
ROA from net income (%)	1.31	1.77	0.29
Turnover from net assets (*x*)	45.45	35.11	121.20
Solvency ratio (from assets) (%)	5.21	4.03	0.97
Solvency ratio (from liabilities) (%)	5.49	4.20	0.98

more is needed. Although BNP Paribas Factor now offers products that can be managed online, it still needs to catch up to the achievements of its competitors. Indeed, the financing solutions offered by BNP Paribas Factor that benefit from 100% digital technology only concern capped offers with small financing lines.

To improve its performance, the historic factor would gain by perfecting its exchange platform with clients to automate numerous tasks, notably assignment and invoice evaluation. While the credit committee remains a reliable risk control tool, algorithms can facilitate specific decision making.

As seen above, a possible rapprochement between Fintech and factors would benefit all market players. These partnerships or takeovers offer the traditional players the possibility of building loyalty and expanding their customer base. The latter could thus choose between the innovative solutions of Fintech and traditional financing solutions.

Finally, Fintech offers can be seen as complementary solutions. Initially created to meet the financing needs of VSEs and SMEs, Fintech offers have established themselves as alternative or complementary solutions to those of traditional players. Thus, the challenge for factoring players is to find solutions adapted to each need while combining responsiveness and simplicity. Whatever the profile of the factor, it must be able to provide liquidity to the company on an ongoing basis while respecting its needs. This situation is where the advantage of Fintech comes into play. While a traditional player requires the member to meet numerous criteria, Fintech does not require any.

According to our analysis, Fintechs' offers are ideally suited to small companies with a one-off need for liquidity. Indeed, for this size of business, financing needs change daily as the business develops, making the no commitment offers suitable. The offers are fast, easy to use, and with tariffs adapted to the income of small structures.

In addition, alliances with credit insurers offer a complete risk management product, mainly thanks to the commercial information Fintech can provide to their members' debtors.

However, the need for this product is becoming more significant and recurrent, and the Fintechs' offers are becoming more costly than traditional factors. These offers are not adapted to the needs of large SMEs. Moreover, the digital process of Fintech does not allow for personalized support in identifying companies' WCR. Thus, Fintech solutions are intended for small companies with a precise idea of their financing needs. For larger companies, these solutions can also be used as a complement to traditional factoring offers.

4.3. Benchmarking with Finexkap

Founded in 2012 but officially launched in early 2015, Finexkap is the first non-banking platform for corporate cash flow financing. It took two years to design the start-up: investment in R&D, a first fundraising round of one million euros, and optimization of its legal and financial terms. In 2014, Fintech organized a second fundraising round for 22.5 million dollars, that is, 18 million euros from GLI Finance, FinSight, and private investors. It is important to note that this fundraising is the third largest in France, behind those of Sarenza and Blablacar.

Finexkap will have raised nearly €32 million between 2014 and 2018. At the beginning of 2019, and since its creation, the Finexkap group financed more than €275 million in invoices.

Motivated by the alarming number of bankruptcies due to late payments and the urgent need for working capital, the co-founders wanted to give their company a clear objective: to give managers back the power over their cash flow. Thus, they have democratized factoring for SMEs whose files are often rejected by traditional factors. Fintech is thus revolutionizing the traditional factoring process, which is cumbersome for entrepreneurs and accumulates costs and additional fees. Finexkap enables companies of all sizes to transfer their outstanding invoices in exchange for a cash advance by offering an entirely dematerialized solution.

Named the best European alternative financing platform at the end of 2015, the start-up mainly targets French companies with a turnover of between one and 20 million euros, that is, VSEs, SMEs, and start-ups. Differentiating from traditional factoring services through its simplicity and flexibility, Finexkap offers receivables transfer service directly accessible from its website.

This platform is based on an investment fund called a "refinancing vehicle," managed by Finexkap Asset Management (AM), a wholly owned subsidiary of Finexkap. This management company, approved by the AMF, was set up jointly with Société Générale, and its role is to act as a custodian for transactions. When customers sell their invoices on the platform, the refinancing vehicle "buys" them and collects the receivables. Cash advances are thus backed by receivables and financed by issuing shares subscribed by investors.

Finexkap was awarded the title of French winner and European runner-up in the Tech5 competition in 2016 and named "Best Fintech start-up" by the J.P. Morgan Award competition in the same year. Finexkap has positioned itself as a leader in its market through its à la carte, no commitment, 100% dematerialized factoring offers, which include financing, collection, and guarantees against non-payment. Since its launch in 2015, Finexkap has financed more than €275 million of cash to over 1,600 customers, including €110 million in 2018. As of May 2018, more than 7,590 businesses have applied to Fintech, and more than 25,961 financings have been granted.

Finexkap offers three financing solutions: "Immediate Cash," "Cash Market," and "Cash Reverse." The first consists of transferring one or more unpaid invoices, with no limit to the number of invoices and no commitment to volume or duration. Thus, the transfer of receivables can be done on a one-off or recurring basis, depending on the company's cash flow needs. This offer enables financing within 48 hours, including collection and credit insurance (Petersen & Rajan, 1997). Unlike traditional factors, Fintech does not charge additional fees for audits and application fees, as the process is 100% digital. Indeed, the entire customer process is done online. This factoring process requires several steps.

Thanks to a robust algorithm, clients can find out in just a few clicks whether their debtors are eligible for the assignment of their receivables without even being registered on the platform. The database is accessible to everyone on the Finexkap homepage.

One of the advantages of the "Immediate Cash" offer, in addition to its speed and simplicity, is its price: a single commission is applied. It can vary between

1.90% and 4.80% of the assigned invoices, with an infinite assignment of receivables. No additional costs are applied. However, in the event of late payment of more than 15 days, Finexkap can claim compensation of 12% of the amount due. Once the debtor has paid, Finexkap pays the remaining 10% to the customer. In addition, it is essential to note that this Fintech applies a holdback of approximately 10% of the face value of the invoices assigned.

The second offer proposed by Finexkap is the "Cash Market." This offer is an invoice financing plug-in, an installed module integrating with B2B marketplaces. This service offers to manage the cash flow financing process, including credit insurance and collection. The offer is aimed at the sellers of these platforms, offering them an à la carte service, with no commitment, to meet their occasional or regular financing needs. Thanks to Finexkap's technology, this solution is directly accessible from the marketplace, making it easier to use.

Once the connection is made between Finexkap and the marketplace, the latter can modify and customize the screen templates provided to adapt the platform to the marketplace's graphic charter. Sellers can then have a financing line in a few clicks. The "Cash Market" offer is remunerated through a single commission, expressed as a percentage of the amount of the financing, with no limit on the number of invoices assigned and no additional fees. This solution makes it possible to manage the credit risk on the B2B marketplace, attract new sellers, retain existing ones, and increase the volume of business processed on the platform.

Finally, the last solution proposed by Finexkap is "Cash Reverse." This offer allows companies to anticipate their suppliers' payments like reverse factoring. As with the "Immediate Cash" offer, this solution is done through a 100% digitalized process, from selecting supplier invoices to granting financing. Once the delivery of goods or service provider has been confirmed, the invoice can be financed within 48 hours. The transfer of invoices is carried out by the supplier, who can manage the payments through Finexkap from a dedicated area. This transfer is a no-obligation, fast, and transparent à la carte financing. The rate for this offer varies according to the quality of the invoices transferred and is paid by the customer himself. The customer must then pay the amount initially due in the invoice to Finexkap after a period set by Fintech, which is often more advantageous than that set by the supplier.

To make itself known, Finexkap has formed partnerships with various players in the financial sector: accountants, brokers, financial advisors, integrators, and associations of CFOs and entrepreneurs. The same applies to brokers, who are paid a percentage of the invoices their client's transfer. Integrators also allow Fintech to integrate its services directly with management and accounting software such as SAGE. In addition, as a member of the French Association of Corporate Treasurers, Finexkap participates in numerous events and thus improves its visibility and promotion. Fintech is also a founder of the France Fintech Association, which brings together more than 75 companies covering the entire financial sphere.

Finexkap has established itself in the factoring market by responding to a cruel lack of adaptation of offers for VSEs and SMEs, the core target of Fintech. The start-up democratizes factoring through its innovative, no-obligation offers and makes it accessible to everyone for one-off or regular needs. Finally, transparency is a significant advantage for Fintechs regarding data processing, transactions, or prices. Nevertheless, the main weakness of Fintech is the need for more visibility Finexkap must face. As factoring Fintech are few and far between, companies are reluctant to use them, mainly because of the 100% digital process.

In summary, the business model of factoring Fintech is complex and requires a knowledge of current and future regulations.

Moreover, the credibility of Fintech is essentially based on the quality and security of its offers. While it is true that digital technology is gaining ground, so is cybercrime. A hack that reveals invoice details, or blocks the provision of finance lines to customers, would be very unpopular with consumers, who would tend to shun Fintech.

A poor risk assessment or algorithmic failure could lower the quality of Finexkap's services. The latter is also threatened by new offers on the market, which in turn revolutionize the Fintech sector.

In conclusion, Finexkap's success is mainly due to the quality of its offers and its revolutionary character. By revolutionizing the sector's business model, mainly through non-bank financing and transparent prices with only one commission, Finexkap is a start-up increasingly attracting entrepreneurs' interest. The à la carte financing, which is not very common among traditional factors, or the financing of B2B marketplaces are working capital financing solutions entirely adapted to SMEs.

4.4. Comparative Analysis Between BNP Paribas Factor and Finexkap

The comparative analysis provides a more profound understanding of the strategies implemented by Fintech Finexkap. From a strategic perspective, the start-up is completely revolutionizing the world of factoring through its process of refinancing receivables and its original internal structure. This situation suggests that with lower fixed costs than traditional factors, Fintech should generate significant profits.

To develop further, Fintechs need to gain consumers' trust, especially regarding data security. Furthermore, these factoring start-ups must prove their maturity and reliability to the market to gain visibility. They will also have to be ready to face the counterattacks of traditional factors increasingly approaching the field of digital offers. The working capital financing solutions proposed by Fintech are therefore revolutionizing the world of factoring strategically. While their offers facilitate factoring for SMEs, companies can use these solutions to complement traditional offers. However, it should be noted that with physical relationships, it is generally easier for Fintechs to advise companies on the working capital financing solutions available to them. Thus, Fintech offerings are primarily aimed at companies that do not require in-depth advice.

The comparative analysis of the offers between BNP Paribas Factor and Finexkap suggests that Fintechs are revolutionizing the factoring world. Thanks to their uncapped, invoice-by-invoice offers and simple, transparent pricing, Finexkap has established itself in this market by breaking the codes of traditional offers. At Finexkap, everything is done online, unlike traditional factors for whom customer relations are significant. Aimed essentially at small businesses, Fintech has established itself in the factoring market despite the monopoly of traditional factors. However, there is still a long way to go before the market shares of Fintech reach the same level as those of factors.

Of course, as BNP Paribas Factor is a reference in the factoring sector, its turnover is expected to be much higher than that of Finexkap, whose activity started in 2014. Although Finexkap's activity is growing slightly, it still has a long way to go before it reaches the same level of turnover as the classic factor.

5. CONCLUSION

Since the crisis of 2007, the control of working capital has become crucial for companies. With the crisis linked to COVID-19, which has further weakened the financial situation of SMEs and VSEs, innovative solutions for financing operating cycles have become a significant issue. Directly affecting the liquidity and performance of companies, working capital management is now an essential tool in corporate finance. WCR can severely impact a company's economic activity and survival if neglected. As described by Padachi (2006) and Peel et al. (2000), the impact of poor working capital management is even more severe the smaller the company. Indeed, too often neglected by SMEs, working capital management is the primary cause of bankruptcy in small companies. Most do not carry out any cash flow forecasting or monitoring.

Our case study has shown that although the strategy of Fintech is revolutionary, its business model has yet to prove itself. The Fintech revolution, therefore, still needs to be won. The keys to success for these factoring start-ups are to gain credibility by proving their maturity and stability. In addition, they must face the counterattack of traditional players trying to compete with Fintech on their ground with increasingly digitalized offers. The future of the factoring sector is still uncertain, and there are still many twists and turns and innovations to come. Therefore, the fate of Fintech has yet to be decided, and there are many opportunities for them (Pollari, 2016). Possible takeovers or alliances between traditional players and factoring start-ups can be envisaged, while the evolution of working capital financing solutions has only just begun.

Our research focused on a case study in the French context. The study could be extended to a panel of international Fintechs specialized in factoring, which could consolidate the results. The study focused on the launch phase of Fintech since it was limited to three pre-Covid-19 accounting periods between 2016 and 2018. As a result, two future avenues of research can be explored: firstly, the evo lution of the Fintechs business model during the different phases of its lifecycle. Secondly, the resilience of Fintechs during the Covid-19 crisis relative to traditional financial industry players is examined.

REFERENCES

Aktas, N., Croci, E., & Petmezas, D. (2015). Is working capital management value enhancing? Evidence from firm performance and investments. *Journal of Corporate Finance*, *30*(1), 98–113.

Allayanis, G., Yemen, G., & Lane, D. (2018). Fintech, payments innovation, and the acquisition of WorldPay. Retrieved from https://ssrn.com/abstract=3198435

Autukaite, R., & Molay, E. (2014). Cash holdings, working capital management and firm value, evidence from France. *Bankers, Markets and Investors*, *132*, 53–62.

Avenier, M. J., & Thomas, C. (2015). Finding one's way around various methodological guidelines for doing rigorous case studies: A comparison of four epistemological frameworks. *Systèmes d'Information et Management*, *20*(1), 61–98.

Banque de France. (2020). Défaillances d'entreprises. *Étude Statistique*, *1*, 119.

Bonin, H. (2016). Dans 50 ans d'affacturage en France. In *Chapitre I: Le temps des pionniers (dans les années 1960–1970)* (pp. 19–43). Publications d'histoire économique et sociale internationale, Librairie Droz.

Bougheas, S., Mateut, S., & Mizen, P. (2009). Corporate trade credit and inventories: New evidence of a trade-off from account payable and receivable. *Journal of Banking and Finance*, *33*, 300–307.

Bouyala, R. (2016). La révolution Fintech. Les essentiels de la banque et de la finance. *Revue Banque*. mars, Kindle Edition.

Clot, A. (2015). Quel avenir pour la Fintechs françaises? *Revue Banque*. Banque & Stratégie n°339, Révolution digitale: menace ou opportunité pour les banques.

Cunat, V. (2007). Trade credit: Suppliers as debt collectors and insurance providers. *Review of Financial Studies*, *20*(2), 491–527.

Effosse, S. (2014). Les débuts de l'affacturage en France, 1961–1973: Un secteur marginal en quête de reconnaissance. *Entreprises et Histoire*, *77*, 114–123.

Eisenhardt, K. M. (1989). Building theories from case study research. *Academy of Management Review*, *14*(4), 532–550.

Eisenhardt, K. M. (2021). What is the Eisenhardt method, really? *Strategic Organization*, *19*, 147–160.

Enqvist, J., Graham, M., & Nikkinen, J. (2014). The impact of working capital management on the firm profitability in different business cycles: Evidence from Finland. *Research in International Business and Finance*, *32*, 36–49.

Fischer, M. (2021). Fintech business models, Applied Canvas Method and Analysis of Venture Capital Rounds. In *Fintech business models*. Berlin: De Gruyter. https://doi.org/10.1515/9783110704907

Garcia-Teruel, P. J., & Solano, M. P. (2007). Effects of working capital management on SME profitability. *International Journal of Managerial Finance*, *3*, 164–177.

Gariglia, A., & Mateut, S. (2010). Inventory investment, global engagement, and financial constraints in the UK: Evidence from micro data. *Journal of Macroeconomics*, *32*, 239–250.

Gill, A., Biger, N., & Mathur, N. A. (2010). The relationship between working capital management and profitability: Evidence from the United States. *Business and Economics Journal*, *2*, 1–9.

Haq, I. U., Sohail, M., Zaman, K., & Alam, Z. (2011). The relationship between working capital management and profitability: A case study of cement industry in Pakistan. *Mediterranean Journal of Social Sciences*, *2*(2), 365–372.

Hornuf, L., Klus, M., Lohwasser, T., & Schwienbacher, A. (2020). How do banks interact with fintech start-ups? CESifo Working Paper Series No. 7170. Retrieved from https://ssrn.com/abstract=3252318

Klapper, L. (2006). The role of factoring for financing small and medium enterprises. *Journal of Banking & Finance*, *30*(11), 3111–3130.

Kumar, S., Srivastava, M., & Prakash, V. (2023). Challenges and opportunities for mutual fund investment and the role of Industry 4.0 to recommend the individual for speculation. In A. Nayyar, M. Naved, & R. Rameshwar (Eds.), *New horizons for Industry 4.0 in modern business. Contributions to environmental sciences & innovative business technology*. Cham: Springer. https://doi.org/10.1007/978-3-031-20443-2_4

Lazaridis, I., & Dimitrios, T. (2006). Relationship between working capital management and profitability of listed companies in the Athens stock exchange. *Journal of Financial Management and Analysis*, *19*(1), 1–12.

Llorca, M. (2017). Les banques aux prises avec les Fintech. *L'Économie Politique*, *75*(3), 43–58.

Mathew, D., Brintha, N. C., & Jappes, J. T. W. (2023). Artificial intelligence powered automation for Industry 4.0. In A. Nayyar, M. Naved, & R. Rameshwar (Eds.), *New horizons for Industry 4.0 in modern business. Contributions to environmental sciences & innovative business technology*. Cham: Springer. doi:10.1007/978-3-031-20443-2_1

Merriam, S. B. (2009). *Qualitative research: A guide to design and implementation* (4th ed.). San Francisco, CA: John Wiley & Sons.

Milian, E. Z., Spinola, M. M., & Carvalho, M. M. (2019). Fintechs: A literature review and research agenda. *Electronic Commerce Research and Applications*, *34*, 100833.

Molina, C. A., & Preve, L. A. (2009). Trade receivables policy distressed firms and its effect on the costs on financial distress. *Financial Management*, *38*(3), 663–686.

Molina, C. A., & Preve, L. A. (2012). An empirical analysis of the effect of financial distress on trade credit. *Financial Management*, *41*(1), 187–205.

Mosa, A., Iraj, S. A., & Maryam, G. (2012). Studying the relationship between working capital management and profitability at Tehran stock exchange: A case study of food industry. *Research Journal of Applied Sciences, Engineering, and Technology*, *4*(13), 868–1874.

Padachi, K. (2006). Trends in working capital management and its impact on firms' performance: An analysis of Mauritian small manufacturing firms. *International Review of Business Research Papers*, 2(*2*), 45–58.

Parashar, B., Sharma, R., Rana, G., & Balaji, R. D. (2023). Foundation concepts for Industry 4.0. In A. Nayyar, M. Naved, & R. Rameshwar (Eds.), *New horizons for Industry 4.0 in modern business. Contributions to environmental sciences & innovative business technology*. Cham: Springer. https://doi.org/10.1007/978-3-031-20443-2-3

Peel, M. J., Nicholas, W., & Carole, H. (2000). Late payment and credit management in the small firm sector: Some empirical evidence. *International Business Journal*, *18*, 17–37.

Petersen, M., & Rajan, R. G. (1997). Trade credit: Theories and evidence. *Review of Financial Studies*, *10*(3), 661–691.

Philippon, T. (2017). L'opportunité de la Fintech. *Revue d'Economie Financiere*, *127*, 127–206.

Pollari, I. (2016). The rise of Fintech opportunities and challenges. *JASSA the Finsia Journal of Applied Finance*, *3*, 15–21.

Raheman, A., & Nasr, M. (2007). Working capital management and profitability: Case of Pakistani firms. *International Review of Business Research Papers*, *3*(1), 279–300.

Salerno, D., Sampagnaro, G., & Verdoliva, V. (2021). Fintech and IPO underpricing: An explorative study. *Finance Research Letters*, *44*(C), 1–3. https://ec.europa.eu/eurostat/data/database

Srivastava, S. (2023). Prospective application of blockchain in mutual fund industry. In A. Nayyar, M. Naved, & R. Rameshwar (Eds.), *New horizons for Industry 4.0 in modern business. Contributions to environmental sciences & innovative business technology*. Cham: Springer. doi:10.1007/978-3-031-20443-2-6

Stake, R. E. (1995). *The art of case study research*. London: Sage Publications.

Torriero, C., Montera, R., & Cucari, N. (2022). How is digitalisation changing the business model of FinTech companies? The case study of an Italian non-bank financial institution. *International Journal of Quality and Innovation*, *6*(1), 7–27.

Tricaud, A. (2018). *Optimisation du BFR par l'affacturage 2.0: Etude du cas FINEXKAP. Mémoire de fin d'étude*. Paris: ESLSCA Business School.

Vasilescu, G. (2010). International factoring: A viable financing solution for firms. *The Young Economists Journal*, *1*(14), 27–34.

Weichert, M. (2017). The future of payments: How Fintech players are accelerating customer-driven innovation in financial services. *Journal of Payments Strategy & Systems*, *11*, 23–33.

Yin, R. K. (2003). *Case study research, design, and methods* (3rd ed.). London: Sage Publications.

Yin, R. K. (2009). *Case study research, design and methods* (4th ed.). London: Sage Publications.

Youssef, W. A. B., & Rakotondratsimba, Y. (2022). Future research avenues for finance in transformation. In S. Boubaker & D. K. Nguyen (Eds.), Financial transformations beyond the COVID-19 health crisis (pp. 697–727). Singapore: World Scientific Publishing.

CHAPTER 5

INVESTIGATING THE ROLE OF BUSINESS MODEL INNOVATION IN THE RELATIONSHIP BETWEEN DIGITALIZATION AND FIRM PERFORMANCE

Imen Belhaj Ammar[a] and Khaled Tamzini[b]

[a]*Faculty of Economic Sciences and Management of Sousse, University of Sousse, Sousse, Tunisia*
[b]*LaREMFiQ, IHEC of Sousse, University of Sousse, Sousse, Tunisia*

ABSTRACT

Digitalization is considered an emerging phenomenon that enables businesses to develop new markets and business models. It helps firms expand the scope of their activities and enables organizations to become more efficient. It is now a reality for firms and contributes to their value creation. Thus, the aim of this paper is to investigate the relationship between digitalization and firm performance through the mediating role of business model innovation (BMI) and to do so, a self-administered questionnaire with a sample of 70 Tunisian firms was conducted for this purpose. The main result of the analysis, confirms that digitalization is positively related to business performance, with BMI mediating this relationship.

Keywords: Digitalization; firm performance; business model innovation; resource-based view (RBV); competitive advantage; value creation

Digital Technology and Changing Roles in Managerial and Financial Accounting: Theoretical Knowledge and Practical Application
Studies in Managerial and Financial Accounting, Volume 36, 53–64

Published under exclusive licence by Emerald Publishing Limited
ISSN: 1479-3512/doi:10.1108/S1479-351220240000036005

1. INTRODUCTION

Over the past decades, digitalization has become increasingly important in business and everyday life. Therefore, it has received increased attention as a key driver of the fourth industrial revolution and its effects on organizations, economies, and societies (Brunetti, Matt, Bonfanti, De Longhi, Pedrini, & Orzes, 2020).

According to Gruia, Roja, Bibu, Nastase, and Cristache (2021), organizations can leverage digitalization to transform their business models and structures, stay competitive, improve productivity, reduce production costs, and make new connections with customers.

In recent years, the advance of digital technology is forcing firms to rethink their organizational models; thus there has been an increase in research focused on digitalization and its impact on business models (Caputo, Pizzi, Pellegrini, & Dabić, 2021). Yet, we still have little understanding of how business models are innovated to adapt to technological changes and disruptive innovations (Caputo et al., 2021). Furthermore, while research on digitalization in the context of business models is receiving increased attention, there is still a gap in the field, as the number of empirical observations is limited (Rachinger, Rauter, Müller, Vorraber, & Schirgi, 2018).

Therefore, the main goal of this study is to investigate if BMI plays a mediating role in the relationship between digitalization and firm performance. The above-discussed research context creates the foundation for the research problem. The identified research gap will be studied with the following research question: Does BMI mediate the relationship between digitalization and firm performance?

The remainder of this paper is structured as follows: In Section 2, a review of theory and literature where the relevant academic literature is presented in order to provide a solid foundation and understanding of the different concepts. In Section 3, the relationships between the theoretical concepts in order to test our research hypotheses and build our conceptual framework is presented. In Section 4, the research methodology and measures are explained. Analysis and research results are provided in Section 5. Section 6 provides a discussion of the results of the study. Finally, the most important practical and theoretical implications, limitations, and future avenues for research are presented in the conclusion section.

2. THEORETICAL BACKGROUND

For this study, the resource-based view (RBV) is selected as the underlying theory in line with the study conducted by Osarenkhoe and Fjellström (2021), which considers the firm as a set of resources and assets that can create competitive advantages when used in a distinctive way. The RBV emphasizes that the firms' resources and capabilities are the primary sources of competitive advantage, leading to superior performance (Barney & Hesterly, 2010).

Berawi et al. (2020) argue that digitalization can create a competitive advantage for firms because it enables them to create new ways to add value to their businesses. Therefore, this study posits that digitalization studies are in line with Grant's RBV (1991), in which digitalization is a specific resource that contributes to a firm's competitive advantage.

3. RESEARCH HYPOTHESES AND THE CONCEPTUAL MODEL

3.1. Digitalization Impact on Firm Performance

In the digital age, new technologies are transforming businesses and providing a multitude of benefits (Ribeiro-Navarrete, Botella-Carrubi, Palacios-Marqués, & Orero-Blat, 2021).

According to Pilinkiene and Liberyte (2021), through digitalization, firms can become more competitive, have more opportunities, and have routine tasks performed faster and more efficiently. Manresa, Bikfalvi, and Simon (2021) have shown that the implementation of different digitalization tools has a positive effect on the operational performance of the firm, for example, the use of digital exchange of product data reduces production lead time and increases the average of orders delivered on time. In addition, digitalization can improve service quality and reduce costs, while improving employee and work efficiency, thus enhancing business performance (Pilinkiene & Liberyte, 2021). Digitalization also offers real-time insights by integrating diverse data sources and enhancing organizational data views (Parviainen et al., 2017). Furthermore, Digitalization enables greater information transparency, benefiting all employees by enhancing their understanding of the business and enabling more informed decision-making (Kuusisto, 2017).

Based on the previous research, the following hypothesis is formulated:

H1. Digitalization has a positive impact on firm performance.

3.2. Digitalization Impact on Business Model Innovation

The rise of digitalization has had an impact on a number of business activities, including business models (BM). In particular, it has enabled firms to develop new forms of cooperation and has given rise to new products and services as well as new relationships with customers and employees (Rachinger et al., 2018).

A study conducted by Legowo et al. (2021) showed that digitalization had a significant role in creating, changing, and improving the values of BMI. For example, digital platform provides added value through new products and services, also innovation increases customers' intention to buy new products/services.

Furthermore, according to Parida, Sjödin, and Reim (2019), digitalization influences the three components of an organization's BMI. First value creation, the value creation dimension of the business model describes what the firm offers to the customer, whether it is a product or a service. Digitalization enabled firms to develop new forms of cooperation and has given rise to new products and services, as well as new relationships with customers and employees (Rachinger et al., 2018). Parida et al. (2019) state that digitalization leads to collaborative value creation by firms and their networks, as well as customer participation in the value creation process, which could have a positive impact on market positioning and competitive advantage, leading to value creation in BMI (Bhuiyan & Yusuph, 2021). Second, is the value delivery dimension which refers to how processes and activities are configured in order to deliver the promised value (Burström, Parida, Lahti, & Wincent, 2021). With digital BM, the value will be delivered to customers in a different way. Third, the value capture dimension focuses on the cost structure and revenue model offerings (Mostaghel, Oghazi, Parida, & Sohrabpour, 2022). A firm can capture value from digitalization in a variety of ways, such as by reducing costs, increasing revenues, or capturing new revenue streams and also by gaining benefits from developing new products/services (Legowo et al., 2021; Parida et al., 2019).

Therefore, the development of *H2*:

H2. Digitalization has a positive impact on business model innovation.

3.3. Business Model Innovation and Firm Performance

The BMI plays a key role in gaining a competitive advantage and improving performance (Anwar, 2018). Pang, Wang, Li, and Duan (2019) argue that BMI can enhance firm performance as it can increase customer satisfaction by delivering new value to customers.

In addition, BMI encourages investment in R&D, which many researchers believe improves business performance. Moreover, BMI allows firms to commercialize their ideas, resources, and products in new ways that are strategically, operationally, and economically beneficial (Pang et al., 2019).

Furthermore, Alshawaaf and Lee (2020) state that the customer creation value dimension improves organizational performance by attracting customers to pay a higher price for an offering or to make frequent purchases. Additionally, new value creation transforms an organization's business model by significantly reducing costs, increasing revenues, or maintaining a competitive advantage.

The above discussion leads us to the following hypothesis:

H3. Business model innovation is positively related to firm performance.

Based on these hypotheses, we developed our conceptual model, as shown in Fig. 5.1.

4. METHODS

In this section, we will provide an overview of the approaches and methods used in this study. Thus, in order to fulfill the purpose of our study and to reach our fundamental objective, our research is placed in a positivist perspective. It is a

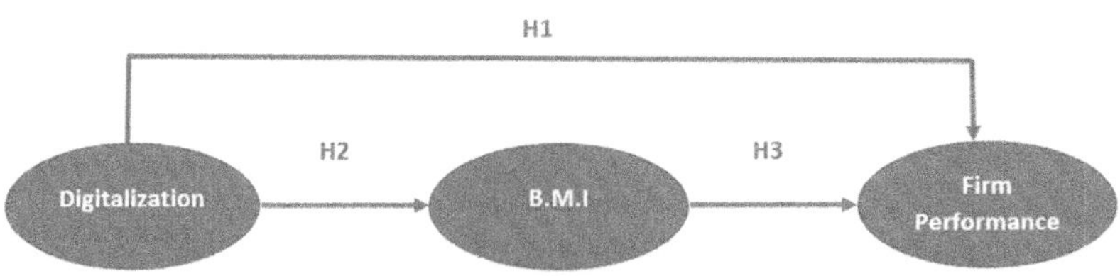

Fig. 5.1. The Conceptual Model.

Table 5.1. Measures of Variables.

Variables	Source	Nature
Digitalization	Abou-foul, Ruiz-Alba, and Soares (2020)	5-Point Likert scale items ranging from "extremely disagree" to "extremely agree"
Firm performance	Wiklund and Shepherd (2003)	5-Point scales ranging from "much lower" to "much higher"
Business model innovation	Latifi, Nikou, and Bouwman (2021)	5-Point Likert scale, ranging from "Very Low" to "Very High"

deductive approach. We have therefore chosen to test our conceptual model using a quantitative approach that aims to collect observable and quantifiable data.

4.1. Data Collection

Data are obtained by questionnaire survey techniques using an online survey and were collected from July 11 to September 11, 2020 via e-mail or LinkedIn message to selected, available, and reachable respondents. We opted for two software programs when processing the data: SPSS 21 and Smart PLS 3.

4.2. Sample

The study was conducted on a convenience sample of 70 Tunisian firms from different activity sectors such as Manufacturing industries, IT services, Banks, and insurance and financial services. Among the respondents, most were directors (34.2%), managers (18.5%), CEO/cofounders (15.6%), heads of departments (15.5%), and others (11%) including engineers and software developers. The average age of respondents is between 35 and 44, with more than five years of experience. The majority of respondents were from SMEs (40% with 10–49 employees, 24.3% with 50–249 employees, 22.9% with 1–9 employees, and 12.9% with more than 250 employees).

4.3. Operationalization of Variables

Table 5.1 summarizes the type and nature of the measurement scales used to operationalize our different research variables, as well as the items in each of these scales.

5. RESULTS

5.1. Measurement Model Evaluation

In this perspective, the estimation of the measurement model corresponds to two types of validity: convergent and discriminant validity.

5.1.1. Convergent Validity

Table 5.2 describes the reliability and validity of the construct.

From this table, we see that the reliability of the different measurement scales of our conceptual model based on CR and Cronbach's *a* is good. In other words, the instrument measures perfectly and only the construct under consideration.

5.1.2. Discriminant Validity

Discriminant validity can be evaluated by initially using the Fornell and Larcker criterion. Table 5.3 illustrates the Fornell–Larcker analysis for discriminant validity.

The Fornell–Larcker criterion was used to test discriminant validity, and it was found that the square root of the mean-variance extracted for each reflective construct was greater than any corresponding correlation involving the constructs. Therefore, the discriminant validity result was satisfactory, demonstrating that each construct shared more variance with its items than any other construct.

5.2. Structural Model Evaluation

5.2.1. Tests of Research Hypotheses

Table 5.4 shows the results of the hypothesis testing in our research.

Based on the above, Table 5.5 provides a summary of the validation of our research hypotheses.

Table 5.2. Reliability and Validity of the Construct.

Variables	AVE	CR
Digitalization	0.613	0.934
Firm performance	0.659	0.946
Business model innovation	0.588	0.909

Table 5.3. The Fornell–Larcker Criterion.

	BMI	Digitalization
BMI	0.767	
Digitalization	0.485	0.783
Performance	0.797	0.626

Table 5.4. Test of Hypotheses.

	Original Sample (O)	Standard Deviation (STDEV)	*T*-statistics (|O/STDEV|)	*p*-values	Decision
Digitalization → performance	0.313	0.118	2.661	0.008	Sig.**
Digitalization → BMI	0.485	0.088	5.547	0.000	Sig.**
BMI → performance	0.645	0.100	6.465	0.000	Sig.**

Significant at ** $p < 0.05$.

Table 5.5. Summary Table of the Results Obtained.

Hypotheses	Results
H1. Digitalization has a positive impact on Firm Performance	Supported
H2. Digitalization has a positive impact on business model innovation	Supported
H3. Business model innovation is positively related to firm performance	Supported

Table 5.6. Coefficient of Determination R^2.

	R^2	Results
BMI	0.236	Low
Performance	0.711	High

Table 5.7. Mediation Effect.

	Original Sample (O)	Standard Deviation (STDEV)	*T* Statistics (|O/STDEV|)	*p* Values	Decision
Digitalization → BMI	0.485	0.506	0.086	5.643	0.000
BMI → performance	0.645	0.643	0.099	6.503	0.000
Digitalization → performance	0.626	0.635	0.083	7.586	0.000
Digitalization → BMI → performance	0.313	0.324	0.074	4.247	0.000

5.2.2. Coefficient of Determination R^2

According to the results of Table 5.6, we can conclude that 23.6% of the variance of BMI is explained by digitalization what is considered to be low. Furthermore, digitalization explains 71.1% of the firm performance variation. Thus, the predictive quality is considered high.

5.3. Study of the Mediation

In this thesis, we examined the mediating role of BMI on the relationship between digitalization and firm performance.

From Table 5.7, it can be seen that BMI plays a mediating role between the independent variable digitalization and the dependent variable firm performance with a high significant *p*-value (<0.05).

Similarly, the indirect effect between digitalization and performance through BMI is significant (p-value $= 0.000 < 0.05$).

Thus, the partial mediation of BMI in the relationship between digitalization and performance is confirmed.

6. DISCUSSION

In this study, we investigated the impact of digitalization on firm performance. Our research showed that digitalization has a positive and significant effect on firm performance. This relationship is supported by Astuti and Augustine (2022) who found that the use of digital technology has a significant impact on business success as well as on organizational performance the same conclusion is also supported by Truant, Broccardo, and Dana (2021) who demonstrated a positive relationship between business performance and digitalization.

This result can be explained by the dynamic and rapidly changing market in which we live today. So, it is no secret that businesses must continually change to remain viable. Organizations around the world are adapting their operations to be digitally enabled; as a result, many firms have realized the importance of digitalization and have already converted or invested in new BM.

The use of digitalization in business has been proven to help many firms succeed, according to the *Harvard Business Review*, "84% of business leaders say new business opportunities have emerged when their firms have made digital transformations."

Also, in a survey conducted by African Manager (2022) among 1,632 Tunisian firms, 82.9% said digitalization could enhance competitiveness. More than 72% of them believe digitalization can increase their market share in the local market and 78% believe it can strengthen their export market share.

Furthermore, our empirical study found that digitalization adoption improves a wide range of business areas, particularly those related to marketing, customer service, strategic planning, human resources, and logistics, which are among the top benefits of digital investments. Thus, we can conclude that firms in Tunisia are more aware than ever of the importance of digitalization, as its processes are now a topic that presents new challenges and opportunities for businesses across industries.

Our study also found that digitalization improves BMI. This result is in line with the results obtained by Legowo et al. (2021). We can explain this outcome by the fact that the use of digital technology positively affects the value creation, value capture, and value delivery of firms. Digitalization has been found to affect value creation by providing more value through the creation of new products and services to customers.

The mechanisms of digitalization also affect value creation, as customers will be able to receive value in a new way through the development of new capabilities and resources, as well as the formation of new alliances with new partners to ensure the delivery of cost-effective offerings.

In terms of how digitalization impacts the value capture dimension, we found that the ability to capture value is affected by improving internal processes that enable profitability and improve revenue streams.

Despite the inconclusive results of recent studies regarding the strength of the relationship between BMI and business performance (Latifi et al., 2021), in this research, a significant and positive relationship between digitalization and business model was found. This result is consistent with the findings of Latifi et al. (2021) and Guo, Tang, Su, and Katz (2017) who also found that BMI is positively related to performance. This can be due to the fact that innovation in BM can create a competitive advantage and thus boost the performance of a firm (Latifi et al., 2021).

Furthermore, the SEM model revealed that BMI partially mediated digitalization and firm performance, with digitalization having an indirect effect on firm performance the results of this hypothesis have no previous related studies. This hypothesis finding is a novelty of this research.

When the BMI was introduced into the model, it served as a strong and significant mediating effect. This proves that digitalization alone is not sufficient to explain the performance. This result can be explained by the fact that Tunisian firms may believe that having innovative technologies is not the only key to success; the business model must also be carefully planned, which means they understand that in order to gain a sustainable competitive advantage and benefit from their technological innovations, they must put in place the appropriate BM and technology strategy, meaning that a firm can have a great innovation, but if the business model has not been properly thought out, the innovator will fail, which will have a negative impact on the performance of the firm.

Additionally, the results can also demonstrate the openness and willingness of Tunisian business leaders to use new technologies to create a new business model or improve the existing one to enhance value creation, value capture, and value delivery for a better understanding of the needs of their customers and also to provide them with better customer service, thus improving their firm performance.

Despite our positive results, Tunisian firms suffer from barriers to investment in digitalization. Our empirical study shows that the main barriers to digitalization in Tunisian firms were insufficient resources and a lack of appropriate skills to manage data, this can be justified by the fact that firms could not bear the additional cost of hiring new skilled employees who are experts in digitalization due to the economic crisis we are experiencing today.

One of the main obstacles is also the low internal acceptance. This may be due to the fact that Tunisian employers fear that the new responsibilities are too demanding for them and that they feel obliged to perform with a totally new tool that they have no experience using.

To overcome these barriers, we believe that Tunisian firms should either hire qualified employees or invest in training their experienced former employees, which can cost less than the hiring process, to hone their strengths, build their confidence, and develop their digital skills in order to help the firm better utilize its technology tools and implement the appropriate digitalization strategies and the appropriate business model as well and therefore develop a competitive advantage and remain successful in the market.

7. CONCLUSION: IMPLICATION, LIMITS, AND FUTURE DIRECTIONS

This study has advanced the conversation on the impact of digitalization on firm performance and BMI, confirming a significant positive relationship. Indeed, the results of this study shed new light on this relationship in the context of Tunisian firms. BMI and digitalization have played a significant role in improving firm performance.

The main objective of this thesis was to critically examine the effects of digitalization on firm performance through the mediating role of BMI, thus advancing the understanding of this topic. By collecting data from various Tunisian firms in different sectors, my research sought to shed light on the mediating effect of the BMI on the relationship between digitalization and firm performance. In an effort to analyze this relationship, we have adopted the positivist epistemological paradigm and opted for a hypothetico-deductive approach.

Our research has several theoretical and practical implications. Concerning theoretical implications, the results provide evidence of the role of digitalization in improving a firm's performance, highlighting the strong relationship between the implementation of digitalization and organizational performance.

In addition, there is a lack of empirical studies on the impact of digitalization on BMI. Therefore, this study adds value to the BMI literature by filling these gaps and providing an avenue for future researchers to extend the research model. Furthermore, the mediating role of BMI between digitalization and performance, to our knowledge is the first study that attempts to explain the role of BMI between digitalization and performance.

From a practical point of view, this study demonstrates how digitalization can improve value creation, capture, and delivery thus encouraging managers to rethink their BM, experiment with new ideas, and even develop new BM that can provide opportunities to learn, stay competitive, and stay ahead of the game. Also, the results have practical implications for managers and other stakeholders seeking to understand the complex relationship between digitalization and firm performance.

The positive results achieved by firms that have implemented digitalization can help motivate decisions by managers to seriously consider investing in digitalization in order to be able to adapt to the changing environment.

In addition, our empirical study gave an idea of the main obstacles to investment in digitalization in Tunisia, which can help managers and leaders seek to better understand these problems and find ways to solve them.

Even though the results of our thesis shed new light on this subject and the obtained results can serve as a basis for future research, they are not without limitations.

The main limitation of this study is related to the sample. Our sample was relatively small (70 firms), also the sampling technique used in this study is convenience sampling. This method limits the generalizability and representativeness of the sample to the overall population. Therefore, we suggest for future research to replicate our research in the same context but with different sample characteristics to increase generalizability. Future research on relevant topics can build on this study.

By expanding existing knowledge, the role of digitalization in BMI and its impact on business performance will help firms flourish in this digital age and remain competitive in a fast-changing environment.

In addition, future studies could explore similar topics in specific types of digital technologies or BM. Also, since our study is based on understanding Tunisian firms only, future studies, therefore, could be particularly interesting to investigate the similar topic from other countries also a comparison between firms from developed and developing countries might be quite interesting to show the differences and peculiarities related to digitalization implementation.

Moreover, the results of this investigation show that even though the research fields of BM and firm performance are not new, due to disruptive innovations and digitalization those topics are more relevant and up-to-date than ever.

Organizations and firms need to embrace digitalization as an essential component of their operations, as it can be considered an opportunity for them to grow their business and boost their performance, which in turn could generate economic growth and reduce unemployment.

Finally, although the use of new digital technologies is a fundamental prerequisite for digitalization, it is not sufficient for its success. Digitalization involves more than digital technologies and data; it requires the restructuring of a firm's business model. Therefore, digitalization should be seen as a strategy to be developed rather than a tool to be implemented. Thus, further analysis is needed to determine the importance and influence of digitalization on firms' strategies and BM.

REFERENCES

Abou-foul, M., Ruiz-Alba, J. L., & Soares, A. (2021). The impact of digitalization and servitization on the financial performance of a firm: An empirical analysis. *Production Planning & Control*, *32*(12), 975–989.

African Manager. (2022). Tunisia: Private companies still struggling to digitalize. Retrieved from https://en.africanmanager.com/tunisia-private-companies-still-struggling-to-digitalize/

Alshawaaf, N., & Lee, S. H. (2021). Business model innovation through digitisation in social purpose organisations: A comparative analysis of Tate Modern and Pompidou Centre. *Journal of Business Research*, *125*, 597–608.

Anwar, M. (2018). Business model innovation and SMEs performance – Does competitive advantage mediate? *International Journal of Innovation Management*, *22*, 1850057.

Astuti, W., & Augustine, Y. (2022). The effect of digital technology and agility on company performance with management accounting system as mediation. *International Journal of Research and Applied Technology*, *2*, 11–29.

Barney, J. B., Hesterly, W. S. (2010). *Strategic management and competitive advantage: Concepts and cases*. Prentice Hall.

Berawi, M., Suwartha, N., Asvial, M., Harwahyu, R., Suryanegara, M., Setiawan, E. A., ... Maknun, I. J. (2020). Digital innovation: Creating competitive advantages. *International Journal of Technology*, *11*, 1076.

Bhuiyan, M. R., & Yusuph, R. G. (2021). Influence of digitalization on business model innovation in the internationalization process of SMEs. Retrieved from http://hdl.handle.net/2077/68819

Brunetti, F., Matt, D. T., Bonfanti, A., De Longhi, A., Pedrini, G., & Orzes, G. (2020) Digital transformation challenges: Strategies emerging from a multi-stakeholder approach. *The TQM Journal*, *32*(4), 697-724.

Burström, T., Parida, V., Lahti, T., & Wincent, J. (2021). AI-enabled business-model innovation and transformation in industrial ecosystems: A framework, model and outline for further research. *Journal of Business Research*, *127*, 85–95.

Caputo, A., Pizzi, S., Pellegrini, M. M., & Dabić, M. (2021). Digitalization and business models: Where are we going? A science map of the field. *Journal of Business Research*, *123*, 489–501.

Gruia, L., Roja, A., Bibu, N., Nastase, M., & Cristache, N. (2021). Approaches to digitalization within organizations. *Indiana International & Comparative Law Review*, *21*(3), 287–297.

Guo, H., Tang, J., Su, Z., & Katz, J. A. (2017). Opportunity recognition and SME performance: The mediating effect of business model innovation. *R&D Management*, *47*(3), 431–442.

Kuusisto, M. (2017). Organizational effects of digitalization: A literature review. *International Journal of Organization Theory and Behavior*, *20*, 341–362.

Latifi, M. A., Nikou, S., & Bouwman, H. (2021). Business model innovation and firm performance: Exploring causal mechanisms in SMEs. *Technovation*, *107*, 102274.

Legowo, B. M., Indiarto, B., Prayitno, D., 2021. Digitalization for Business Model Innovation: Create, Change, and Improve for Values. pp. 192–197. https://doi.org/10.1109/IC2IE53219.2021.9649340

Manresa, A., Bikfalvi, A., & Simon, A. (2021). Investigating the impact of new technologies and organizational practices on operational performance: Evidence from Spanish manufacturing companies. *Central European Journal of Operations Research*, *29*, 1317–1327. https://doi.org/10.1007/s10100-020-00692-8

Mostaghel, R., Oghazi, P., Parida, V., & Sohrabpour, V. (2022). Digitalization driven retail business model innovation: Evaluation of past and avenues for future research trends. *Journal of Business Research*, *146*, 134–145.

Osarenkhoe, A., & Fjellström, D. (2021). The oxymoron of digitalization: A resource-based perspective. *Journal of Information Technology Research*, *14*(4), 122–138.

Pang, C., Wang, Q., Li, Y., & Duan, G. (2019). Integrative capability, business model innovation and performance: Contingent effect of business strategy. *European Journal of Innovation Management*, *22*(3), 541–561.

Parida, V., Sjödin, D., & Reim, W. (2019). Reviewing literature on digitalization, business model innovation, and sustainable industry: Past achievements and future promises. *Sustainability*, *11*(2), 391.

Parviainen, P., Tihinen, M., Kääriäinen, J., & Teppola, S. (2017). Tackling the digitalization challenge: How to benefit from digitalization in practice. *International Journal of Information Systems and Project Management*, 5(1), 63–77.

Pilinkiene, V., & Liberyte, M. (2021, August 24–27). Conceptualization of business digitalization and its impact on economics. In *IEEE international conference on technology and entrepreneurship (ICTE)* (pp. 1–6). Piscataway, NJ: IEEE.

Rachinger, M., Rauter, R., Müller, C., Vorraber, W., & Schirgi, E. (2018). Digitalization and its influence on business model innovation. *Journal of Manufacturing Technology Management*, *30*(8), 1143–1160.

Ribeiro-Navarrete, S., Botella-Carrubi, D., Palacios-Marqués, D., & Orero-Blat, M. (2021). The effect of digitalization on business performance: An applied study of KIBS. *Journal of Business Research*, *126*, 319–326.

Truant, E., Broccardo, L., & Dana, L. P. (2021). Digitalisation boosts company performance: An overview of Italian listed companies. *Technological Forecasting and Social Change*, *173*, 121173.

Wiklund, J., & Shepherd, D. (2003). Knowledge-based resources, entrepreneurial orientation, and the performance of small and medium-sized businesses. *Strategic Management Journal*, *24*(13), 1307–1314.

CHAPTER 6

USER'S CONTINUANCE INTENTION TOWARDS BANKER'S CHATBOT SERVICE – A TECHNOLOGY ACCEPTANCE USING SUS AND TTF MODEL

C. Nagadeepa[a], A. Pushpa[a], K. P. Jaheer Mukthar[a], Roger Rurush-Asencio[b], Jose Sifuentes-Stratti[b] and Jose Rodriguez-Kong[c]

[a]*Kristu Jayanti College, Autonomous, Bengaluru, India*
[b]*Universidad Nacional Santiago Antunez de Mayolo, Huaraz, Peru*
[c]*Universidad Señor de Sipán, Chiclayo, Peru*

ABSTRACT

Chatbot technology is growing swiftly across the banking and finance industry. The study aims to explore the influence of Task-Technology Fit (TTF), system suitability, perceived usefulness, social influence and satisfaction on respondents' continuance intention among the chatbot-users. A total of 250 responses were collected using a structured questionnaire via social media across India. The measurement model was proposed based on the system usability (SUS) and TTF model with other constructs, and the hypothesis was tested using a structural equation model. The findings of the study highlighted and confirmed

Digital Technology and Changing Roles in Managerial and Financial Accounting: Theoretical Knowledge and Practical Application
Studies in Managerial and Financial Accounting, Volume 36, 65–77

Published under exclusive licence by Emerald Publishing Limited
ISSN: 1479-3512/doi:10.1108/S1479-351220240000036006

the association among five constructs: TTF, SUS, perceived usefulness, social influence, on satisfaction and continuance intention in the context of chatbots usage in banking.

Keywords: Chatbot; Task-Technology Fit; system usability; perceived usefulness; technology acceptance; SUS; TTF

1. INTRODUCTION

In today's remote era, chatbots have become a competitive necessity and a game changer for banking industry. Chatbots are artificial intelligence (AI) programme intended to stimulate communication with customers directly through voice applications or chat windows. Digitalisation is a new dimension that has led most sectors go online, and banking sector is no exception and this increases demand for online help. The onset of pandemic-led businesses confronts unprecedented issues compelling industries accelerate digital transformation. In the wake of COVID-19, worldwide lockdown and general workspace restriction have directly affected availability of manpower availability, coercing businesses streamline their operations. The new social norm social distancing forced customer's transit online driving businesses go digital in creating customer experience embracing automation and chatbots. Automation and AI chatbots gained prominence as they provide 24/7 support in resolving queries automatically without human intervention. The chatbots enable financial institutions handle millions of customers on many touch points and alert customers on upcoming payments and issues. Customers favour digital banking as they continue to avoid visiting branches, expecting banks to launch more virtual assistants.

World's prominent banks have integrated live chats into their websites and use of live chats, WhatsApp chatbots to engage their customers. Impeding use of chatbots in banking functions – conversational banking – leads to improved efficiency and better customer experience assisting banks in interacting with clients at all stages of customer life cycle. Studies demonstrate automation of 90% of customer's interaction in banking system through AI chatbots indicating the positive response from customers towards the usage of chatbots. Tech savvy customers, the millennials dearth every solution over the internet. Conversational AI-powered chatbots are smart solutions from the sophistication in technology redefining the customer support landscape that allow banks support their customers' needs with visual search to automated messages. Chatbots as an innovative tool for customer service interaction has gained tremendous relevance in the past few years. However, existent literature is unclear on impact of usage of chatbots on customer service perception and other relevant metrics indicating the requisite to develop insights on chatbots usage (Reshmi & Balakrishnan, 2018).

With this backdrop the study identifies the need to measure and identify insights on other metrics impacting usage of chatbots. The study aims exploring the influence of TTF, system suitability, perceived usefulness, social influence and satisfaction on continuance intention among the chatbot-users. The rest of the study in organised as follows: Section 2 briefs the review for the background of research; Section 3 illustrates research methodology; Section 4 presents the analysis and results testing the proposed model and Section 5 discusses the implications, limitations and future research implications.

2. THEORETICAL FOUNDATION

A conversational AI system that enables communication among persons is termed as chatbot using natural language. Chatbots assist online users on various platforms to attain best services while dealing with service providers.

2.1. Task-Technology Fit

The TTF reveals the link amid information systems (IS) and users' performance; denoting the behaviour or aspects that users expect to complete a goal (Fuller et al., 2009) and technology refers to the device to execute or complete a task. It refers to the degree a technology can assist its users in performing their tasks, the degree of TTF is put up to the requirements of the task, functionality and ability of the technology. Tasks vary in numerous dimensions, and it may include interdependent tasks, critical tasks and non-routine tasks. The present study considers usage of chatbot as a task characteristic that affects its utilisation and performance. The characteristics have an impact on how users evaluate technology fit, forming the foundation for assessing usage among users within an organizational context. Prior researches have devoted on extending the TTF model to different context in IS like group support system; data base management system; impact on adoption (Rai et al., 2019); wireless technology (Yen et al., 2010); performance (El-Gayar, 2010); learning performance (Marikyan & Papagiannidis, 2022); mitigating technostress. Thus, TTF-linked measure of performance can be used in a larger context of measuring the impact of chatbots on users' task performance. The study proposes content characteristics as an additional determinant of fit, contributing to the explanation of impact on satisfaction leading to continuance usage. Consequently, the following hypothesis was formulated based on TTF constructs relationship with satisfaction of chatbot usage and continuance usage.

H1. TTF has a positive impact on user's satisfaction.

2.2. System Usability

SUS also refers to perceived usability of a system, and it is associated with the travail needed to use an information system, computer system, website or a product. Perceived SUSis the user's ability to use it to reach out one's goals with proficiency, efficacy and satisfaction in a quantified context of use (Flavián, Guinaliu, & Gurrea, 2006). The SUS was developed by John Brook in 1986 and used in usability of electronic office systems. Extant literature unveils usability from different context like consumer perceptions about formations (Anu, 2002), effect of website attributes on potential consumers (Flavián et al., 2006) and access to desire to information from a website. Few studies have evidenced that consumer's satisfaction is solely achieved because of usability and is considered as a key factor in organisations based on internet (Chandrasekaran & Ganapathy, 2002; Kim & Eom, 2002; Naomi & Johnson, 1999). Usability plays an important role in predicting intentions to use. Thus, the study claims that usability improves satisfaction and consequently the following hypothesis was framed.

H2. System usability has a positive impact on user's satisfaction.

2.3. Perceived Usefulness

Perceived usefulness (PU) is understood as user's perception if a new technology can change the way one performs and enhance one's performance (Ajzen, 1991; Raman & Aashish, 2017). It is one of the essential precursors of innovation usage that relates to the extent to which technology users accept using IT creates utilitarian value (Rouibah, Abbas, & Rouibah, 2011); online education classes. Previous researchers have found PU as significant precursor of customer satisfaction (Amin, Rezaei, & Abolghasemi, 2014; Park, Kim, & Del Pobil, 2013) on Facebook users (Sibona & Choi, 2012) and computer industry (Wilson, Keni, & Tan, 2021). Studies have shown Pu as a significant precursor of user's continuance intention to use adoption of hotel services online shopping intention to accept matching services Sports app acceptance intention. Based on the explanation, it is important to gain insights relationship between PU and satisfaction and it consequently frames the hypothesis:

H3. Perceived usefulness has a positive impact on customer satisfaction.

2.4. Social Influence-Subjective Norms

Social influence is a predictor of technology adoption and was included in the extended technology acceptance model (TAM). The theory of reasoned action predicted social influence as a result of people's expectations that is significantly what others expect them to be or to behave differentiated social influence as injunctive social norm and descriptive social norm. Injunctive norm infers what most of the people favour or object, descriptive norm infers to what most of them normally do. Ajzen (1991) defined subjective norm as perception of a people the need to behave in a certain way due to social pressure claimed subjective norm as a predictor of users' intentions to use fitness apps. Researchers have explored the social influence in a non-pandemic context. The study considers Covid-19 fear as a subjective norm as people were forced to follow the Covid-19 protocol of social distancing and contactless dealings that lead to social isolation. Outbreak of COVID-19 has significantly added to change in the attitude and behaviour intention. Hence the study included injunctive and subjective social norms to explain the inclination to use chatbots, and it is highly likely that the situation of COVID-19 fear experience would indulge people continue the usage of chatbots to interact with the service providers and might provide new insights to academicians and practitioners, thereby proposing the following hypothesis:

H4. Social Influence has a positive impact on customer satisfaction.

2.5. Satisfaction and Continuance Intention

Customer satisfaction is a key parameter in the study of consumer behaviour. User satisfaction is one's feeling of discomfort/contentment parallel to his or her belief of an outcome that partakes a strong impact on repurchase decision of users (Bhattacherjee, 2001; Weng, Tsai, & Weng, 2015). User's future decision to use is based on his/her experience the outcome of user satisfaction (Raman & Aashish, 2021). As researchers have confronted a strong association among satisfaction and continuance among users, the study deliberated the same from different contexts of IS not restricted to e-commerce mobile payments (Mouakket, 2020); m-banking e-training (Garg & Sharma, 2020); m-campus (Razak, Mokhtar, Rahman, & Abidin, 2021); e-learning (Fleming, Becker, & Newton, 2017). In addition, studies have deliberated the existence of association between the two factors (Cronin, Brady, & Hult, 2000; Rahman et al., 2017; Weng et al., 2015). The study claims that the users' continuance intention is influenced by his or her satisfaction in the context of chatbot in information system. Thus, the following hypothesis is framed.

H5. Users' satisfaction has a positive impact on users' continuance intention.

3. RESEARCH MODEL AND METHODOLOGY

Technology made things very easy and people expected to do things very fast. Nowadays, time is considered more precious than money. To save time and make things easy many researchers invent new technology to attract and get new customers. Chatbot is also one of the new technologies and bankers introduced this service to enhance their services to the customers. People hate long queues. Due to heavy traffic, and to save time, they seek information from their place wherever they are. They search for information and need the answer from the banks. Chatbot is one of the human-free service providers which gives solution for the customer's queries. This research is an effort to understand the user's satisfaction towards chatbot and continuation of this service in future. To know this, a framework was formulated using TTF model, system usability model (SUM), TAM and continuation model. TTF is used in this framework to examine the users' satisfaction towards the chatbots services, whether the technology is completing the given task or not. The usability and TAM model is altered to find out the satisfaction towards its usability and usefulness regarding their banking queries.

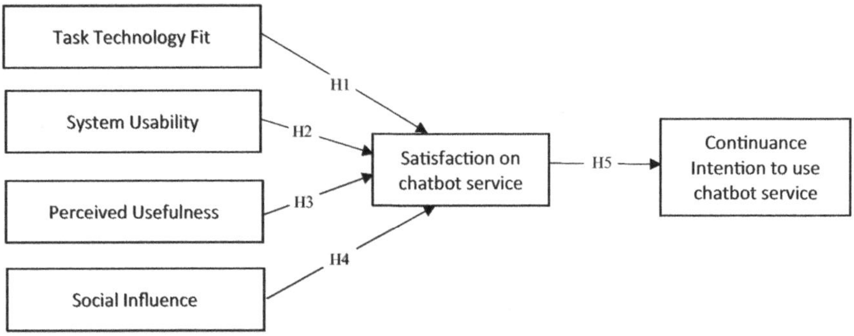

Fig. 6.1. Conceptual Framework – Continuance Intention of Bankers' Chatbot Service. Authors' compilation.

Finally, the respondents' intention to continue the facility is examined with satisfaction and continuance usage of chatbot services in banking sector (refer to Fig. 6.1).

The research is based on descriptive research design and it was carried out using convenient sampling method. The data were collected via structured questionnaire and circulated via social media across India. The people who experienced the chatbot facility were considered for this study as respondents. Two hundred and fifty respondents were participated and filled the questionnaire. The questionnaire has two parts: the first part is related to the respondent's demographic information and the second part has 22 questions to measure the chatbot user's intention to continue the services in the banking sector. Table 6.1 shows the various questions asked to the respondents to measure their satisfaction level of chatbots used by them to get the information from various banks. To determine whether the chatbot's performance met respondents' expectations for the assigned task, six questions were posed. In a similar manner, satisfaction with technological usability, convenience of use and social influence were evaluated by posing four, three and three questions, respectively. Finally, they were asked to give their opinion to continue using this chatbot technology further in the future. They were then prompted to express their views on whether chatbot technology should be used moving forward.

4. ANALYSIS AND INTERPRETATION OF RESULTS

Table 6.1 shows the respondent's profile.

The maximum respondents are male (62%) and maximum of them fall under the age group of 25–35 (37%). Majority of the respondents are degree holders. Most of the respondents (35%) are employed under private and public sectors and 30% of them are doing own business; 37% of them are using chatbots often and only 2% of them are using frequently; 44% of them have both business and personal account.

Table 6.1. Profile of the Sample Chatbot-Users.

Particulars of Sample Respondents		Frequency	Percentage
Gender	Male	156	62
	Female	94	38
Age	<25	56	22
	25–35	92	37
	36–45	37	15
	Above 45	65	26
Education	High school	25	10
	Degree	97	39
	Masters	75	30
	Others	53	21
Occupation	Student	35	14
	Employed	88	35
	Business	75	30
	Others	52	21
Frequency of using chatbot	Always	5	2
	Often	95	37
	Sometimes	77	31
	Rarely	73	30
Use of chatbots for different types of banking	Personal Account	75	30
	Business Account	66	26
	Both	109	44

Source: Primary data.

4.1. Measurement of the Model

To test the reliability questions were measured using Cronbach's α to find out the internal consistency of the items. Table 6.2 shows the Cronbach's α of each construct. It is inferred that all the items are above the recommended value 0.7, and it shows that the subscales of all the variables are highly reliable.

The KMO (Kaiser–Meyer–Olkin) test was conducted to measure the adequacy of the sampling for all the factors. The results of the test supplied the adequate factor loading which are shown in Table 6.2.

4.2. Hypotheses Test Results

The suggested measurement model was tested using the data collected through questionnaire from the respondents. Structural equation modelling (SEM) was used to measure and prove the hypotheses framed using AMOS. The first step in the SEM is to measure the model fit comparing the various model fit indices. Table 6.3 shows the various model indices of the proposed model.

The result shows the fitness of the final SEM developed to assess the impact of chosen independent variables on the dependent variable. The result shows that all the indicators of model fit attain the threshold limit. Hence the developed model is considered fit. The first fit is the minimal fit, that is, chi-square. For the model, the chi-square data is 351.045 with 154 degrees of freedom is 2.21 which shows an adequate fit. The Goodness of Fit Index achieved is

Table 6.2. Survey Item and Factor Loading.

Constructs	Code	Measurement items	Loading	Cronbach's α
Task-technology fit (TTF)	TTF1	It provides the accurate answer to the question.	0.79	0.87
	TTF2	The answer of the queries through chatbot is presented in a useful format and manner.	0.85	
	TTF3	I need some special training to use the chatbot	0.74	
	TTF4	The chatbot is available whenever I need it	0.88	
	TTF5	I am able to get the information what I want from the banks through this chatbot without any human interaction.	0.79	
	TTF6	The chatbot addresses the issue what I had.	0.87	
System usability (SU)	SU1	I like to use chatbot frequently to know my banking-related information	0.91	0.83
	SU2	I need the support of a technical person to use chatbot service	0.72	
	SU3	I learn to use this chatbot services very quickly	0.77	
	SU4	I felt very confident using the chatbot service	0.82	
Perceived usefulness (PU)	PU1	This chatbot saves me time in finding information	0.78	0.91
	PU2	It is good practice to use chatbot to get bank-related queries	0.72	
	PU3	Chatbot is very useful technology to get the information	0.92	
Social influence (SI)	SI1	It is good to use chatbot during pandemic situations	0.96	0.86
	SI2	I am worrying about pandemic, so I am using chatbot to get information	0.88	
	SI3	My hair palpitates when I think about getting diseases, hence I am using chatbots	0.75	
Satisfaction (SAT)	SAT1	I am happy about the overall experience with chatbot	074	0.85
	SAT2	Chatbot meets my expectation	0.89	
	SAT3	I am satisfied with information provided by the chatbot	0.91	
Continuance intention (CI)	CI1	Will continue using chatbot in future	0.88	0.79
	CI2	I will recommend chatbot for others to use it	0.78	
	CI3	I will keep using the chatbot service to get information after pandemic too	0.82	

Source: Primary data.

Table 6.3. Various Indicators of Chatbot Acceptance Model.

Fit Indices	Proposed Model Value	Standard Value
CMIN/DF	2.21	≤3
P	0.06	>0.05
GFI	0.93	>0.9
AGFI	0.912	>0.9
NFI	0.902	>0.9
CFI	0.962	>0.95
RMSEA	0.048	≤0.08
TLI	0.952	>0.95

Source: Primary data.

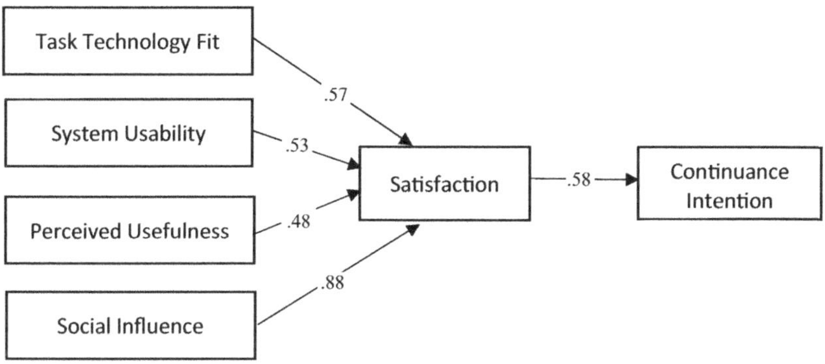

Fig. 6.2. Conceptual Framework. Authors' compilation.

0.930, while the Goodness of Fit Adjusted Index) is 0.912, above the required 0.90. The Comparatives Fit Index (CFI) and Normal Fit Index values computed are more than 0.90, indicating that the model fits perfectly with the data. It was discovered that RMSEA is 0.038, which is lower than 0.08, and that it confirms the model fit. SEM was employed to examine the proposed model. Fig. 6.2 and Table 6.4 show the result of the hypotheses and their relationship clearly.

The regression estimates and their significance for the entire path are calculated. Each estimate represents the amount of change in its dependent variable for each one-unit change in the variable predicting it. The relative contribution of each predictor variable to each dependent variable is given by the standardised estimates in Table 6.4. The results of the model show that all the independent variable has an impact on dependent variable.

4.3. Task-Technology Fit and Satisfaction of Bank's Chatbot Services

The impact of Banker's chatbot services has a significant and positive impact on user's satisfaction (estimator = 57% – 0.057) as the *p*-value is less than

Table 6.4. Regression Weights of Estimated Model.

DV	INF	INDV	Estimate	SE	CR	*p*	Result
Satisfaction	←	Task-technology fit	0.57	0.079	2.170	*	Accepted
Satisfaction	←	System usability	0.53	0.061	2.527	**	Accepted
Satisfaction	←	Perceived usefulness	0.48	0.090	4.452	*	Accepted
Satisfaction	←	Social influence	0.88	0.060	2.507	**	Accepted
Continuance intention	←	Satisfaction	0.58	0.104	2.403	**	Accepted

Source: Primary data.
$*p < 0.05$; $**p < 0.01$.

0.05 ($p = 0.002$) with CR 2.170. The chatbots are performing the given task by the respondents, and it significantly impacts on satisfaction towards it, which is similar with the study conducted by Lin (2012). At the same time Ouyang, Tang, Rong, Zhang, Yin, and Xiong (2017) found insignificance between TTF and student's satisfaction towards MOOCs.

4.4. SUS and Satisfaction of Bank's Chatbot Services

The chatbot-users have a significant satisfaction towards its usability as its *p*-value is less than 0.05 ($p = 0.02$) with the estimator of 0.53, SE of 0.61 and CR of 2.527. It is inferred that the perceived chatbot usability has a significant impact on respondents' satisfaction. This result is similar to the study conducted by Pal et al. (2020), and respondents' perceived usability (SUS) of Microsoft Teams is quite interesting when they work with the new technology.

4.5. Perceived Usefulness and Satisfaction of Bank's Chatbot Services

Respondent's PU of chatbots has a significant impact on user's satisfaction as the *p*-value is less than 0.05 ($p = 0.010$), with estimator value of 0.48, SE of 0.090 and CR of 2.542. Chatbot is very useful and there is no need of more technical knowledge use in this technology. Hence, there is significant impact of ease of use on satisfaction of this chatbot service. This result is similar to the study by den Hollander (2020).

4.6. Social Influence and Satisfaction of Bank's Chatbot Services

Social distancing and pandemic fear are the social influences that motivated the users to use chatbots. The *p*-value of 0.012, which is less 0.05, signifies that the social influence has a significant impact on chatbot user's satisfaction towards its services. Pandemic isolation is one of the social influences that forced the respondents to have direct contact with banks and bankers. The results showed that there is a high impact of social influence on satisfaction level of chatbot services. This result is similar to the study conducted by Jure

(2022), who proved that social isolation made the people go for online shopping during COVID-19.

4.7. Satisfaction and Continue Intention of Bank's Chatbot Services

Finally, user's satisfaction of chatbot services has significantly influenced the people to use the service in future too (continuance intention), as its p-value is less than 0.05 ($p = 0.016$) with the estimator of 0.58 (SE is 0.104) and CR of 2.403. Hence, the satisfaction of chatbot services leads to continue intention towards its services. To avoid long queue, save time and completion of task the respondents are motivated to continue to use this service.

5. CONCLUSION

The main persistence of the study was to confirm the association among five constructs: TTF, SUS, PU, social influence, on satisfaction and continuance intention in the context of chatbots usage in banking. The study integrated the SUS and TTF model to recommend the proposed model. Expanding the study to include COVID-19 fear as a variable assumes that the experience of fear related to COVID-19 induces people to use chatbots for interacting with service providers. This experience may, in turn, lead to continuance intention, thus offering new insights to academics and practitioners.. The results of the study revealed a significant association among the dependent and the independent constructs at 5% and 1% level of significance. The findings of the study have strong implication to practitioners especially the bank managers, as the study has integrated constructs of SUS and TTF model to study the technology acceptance and identified new path relationships. The results provide new insights to practitioners that may be fundamental in developing stratagems that directly or indirectly enhance user's experience that leads to satisfaction and continuance intention in future transaction. Bankers should ensure that customers perceive chatbots useful, understand its usage and build trust that chatbots improve their services. The study verdicts need to be deliberated in the light of few limitations and this indeed serves as prospects for further investigation. Firstly, results cannot be generalised as results are based on convenience sampling insisting future research using probability sampling technique. Secondly, the study is from the context of chatbots in banking, and it is recommended to replicate the study with respect to other contexts such as education sector, e-wallets, investment apps, generalising the results.

REFERENCES

Ajzen, I. (1991). The theory of planned behavior. *Organizational Behavior and Human Decision Processes*, *50*(2), 179–211.

Amin, M., Rezaei, S., & Abolghasemi, M. (2014). User satisfaction with mobile websites: The impact of perceived usefulness (PU), perceived ease-of-use (PEOU) and trust. *Nankai Business Review International*, *5*(3), 258–274.

Anu, R. (2002). The consumer benefits and problems in the electronic grocery store. *Journal of Retailing and Consumer Services*, *9*(2), 107–113.

Bhattacherjee, A. (2001). Understanding information systems continuance: An expectation-confirmation model. *MIS Quarterly*, *25*(3), 351–370.

Chandrasekaran, R., & Ganapathy, S. (2002). Key dimensions of business-to-consumer web sites. *Information and Management*, *39*(6), 457–465.

Chen, Y. S. (2013). Towards green loyalty: Driving from green perceived value, green satisfaction, and green trust. *Sustainable Development*, *21*(5), 294–308.

Cronin, J., Brady, M., & Hult, G. (2000). Assessing the effects of quality, value, and customer satisfaction on behavior intentions in service environments. *Journal of Retailing*, *76*(2), 193–218.

den Hollander, D. (2020). *The influence of a personal conversational recommendation on the user experience in chatbots*. The Netherlands: Radbound University.

Flavián, C., Guinalíu, M., & Gurrea, R. (2006). The role played by perceived usability, satisfaction and consumer trust on website loyalty. *Information & Management*, *43*(1), 1–14. doi: 10.1016/j.im.2005.01.002.

Fleming, J., Becker, K., & Newton, C. (2017). Factors for successful e-learning: Does age matter? *Education + Training*, *59*(1), 76–89. http://doi.org/10.1108/ET-07-2015-0057

Garg, S., & Sharma, S. (2020). User satisfaction and continuance intention for using e-training: A structural equation model. *Vision: The Journal of Business Perspective*, *24*(4). doi:10.1177/0972262920926827.

Kim, E. B., & Eom, S. B. (2002). Designing effective cyber store user interface. *Industrial Management & Data Systems*, *102*(5), 241–51.

Marikyan, D., & Papagiannidis, S. (2023). *Technology Acceptance Model: A review*. In S. Papagiannidis (Ed.), *TheoryHub*. http://open.ncl.ac.uk

Mouakket, S. (2020). Investigating the role of mobile payment quality characteristics in the United Arab Emirates: Implications for emerging economies. *International Journal of Bank Marketing*, *38*(7), 1465–1490.

Naomi, M., & Johnson, E. (1999, February 2). Constructing preferences online: Can web pages change what you want? *Arbeitspapier*.

Ouyang, Y., Tang, C., Rong, W., Zhang, L., Yin, C., & Xiong, Z. (2017, January 4–7). Task-technology fit aware expectation-confirmation model towards understanding of MOOCs continued usage intention. In *Proceedings of the 50th Hawaii international conference on system sciences*, Hawaii, USA.

Ozecan, M., & Arikan, E. (2022). An integrative model on user satisfaction and continuance intention for using M-banking. *Business and Economics Research Journal*, *13*(3), 465–482. doi:10.20409/berj.2022.384

Park, E., Kim, K. J., & Del Pobil, A. P. (2012). An examination of psychological factors affecting drivers' perceptions and attitudes toward car navigation systems. In Kim, K., Chung, KY. (Eds.), *IT convergence and security* (Vol 215, pp. 555–562). The Netherlands: Springer. https://doi.org/10.1007/978-94-007-5860-5_66

Rai, R. S., & Selnes, F. (2019). Conceptualizing task-technology fit and the effect on adoption – A case study of a digital textbook service. *Information & Management*, *56*(8), 103161. doi: 10.1016/j.im.2019.04.004

Raman, P., & Aashish, K. (2021). To continue or not to continue: A structural analysis of antecedents of mobile payment systems in India. *International Journal of Bank Marketing*, *39*(2), 242–271.

Razak, F. Z. A., Mokhtar, A. E., Rahman, A. A., & Abidin, Z. Z. (2021). *Journal of Physics: Conference Series*, 1793. doi:10.1088/1742-6596/1793/1/012019.

Reshmi, S., & Balakrishnan, K. (2018). Empowering chatbots with business intelligence by big data integration. *International Journal of Advanced Research in Computer Science*, *9*, 627.

Rouibah, K., Abbas, H., & Rouibah, S. (2011). Factors affecting camera mobile phone adoption before e-shopping in the Arab world. *Technology in Society*, *33*(3/4), 271–283.

Sibona, C., & Choi, J. H. (2012, June 4–7). Factors affecting end-user satisfaction on Facebook. In *Paper presented in sixth international AAAI conference on weblogs and social media*, Dublin, Ireland.

Weng, C., Tsai, C. C. & Weng, A. (2015). Social support as a neglected e-learning motivator affecting trainee's decisions of continuous intentions of usage. *Australasian Journal of Educational Technology*, *31*(2), 177–192.

Wilson, N., Keni, K., & Tan, P. H. (2021). The role of perceived usefulness and perceived ease-of-use toward satisfaction and trust which influence computer consumers' loyalty in China. *Gadjah Mada International Journal of Business*, *23*, 262–294. doi:10.22146/gamaijb.32106

CHAPTER 7

THE VALUE OF INFORMATION AND COMMUNICATION TECHNOLOGY IN HUMAN RESOURCE MANAGEMENT

Arti Singh[a], Raja Kamal Ch[a] and Sanjeev Chauhan[b]

[a]*Kristu Jayanti College, Bangalore, India*
[b]*Institute of Business Management, GLA University, Mathura, India*

ABSTRACT

Over the last several years, it has been clear that HR departments rely heavily on their own pieces of technological infrastructure. For improved time management, efficiency in working, productivity, managing remuneration, assessing personnel, recruiting candidates via online methods, etc., technology is being used across all areas of human resources. All of this require technology, and in this qualitative study, the author has attempted to compile the technologies used across all of the verticals, as well as their impact on HR functioning and the ways in which the Human Resource Information System (HRIS) is used within the organization. HRIS have modified HR administrative work and improved the business, allowing HR to rise from the tiers of management, administration, and maintenance to the level of core business and strategy.

Keywords: HR technologies; performance; productivity; workforce analytics

Digital Technology and Changing Roles in Managerial and Financial Accounting: Theoretical Knowledge and Practical Application
Studies in Managerial and Financial Accounting, Volume 36, 79–85

ISSN: 1479-3512/doi:10.1108/S1479-351220240000036007

1. INTRODUCTION

HRIS have been more popular in the recent decade as a means of gathering and analyzing HR data in a variety of organizations (Beckers & Bsat, 2002). Numerous pieces of software aid in the following areas of human resources:

Internet-based registration, hiring, and enlistment:

- Keeping an Eye on the Staff
- Tracking Progress
- E-Learning
- Compensation and Advantages
- Effective Human Resource Management

Human resources departments use technological tools to improve the quality of their strategic planning and the efficiency and effectiveness of their operational procedures. Numerous studies have shown that using an HRIS may help businesses save money via process automation and time through the elimination of mundane tasks. Furthermore, this would result in a decrease in the number of HR specialists in a firm while simultaneously increasing productivity. The following benefits would result from doing so:

- Employee data and documentation.
- Managers can see all essential data.
- Data analysis becomes manageable.
- Data-driven judgments.
- Worker communication.

HR professionals must comprehend the linkages between innovation and HRM demonstrated in Fig. 7.1. As HR moves from clerical support in manufacturing to management support in IT, competency requirements for HR professionals are shifting. HR experts will need an authority of the conduct and mental establishment of HRM, a vital direction with expansive knowledge of the legal climate and hierarchical structure and measures, and an arrangement and authority of the new advancements that are affecting the plan of establishments, work, and HR frameworks to address the issues of this emerging type of HRM.

The focus on HR's basic components (Breaugh, 1992) and the tendency to see HR as applied authoritative behavior (OB) (Brockbank & Ulrich, 2000) indicate that HR experts' education and training now prioritize the first two skills. Brown (2002) noted that most corporate HR departments' specialized demands and abilities are in the third competency. Human resources professionals should study and apply innovative skills to exhibit expertise.

2. METHODOLOGY

The major focus of this descriptive investigation is on secondary sources of information. Journals, periodicals, websites, articles, blogs, and publications on the use of technology in human resources were mined for secondary material for this study.

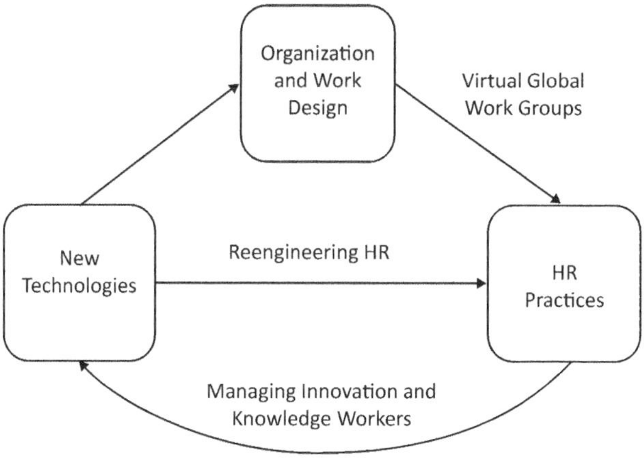

Fig. 7.1. The Perplexing Establishments Among Innovation and HRM Outlined.

2.1. Objectives

This study demonstrates on following objectives:

- Recognizing the benefits of HR technology on productivity and effectiveness.
- Locating HR tools that improve productivity in the workplace.

2.2. Research Objectives

- To demonstrate the efficiency and usefulness of HR technologies.
- To improve organization performance, identify HR technology.

2.3. Analysis Technology in E-Recruitment and& Selection

Those looking for work may find it through online businesses. E-recruitment refers to the practice of looking for a job using the internet. E-enrolment includes applicant screening, communication, and administration that take place entirely online (Bussler & Davis, 2002). E-recruitment include posting openings online, collecting resumes, and maintaining databases of potential employees.

Internet usage has significantly impacted HR, said Casper (1985). Chapman and Webster (2003) note an increase in online recruitment. Employers and job-seekers alike may use the internet-based HR Portal 2003 to look up applicants, administer tests, and get in touch with those who passed.

Below listed are the benefits of the online hiring:

- The price of hiring is quite inexpensive.
- Possibility of finding and hiring superior candidates.

According to Cullen (2001), a competitive atmosphere is needed to hire the finest employees, and online exams provide a simple and affordable approach for firms to locate qualified applicants. They recruit applicants online. E-HRM is changing the HR business and needs acknowledgment as a real and major innovation (Edelman, 2004; Faiz, 2001). E-recruitment attracts competent candidates and persuades them to apply.

3. TECHNO-COMMUNICATION

Human resources rules and procedures on the intranet need reliable means of internal communication. New rules and responsibilities are made clearer via intranets (Gallagher, 1997). Any prospective applicant may quickly and easily see, recover, and modify any policy. You may get information from other departments without having to physically go or phone in, thanks to the intranet. This is what you use to send birthday wishes, check your email, and organize your inbox. It takes care of the staff directory and automatically generates birthday greetings. Employees are more likely to experience a sense of pride in their work when they get a birthday greeting from upper management (Gara, 2001), this is because the system automatically created the message after identifying the employee's email address in the database. When a new employee is hired, HRIS sends out a security email, audits the phone system, and notifies legal of any compliance or registration concerns.

It is the engine behind the following features:

- Vacations and Sick Days
- Taxation
- Mortgage and car loan statements (if applicable)
- Overtime
- Pay slip
- PF statement

It used to take a lot of time to get back to employees who had questions. Now, though, this might end up saving a lot of time for the HR department. Some of the talents fostered by implementing technology inside the business.

- Costs that are minimal.
- The availability and ease of access to more data.
- Positive interactions among workers; improved, timely dialogue.
- Upgraded feedback mechanism.
- Internal departmental collaboration is simplified with documentation.
- Improved focus group discussions.

3.1. Technology in Workflow Advancements (Business Process Management)

Representative access requires workflow management. Workflow technology lets someone quickly develop a process change approval process (Gatewood, Gowan, & Lautenschlager, 1993). When employees want a break, managers and HR decide. Directors may appoint a replacement approver while absent.

3.2. Technology and Applicant Tracking Systems

Every day, businesses must contend with fierce competitiveness for few resources, even as they pare down their own recruiting budgets and cut staff in order to keep up with the demand. The association for human resource management's Gentner's 1984 publication "Workplace trends" suggests/indicates that:

- A greater need has arisen for qualified workers.
- Online methods of hiring are in high demand.
- Increased rivalry for a shrinking pool of available workers.
- The expansion of app developers.
- Recruitment as part of a larger BPO.
- Increased reliance on evaluations in the hiring process.

3.3. Technology in Performance Management System (PMS)

Staff evaluations are streamlined under the new PMS. Since technology permeates every industry, PMS tools are widely used. Human resource managers may oversee company image and employee interactions (Gourley & Connolly, 1996). The functions of performance management software include:

- Performance assessments.
- Notes by Email.
- Aligning competency mapping with business objectives.
- Management technique for the self and the workplace.
- Reporting on productivity growth.

3.4. Automation of Performance Management Workflow/System

Infosys' Performagic, a cloud-based BPO PMS, is fully automated. It was developed by Infosys Tech. In addition, Infosys only utilizes it twice a year for evaluations, and only internally. Through the company intranet, it facilitates communication across divisions. Moreover, it also

- Appraisal feedback capturing and analysis.
- Performance history records.
- Evaluation based on a comparison to historical results.
- All policies and forms are kept strictly confidential.
- Appraisal history may be tracked at any moment.
- Timeliness and open communication are essential.

3.5. Technology in Compensation and Payroll

The payroll model automates payroll by collecting employee data such attendance, reporting time, deductions, and taxes to create pay stubs and tax returns. Greer (1995) recommends this since it saves the HR administrator time when inputting data for the reports. In 2007, payroll began sending accounting data to the general ledger. The biggest advantage is being able to run all these reports on demand, making last-minute changes without effort, saving time, and ensuring correctness. These flexible options:

- Reduced complicatedness of payment handling.
- Detailed documentation.
- Create a check.
- Cash payment for managing expenses.

3.6. Technology Trends and Technological Implications

Management repercussions of business decisions and strategy frameworks have received a lot of attention from both the HR and technological sectors. The following are some of the ramifications:

- E-recruitment is a great way to find new employees.
- Online applications for human resources management.
- The use of online courses increases.
- Protecting personnel records is crucial.
- Enhanced performance.
- Strategic HR transactions are applied using HRIS software/application.
- HRMS outsourcing.
- The return on investment for HR software is determined.

4. CONCLUSION

This research explored how technology influences HR management and HR information systems on HR and business excellence. Technology freed HRs to focus on strategy rather than support. HRIS improved workflow and operations strategically. HRIS enhances cycle efficiency and makes HR a genuine partner, enabling long-term success. HRIS may boost corporate performance. This technological option gives leaders swift access to job-relevant data and a good platform to disseminate it to its employees, improving productivity, viability, consistency, competence, association adaptability, and client-centered and benefit duty. High-tech may increase business and human capital.

REFERENCES

Beckers, A. M., & Bsat, M. Z. (2002). A DSS classification model for research in human resource information systems. *Information Systems Management*, *19*, 41–50.

Breaugh, J. A. (1992). *Recruitment: Science and practice*. Boston, MA: PWS-Kent.

Brockbank, W., & Ulrich, D. (2000). *Competencies of new HR*, *2*(Is), 21–39. Arlington, VA: Society of Human Resource Management.

Brown, D. (2002). EHR – Victim of unrealistic expectations. *Canadian HR Reporter*, *15*(16), 1–6.

Bussler, L., & Davis, E. (2002). Information systems: The quiet revolution in human resource management. *Journal of Computer Information Systems*, *42*(2), 17-20.

Casper, R. (1985). Online recruitment. *Personnel Journal*, *64*(5), 4–5.

Chapman, D., & Webster, J. (2003). The use of technologies in recruiting, screening, and selection processes for candidates. *International Journal of Selection and Assessment*, *11*(2/3), 113–20.

Cullen, B. J. (2001). *Winning the war for talent: E-recruiting best practices*, *3*(2), 59–72. Boston, MA: Cambria Consulting.

Edelman, D. (2004, November). Engaging your employees in new technology launches. *Employee Thinking*, *1*(1), 41–49.

Faiz, A. (2001). *Leveraging IT in HR*, *2*, 39–47. Mumbai: Indian Express Newspapers Limited.

Gallagher, S. (1997). *Human resource management software*, 59–72. London: Conspectus, PMP Ltd.

Gara, S. J. (2001). *How an HRIS can impact HR: A complete paradigm shift for the 21st century*, *1*(4), 22–33. Alexandria, VA: Society for Human Resource Management (SHRM).

Gatewood, R. W., Gowan, M., & Lautenschlager, G. (1993). Corporate image, recruitment image and initial job choice decision. *Academy of Management Journal*, *36*(2), 14–22.

Gentner, C. (1984). The computerized job seeker. *Personnel Administrator*, *29*(8), 107–117.

Gourley, S., & Connolly, P. (1996). HRM and computerized information systems – Have we missed a link? In Paper presented at conference – Strategic direction of HRM, (1), 1–21.

Greer, C. (1995). *Strategy and human resources: A general managerial perspective*. Englewood Cliffs, NJ: Prentice Hall.

Grossman, R. J. (2000). Measuring up: Appropriate metrics help HR prove its worth. *HR Magazine*, *45*(1), 28–35.

CHAPTER 8

THE IMPACT OF GREEN INNOVATION ON THE FINANCIAL PERFORMANCE OF COMPANIES: CONTEXT OF MENA COUNTRIES

Naziha Kasraoui[a], Kais Ben-Ahmed[b,c] and Amira Feidi[a]

[a]*IFGT Laboratory, Faculty of Economic Sciences and Management of Tunis, University of Tunis El-Manar, Tunisia*
[b]*Department of Finance and Economics, University of Jeddah, College of Business, Jeddah, Saudi Arabia*
[c]*Higher Institute of Managment, ISG, University of Sousse, Tunisia*

ABSTRACT

This study focuses on the impact of green innovation on oil and gas firms' performance in the MENA region from 2010 to 2020. Return on assets (ROA) was used to measure the financial performance of firms. However, green innovation was measured using two different scores, namely the environmental pillar and the innovation scores. Additionally, we introduced an oil price-moderated variable to examine its effect on the firm's performance and the green innovation nexus. We collected data from the DataStream database. Regarding our empirical part, we use the generalized least squares method to carry out the analysis. Results showed a positive impact between green innovation scores and the firm's performance in the MENA region. Also, we found that green innovation has a linear effect on firm performance. Finally, a negative, moderated effect of crude oil prices on green innovation and the firm's financial performance nexus has been found.

Digital Technology and Changing Roles in Managerial and Financial Accounting: Theoretical Knowledge and Practical Application
Studies in Managerial and Financial Accounting, Volume 36, 87–94

Published under exclusive licence by Emerald Publishing Limited
ISSN: 1479-3512/doi:10.1108/S1479-351220240000036008

Keywords: Green innovation; financial performance; pillar score; innovation score; MENA region; financial technology

1. INTRODUCTION

Green finance appeared when the European Bank launched the green bond market (EIB) in 2007. Then, in March 2013, we saw the growing importance of green bonds issued by several countries, such as the USA, China, France, and Massachusetts (a state part of the New England region). More precisely, in 2019, the Green Finance Institute helped companies access green investment rules. Green finance aims to collect green funds, allowing investors to invest, in particular, in renewable energy projects, energy and environmental transition, and activities contributing to ecological transition projects that respect the environment. Green finance directs the use of natural resources toward improving human well-being. According to Kemps and Pearson (2007), the evolution of "green innovation" appeared through new concepts such as environmental innovation, eco-innovation, and eco-efficiency.

For McKeown et al. (2008), environmental innovation has recently emerged because of global environmental challenges. Based on the work of Bansal (2005), Etzion (2007), and Starik and Kanashiro (2013), companies must operate in an environmentally responsible way to contribute to the well-being of society while ensuring their financial performance. Similarly, Dangelico and Pujari (2010) showed that green innovation affects performance, environmental sustainability, and quality of life. In this research work, we aim to unveil the nature of green innovation's effect on business performance. Admittedly, the ideal innovation, or "green innovation," favors respect for the environment and aims to reduce the number of resources used and, above all, the overall reduction of greenhouse gas emissions. For this reason, we now speak of a carbon market that presents an essential destination based on the allocation of "pollution rights," which can then be exchanged on the market to guarantee revenues. Thus, companies wishing to pollute more must buy additional rights. Also, the market fulfills its role in carbon taxation, increasing the cost of greenhouse gas emitting activities to encourage companies to find alternative energy sources.

Several research studies have examined the relationship between green innovation and firm performance. Indeed, green innovation can help companies improve the overall quality of life while increasing profits through increased efficiency. For example, Hart (1995, 2002) shows the increased demand for products from social consumers in the environment (King & Lenox, 2002).

According to Bansal (2005), environmental activities provide companies with a good brand image or reputation, so the firm will have the chance to benefit from higher prices and better sales, increasing turnover because of an increased social approach.

Du and Li (2019) examined the effect of the intensity of green innovation on the financial performance of multinational companies and introduced internationalization as a mediating variable; the results reveal the existence of a positive association since companies that implement green innovation could improve their financial performance by focusing on cost leadership and product differentiation.

Similarly, based on the work of Xie et al. (2019), green innovation positively affects business performance. Indeed, it improves both the return on equity and assets. In addition, Miroshnychenko et al. (2017) argued that the development of green products has a favorable (positive) impact on the company's stock market performance as measured by Tobin's *Q*, so there will be a better return on investments.

In these senses, the authors add that the profitability of companies depends on the availability of ecological articles. The work of Fernando, Jabbour, and Wah (2009) shows a negative link between green innovation and business performance. They point out that green business strategies do not contribute to increasing a firm's market value. In addition, companies that emphasize green innovation face the risk of permanent government subsidies; thus, leaders will only be able to achieve environmental gains. In this sense, Yu-Shan, Shyh-Bao, and Chao-Tung (2006) state that even if companies overcome obstacles because of the development of environmentally friendly technologies, these advances do not always translate into improved financial performance.

The rest of this chapter is as follows: Section 2 stands for method and data sources, Section 3 provides results, and Section 4 concludes.

2. METHODOLOGY AND DATA SOURCES

Available data were collected from 2002 up to the end of 2020 from DataStream. Additionally, we considered companies from the oil and gas industry and those that reported environmental scores for 2012–2020. We collected this sofa data from Environmental, Social, and Governance (ESG). The sample comprises 13 companies from the MENA region, distributed according to 11 countries. Considering the previous theory, we test the following hypothesis:

H0. Green finance positively impacts firm performance.

H1. Green finance hurts firm performance.

Following Refinitiv (2020), we used ESG to measure green innovation. Moreover, the ROA was used to quantify financial performance. Noticeably, the ROA variable has been widely used to measure firms' financial success (Xie et al., 2019). The looter score contains three types of information:

- Resource consumption.
- Reducing emissions.
- Company innovation scores.

The resource consumption score measures a company's ability to decrease material or, more often, energy or water consumption. However, the emission reduction score shows the commitment of such a company to reducing environmental emissions in production and operational processes. We weighed these three variables according to their relative significance to the industry group getting the final environmental pillar score (Refinitiv, 2020). Finally, we apply the Pillar score and its third subcategory (innovation score) to evaluate the green innovation efforts of gas and oil companies.

In this study, the independent variable was the ROA, which measures the company's performance. However, the independent variables comprise firm size, leverage-to-debt ratio, oil price, green innovation, and a dummy variable (see models 1–6). The variables included in the model, and their acronyms are briefly defined in Table 8.1.

Therefore, we used six different panel models in the analysis and proceeded as follows:

$$\mathrm{ROA}_{it} = \beta_0 + \beta_1 \mathrm{S}_{it} + \beta_2 \mathrm{Lev}_{it} + \beta_3 \mathrm{OP}_{it} + \beta_4 \mathrm{D}_t + \varepsilon_{it} \quad (1)$$

Model 2 is a simple regression containing green innovation variables:

$$\mathrm{ROA}_{it} = \beta_0 + \beta_1 \mathrm{IS}_{it} + \varepsilon_{it} \quad (2)$$

Because of the multicollinearity of the variables, models 1 and 2 were estimated to identify whether there is an excessively strong correlation between the various explanatory factors.

In model 3, we introduce the innovation score variable as a control variable to examine the impact of green innovation level on firm performance:

$$\mathrm{ROA}_{it} = \beta_0 + \beta_1 S_{it} + \beta_2 \mathrm{Lev}_{it} + \beta_3 \mathrm{OP}_{it} + \beta_4 \mathrm{D}_t + \beta_5 \mathrm{IS}_{it} + \varepsilon_{it} \quad (3)$$

The curvilinear relationship between green innovation and firm performance was verified by introducing a quadratic term, green innovation, on the right-hand side of model 4:

$$\mathrm{ROA}_{it} = \beta_0 + \beta_1 S_{it} + \beta_2 \mathrm{Lev}_{it} + \beta_3 \mathrm{OP}_{it} + \beta_4 \mathrm{D}_t + \beta_5 \mathrm{IS}_{it} + \beta_6 \mathrm{IS}_{it}^2 + \varepsilon_{it} \quad (4)$$

To stress the moderating effect of OP on the relationship between IS and OP, we introduce IS–OP interaction on the right-hand side of model 5:

Table 8.1. Summary of Variables Study.

Variable	Symbol	Definition
Firm size	S	Firm size in the natural logarithm of total assets
Leverage-to-debt ratio	Lev	Percentage ratio of total debt to total capital to account for the business' risk level
Oil price	OP	The financial performance of gas companies and their revenue components is based on the product's price and the number of sales (Bagirov & Mateus, 2019)
Green innovation	GI	The environmental pillar (PS) and innovation scores (IS) measured it
Dummy variable	D	This variable is 1 for the 2014–2015 oil crisis and zero otherwise

$$\mathrm{ROA}_{it} = \beta_0 + \beta_1 S_{it} + \beta_2 \mathrm{Lev}_{it} + \beta_3 \mathrm{OP}_{it} + \beta_4 D_t + \beta_5 \mathrm{IS}_{it} + \beta_6 \mathrm{IS}_{it}\mathrm{OP}_{it} + \varepsilon_{it} \quad (5)$$

Model 6 includes all variables studied and is used as a robustness check to validate the estimation results further.

$$\begin{aligned}\mathrm{ROA}_{it} = \beta_0 + \beta_1 S_{it} + \beta_2 \mathrm{Lev}_{it} + \beta_3 \mathrm{OP}_{it} + \beta_4 \mathrm{D}_t + \beta_5 \mathrm{IS}_{it} + \\ \beta_6 \mathrm{IS}_{it}\mathrm{OP}_{it} + \beta_7 \mathrm{IS}_{it}^2 + \varepsilon_{it}\end{aligned} \quad (6)$$

It is important to notice that i denotes firm and t denotes year in models 1–6.

3. RESULTS

Table 8.2 shows that the ROA variable is, on average, 0.031; it reaches a maximum value of 1.607 but a negative minimum value, which amounts to a decrease in assets within a few companies after the oil crisis of 2015. The size of the firm was, on average, 17.56, and it can reach a maximum value of over 23. These values show that most enterprises are large. The price of oil varies between 1.8 and 6.5. This variable is widely fluctuating. Suddenly, it has a standard deviation (1.02) lower than the average of 4.11. Environment and innovation scores vary between 0.19 and 0.76. They have averages of 0.47 and 0.41, respectively.

We apply a generalized least squares model for the estimates, allowing us to control for heteroscedasticity and autocorrelation of errors. This method also excludes the potential endogeneity that could impact a firm's performance.

Table 8.3 reports the results of models 1 and 2. However, Table 8.4 presents the results of estimating models 4–6. The innovation score positively impacts the financial performance of oil and gas firms in the MENA region. One might, therefore, support efforts to develop new and environmentally friendly products that could ensure a company's long-term survival by maintaining its competitiveness. Aastvedt, Behmiri, and Lu (2021) investigate the impact of green innovation on the financial performance of oil and gas companies. The authors found that green innovation significantly and positively affects firms' performance in the US. However, the authors showed that the environmental pillar score is not linear. The authors also found that low environmental pillar scores positively affect firm performance in the US. However, the effect changes at higher levels.

In contrast, low levels of the environmental pillar score negatively affect firms' performance in Europe. Similarly, the effect changes sign when the environmental

Table 8.2. Summary Statistics.

Variable	Mean	SD	Min.	Max.
ROA	0.031	0.175	–0.498	1.607
S	17.561	2.941	10.096	23.359
Lev	24.674	84.365	0.006	927.778
OP	4.108	1.024	1.833	6.53
PS	0.474	0.12	0.185	0.762
IS	0.411	0.102	0.183	0.653

Table 8.3. Model Linear Estimation.

	Model 1	Model 2		Model 3	
Variables	Controls	PS	IS	PS	IS
S	0.0111****			0.00798**	0.0108***
	(0.00302)			(0.00359)	(0.00300)
Lev	0.00139***			0.00141***	0.00135***
	(0.000324)			(0.000318)	(0.000319)
OP	0.00980***			0.0415***	
	(0.00352)			(0.0147)	
D	−0.00117			−0.00118	
	(0.00563)			(0.00581)	
PS		−0.0682		0.283**	
		(0.0478)		(0.132)	
IS			−0.205***		0.0924***
			(0.0489)		(0.0344)
Constant	−0.224***	−0.0133	0.0324	−0.173***	−0.220***
	(0.0586)	(0.0256)	(0.0238)	(0.0664)	(0.0583)
Observations	143	143	143	143	143
Number of id	13	13	13	13	13

Table 8.4. Estimation Results of Models 4–6.

	Model 4		Model 5		Model 6	
Variable	PS	IS	PS	IS	PS	IS
S	0.00778***	0.00968***	0.00772*	0.00968*	0.00772***	0.00968***
	(0.000595)	(0.000775)	(0.000611)	(0.000775)	(0.000611)	(0.000775)
Lev	0.00139***	0.00137***	0.00139***	0.00137***	0.00139***	0.00137***
	(9.29e–05)	(5.94e–05)	(9.61e–05)	(5.94e–05)	(9.61e–05)	(5.94e–05)
OP	0.0315***	0.221***	0.0242	0.221***	0.0242	0.265***
	(0.00300)	(0.00657)	(0.0175)	(0.00657)	(0.0175)	(0.00661)
D	0.0225***	0.0224***	0.0213**	0.0213**	0.0224**	0.0106**
	(0.00215)	(0.00114)	(0.00215)	(0.00114)	(0.00215)	(0.00057)
PS	−1.859***		−1.888***		−1.888***	
	(0.121)		(0.200)		(0.200)	

pillar score has higher levels. Finally, higher crude oil prices negatively moderated European innovation scores and the financial performance nexus.

The effect of the environmental score is positive, but with a decreasing rate in the MENA region. As a result, green innovation efforts can positively impact other operational activities that use fewer resources (Wagner, 2005). These findings are consistent with the study by Trump and Guenther (2017). However, innovation can negatively affect financial performance because of the high risk involved (D'Oliveria & Terence, 2018). Firms will operate with increased costs and lower profits if innovation fails.

Our results show that all moderated effects are significant for crude oil prices based on the strength of the environmental score and financial performance nexus. However, in MENA firms, innovative scores and financial performance relationships decrease with increasing crude oil prices.

Concerning the environmental score, we found that when crude oil prices are high, oil and gas firms should focus on their conventional activities rather than allocating resources to green innovation practices. The high price of crude oil supports the idea that supply is short, and demand from the consumer side is vital. As resources are scarce, investing in green practices would have a high opportunity cost. The negative opportunity cost of investment in green innovation increases the negative effect of environmental regulations. Therefore, when oil prices rise, the positive effect of higher green innovation practices on financial performance becomes lower.

Financial leverage is significant in external financing modes. Financial leverage shows that a business needs finance to purchase a new asset or enhance its production or operational activities; financial leverage is one of the best ways for an organization to achieve its goal; with the help of financial leverage, a company can not only achieve its goals but also maximize the value of its shareholders. Iqbal and Usman (2018) showed that financial leverage positively impacts the ROA of firms in Pakistan.

4. CONCLUSION

Through this study, we aimed to know if the environmental index and the innovation score positively affect performance, which helps to fight against pollution and excessive gas emissions on the one hand and provides the durability of oil and gas firms since oil and gas do not have removable resources. To do so, we used a sample of 13 oil and gas firms in the MENA region over a period ranging from 2010 to 2020. The method of fixed effect, which makes it possible to control the firm's heterogeneity level, estimated the parameters possible.

We also used the Breush-Pagan and Cook-Wesihery tests based on heteroscedasticity knowledge like the Goldfield and Qwandt tests. However, the difference between them is that the normality of the errors is unnecessary and that we can test several variables that apply in our world since our sample size is less than 15 (13 oil firms from 11 countries in the MENA region). The econometric results showed a linear effect of green innovation on financial performance, a positive effect of the environmental pillar score on financial performance, and a negative moderated effect of crude oil price on the green innovation and the firm's financial performance nexus.

REFERENCES

Aastvedt, T. M., Behmiri, N. B., & Lu, L. (2021). Does green innovation damage financial performance of oil and gas companies. *Resources Policy*, *73*, 102235. doi:10.1016/j.resourpol.2021.102235

Bagirov, M., & Mateus, C. (2019). Oil prices; stocks markets and firm performance: Evidence from Europe. *International Review of Economic and Finance*, *61*, 270–288.

Bansal. P. (2005). Evolving sustainability: A longitudinal study of corporate sustainable development. *Strategic Management Journal*, *26*(3), 197–218.

D'Oliveria. P. H., & Terence, A. C. F. (2018). Innovation practices in small technology-based companies during incubation and port incubation periods. *Innovation and Management Review*, *15*(2), 174–188.

Dangelico. R. M., & Pujari, D. (2010). Main streaming green product innovation: Why and how companies integrate environmental sustainability. *Journal of Business Ethics*, *95*, 471–486.

Du, K., & Li, J. (2019). Towards a green world: How do green technology innovations affect total-factor carbon productivity. *Energy Policy*, *131*, 240–250.

Etzion, D. (2007). Research on organizations and the natural environment, 1992–present: A review. *Journal of Management*, *33*, 637–664.

Fernando, Y., Jabbour, C. J. C., & Wah, W. X. (2019). Pursuing green growth in technology firms through the connections between environmental innovation and sustainable business performance: Does service capability matter? *Resources; Conservation and Recycling*, *141*, 8–20.

Hart, S. L. (1995). A natural resource-based view of the firm. *Academy of Management Review*, *20*, 986–1014.

Hart, S. L., & Christensen, C. M. (2002). The great leap: Driving innovation from the base of the pyramid. *MIT Sloan Management Review*, *44*(1), 51.

Iqbal, U., & Usman, M. (2018). Impact of financial leverage on firm performance: Textile composite companies of Pakistan. *Sisense Journal of Management*, *1*(2), 70–78.

Kemp, R., & Pearson, P. (2007). Final report MEI project about measuring eco-innovation, deliverable 15 of MEI project D 15. Project report, Masstricht, 45 p.

King, A., & Lenox, M. (2002). Exploring the locus of profitable pollution reduction. *Management Sciences*, *48*, 289–299.

McKeown, N., Anderson, T., Balakrishnan, H., Parulkar, G., Peterson, L., Rexford, J., … Turner, J. (2008). OpenFlow: Enabling innovation in campus networks. *ACM SIGCOMM Computer Communication Review*, *38*(2), 69–74.

Miroshnychenko, I., Barontini, R., & Testa, F. (2017). Green practices and financial performance: A global outlook. *Journal of Cleaner Production*, *147*, 340–351. doi:10.1016/j.jclepro.2017.01.058

Refinitiv. (2020). Environmental, social and governance (ESG) scores from refinitiv. Retrieved from https://www.refinitiv.com/content/dam/marketing/en_us/documents/methodology/esg-scores-methodology.pdf. Accessed on April 19, 2020.

Starik, M., & Kanashiro, P. (2013). Toward a theory of sustainability management. *Organization & Environment*, *26*(1), 7–30. doi:10.1177/1086026612474958.

Trump, C. T., & Guenther, T. (2017). Too little or too much? Exploring the U-shaped relationship between corporate environmental performance and corporate financial performance. *Business Strategy and the Environment*, *26*(1), 49–68.

Wagner, M. (2005). How to reconcile environmental and economic performance to improve corporate sustainability: Corporate environmental strategies in the European paper industry. *Journal of Environmental Management*, *76*(2), 105–118. doi:10.1016/j.jenvman.2004.11.021

Xie, X., Huo, J., & Zou, H. (2019). Green process innovation, green product innovation, and corporate financial performance: A content analysis method. *Journal of Business Research*, *101*, 697–706.

Yu-Shan, C., Shyh-Bao, L., & Chao-Tung, W. (2006). The influence of green innovation performance on corporate advantage in Taiwan. *Journal of Business Ethics*, *67*(4), 331–339.

PART II

DIGITALIZATION OF BANKING SERVICES AND THE ROLE OF MANAGERIAL ACCOUNTING, ACCOUNTABILITY, AND TRANSPARENCY

CHAPTER 9

SERVICE DIGITALIZATION DIMENSIONS AND BANKS COMPETITIVENESS: AN INSTITUTIONAL-FOCUSED PLS-SEM APPROACH

AlaEldin Awawdeh[a], Ahmad Al-Hiyari[b] and Abdussalaam Iyanda Ismail[c]

[a]*Department of Management, Liwa College of Technology, Abu Dhabi, UAE*
[b]*College of Business Administration, University of Khorfakkan, Sharjah, UAE*
[c]*College of Business Administration, Ajman University, Ajman, UAE*

ABSTRACT

The transition in the Nigerian financial environment can be directly linked to digitalization as banks are racing to digital complexity. Historically in Nigeria, the utilization of digital operations by financial institutions is to reduce the burden of long queues in the banking hall and the pressure of carrying cash all the time. The goal of financial technology was to enable bank customers to use digitalized banking services. Hence, the purpose of this paper is to establish an empirical analysis evaluating the effect of service digitalization (internet banking, mobile banking, and automated teller machine) on bank competitiveness. Survey data were collected from 118 banks employees and hypothesized relationships were assessed through SMART-PLS structural equation modeling tool version 3.3.3. The study found a positive and significant impact of internet banking and automated machines on bank competitiveness. The findings also

Digital Technology and Changing Roles in Managerial and Financial Accounting: Theoretical Knowledge and Practical Application
Studies in Managerial and Financial Accounting, Volume 36, 97–106

ISSN: 1479-3512/doi:10.1108/S1479-351220240000036009

revealed that mobile banking has an insignificant effect on bank competition, although the outcome was positive. Overall, both the regulators and bankers should formulate and integrate their digitalized banking system by focusing on the attributes that are required for effective and safe digital-based banking.

Keywords: Service digitalization; bank competitiveness; Internet banking; PLS-SEM; automated teller machine; mobile banking

1. INTRODUCTION

With the advent of technology in the current competitive market environment, service digitalization has become essential as businesses and institutions, including commercial banks, seek to embrace improved and more efficient methods of service provision for their clients and day-to-day customers (More, 2023; Srivastava, 2023). Owing to fast technological advancement, financial service industries, in general, and the banking industry, in particular, are increasingly moving toward online and digital value creation (Niemand, Rigtering, Kallmünzer, Kraus, & Maalaoui, 2021). This development has resulted from a supportive political environment, technological development, increased financial inclusion and the proliferation of new means of service distribution. In spite of a strong move to digitalize operational efficiency and delivery methods, it is important to note that some financial institutions still see the whole digitalization process as challenging and complicated (Carbó-Valverde, 2017). In the banking industry, digitalization is a global innovation that allows customers to rapidly embrace digital banking and services as a new approach, and over the last few years, the global banking and financial industry has undergone drastic changes and improvements in the state of growth as regards to technological advancement in carrying out service delivery to their customers (Gartner, 2016).

However, it is worth mentioning that the banking industry has traditionally lever-aged on technology to enhance their performance and service offerings to their customers, but rapid progress and advancements in payment systems, internet banking, mobile banking, perceived ease of use (PEOU), consumer engagement networks, and media communication have resulted in much broader consequences on how banks engage customers (Cuesta, Ruesta, Tuesta, & Urbiola, 2015). This movement from conventional banking to advanced and modernized banking is triggered as a result of complex customer needs and the challenges of globalization. Nigeria, for example, is one of the developing countries that has rapidly accelerated the digital payment platform revolution by joining other countries, especially in the banking industry. Deposit money banks dominate the banking industry in Nigeria, and at the time of writing the operational number of the banks stands at 22 (CBN, 2010). The existence of this institution is important and relevant in society as they facilitate and promote the flow of cash from the surplus or excess unit to the deficit unit while providing a wide range of financial products and services (Kimutai & Ambrose, 2013). However, as the digital payment revolution has spread to other sectors of the economy, its impact is transformative in nature, based on exploring the opportunities of the technological era and customers are now hunting for quicker and more reliable technology with a more fulfilling banking experience (Taiwo & Agwu, 2017). According to the technology acceptance model, PEOU and perceived usefulness are two factors that influenced users' decisions when using a specific technology framework such as mobile banking, automated teller machines, internet banking, point of sales, and other forms of electronic banking systems as a result of digitalization (Surendran, 2012). Furthermore, the adoption and integration of digital technology into business strategies or models are essential for banks to reach a larger scale, enter new markets rapidly, and fully understand customers' needs leading to higher profitability and competitiveness (Peppers & Rogers, 2016).

The statistics from the Central Bank of Nigeria on industry e-payment figures from January to December 2019 show that Internet banking, automated teller machines (ATM), mobile banking, and point of sales accounted for over N 478 trillion, N 6 trillion, N 5 trillion, and N 3 trillion, respectively, in 2019 (NBC, 2019). Based on the aforementioned statistics, it is obvious that the introduction of a cashless policy in Nigeria has emerged among the policy makers and the citizens leading to the digitalization of the economy. However, customers are still facing different kinds of difficulties with banks in the conduct of daily banking transactions. Nigerian commercial banks may have digitalized their business procedures, but there is still a range of constraints experienced by the customers. Customers are also very restricted when they perform their daily banking transactions such as still filling out physical forms to figure out problems that should have been resolved digitally or electronically via the digitalized service platforms (Agboola et al., 2019).

Various scholars have conducted research on the myriad digital channels used by deposit money banks in Nigeria and the literature reviewed concentrated on some specific digital channels that form the digitalization framework and the majority of those studies are customer-focused. These particular digital systems that have been examined in the past contain agency banking, internet banking, and mobile phone technology banking. However, deposit money banks in Nigeria have not restricted themselves to using a single type of digital platform as they engaged in using a wide range of digital channels. To the best of the researchers' knowledge, at the time of the review, many studies have not integrated different forms of service digital channels based on the digitalization definition in evaluating the competitiveness of the deposit money banks in Nigeria. Although deposit money banks in Nigeria are actively developing new business models on how to carry out business operations digitally, based on the aforementioned problems, the researchers sought to bridge this existing research lacuna by integrating the three most used service digitalization dimensions by banks in investigating the competitiveness of the deposit money banks in Nigeria.

This study aims to provide answers to the following questions: (1) is service digitalization successful in the banking industry? (2) is the competitiveness advantage within the banking industry dependent on service digitalization? The primary objective of this paper is to examine the effect of service digitalization dimensions on banks' competitiveness. More precisely, the study examines the degree to which the digitalization system of banking services relates to the competitiveness of the deposit money banks in Nigeria.

2. HYPOTHESES DEVELOPMENT

In relationship to the above research questions, this study seeks to test the following three hypotheses:

H1. Internet banking has a positive and significant influence on bank competitiveness.

H2. Mobile banking positively and significantly influences bank competitiveness.

H3. Automated teller machine (ATM) has a positive and significant effect on bank competitiveness.

Our theoretical framework is depicted in Fig. 9.1.

3. RESEARCH METHODOLOGY

The population of the study comprises the employees of the selected banking firms situated in Lagos, the commercial hub of Nigeria. The respondents selected were perceived to perform a significant responsibility influencing the preference of technology adoption by their customers and were knowledgeable of its consequence. The study adopted a cross-sectional survey design to collect the primary data from the firm level in order to establish the relationship between the study's variables. The banking firms make up the sample for the current study since this financial institution has a broader adoption of technology, hence leading to the digitalization of their operation. Currently, there are 22 functioning commercial banks in Nigeria, but 5 of these banks which are Guarantee Trust Bank Zenith Bank, Access Bank, United Bank for Africa, and First Bank were selected based on their customer base and performance level in the previous years. A total sample of 118 was achieved. A convenience sampling technique was employed in

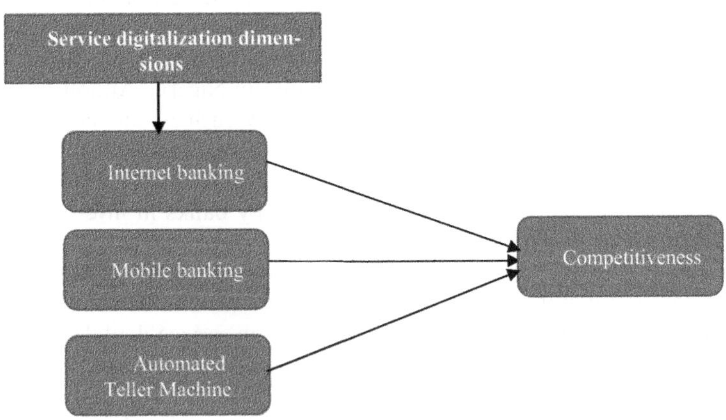

Fig. 9.1. Research Model.

selecting the respondents who are employees in the selected banks and survey questionnaires were distributed to gather data from the sampled respondents. The questionnaire used a 5-point Likert scale from "1" referring to "strongly disagree" to "5" referring to "strongly agree." Internet banking constructs comprise five indicators and were adapted from Ohiani (2021), Mobile banking constructs also comprise five indicators and were adapted from Sigalas, Economou, and Georgopoulos (2013), while ATM and firm competitiveness were both measured with six and five items which were adopted from the studies of (Mueni, 2017). In addition, it is important to note that all the construct indicators were measured reflectively.

4. DATA ANALYSIS AND RESULTS

4.1. Structural Model Evaluation

The following step in our analysis was to examine the structural model. This presents the paths hypothesized in the research model. The direct relationships of the variables were examined based on R^2 and predictive relevance (Q^2) (Geisser, 1974; Stone, 1974). The R^2 measures the variance, which is explained in the endogenous latent variable, and also describes the model's explanatory power (Shmueli & Koppius, 2011). The R^2 is also termed as the in-sample predictor power (Rigdon, 2012). The results from the analysis were presented in detail in Table 9.1. The goodness of the model is evaluated through the strength of the structural path (see Fig. 9.2) determined by R^2 for the dependent variable, the value for the R^2 should be equal to or over 0.1. The result in Table 9.1 shows that the R^2 value is above the threshold value of 0.1. Hence, the predictive capability is attained. In addition, the Q^2 establishes the predictive relevance of the endogenous variable (Shmueli, Ray, Estrada, & Chatla, 2016). According to Hair, Black, Babin, Anderson, and Latham (2010), a Q^2 value above 0 shows that the model has predictive relevance. Hence, the result (see Table 9.1) shows that there is significant predictive relevance of the PLS-path model.

Consequently, the hypotheses were tested to establish the relationship between the variables. *H1* examined whether IB has a significant impact on firm competitiveness (FC). The results revealed that IB has a significant impact on FC ($\beta = 0.419$, $t = 4.366$, $p = 0.000$). Hence, *H1* was supported and accepted. Furthermore, *H2* evaluates whether MB has a significant impact on FC. The results found that MB has a positive but insignificant impact on FC ($\beta = 0.047$, $t = 0.334$, $p = 0.738$). Hence, *H2* was not supported. Lastly, *H3* tests whether ATM has a significant impact on FC. The findings revealed that ATM has a positive and significant impact on FC ($\beta = 0.120$, $t = 2.195$, $p = 0.0029$). Hence, *H3* was supported. More importantly, as depicted in Fig. 9.2 and Table 9.1, it revealed that the R^2 value of 0.384 (see Fig. 9.2) shows that, in the model, exogenous latent variables which are, internet banking, mobile banking, and ATM explains 38% of the variance of the endogenous latent variable (i.e., firm competitiveness). The results are presented in Table 9.1.

Table 9.1. Direct Relationships (*H1–H3*).

Hypotheses	Path coefficient (*β*)	SD (STDEV)	*t*-value (bootstrap)	*p*-values	BI [2.5%; 97.5%]	Decision
IB → FC	0.419	0.096	4.366	0.000	[0.012; 0.471]	Supported
MB → FC	0.047	0.142	0.334	0.738	[0.246; 0.621]	Rejected
ATM → FC	0.263	0.120	2.195	0.029	[−0.24; 0.298]	Supported
	R^2	Q^2				
FC	0.384	0.186				

BI, bias corrected confidence interval; IB, internet banking; MB, mobile banking; ATM, automated teller machine; FC, firm competitiveness.

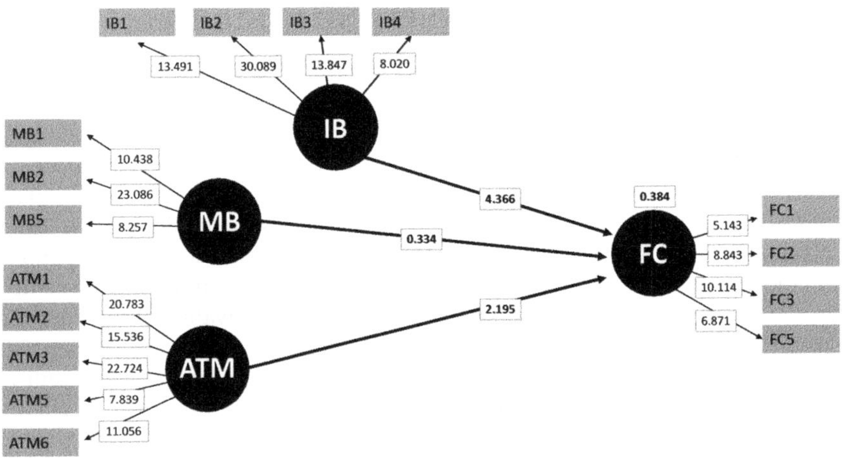

Fig. 9.2. Structural Model.

5. DISCUSSION AND CONCLUSION

The emergence of information technology, along with the advent of the internet across the world, has contributed to the rise of services digitalization in the banking sector. Service digitalization has been advocated as the creative solution and workable approach to extending banking operations geographically at a comparatively lower cost by offering self-service solutions to fulfill customer requirements and preferences. Nevertheless, the deficiency of empirical evidence to justify the assertions of the advantage of services digitalization dimensions has frequently been recognized by literature (Kwateng, Osei-Wusu, & Amaner, 2020). Moreover, the limited empirical studies performed have primarily focused on industrialized economies with substantial use of financial metrics for calculating the competitiveness and efficiency of banks. It is on the aforementioned gap in the empirical literature that we conducted the current study. The study examined the impact of the service digitalization process measured through (internet banking, mobile banking, and ATM) on FC.

First, the result of the first hypothesis signifies that Internet banking has a positive impact on FC. This finding could be attached to the assertion that the majority of banking customers find it easy to use the Internet to carry out their banking services. This finding is in tandem with the studies (Akyuz, Tony, & Opusunju, 2019; Callaway, 2011; Mateka, Gogo, & Omagwa, 2016; Rahi, Mansour, Alghizzawi, & Alnaser, 2019; Stoica, Mehdian, & Sargu, 2015; Taiwo & Agwu, 2017) who also found a positive significant relationship between internet banking and bank performance. Therefore, to establish, and sustain, market penetration with customer relationships, internet banking is therefore obviously crucial for banks. In addition, the management of banking institutions needs to embrace a strategic marketing campaign to aggressively promote awareness of Internet banking and foster customer acceptance. The insignificant effect of mobile banking could be a result of low customer engagement with mobile applications along with incompetent in-house capabilities.

As such, it is expected that mobile banking's competitive edge needs to be readdressed in order to be a component of the strategic plans of banks. This finding corroborates with the study of Iwari, Buse, and Herstatt (2006) and Okoro (2014) who confirmed that the absence of potential competitive advantage of mobile banking may have prompted banks to ignore it as a lengthy strategic target. In addition to our result on mobile banking, Jalal-Karim and Hamdan (2010) and Massoud and Scholnick (2003) in their studies also established that mobile banking has negative effects on banking performance indicators. However, contrary to Bradley and Stewart (2002), who found mobile banking to have significant and positive effects on the performance of banking institutions and further stated that mobile banking is an umbrella of competitiveness in the banking sector.

Lastly, hypothesis three tested the impact of ATMs on bank competitiveness. It was found in the current study that the utilization of ATMs has a positive and significant impact on bank competitiveness which then leads to the acceptance of hypothesis three. This finding is consistent with some previous studies on the adoption of ATMs (e.g., Chaouali & Hedhli, 2019; Kumar, Malathy, & Ganesh, 2011; Mwatsika, 2016; Narteh, 2015) who found ATMs to be performance effective in the banking sector. But contrary to the above findings, Jegede (2014) submitted that the benefits that accompanied ATMs are far less than the improvement in performance due to the incessant rate of fraud associated with it. To proffer answers to the questions raised in the first part of this study, according to the results of this study, we can, therefore, say that service digitalization has been successful in the Nigerian banking industry and influence competitiveness within the banking industry. It is therefore concluded, relying on the results of this study, that service digitalization has a major effect as regards competitiveness among banking firms. Hence, there is a need for banking firms to pay more attention to their service digitalization process to suit the demands of their customers. If the banking service digitalization mechanisms are optimized the problems associated with customers visiting banking halls will lessen.

This study makes several contributions practically and theoretically. To start with, it contributes to the existing body of knowledge relating to service digitalization in the banking sector. Whereby both the regulators and bankers are advised to formulate and integrate their digitalized banking system by focusing on the attributes that are required for effective and safe digital-based banking. Digitalization literature in the banking sector is of two empirical analyses: customer-focused and institutional-focused. There have been many studies that analyzed customer-focused (i.e., customer perspective studies) as opposed to institutional-focused (i.e., organizational perspective). Hence, this study will add theoretically to the few studies that were institutionally focused. In addition, the study expands the established understanding of technology acceptance in the financial sector by adding to the bank's studies from the organization's perspective. Furthermore, the current study strengthens and updates prior information about the adoption of service digitalization in the banking sector. This study further outlines key service digitalization dimensions (internet banking, mobile banking, and ATM) that influence customers' engagement which has theoretical and practical implications in the digital banking platform. Bank executives can use the findings of the current study to enhance their marketing campaigns and services provided to make them more appealing to users to increase the usage rate.

This study is also not far from limitations. Firstly, the sampled scope is limited to five banks in a single country (Nigeria), although the selected banks are the leading banks in terms of customer base and performance level. For that reason, the study's findings cannot be generalized to other countries with higher levels of information technology adoption rates. Hence, future studies can be tailored to other banks or other developing nations to generalize the findings. For example, in African nations, service digitalization could be instrumental and advantageous due to the high local population. For further reference, the study findings can be evaluated through customer-focused studies. Furthermore, this study was conducted in the banking sector, and it would be interesting to replicate the study framework in other sectors where service digitalization is utilized.

REFERENCES

Agboola, M. G., Awobajo, K. A., Oluwatobi, S. O., Akinbode, M. O., Fagbohun, M. O., Esse, U. C., … Betek, C. M. (2019, May 27–June 6). Effect of digitalization on the performance of commercial banks in Nigeria. In *IOP conference series: Earth and environmental science*, Russian Federation, Moscow.

Akyuz, M., Tony, L. W., & Opusunju, M. I. (2019). Impact of bank verification number (BVN) on corrupt business practices in United Bank for Africa in Abuja. *International Journal of Management Studies and Social Science Research*, *51*, 39–52.

Bradley, L., & Stewart, K. (2002). A Delphi study of the drivers and inhibitors of Internet banking. *International Journal of Bank Marketing*, *20*(6), 250–260.

Callaway, S. K. (2011). Internet banking and performance: The relationship of web site traffic rank and bank performance. *American Journal of Business*, *26*(1), 12–25.

CarbÓ-Valverde, S. (2017). The impact on digitalization on banking and financial stability. *Journal of Financial Management, Markets and Institutions*, *5*(1), 133–140.

CBN. (2010). List of financial institutions. Retrieved from https://www.cbn.gov.ng/Supervision/Inst-DM.asp. Accessed on October 27, 2020.

Chaouali, W., & Hedhli, K. El. (2019). Toward a contagion-based model of mobile banking adoption. *International Journal of Bank Marketing*, *37*(1), 69–96.

Cuesta, C., Ruesta, M., Tuesta, D., & Urbiola, P. (2015). The digital transformation of the banking industry. *BBVA Research*, *1*, 1–10.

Geisser, S. (1974). A predictive approach to the random effect model. *Biometrika*, *61*(1), 101–107.

Hair, J. F., Black, W. C., Babin, B. J., Anderson, R. E., & Latham, R. (2010). *Multivariate data analysis* (6th ed.). Upper Saddle River, NJ: Pearson.

Iwari, R., Buse, S., & Herstatt, C. (2006). Mobile banking as business strategy: Impact of mobile technologies on customer behaviour and its implications for banks. *In 2006 Technology management for the Global future-PICMET 2006 conference*, 1935–1946.

Jalal-Karim, A., & Hamdan, A. M. (2010). The impact of information technology on improving banking performance matrix: Jordanian banks as case study. In *European, Mediterranean & Middle Eastern conference on information systems* (pp. 21–33).

Jegede, C.A. (2014). Effects of automated teller machine on the performance of Nigerian banks. *American Journal of Applied Mathematics and Statistics*. 2(1), 40–46.

Kimutai, C. J., & Ambrose, J. (2013). Factors influencing credit rationing by commercial banks in Kenya. *International Journal of Humanities and Social Science*, *3*(20), 244–252.

Kumar, L., Malathy, D., & Ganesh, L. S. (2011). The diffusion of ATM technology in Indian banking. *Journal of Economic Studies*, *38*(4), 483–500.

Kwateng, K. O., Osei-Wusu, E. E., & Amanor, K. (2020). Exploring the effect of online banking on bank performance using data envelopment analysis. *Benchmarking: An International Journal*, *27*(1), 137–165.

Massoud, N., & Scholnick, B. (2003). *Is there a customer relationship effect from bank ATM surcharges?* NYU Working Paper No. S-FI-03-05. Available at SSRN: https://ssrn.com/abstract=1297768

Mateka, M., Gogo, J., & Omagwa, J. (2016). Effects of internet banking on financial performance of listed commercial banks in Kenya. *American Journal of Finance*, *1*(2), 53–71.

More, A. B. (2023). Implementing Digital age experience marketing to make customer relations More sustainable. In *New Horizons for Industry 4.0 in modern business* (pp. 99–119). Cham Berlin: Springer International Publishing.

Mueni, M. B. (2017). *The Influence of digitalization on the performance of digitalized commercial banks in Kenya*. San Diego, CA: United States International University.

Mwatsika, C. (2016). Impact of ATM banking performance on customer satisfaction with the bank in Malawi. *International Journal of Business and Economics Research*, *5*(1), 1–9.

Narteh, B. (2015). Perceived service quality and satisfaction of self-service technology: The case of automated teller machines. *International Journal of Quality & Reliability Management*, *32*(4), 361–380.

NBC. (2019). E-Payment statistics. Retrieved from https://www.cbn.gov.ng/Paymentsystem/ePayment-Statistics.asp

Niemand, T., Rigtering, C., Kallmünzer, A., Kraus, S., & Maalaoui, A. (2021). Digitalization in the financial industry: A contingency approach of entrepreneurial orientation and strategic vision on digitalization. *European Management Journal*, *39*(3), 317–326.

Ohiani, A. S. (2021). Technology innovation in the Nigerian banking system: Prospects and challenges. *Rajagiri Management Journal*, *15*(1), 2–15.

Okoro, A. S. (2014). Impact of electronic banking instruments on the intermediation efficiency of the Nigerian economy. *International Journal of Accounting Research*, *42*(1480), 1–8.

Peppers, D., & Rogers, M. (2016). *Managing customer experience and relationships: A strategic framework*. Hoboken, NJ: John Wiley & Sons.

Rahi, S., Mansour, M. M. O., Alghizzawi, M., & Alnaser, F. M. (2019). Integration of UTAUT model in internet banking adoption context: The mediating role of performance expectancy and effort expectancy. *Journal of Research in Interactive Marketing*, *13*(3), 411–435.

Shmueli, G., & Koppius, O. R. (2011). Predictive analytics in information systems research. *MIS Quarterly*, *35*(3), 553–572.

Shmueli, G., Ray, S., Estrada, J. M. V., & Chatla, S. B. (2016). The elephant in the room: Predictive performance of PLS models. *Journal of Business Research*, *69*(10), 4552–4564.

Sigalas, C., Economou, V. P., & Georgopoulos, N. B. (2013). Developing a measure of competitive advantage. *Journal of Strategy and Management*, *6*(4), 320–342.

Srivastava, S. (2023). Prospective application of blockchain in mutual fund industry. In *New horizons for Industry 4.0 in modern business* (pp. 121–148). Cham Berlin: Springer International Publishing.

Stoica, O., Mehdian, S., & Sargu, A. (2015). The impact of Internet Banking on the performance of Romanian banks: DEA and PCA Approach. *Procedia Economics and Finance*, *20*, 610–622.

Stone, M. (1974). Cross-validatory choice and assessment of statistical predictions. *Journal of the Royal Statistical Society: Series B (Methodological)*, *36*(2), 111–133.

Surendran, P. (2012). Technology acceptance model: A survey of literature. *International Journal of Business and Social Research*, *2*(4), 175–178.

Taiwo, J. N., & Agwu, M. E. (2017). The role of e-banking on operational efficiency of banks in Nigeria. *Journal of Business Management and Accounts*, *6*(1), 1–10.

CHAPTER 10

USE OF CHATBOTS AND ITS ROLE IN ENHANCING CUSTOMER EXPERIENCE: A STUDY OF THE BANKING INDUSTRY

Mohammed Salem

University College of Applied Sciences, Gaza, Palestine

ABSTRACT

This study examines how chatbots could improve the client experience in the banking sector. Due to their quick and effective customer service, chatbots are becoming more and more popular, but it is still unknown whether they can improve the customer experience. In order to gather data from a simple random sample of Palestinian banking clients in the Gaza Strip, a survey was conducted utilizing the explanatory technique. To test hypotheses, data collected from 337 individuals was evaluated using simple regression analysis. According to the results, chatbots may enhance the customer experience by offering 24/7 availability, prompt support, and customized replies. However, issues with data privacy, lack of human interaction, and chatbot accuracy were also noted. The study comes to the conclusion that chatbots may be an effective tool for increasing customer experience in the banking sector, but their design, deployment, and interaction with current customer service channels must be carefully considered. This study significantly adds to the body of

Digital Technology and Changing Roles in Managerial and Financial Accounting: Theoretical Knowledge and Practical Application
Studies in Managerial and Financial Accounting, Volume 36, 107–114

ISSN: 1479-3512/doi:10.1108/S1479-351220240000036010

knowledge on chatbots and their potential influence on customer experience. The study offers useful insights into the particular difficulties and potential of employing chatbots in a highly regulated and customer-focused industry by concentrating exclusively on the banking sector. The results show that chatbot implementation in banking needs to be approached thoughtfully and strategically to maximize their potential for improving customer experience while limiting any possible downsides.

Keywords: Chatbots; customer experience; banking industry; simple regression; Gaza strip; Palestine

1. INTRODUCTION

In recent years, chatbots have gained popularity as a way to improve customer experience across a variety of businesses, including banking. Computer programs known as "chatbots" are used to quickly and effectively address consumer questions and issues by simulating human communication (Eren, 2021; Hsu & Lin, 2023). Chatbots have become more prevalent as a possible tool for enhancing customer experience and lowering operating expenses as digital channels for banking become more widely used. Uncertainty persists over chatbots' ability to improve the client experience in the banking sector (Jang, Jung, & Kim, 2021; Sarbabidya & Saha, 2020).

The purpose of this study is to examine how chatbots may improve customer experience in the banking sector. This chapter specifically attempts to respond to the following research questions: (1) What are the advantages and difficulties of chatbot use in the banking sector? (2) How do clients see the integration of chatbots into the banking process? and (3) How do banking professionals view chatbots as a means of increasing the client experience?

The study is important in a number of ways. First, it adds to the expanding corpus of research on the use of chatbots to improve customer experience in the banking sector. Second, the study specializes in the Palestinian banking sector, which has not gotten much attention in the literature too far. Third, the study uses a quantitative method approach to provide a thorough knowledge of the advantages and disadvantages of employing chatbots in banking from the viewpoints of customers. The study's overall goal is to offer useful information to banking professionals, decision makers, and researchers about how chatbots might improve the customer experience in the banking sector.

The remainder of the chapter is structured as follows. An overview of the literature on chatbot use in customer service and the banking sector is presented in Section 2. The methodology for the study, including the sampling method, data collecting, and analysis, is described in Section 3. The study's findings are presented in Section 4 together with consumer implications of chatbots, banking industry attitudes, and perceptions of chatbots, as well as the advantages and disadvantages of employing chatbots in banking.

2. THEORETICAL BACKGROUND

2.1. Customer Experience

Customer experience is the collective term for all interactions and touchpoints that occur throughout a customer's relationship with a business or organization. Customer experience is playing a bigger role in customer loyalty and retention as customers are more inclined to stick with businesses that provide them a good experience (Bhattacharya & Sinha, 2022; Trivedi, 2019). Customer experience is crucial in the banking sector because of the fierce competition and the delicate nature of financial transactions. As a result, improving customer experience is a crucial strategic objective for banking organizations, and using chatbots has the ability to help with this objective (El Bakkouri, Raki, & Belgnaoui, 2022).

The customer experience might be improved by chatbots in a number of ways (Chen, Le, & Florence, 2021; Daqar & Smoudy, 2019). First, chatbots may respond quickly and effectively to client enquiries, speeding up response times and cutting down on wait times. Increased client satisfaction and loyalty may result from this. Second, chatbots may give tailored replies based on past interactions and preferences of users, giving them a more tailored and interesting experience. This can strengthen the bank's reputation as a whole and foster enduring ties with its clients. Last but not least, chatbots can offer a 24/7 accessibility, enabling users to access financial services from any location and at any time. Customers may see this as frictionless and convenient, increasing their level of happiness and loyalty.

2.2. The Use of Chatbots

To improve customer experience, chatbots are being used more and more often in a variety of sectors, including banking. Instant support and tailored replies are offered by chatbots, which can increase customer happiness and loyalty. Chatbots can also lower operating expenses by answering common questions, freeing up human customer care personnel to handle more complicated problems (Abdulquadri, Mogaji, Kieu, & Nguyen, 2021).

Chatbots in the banking sector can offer 24/7 accessibility, enabling users to access financial services from any location and at any time. Inquiries about balances, cash transfers, and bill payments are just a few of the fundamental banking tasks that chatbots may help with, which can save wait times for customers and increase productivity (Rani, Kanda, Chanchal, & Vij, 2023). Additionally, chatbots can assist banking organizations in gathering client feedback and insights that can be used to enhance customer service and create new goods and services. To guarantee the success of chatbot deployment, issues about accuracy, data privacy, and the absence of human connection are also raised by the use of chatbots in banking. These concerns must be properly studied and addressed (Ngai, Lee, Luo, Chan, & Liang, 2021; Satheesh, Samala, & Rodriguez, 2020). Based on the above, we set the following hypothesis:

H1. Use of chatbots positively affects the Palestinian customer experience in the banking sector.

3. METHODOLOGY

3.1. Participants

As seen in Fig. 10.1, 337 respondents completed the questionnaire and returned it. Fig. 10.1 showed the results for the demographic variables.

3.2. Procedures

The major instrument utilized to gather data for the study was a face-to-face questionnaire. The original questionnaire was appropriately translated into Arabic because Arabic is a language that is widely spoken in Palestine. After that, a pilot test and accuracy testing were conducted by two native Arabic speakers. In order to analyze the statistical data, IBM SPSS version 23 was used.

3.3. Measures

For the survey, a 5-point Likert scale was used. Three sections made up the survey. To assess the use of chatbots in the first section, seven questions based on Sarbabidya and Saha (2020), Jang, Jung, and Kim (2021), and Rani, Kanda, Chanchal, and Vij (2023) are employed. The customer experience is examined in the second section using four questions based on Trivedi (Trivedi, 2019), Bhattacharya and Sinha (Bhattacharya & Sinha, 2022), and El Bakkouri, Raki, and Belgnaoui (2022). In the final part, the demography-related aspects are covered.

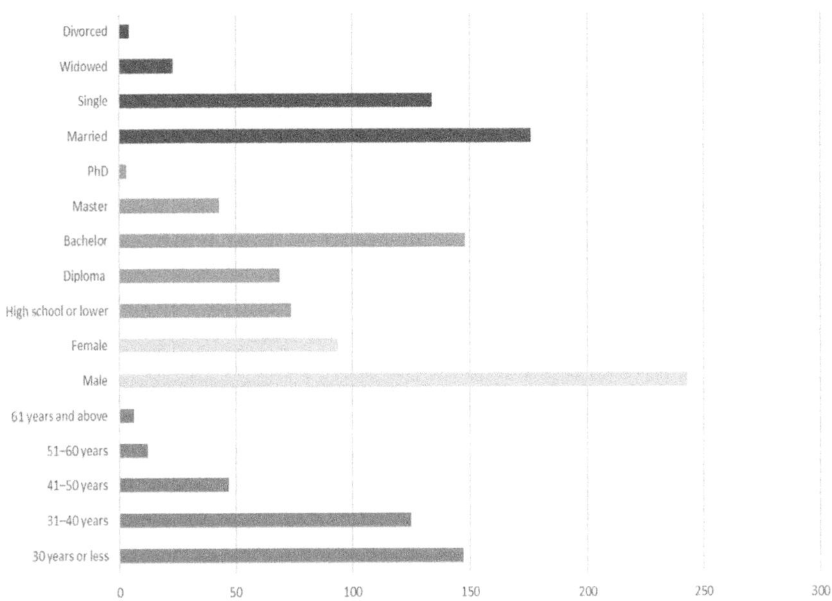

Fig. 10.1. Respondents' Personal Information ($n = 337$).

4. RESULTS

4.1. Factor Analysis

By using the KMO and Bartlett's tests, we were able to determine if the factor analysis was applicable for our research. The dependability test must be passed with a minimum score of 0.7. Bartlett's sphericity test results frequently fall below the threshold of 0.05. The KMO result is more than the permissible cutoff level of 0.000, indicating that the data analysis is adequate for the research's goals.

Using the varimax normalization approach, the principal component analysis factor score coefficient matrix from Table 10.1 has been rotated by one primary factor (Raab, Salem, & Wagner, 2021; Salem, 2010, 2019; Salem & Al Najdawi, 2023; Salem & Baidoun, 2022; Salem & Yousif, 2023). The factor is composed of 17 items. Prior research has shown that factor loadings on a variety of scales should satisfy a minimum loading criterion of 0.30 (Baidoun & Salem, 2023; Baidoun, Salem, & Wagner, 2023; Raab, Wagner, Ertz, & Salem, 2022; Salem, Baidoun, Wady, Alhajsaleh, & Hamouda, 2022; Salem & Ertz, 2023; Salem et al., 2022). The loadings in Table 10.1 are all more than 0.30, indicating that the construct validity of the scales has been maintained.

4.2. Hypotheses Testing

Simple regression analysis was carried out to look at the relationship between the dependent variable (customer experience) and the independent variables (use of chatbots). Table 10.2 demonstrates that independent factor account for 56.3% of the variation in customer experience, with an adjusted R^2 value of 0.563. Table 10.2 displays a link between customer experience and the use of chatbots ($t = 2.972$, $p = 0.000$). As a result, it was determined that *H1* was strongly supported by the data.

Table 10.1. The Constructions' Reliability and Factor Loading.

Construct	Item	MV	SD	FL	Cronbach's α
Use of chatbots	1	3.57	0.76	0.764	0.784
	2	3.38	0.73	0.742	
	3	3.45	0.82	0.753	
	4	3.55	0.84	0.767	
	5	3.61	0.87	0.784	
	6	3.53	0.74	0.745	
	7	3.34	0.79	0.737	
Customer experience	8	3.46	0.86	0.762	0.791
	9	3.54	0.78	0.756	
	10	3.42	0.84	0.747	
	11	3.65	0.86	0.769	
	12	3.41	0.74	0.744	
	13	3.56	0.76	0.758	

Table 10.2. Simple Regression Analysis Outputs.

Model	Unstandardized coefficients		Standardized Coefficients	t	Sig.
	β	SE	β		
1 (Constant)	0.094	0.228		0.426	0.237
Use of chatbots	0.345	0.082	0.234	2.972	0.000

Note: Dependent variable: Customer experience; adjusted $R^2 = 0.563$, $F = 114.539$, and sig.= 0.000

5. DISCUSSION

According to the study's conclusions, chatbot adoption in the banking sector can improve customer experience but also present a number of difficulties. The advantages of chatbots in banking include quicker response times, tailored replies, and availability around-the-clock. However, accuracy, data privacy, and a lack of human connection are obstacles. Therefore, for chatbot deployment in banking to be effective, significant thought and preparation are required.

Response times may be improved, which is one of chatbots in banking's main advantages. Customers want prompt, effective solutions to their questions, and chatbots may offer this without the need for human support. This can shorten wait times for customers, increasing their pleasure and loyalty. Additionally, chatbots can offer customized responses based on customer preferences and history, giving users a more interesting and tailored experience. This may facilitate the development of enduring connections with clients and enhance clients' perceptions of the bank generally.

Chatbots, however, can present a number of difficulties. Since inaccurate answers can harm customer trust and perception of the bank, accuracy is a crucial issue. As a result, in order for chatbots to offer precise and pertinent replies, they must be properly created and programmed. Another issue is data privacy since chatbots could have access to private client data. To secure consumer data, the necessary security procedures must be implemented. Last but not the least, a lack of human contact might result in a lack of understanding and empathy for client issues. As a result, chatbots ought to be programmed to forward difficult questions to real customer support agents as needed.

Chatbots have the ability to greatly improve the client experience in the banking sector despite these difficulties. Customers demand efficiency and convenience, which chatbots may deliver while saving banks money on operating expenses. Additionally, chatbots may offer insightful information about client requirements and preferences that can be utilized to enhance customer care and create new goods and services.

While this study on the use of chatbots and their contribution to improving customer experience in the banking sector offers insightful information, it is important to recognize its limitations. These include potential bias in sample selection, contextual elements unique to particular banks, arbitrary measurement constructs, and practical constraints. Future research should concentrate on customer segmentation to cater to diverse needs, investigate the integration of chatbots with human support, look into trust and privacy issues, look into the multichannel experience, and evaluate the long-term customer outcomes of chatbot interactions in order to further our understanding. By addressing these issues, we can get a deeper knowledge of how chatbots may improve the customer experience in the banking sector and provide direction for the creation and use of chatbot strategies that will increase consumer satisfaction and loyalty.

In conclusion, the banking sector may benefit from the deployment of chatbots by increasing operational effectiveness and improving customer experience. To achieve a successful chatbot adoption, nevertheless, much thought and planning are required. In the creation and training of chatbots, banks must place a high priority on accuracy, data privacy, and human engagement. Banks must also be aware of the wants and demands of their customers in order to employ chatbots to provide individualized and interesting experiences. The introduction of chatbots in the banking sector must also coincide with a culture shift toward digital transformation, as clients demand more smooth and practical digital interactions.

REFERENCES

Abdulquadri, A., Mogaji, E., Kieu, T. A., & Nguyen, N. P. (2021). Digital transformation in financial services provision: A Nigerian perspective to the adoption of chatbot. *Journal of Enterprising Communities: People and Places in the Global Economy*, *15*(2), 258–281.

Baidoun, S. D., & Salem, M. Z. (2023). The moderating role of perceived trust and perceived value on online shopping behavioral intention of Palestinian millennials during COVID-19. *Competitiveness Review: An International Business Journal*. https://doi.org/10.1108/CR-10-2022-0161

Baidoun, S. D., Salem, M. Z., & Wagner, R. (2023). The moderating role of narcissism in predicting the behavior intention of the Palestinian university students towards adopting the new Facebook currency. *Online Information Review*. https://doi.org/10.1108/OIR-12-2021-0666

Bhattacharya, C., & Sinha, M. (2022). The role of artificial intelligence in banking for leveraging customer experience. *Australasian Accounting, Business and Finance Journal*, *16*(5), 89–105.

Chen, J. S., Le, T. T. Y., & Florence, D. (2021). Usability and responsiveness of artificial intelligence chatbot on online customer experience in e-retailing. *International Journal of Retail & Distribution Management*, *49*(11), 1512–1531.

Daqar, M. A. A., & Smoudy, A. K. (2019). The role of artificial intelligence on enhancing customer experience. *International Review of Management and Marketing*, *9*(4), 22–31.

El Bakkouri, B., Raki, S., & Belgnaoui, T. (2022). The role of chatbots in enhancing customer experience: Literature review. *Procedia Computer Science*, *203*, 432–437 (2022).

Eren, B. A. (2021). Determinants of customer satisfaction in chatbot use: Evidence from a banking application in Turkey. *International Journal of Bank Marketing*, *39*(2), 294–311.

Hsu, C. L., & Lin, J. C. C. (2023). Understanding the user satisfaction and loyalty of customer service chatbots. *Journal of Retailing and Consumer Services*, *71*, 103211.

Jang, M., Jung, Y., & Kim, S. (2021). Investigating managers' understanding of chatbots in the Korean financial industry. *Computers in Human Behavior*, *120*, 106747.

Ngai, E. W., Lee, M. C., Luo, M., Chan, P. S., & Liang, T. (2021). An intelligent knowledge-based chatbot for customer service. *Electronic Commerce Research and Applications*, *50*, 101098.

Raab, K., Salem, M., & Wagner, R. (2021). Antecedents of daily disposal routines in the Gaza Strip refugee camps. *Resources, Conservation and Recycling*, *168*, 105427.

Raab, K., Wagner, R., Ertz, M., & Salem, M. (2022). When marketing discourages consumption: De-marketing of single-use plastics for city tourism in Ottawa, Canada. *Journal of Ecotourism*, *22*(3), 375–405.

Rani, R., Kanda, J., Chanchal, C., & Vij, T. S. (2023). A study on chatbots in the Indian banking sector. In S. Grima, K. Sood, & E. Özen (Eds.), *Contemporary studies of risks in emerging technology, Part A* (*Emerald Studies in Finance, Insurance, and Risk Management*, pp. 35–47). Leeds: Emerald Publishing Limited. doi.org/10.1108/978-1-80455-5

Sarbabidya, S., & Saha, T. (2020). Role of chatbot in customer service: A study from the perspectives of the banking industry of Bangladesh. *International Review of Business Research Papers*, *16*(1), 231–248.

Salem, M., & Baidoun, S. (2022). Factors affecting Palestinian consumer behavioral intentions toward online shopping during COVID-19: The moderating role of perceived trust. In S. G. Yaseen (Ed.), *Digital economy, business analytics, and big data analytics applications* (*Studies in Computational Intelligence*, Vol. 1010, pp. 673–687). Cham: Springer International Publishing. https://doi.org/10.1007/978-3-031-05258-3_52

Salem, M., Baidoun, S., Abu Sharekh, N., Sammour, N., Alnajar, G., Alasttal, F., … Saqer, H. (2022). Factors affecting Arab consumers' attitudes toward online shopping in light of COVID-19: the moderating role of digital marketing. *Journal of Enterprise Information Management*, *36*(2), 480–504.

Salem, M., Baidoun, S., Wady, R., Alhajsaleh, N., & Hamouda, M. (2022). Factors affecting consumer attitudes towards SMS advertising in the Palestinian banking sector. The moderating role of national culture. *Journal of Marketing Communications*, 1–22.

Salem, M. Z. (2019). Effects of formula milk packaging design on breastfeeding Palestinian women's purchasing decisions. *Ethiopian Journal of Health Development*, *33*(1), 1–3.

Salem, M. Z., & Al Najdawi, S. (2023). Would demarketing strategies rationalize household food waste consumption? *Journal of Statistics Applications & Probability*, *12*(1), 207–213.

Salem, M. Z., & Ertz, M. (2023). Water consumption rationalization using demarketing strategies in the Gaza Strip, Palestine. *Water Resources and Economics*, *43*, 100227.

Salem, M. Z., & Yousif, M. (2023). Strategic employees satisfaction toward human resource management information system in higher education institutions. *Journal of Statistics Applications & Probability*, *12*(1), 61–70.

Salem, M. Z. Y. (2010). Factors affecting the demarketing of cigarette smoking in Palestine. *International Journal of Arab Culture, Management and Sustainable Development*, *1*(4), 340–358.

Satheesh, M. K., Samala, N., & Rodriguez, R. V. (2020). Role of AI-induced chatbot in enhancing customer relationship management in the banking industry. *ICTACT Journal on Management Studies*, *6*(4), 1320–1323.

Trivedi, J. (2019). Examining the customer experience of using banking chatbots and its impact on brand love: The moderating role of perceived risk. *Journal of Internet Commerce*, *18*(1), 91–111.

CHAPTER 11

FACTORS INFLUENCING THE MOBILE BANKING USAGE: MEDIATING ROLE OF PERCEIVED USEFULNESS

Nabil Hussein Al-Fahim, Ali Ahmed Ateeq, Zahida Abro, Marwan Milhem, Mohammed Alzoraiki, Tamer M. Alkadash and Muskan Nagi

College of Administrative & Financial Sciences, Gulf University, Sanad, Bahrain

ABSTRACT

The purpose of this research was to investigate at the influence of technology acceptance model (TAM) characteristics including perceived ease of use, perceived compatibility, and perceived security on the perceived utility and actual use of mobile banking among Yemeni academics. It also investigated the function of perceived utility as a moderator in the link between TAM variables and mobile banking adoption. The sample size was 251 respondents who worked at universities in Yemen and were chosen using stratified random selection. According to the findings, perceived compatibility and perceived security had a substantial positive influence on perceived usefulness and real mobile banking use; however perceived simplicity of use had no effect on mobile banking usage. According to the results, perceived usefulness slightly mediated the association between perceived ease of use and security and mobile banking use, whereas it completely mediated the relationship between perceived compatibility and

Digital Technology and Changing Roles in Managerial and Financial Accounting: Theoretical Knowledge and Practical Application
Studies in Managerial and Financial Accounting, Volume 36, 115–128

ISSN: 1479-3512/doi:10.1108/S1479-351220240000036011

mobile banking usage. Overall, the research proved the significance of TAM elements in academics' use of mobile banking in Yemen, offering a credible empirical framework for studying mobile banking usage in this setting.

Keywords: Ease of use; compatibility; security; usefulness; mobile banking; University; Yemen

1. INTRODUCTION

In the past few decades, the pervasive use of mobile phones has transformed human interaction, and smartphones and tablets have become indispensable instruments for accessing the internet, undertaking transactions, and obtaining information (Purwanto, Deviny, & Mutahar, 2020). To meet the daily requirements of consumers, the term m-banking has become popular, with mobile banking defined as the use of wireless portable devices to conduct online transactions such as online banking, product or service purchases, and bill payment. These activities are further categorized as mobile banking, mobile payments, and mobile banking (Sharma & Sharma, 2019).

Implementing mobile banking as a marketing strategy is crucial because it provides consumers with an alternative banking channel. Mobile banking, or m-banking, refers to the use of wireless portable devices for online transactions, including the purchase of goods and services, online banking, and bill payment (Karjaluoto, Glavee-Geo, Ramdhony, Shaikh, & Hurpaul, 2021).

The previous studies have identified several gaps in understanding the factors that can affect customer satisfaction when using mobile banking. The design of mobile apps plays a crucial role in the satisfaction of university employees. The mobile app should be user-friendly and easy to use, but it is important to note that not all mobile devices support this type of technology, as only smart devices can be used for this (Pakurár, Haddad, Nagy, Popp, & Oláh, 2019).

Yemeni universities are only starting to use m-banking adoption (Hadi, Huafei, Khan, Abdulrab, & Yan, 2021). Due to low technology utilization, lack of competent employees to build, install, and operate business websites, and limited financial resources, the organization has delayed implementing a more modern m-banking solution. Yemeni University staff may use e-business less due to a shortage of computer software and hardware (Abdullah, Thomas, Murphy, & Plant, 2018).

Hence, the study analyzes mobile banking use and perceived ease of use, compatibility, security, and usefulness. It also investigates how perceived utility mediates these characteristics and mobile banking use among Yemeni University professors. The study will reveal how this demographic utilizes mobile banking and its effects.

2. RESEARCH QUESTIONS

- Does perceived ease of use have a significant and positive influence on the actual usage of m-banking?
- Does perceived compatibility have a significant and positive influence on the actual usage of m-banking?

- Does perceived security have a significant and positive influence on the actual usage of m-banking?
- Does perceived ease of use have a significant and positive influence on the perceived usefulness of m-banking?
- Does perceived compatibility have a significant and positive influence on the perceived usefulness of m-banking?
- Does perceived security have a significant and positive influence on the perceived usefulness of m-banking?
- Does perceived usefulness have a significant and positive influence on the actual usage of m-banking?
- Does perceived usefulness mediate the relationship between TAM factors (perceived ease of use, perceived compatibility, and perceived security) and the actual usage of m-banking?

2.1. Research Objectives

- Determine the impact of perceived ease of use on the actual usage of m-banking.
- Assess the influence of perceived compatibility on the actual usage of m-banking.
- Examine the effect of perceived security on the actual usage of m-banking.
- Investigate the relationship between perceived ease of use and perceived usefulness in the context of m-banking.
- Explore the relationship between perceived compatibility and perceived usefulness in the context of m-banking.
- Analyze the relationship between perceived security and perceived usefulness in the context of m-banking.
- Evaluate the impact of perceived usefulness on the actual usage of m-banking.
- Investigate the mediating role of perceived usefulness in the relationship between TAM factors (perceived ease of use, perceived compatibility, and perceived security) and the actual usage of m-banking.

By addressing these research objectives, this study aims to provide valuable insights into the factors influencing the adoption and usage of m-banking, as well as the role of perceived usefulness as a mediating factor. The findings will contribute to the existing body of knowledge on technology acceptance and provide practical implications for improving m-banking services and enhancing user experience.

3. LITERATURE REVIEW

Many researchers have tried to understand consumer acceptance of mobile technology due to its rapid advancement and incorporation into banking transactions and services. The TAM has been practically and conceptually explained and supported (Su, Nguyen, Nguyen, & Luu, 2022). Mobile banking uses the TAM extensively. The approach does not account for all technological adoption and usage aspects. Researchers advise evaluating how external factors affect TAM's core components, such as perceived utility and perceived ease of use (Assaker, 2020). TAM originally contained the attitude concept, but empirical research has shown that it may not sufficiently moderate the effect of perceived ease of use and perceived usefulness on intention (Nguyen, Nguyen-Phuoc, & Johnson, 2023). Customer attitude may not affect mobile service uptake. Thus, TAM's main constructs are important for understanding mobile banking adoption, but other constructs may also matter.

Mobile banking is the new frontiers of banking which allow customers to access banking services anywhere and anytime with the help of a mobile device (Sharma, 2019). It offers a variety of services such as mobile payments, money transfers, account balance checking, and more. Due to its advantages, the adoption rate of mobile banking has increased significantly over the years. It is important to understand the factors that contribute to the adoption of mobile banking by customers (Shaikh, Alamoudi, Alharthi, & Glavee-Geo, 2023). Factors of the adoption of mobile banking are compatibility (COMP), perceived usefulness, and perceived security.

In terms of COMP, it is the degree to which technology is seen to be compatible with existing user standards. It can also be described as the extent to which technology is compliant with existing facilities and procedures (Kumar, Engle, & Tucker, 2018). The study of factors that act as drivers for mobile banking adoption in Jordan found that compatibility influenced consumers' mobile banking intention to use (Gharaibeh & Arshad, 2018). Similarly, the study of Kapoor and Dwivedi (2020) also determined compatibility as an important factor that influenced mobile phone users' intention to adopt mobile marketing services.

Regarding the perceived usefulness, Leem and Eum (2021) defined perceived usefulness in the TAM model as the extent to which an individual believes that applying an innovation increases job performance. This definition originates from the word useful, which means the ability to be used advantageously. Ammenwerth (2019) confirmed that perceived security and perceived usefulness served as influencing factors that impact m-banking adoption in Bangladesh. Similarly, Sankaran and Chakraborty (2021) claimed that perceived usefulness and emotion played significant roles in accounting for both the usage and intention to use m-banking through perceived value.

Perceived security was first established by Rattanaburi and Vongurai (2021) as uncertainty and consequence related to customers' activities. Perceived security and behavioral intention are linked in many research. Li et al. (2023) found that perceived security was adversely connected with behavioral intention to use services from a tourist business, meaning managers are less likely to utilize e-banking if system security is high.

Fig. 11.1 displays all causal relationships among variables and analyzes the factors that influence perceived usefulness and the actual usage of m-banking applications among university academics in Yemen. The theoretical and conceptual frameworks describe the path of the study, create the ground theory and construct the variables. The framework's overall purpose is to make the study results more relevant, accessible to theoretical constructs in research and promote generalization (Ali, Yusoffii, & Ali, 2019; Habtoor & Ali, 2022). The conceptual framework variables include actual usage, compatibility, perceived cost, perceived usefulness, perceived ease-of-use and perceived security.

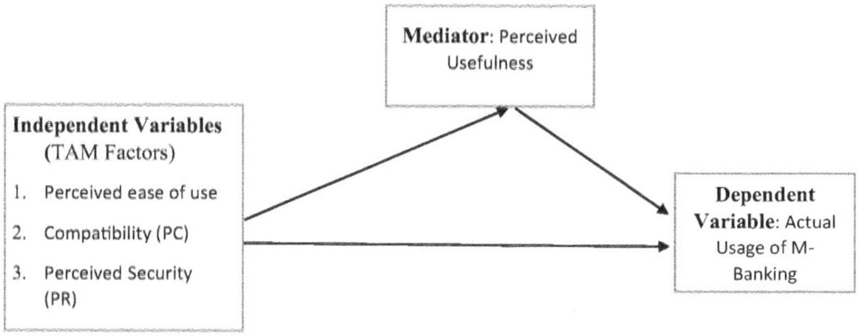

Fig. 11.1. Conceptual Framework and Hypotheses Testing.

H1. Perceived Ease of use has a significant and positive influence on actual usage of m-banking.

H2. Perceived compatibility (PC) has a significant and positive influence on actual usage of m-banking.

H3. Perceived Security (PR) has a significant and positive influence on actual usage of m-banking.

H4. Perceived ease of use has a significant and positive influence on perceived usefulness to use MB.

H5. PC has a significant and positive influence on perceived usefulness to use MB.

H6. Security (Na, Heo, Han, Shin, & Roh, 2022) has a significant and positive influence on perceived usefulness to use MB.

H7. Perceived Usefulness has a significant and positive influence on actual usage of MB.

H8. Perceived Usefulness mediates the relationship between TAM factors and actual usage of m-banking.

4. RESEARCH METHODOLOGY

The present study would benefit most from a quantitative approach to its research design. This is due to the fact that it intends to test hypotheses in order to investigate the effect of project success such as through self-assessment and information and communication as a mediating role. In order to do this, it will be using a quantitative technique to deal with the data, which is a necessary precondition for the testing of hypotheses (Al Balushi, Ali, & Alzoraik, 2023; Ateeq, 2022; Ateeq, Ebrahim, & Al-Ghatam, 2022; Alzoraiki et al., 2023; Galdeano, Fati, Ogalo, & Abro, 2019).

Using a self-administered survey and stratified random sample, 251 Yemeni university professors were surveyed. The survey consisted of two parts: demographic information and research factors like real use, ease of use, perceived security, perceived expense, perceived utility and actual utilization. The research examined causal links between latent variables using structural equation modeling. The research had a 79% response rate and 251 participants, which meets acceptable ratios of observations to parameters.

5. RESULTS

In terms of correlation matrix between variables, it was seen from the study's results that the maximum relation (correlation) between (Mahaputra & Saputra, 2021) and the (Galdeano, Fati, Ogalo, & Abro, 2019) is 0.545, (PEOU) and (PC) is 0.491 and *p*-value was 0.000. Contrarily, the lowest correlation between the variables was (Pratt & Gladue, 2022) and (Ali, AlZgool, Alzoraiki, Milhem, & Al-Absy, 2023; Galdeano, Fati, Ogalo, & Abro, 2019) with 0.278. It is shown from the correlation matrix that the values of the correlation are less than 0.80 and are varied from the 0.545 and 0.278 (Al-Refaei, Ali, Ateeq, & Alzoraiki, 2023; Ateeq, Yusoff, & Ali, 2019). The findings of the study verified that the multicollinearity is not considered as a problem between the study model's constructs. Table 11.1 represents the correlation matrix among the variables.

The research calculated mean and standard deviation of measuring scales using a 5-point Likert scale from "1" strongly disagree to "5" strongly agree to describe latent components. Mobile banking and perceived usefulness had the highest mean scores, 67.9% and 67.8%, respectively. Security had the lowest mean value, 63%; 65% of ratings were 3.36. All variables had standard deviations between 0.879 and 1.176, suggesting acceptable data set variability. Table 11.2 shows variable descriptive data. Between intention and use, analyze the impact of each security factor.

The measurement model's construct, convergent, and discriminant validity was assessed using a two-stage SEM analysis. Convergent validity was proven

Table 11.1. Pearson Correlation Among the Variables.

	MB	PU	PEOU	PC	PR
MB	1				
PU	0.545**	1			
PEOU	0.326**	0.357**	1		
PC	0.341**	0.425**	0.491**	1	
PR	0.278**	0.413**	0.383**	0.329**	1

Note: MB, mobile banking; PU, perceived usefulness; PEOU, perceived ease of use; PR, perceived security; PC, compatibility.

** Indicates a high level of statistical significance.

Table 11.2. Descriptive Statistics for Study Variables (Mean and SD).

Variable	Mean	%	SD
Use of mobile banking	3.3974	67.948	1.01227
Perceived usefulness	3.3929	67.87	0.87985
Perceived ease of use	3.3884	67.768	1.09818
Compatibility	3.2470	64.94	1.12661
Perceived security	3.1584	63.168	1.17625
Overall	3.3621	65.521	0.88860

Table 11.3. Cronbach's Alpha, Composite reliability.

Variables	Cronbach's α	rho_A	CR
Compatibility	0.789	0.794	0.863
Mobile banking	0.887	0.887	0.910
Perceived ease of use	0.814	0.820	0.877
Perceived security	0.750	0.753	0.841
Perceived usefulness	0.808	0.809	0.866

Source: Computed data Analysis.

Table 11.4. Items Loading.

Variable	Item	Loading	Variable	Item	Loading
Use of mobile banking	MB1	0.787	Compatibility	COMP1	0.734
	MB2	0.765		COMP2	0.766
	MB3	0.747		COMP3	0.746
	MB4	0.790		COMP4	0.774
	MB5	0.769			
	MB6	0.700	Perceived security	PR1	0.769
	MB7	0.715		PR2	0.757
	MB8	0.703		PR3	0.748
				PR4	0.742
Perceived usefulness	PU1	0.757	Perceived ease of use	PEOU1	0.814
	PU2	0.726		PEOU2	0.832
	PU3	0.756		PEOU3	0.787
	PU4	0.770		PEOU4	0.767
	PU5	0.748			

Source: Computed data analysis.

when items loaded substantially, the average variance extracted was at least 0.5, and composite reliability values were above 0.70; 0.750–0.887 was the reliability range (refer Table 11.3).

In terms of convergent validity, the factor loading for the items are more than 0.50 and are acceptable if the study sample is more than 200 respondents (Ali, Alzoraiki, Al-shaibath, & Almaamari, 2022). This, in turn, is sufficient evidence of convergent validity. The factor loading ranged between MB8 (0.703) and PEOU (0.832) (refer Table 11.4). Therefore, all indicators in the present study are related to their particular constructs, and thus there is satisfactory proof of the convergent validity of the model (as mentioned in Fig. 11.2).

6. MEDIATING EFFECT (INDIRECT HYPOTHESES RESULTS)

Perceived usefulness mediated the TAM-mobile banking link in the research. Perceived utility partly moderated the association between ease of use, security, and mobile banking. PC did not affect mobile banking via perceived utility. *H8*, *H10*, and *H11* were confirmed. Tables 11.5 and 11.9 showed varying impacts directly and indirectly.

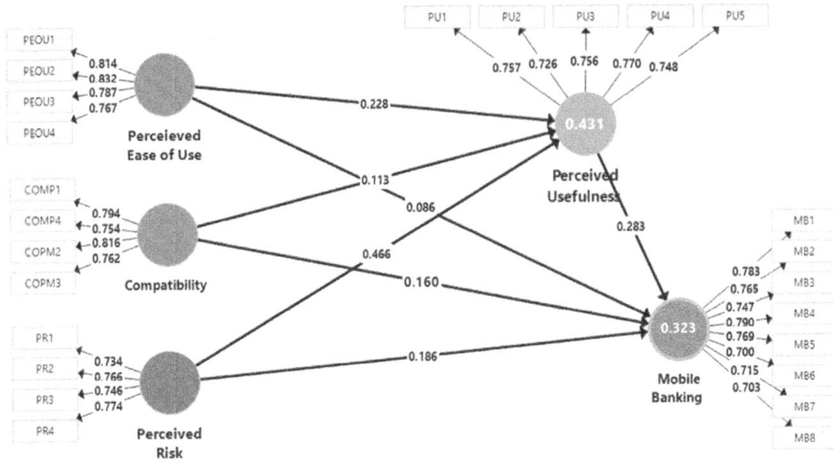

Fig. 11.2. Measurement Model/Outer Model.

Regarding the Discriminant validity, it gives the extent to which a construct is truly distinct from other constrDiscriminant validity is evaluated by using average variance extracted for every construct that exceeds the squared correlation among other constructs. Discriminant validity gives the extent to which a construct is truly distinct from other constructs (Alzoraiki, 2021). Discriminant validity is evaluated by using average variance extracted for every construct that exceeds the squared correlation among other constructs. In this chapter, AVE values were more than 0.50 and ranged between 0.565 and 0.641, suggestion acceptable values indicating an adequate convergent validity. Thus, the convergent validity was confirmed in the study (see Table 11.5).

PLS-SEM was used to examine the predicted correlations between study variables (Table 11.6), and the findings fit well. The coefficient of determination (R^2) values showed that the model had a minimal degree of explanatory power, explaining a considerable percentage of the dependent variable variation. Mobile banking use explained 42.5% of the variation in project management among university professors. Security management techniques explained 39.2% of internal control among Yemeni university professors (Alzoraiki, Rahman, & Mutalib, 2018; Gohar, Chang, Derindag, & Abro, 2022) (refer Table 11.7).

Effect size (*f*2) analysis was performed to estimate the latent variable effects on dependent variables. Effect size was calculated using Cohen's (1988) method. Perceived ease of use had a minor impact size of 0.046 on perceived usefulness, but perceived security had a big effect size of 0.324. Perceived security and usefulness showed negligible effects on mobile banking use, 0.33 and 0.067, respectively (Ateeq, Alzoraiki, & Milhem, 2023). The results are presented in Table 11.8.

The empirical study tested four hypotheses related to the aim of the study. According to the results in Table 11.5, compatibility and perceived security are the important factor influence on mobile banking and usefulness among universities academics in Yemen. Therefore, *H2*, *H3*, *H5* and *H6* are supported (as mentioned in Fig. 11.3).

Table 11.5. Summary of Hypotheses Testing for the Indirect Effect (Mediating Results).

Hypotheses	Relation	Original Sample (β)	Standard Deviation	*T*-value	*p*-Value	Result
H8	PEOU → PU → MB	0.064	0.024	2.677	0.008	Supported
H9	COMP → PU → MB	0.032	0.019	1.719	0.087	Not supported
H10	PR → PU → MB	0.132	0.042	3.138	0.002	Supported
H11: Main Indirect Hypothesis	TAM → PU → MB	0.206	0.059	3.497	0.001	Supported

Note: MB, mobile banking; PU, perceived usefulness; PEOU, perceived ease of use; PR, perceived security; PC, compatibility.

Table 11.6. Discriminant Validity and for Latent Variables.

	AVE	Compatibility	Mobile Banking	Perceived Ease of Use	Perceived Security	Perceived Usefulness
Compatibility	0.612	0.782				
Mobile banking	0.559	0.405	0.747			
Perceived ease of use	0.641	0.690	0.399	0.800		
Perceived security	0.570	0.344	0.439	0.365	0.755	
Perceived usefulness	0.565	0.430	0.502	0.475	0.588	0.752

Source: Computed data analysis.

Table 11.7. Coefficient of Determination Result R^2.

Independent Variable	Dependent Variable	R^2	Adjust R^2
Perceived ease of use, perceived compatibility, and perceived security	Perceived usefulness	0.431	
Perceived ease of use, perceived compatibility, perceived security, and perceived usefulness	Mobile banking usage	0.323	

Table 11.8. Effect Size.

Variable	Effect Size			
	Using of Mobile Banking	Rating	Perceived Usefulness	Rating
Perceived ease of use	0.005	Non	0.046	Small
Compatibility	0.019	Small	0.011	Non
perceived security	0.033	Small	0.324	Large
Perceived usefulness	0.067	Small	–	–

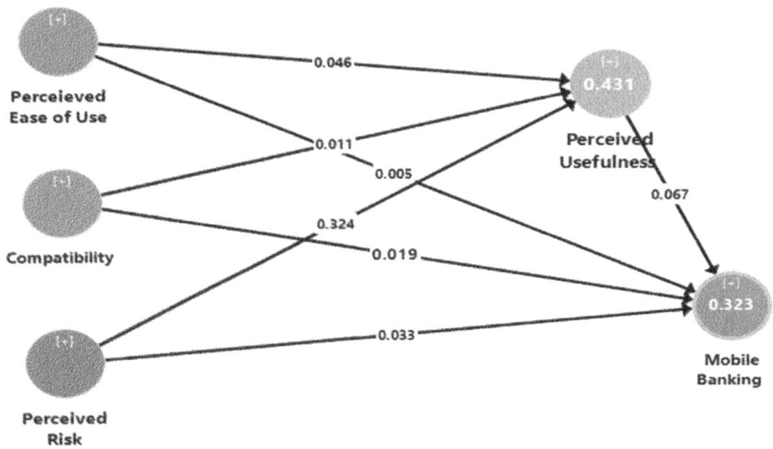

Fig. 11.3. Measurement Model With (R^2) and (Algorithm).

Table 11.9. Summary of Structural Model for Direct Hypotheses Results.

H	Exog.	⇨	Endo.	Original Sample (β)	Standard Deviation (STDEV)	*t*-value (CR)	*P*-value	Result
H1	PEOU	⇨	MB	0.086	0.075	1.138	0.256	Not Supported
H2	COMP	⇨	MB	0.160	0.066	2.402	0.017	Supported
H3	PR	⇨	MB	0.186	0.068	2.742	0.007	Supported
H4	PEOU	⇨	PU	0.228	0.062	3.668	0.000	Supported
H5	COMP	⇨	PU	0.113	0.055	2.051	0.042	Supported
H6	PR	⇨	PU	0.466	0.059	7.887	0.000	Supported
H7	PU	⇨	MB	0.283	0.074	3.825	0.000	Supported

Note: MB, mobile banking; PU, perceived usefulness; PEOU, perceived ease of use; PR, perceived security; PC, compatibility.

** Significant at $p < 0.01$. *Significant at bootstrapping $p < 0.05$.

The result indicates that perceived usefulness had a significant and positive impact on mobile banking ($\beta = 0.283$; CR =3.825; $P = 0.000$); thus, *H7* is supported.

On the other hand, perceived ease of use was not significantly effect on mobile banking; thus *H1* is not supported ($\beta = 0.086$; CR = 1.138; $P = 0.265$). Table 11.9 presents that the direct hypotheses results (and refer to Fig. 11.4).

7. DISCUSSION AND CONCLUSION

This study intended to examine the impact of TAM variables, including perceived utility, convenience of use, perceived security, and compatibility, on academics'

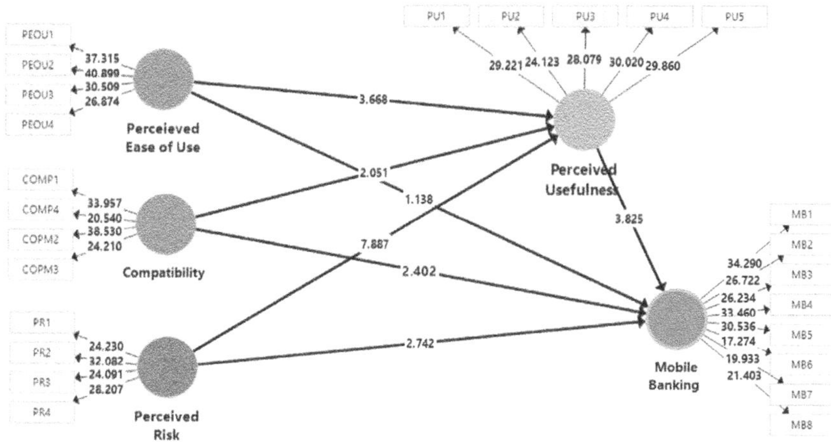

Fig. 11.4. Structural Model With (Bootstrapping) (Hypotheses Results).

use of mobile banking services in Yemen (Obaid, 2021). The findings revealed that perceived security and compatibility had a considerable positive effect on perceived utility and mobile banking usage. Additionally, it was discovered that usability has a significant impact on perceived utility. Prior research has emphasized the significance of information and guidance provided by institutions to reduce usage, value, and security barriers. The study's findings are consistent with this emphasis. In addition, the findings imply that a greater awareness of mobile banking services and concrete information may reduce security concerns among Yemeni university professors. The mediating effect of perceived utility was also found to influence the utilization of mobile banking services via the TAM constructs (Nelwan, Yasa, Sukaantmadja, & Ekawati, 2021).

The results of this study are consistent with previous research that demonstrates the significance of usability in determining perceived utility in the context of internet banking. The original TAM proposed that perceived simplicity of use predicts perceived utility, and that both variables are predictors of technology adoption(Pitafi, Kanwal, & Khan, 2020). In this study, perceived simplicity of use was found to be a significant predictor of the perceived utility of mobile banking among Yemeni university professors.

This is consistent with previous researches (Mutahar, Aldholay, Isaac, Jalal, & Alkibsi, 2022; Mutahar et al., 2021; Rezvani, Heidari, Roustapisheh, & Dokhanian, 2022) in a different context and application, reporting on the significant positive influence of perceived ease of use on perceived usefulness. Potential users of the mobile banking system in Yemen perceive that when the mobile banking services system is easy to use, their perception of the usefulness of the same system is increased as well. This will consequently increase their intention to use mobile banking services. The results of this study are consistent with Mutahar, Aldholay et al. (2022), Mutahar, Norzaidi et al. (2021), and Aslam, de Luna, Asim, and Farhat (2023) all of whom showed empirically that perceived usefulness and ease of use have a positive influence on the intention to use mobile banking services. Based on the above.

7.1. Recommendations and Suggestion

There are drawbacks to this study that need to be worked out in other studies. Perceived security and compatibility were added to TAM, but more elements should be included to present a fuller picture of mobile banking and better enable forecast of uptake. It's possible that the chosen technique of sampling is not providing accurate representation of the population; other approaches should be considered. The privacy and safety implications of TAM should be studied independently in the future. The research is limited since it measures only desire to change behavior rather than actual changes or rates of adoption. The effects of each of the suggested security characteristics should be studied independently in future studies, and the causal relationship between purpose and behavior should be explored.

REFERENCES

Abdullah, A., Thomas, B., Murphy, L., & Plant, E. (2018). An investigation of the benefits and barriers of e-business adoption activities in Yemeni SMEs. *Strategic Change*, *27*(3), 195–208.

Al Balushi, F. S. M., Ali, A. A. A., & Alzoraik, M. (2022). The impact of forecasting strategy and training and development strategy on preparing leadership competencies administrative support in the Sultanate of Oman. *Resource*, *3*(1), 34–41.

Al-refaei, A. A.-A., Ali, H. B., Ateqe, A. A., & Alzoraiki, M. (2023). An integrated mediating and moderating model to improve service quality through job involvement, job satisfaction, and organizational commitment. *Sustainability*, *15*(10), 7978.

Ali, A. A. A., AlZgool, M., Alzoraiki, M., Milhem, M., & Al-Absy, M. S. M. (2023). Moderating effect of strategic planning on the relationship between career path planning and job performance. *Sustainability*, *15*(11), 8490.

Ali, A. A. A., Yusoffii, S. H., & Ali, K. (2019a, July 29). Fundamental of equal opportunities in employee's performance: A critical review. In *5th world conference on integration of knowledge*, Bangi Selangor, Malaysia.

Ali, A. A. A., Yusoff, S. H., & Ali, K. (2019b). The relationship between equal opportunities and employee performance: A special reference to with specific refence to BDF Hospital in the Kingdom of Bahrain. *International E-Journal of Advances in Social Sciences*, *5*(14), 1200–1206.

Alzoraiki, M., Ahmad, A. R., Ateeq, A. A., Naji, G. M. A., Almaamari, Q., & Beshr, B. A. H. (2023). Impact of teachers' commitment to the relationship between transformational leadership and sustainable teaching performance. *Sustainability*, *15*(5), 4620.

Alzoraiki, M., Rahman, O. b. A., & Mutalib, M. A. (2018). The effect of the dimensions of transformational leadership on the teachers' performance in the Yemeni public schools. *European Scientific Journal*, *14*(25), 322.

Alzoraiki, M. S. M. (2021). Towards the sustainable teaching quality through school culture and teachers' commitment using PLS-SEM approach. *Asia Proceedings of Social Sciences*, *8*(2), 84–87.

Ammenwerth, E. (2019). Technology acceptance models in health informatics: TAM and UTAUT. *Studies in Health Technology and Informatics*, *263*, 64–71.

Aslam, W., de Luna, I. R., Asim, K., & Farhat, K. (2023). Do the preceding self-service technologies influence mobile banking adoption? *IIM Kozhikode Society & Management Review*, *12*(1), 50–66.

Assaker, G. (2020). Age and gender differences in online travel reviews and user-generated-content (UGC) adoption: Extending the technology acceptance model (TAM) with credibility theory. *Journal of Hospitality Marketing & Management*, *29*(4), 428–449.

Ateeq, A., Ebrahim, S., & Al-Ghatam, R. (2022). The impact of stress and its influencing factors among dentists during the COVID-19 pandemic in Kingdom of Bahrain. *F1000Research*, *11*, 930.

Ateeq, A. A. (2022). *The relationship between Islamic work ethics and employee performance among medical staff in the public health sector in Bahrain: Employee commitment as mediating variable*. Malaysia: Universiti Sains Islam Malaysia.

Ateeq, A. A., Alzoraiki, M., Al-shaibah, M., & Almaamari, Q. (2022). Enhancing contextual performance through Islamic work ethics with mediating role of normative commitment. *Mathematical Statistician and Engineering Applications*, *71*(4), 8668–8683.

Galdeano, D. M., Fati, M., Ogalo, H. S., & Abro, Z. (2019). Social media and purchase intention: Findings for future empirical directions. *Humanities & Social Sciences Reviews*, *7*(4), 141–150.

Gharaibeh, M. K., & Arshad, M. R. M. (2018). Determinants of intention to use mobile banking in the North of Jordan: Extending UTAUT2 with mass media and trust. *Journal of Engineering and Applied Sciences*, *13*(8), 2023–2033.

Gohar, R., Chang, B. H., Derindag, O. F., & Abro, Z. (2022). Nexus between consumption, income, and price changes: Asymmetric evidence from NARDL model. *Etikonomi*, *21*(2), 213–228.

Habtoor, N. H., & Ali, E. S. (2022). Human side of total quality management: A critical review. *International Journal of Intellectual Human Resource Management (IJIHRM)*, *3*(2), 27–32.

Hadi, J., Huafei, W., Khan, M. S., Abdulrab, M. A., & Yan, Z. S. (2021). The impact of mobile banking application on client interaction with Yemen banks. *International Journal of Business Strategies*, *6*(1), 58–68.

Kapoor, K. K., & Dwivedi, Y. K. (2020). Sustainable consumption from the consumer's perspective: Antecedents of solar innovation adoption. *Resources, Conservation and Recycling*, *152*, 104501.

Karjaluoto, H., Glavee-Geo, R., Ramdhony, D., & Shaikh, A. A. (2021). Consumption values and mobile banking services: Understanding the urban–rural dichotomy in a developing economy. *International Journal of Bank Marketing*, *39*(2), 272–293.

Kumar, G., Engle, C., & Tucker, C. (2018). Factors driving aquaculture technology adoption. *Journal of the World Aquaculture Society*, *49*(3), 447–476.

Leem, B.-H., & Eum, S.-W. (2021). Using text mining to measure mobile banking service quality. *Industrial Management & Data Systems*, *121*(5), 993–1007.

Li, C., Khaliq, N., Chinove, L., Khaliq, U., Ullah, M., Lakner, Z., & Popp, J. (2023). Perceived transaction cost and its antecedents associated with fintech users' intention: Evidence from Pakistan. *Heliyon*, *9*(4), e15140.

Mahaputra, M. R., & Saputra, F. (2021). Literature review the effect of headmaster leadership on teacher performance, loyalty and motivation. *Journal of Accounting and Finance Management*, *2*(2), 103–113.

Mutahar, A. M., Aldholay, A., Isaac, O., & Jalal, A. N. (2022). The moderating role of perceived risk in the technology acceptance model (TAM): The context of mobile banking in developing countries. In *Proceedings of international conference on emerging technologies and intelligent systems (Vol. 1)*. Berlin: Springer.

Mutahar, A. M., Aldholay, A., Isaac, O., Jalal, A. N., & Alkibsi, S. (2022). Predicting intention to use mobile banking services among Yemeni banks' clients: Is perceived value important? In *Proceedings of international conference on emerging technologies and intelligent systems (Vol. 1)*. Berlin: Springer.

Na, S., Heo, S., Han, S., Shin, Y., & Roh, Y. (2022). Acceptance model of artificial intelligence (AI)-based technologies in construction firms: Applying the technology acceptance model (TAM) in combination with the Technology–Organisation–Environment (TOE) framework. *Buildings*, *12*(2), 90.

Nelwan, J., Yasa, N. N. K., Sukaantmadja, I. P. G., & Ekawati, N. W. (2021). Antecedent behaviour and its implication on the intention to reuse the internet banking and mobile services. *International Journal of Data and Network Science*, *5*(3), 451–464.

Nguyen, M. H., Nguyen-Phuoc, D. Q., & Johnson, L. W. (2023). Why do parents intend to permit their children to ride e-bikes? Empirical evidence from Vietnam. *Travel Behaviour and Society*, *32*, 100586.

Obaid, T. (2021). Predicting mobile banking adoption: An integration of TAM and TPB with trust and perceived risk. Retrieved from SSRN 3761669.

Pakurár, M., Haddad, H., Nagy, J., Popp, J., & Oláh, J. (2019). The service quality dimensions that affect customer satisfaction in the Jordanian banking sector. *Sustainability*, *11*(4), 1113.

Pitafi, A. H., Kanwal, S., & Khan, A. N. (2020). Effects of perceived ease of use on SNSs-addiction through psychological dependence, habit: The moderating role of perceived usefulness. *International Journal of Business Information Systems*, *33*(3), 383–407.

Pratt, Y. P., & Gladue, K. (2022). Re-defining academic integrity: Embracing Indigenous truths. In *Academic integrity in Canada: An enduring and essential challenge* (pp. 103–123). Cham: Springer International Publishing.

Purwanto, E., Deviny, J., & Mutahar, A. M. (2020). The mediating role of trust in the relationship between corporate image, security, word of mouth and loyalty in M-banking using among the millennial generation in Indonesia. *Management & Marketing. Challenges for the Knowledge Society*, *15*(2), 255–274.

Rattanaburi, K., & Vongurai, R. (2021). Factors influencing actual usage of mobile shopping applications: Generation Y in Thailand. *The Journal of Asian Finance, Economics and Business*, *8*(1), 901–913.

Rezvani, S., Heidari, S., Roustapisheh, N., & Gokhanian, S. (2022). The effectiveness of system quality, habit, and effort expectation on library application use intention: The mediating role of perceived usefulness, perceived ease of use, and user satisfaction. *International Journal of Business Information Systems*, *1*(1), 1–18.

Sankaran, R., & Chakraborty, S. (2021). Factors impacting mobile banking in India: Empirical approach extending UTAUT2 with perceived value and trust. *IIM Kozhikode Society & Management Review*, *11*(1), 7–24.

Shaikh, A. A., Alamoudi, H., Alharthi, M., & Glavee-Geo, R. (2023). Advances in mobile financial services: a review of the literature and future research directions. *International Journal of Bank Marketing*, *41*(1), 1–33.

Sharma, S. K. (2019). Integrating cognitive antecedents into TAM to explain mobile banking behavioral intention: A SEM-neural network modeling. *Information Systems Frontiers*, *21*(4), 815–827.

Sharma, S. K., & Sharma, M. (2019). Examining the role of trust and quality dimensions in the actual usage of mobile banking services: An empirical investigation. *International Journal of Information Management*, *44*, 65–75.

Su, D. N., Nguyen, N. A. N., Nguyen, L. N., & Luu, T. T. (2022). Modeling consumers' trust in mobile food delivery apps: Perspectives of technology acceptance model, mobile service quality and personalization-privacy theory. *Journal of Hospitality Marketing & Management*, *31*(5), 535–569.

CHAPTER 12

BUSINESS STRATEGY AND EARNINGS MANAGEMENT: FINANCIAL VERSUS NON-FINANCIAL FIRMS

Taqwa Al Mawaali, Omar Nasser Khamis Al Hashar, Noof Al Alawi, Tamanna Dalwai, Syeeda Shafiya Mohammadi and Maroua Ben Maaouia

Muscat College, Ruwi, Sultanate of Oman

ABSTRACT

This study investigates the impact of business strategy on earnings management practices for financial and non-financial firms in Oman. To assess the research objective, 430 firm-year observations from 2015 to 2019 were employed in the study. Using regression analysis, the findings suggest that differentiation strategy positively affects earnings management in financial sector firms. In addition, cost leadership strategy positively affects earnings management in non-financial sector firms. This indicates that business strategy is associated with company leaders managing their earnings while they are trying to survive through competition. These findings are useful for regulators, as they can

Digital Technology and Changing Roles in Managerial and Financial Accounting: Theoretical Knowledge and Practical Application
Studies in Managerial and Financial Accounting, Volume 36, 129–139

Published under exclusive licence by Emerald Publishing Limited
ISSN: 1479-3512/doi:10.1108/S1479-351220240000036013

introduce mechanisms to curb earnings management practices and instil more faith in investors.

Keywords: Business strategy; earnings management; emerging country; financial sector; non-financial sector; cost leadership; differentiation

1. INTRODUCTION

According to Magerakis and Habib (2021) business strategy defines the organization's strategic moves intended to acquire a competitive advantage (Hambrick & Mason, 1984; Porter, 1980). Having a well-defined, clear business strategy in place impacts any organization with certainty and, moreover, has great importance in aiding an organization's success(Patra & Roy, 2023). In order to achieve better business functioning, strategies are generally concentrated on the actions required to create customer value in the firm's target markets. Numerous studies examine and reach conclusions on how various business strategies impact a company's success in several countries, although a lack of data is apparent on listed firms predominantly in the Sultanate of Oman. Therefore, this chapter investigates this objective to close the gap. In a study examining publicly traded Chinese firms, it was found that prospectors and companies with an innovation-based strategy had a greater wage disparity than those with a cost leadership approach, also known as defenders (Kong, Yang, Liu, & Yang, 2019).

The use of accounting methods to create financial statements that positively overstate a company's business operations and financial situation is known as earnings management. According to agency theory (Wu, Gao, & Gu, 2015), the primary reason for having earnings management is a dispute or disagreement between management and the owners in an organization. Due to the discrepancies in contracts, and lack of accurate information, management may have strong reasons to participate in earnings management to match analysts' forecasts and smooth overall outcomes. The distinctive tone used specifically during earnings conference calls and the increased usage of earnings management by businesses to exceed or meet a firm's earnings were found to be positively correlated, according to a study on tone and earnings management conducted in the UK by Kayed and Meqbel (2022). This illustrates how tone modulation can be used to successfully manage audience perception. In terms of cost leadership and differentiation business strategies, earnings management and firm bankruptcy risk are interrelated, therefore both techniques significantly lower the chance of bankruptcy (Agustia, Muhammad, & Permatasari, 2020). The overall long-term business strategy may incorporate earnings management, which is considered an opportunistic and resourceful tool for enterprises (Dokas, Leontidis, Eriotis, & Hazakis, 2021). Martínez-Ferrero, Banerjee, and García-Sánchez (2016) have uncovered that corporate social responsibility (CSR) has a stronger positive influence on the cost of capital in companies that demonstrate earnings management, indicating that the market is unaware of situations in which CSR approaches are used to conceal earnings management.

This study adds to the body of knowledge by investigating the impact of various business strategies, primarily cost-based and differentiation strategies, on earnings management in financial and non-financial listed firms in the Sultanate of Oman. The 2040 vision of Oman states long-term goals, which include targets to encourage all Omani-based businesses to develop efficient business plans and strategies to focus on diversifying the nation's economy and lessen its current reliance on the Omani oil sector, thus representing the importance of strategic goals in business. According to Dalwai and Salehi (2021) organizations must adapt to survive and make the most of the environmental prospects based on their strengths and shortcomings since business strategies aim to increase the competitive position of the company's offerings in its sector. Despite the economic, social, and cultural importance of emerging economy businesses around the world and in Oman, there is a shortage of literature that helps to understand how these businesses operate in emerging economy markets, and how strategy implementation and market forces might help to enhance their earnings management. Over the past 20 years, several authors have developed typologies to differentiate companies according to their strategies (Miller & Friesen, 1986; Miles, Snow, Meyer, & Coleman, 1978; Porter, 1991; Scafarto, Dalwai, Ricci, & della Corte, 2023). A company's strategy represents choices of objectives and means that strategic units decide to implement them after an assessment of their strengths and weaknesses both internally and in their external environment (Miles et al., 1978). Two typologies aim to classify business organizations according to their competitive strategy (Mileas et al., 1978; Porter, 1991). This study aims to identify the different business strategies related to earning management. The research attempts to identify which strategy and market forces are the most influential on strategy and business performance in the context of Oman.

The remainder of the chapter is organized as follows: Section 2 presents the literature review and hypothesis development. Section 3 discusses the methodology presented in the study. Section 4 presents the results and discussion of the data analyzed. Lastly, Section 5 discusses the conclusion and recommendations.

2. LITERATURE REVIEW

2.1. Business Strategy

The literature in strategic management has given rise to the concept of business strategy and led to numerous typologies intended to define and categorize these business strategies. This development began with the observation that several firms using very different strategies achieve a high level of performance in a given field of activity(Parnell & Wright, 1993). Among these typologies, those of Porter (1980), Miles, Snow, Meyer, and Coleman (1978), and Youndt and Snell (2004) come up more particularly in management books and practices because of their accuracy, ease of implementation, and explanatory power. Porter (1980) typology refers to three fundamental strategies: cost dominance, differentiation, and focus strategy. The Miles et al.'s (1978) typology proposes four types of strategic configuration (prospectors, defendants, analysts, and reagents) based on their organization, efficiency, process, responsiveness, and products. Finally, the typology of Youndt and Snell (2004) distinguish three types of strategies: cost strategies, quality strategies, and flexibility strategies. Besides, it has already been established that strategy plays a key role in the development of earning management systems(Govindarajan & Fisher, 1990; Parnell & Wright, 1993). The objective of this article is to try to understand the extent to which a company's strategy influences decisions about earning management measures, established in management accounting systems using Porter (1980) framework.

2.2. Hypothesis Development

Porter [14] claims that the cost leadership strategy and the differentiation strategy are two different types of business strategies. To compete in the market, the cost leadership strategy emphasizes cost efficiency (Agustia et al., 2020; Wu et al., 2015). Cost-effectiveness is attained by limiting the expenses associated with the business' operating activities. High-cost tasks are typically avoided using this method. The cost leadership technique is frequently applied to minimize production costs in developing nations like Indonesia, where labour costs are low. The differentiation strategy places a focus on the uniqueness that enhances the value of a good or service. To set the company's product or service apart from its rivals, it can offer uniqueness in the form of design, features, technology, or customer service. Businesses that adopt a product differentiation approach frequently make significant investments in the facilities or activities that support this strategy, such as R&D, employee development, and brand creation (Agustia et al., 2020; Mathew, Brintha, & Jappes, 2023). As a result, the production costs associated with this differentiation strategy are typically high. Business strategy may be regarded as an important factor in motivating managers to use earnings management (Bentley, Omer, & Sharp, 2013). The choice of an earnings management approach can vary depending on variances in business strategies like cost leadership and differentiation initiatives.

Earnings management is the process of modifying accrual earnings to reflect the desired corporate performance, influencing the favorable opinions of users of the company's financial statements (Purba, Fransisca, & Joshi, 2022). Earnings management practices can be carried out through accruals or the company's actual activities (Cohen, Dey, & Lys, 2008; Cohen & Zarowin, 2010). Managerial discretionary accruals are used to manage accrual earnings. In this scenario, managers have the authority to choose accrual policy decisions, such as the depreciation method, uncollectible accounts, inventory, and policy estimations in provisions. The methodology and volume of accrual transactions are subject to some managerial discretion. Prior to the release of financial statements, accrual adjustments are often used to perform accrual earnings management. As a result, this type of earnings management does not affect cash flow (Cohen & Zarowin, 2010; Zang, 2012). Managers use accrual forms of earnings management to either reduce costs or increase profits.

Real earnings management is the activity taken by a manager to achieve profit goals through operational or real-world, decision making. To reach the required sales statistics, true earnings management practices are used, such as providing exorbitant discounts or more accommodating credit conditions, resulting in increased profits. Real profit management can also be accomplished by raising or lowering discretionary spendings like R&D, marketing and advertising, and general and administrative expenses to meet profit goals. The management of real earnings can be done at any time of the year and directly affects the company's cash flow. Previous studies (Badertscher, 2011; Braam, Nandy, Weitzel, & Lodh, 2015; Zang, 2012) claimed that real-world earnings management practices were more expensive than accrual earnings management.

Therefore, after having reviewed the prior studies, the following relationship is hypothesized:

H1. The cost leadership strategy is positively related to earnings management.

H2: Differentiation strategy is negatively related to the level of earnings management.

3. METHODOLOGY

This study uses data from the S&P Capital IQ database. The sample has been collected for financial and non-financial firms listed in the Muscat Stock Exchange, that is, there are 430 firm observations (130 financial and 300 non-financial firms) for five years from 2015 to 2019. To execute the research model and classify an association between the dependent variable and the independent variable, STATA version 17 software is used for conducting multiple linear regression analysis.

3.1. Research Model

$$\begin{aligned}\text{Earnings Management}_{i,t} = {} & \beta_0 + \beta_1 \text{ Cost Leadership}_{i,t} + \beta_2 \text{ Differentiation}_{i,t} \\ & + \beta_3 \text{ Cash Holding}_{i,t} + \beta_4 \text{ ROA}_{i,t} + \beta_5 \text{ Firm Size}_{i,t} \\ & + \beta_6 \text{ Leverage}_{i,t} + \beta_7 \text{ Tangibility}_{i,t} + \beta_6 \text{ SalesGrowth}_{i,t} \\ & + \beta_6 \text{ Firm Age}_{i,t} + \alpha \qquad \text{(Equation 1)}\end{aligned}$$

Earning management (EM) is dependent, while the business strategy variables cost leadership and differentiation strategy are independent research variables. EM is the discretionary accruals measure that is derived from the prior study of Kothari, Leone, and Wasley (2005). As suggested by the work of Hambrick (1983) and David, Hwang, Pei, and Reneau (2002), cost leadership is a technique employed by cost leaders to establish a competitive advantage in pricing through the reduction of costs carried together by the development of operational excellence. It is measured with the proxy of asset turnover of operations, which is the ratio of operating sales divided by average operating assets. The differentiation business strategy aims to gain a competitive advantage over competitors by making products and services that differentiate themselves from their competitors. Differentiation is measured using the proxy of profit margin, calculated with the formula operating income plus R&D expenses divided by sales (Wu et al., 2015).

In addition to the independent and dependent variables already indicated, the study model also includes several control variables chosen in light of the existing literature (Agustia et al., 2020; Habib & Hasan, 2021; Wu et al., 2015). Leverage is the ratio of a company's total liabilities to its total assets and is a measure of its utilization of debt from creditors in the capital structure of the company (Dalwai & Sewpersadh, 2023). The size of a firm is calculated using the natural logarithm of the firm's total assets to determine its relative size in comparison to other businesses operating in the same industry (Dalwai, Habib, Mohammadi, & Hussainey, 2023). When a company's total assets are higher, the size of the company is larger, which in turn correlates to different patterns of behavior and different financial conditions, and should comply with different regulatory requirements that the company has. The return on assets (ROA), which is calculated as net profit divided by total assets, is used as the control variable in this study (Maji & Goswami, 2016). ROA quantifies the productiveness of asset use over earning profits. The natural logarithm of the firm's age represents the age of the company (Habib & Dalwai, 2023).

4. RESULTS AND DISCUSSION

4.1. Descriptive Statistics

Table 12.1 presents the descriptive statistics of the variables in Equation (1). The mean value of earnings management is −0.029 for the financial sector and in comparison a positive mean value of 0.013 is shown for the non-financial thus reflecting the varying degrees of EM of listed companies vary greatly across the firms. The mean value for the independent variables, that is, cost leadership and differentiation is 0.801 and 0.088, respectively, for the financial sector while the mean value is 0.880 and 0.071, respectively, for the non-financial sector. The data suggests that financial sector firms are generally large-sized (size) in comparison to the non-financial sector. Non-financial sector firms hold more tangible assets in comparison to the financial sector.

4.2. Regression Analysis

Table 12.2 presents the regression results of business strategies' impact on earnings management practices of financial and non-financial sector-listed companies in Oman. Result 1 is for 130 firm-year observations related to financial sector companies, and the R^2 of 34.3% suggests the model's predictive power in explaining the variation in earnings management. As seen from the table the differentiation strategy is positively and statistically significant in its association with earnings management. Thus, financial sector firms are more reliant on differentiation strategies, and this leads to managers being encouraged to undertake more earnings management practices. This finding is consistent with Indonesia's listed non-financial firms, whose differentiation strategy is associated with earnings management (Purba, Fransisca, & Joshi, 2022). However, other prior studies indicated that a differentiation strategy could result in good financial performance without engaging in real earnings management (Chun & Cho, 2017; Widuri & Sutanto, 2019). Results 2 for 300 firm-year observations of non-financial sector firms have an explanatory power

Table 12.1. Descriptive Statistics.

	Financial sector			Non-financial sector		
Variables	*N*	Mean	SD	*N*	Mean	SD
Earnings management	130	−0.029	0.075	300	0.013	0.093
Cost leadership	130	0.801	0.240	300	0.880	0.176
Differentiation	130	0.088	0.166	300	0.071	0.151
Cash holding	130	0.129	0.140	300	0.118	0.163
ROA	130	1.343	1.897	300	2.221	3.740
Size	130	5.574	0.776	300	4.960	0.615
Leverage	130	0.288	0.392	300	0.301	0.345
Tangibility	130	0.095	0.230	300	0.477	0.306
Sales growth	130	0.932	19.031	300	−2.476	16.447
Firm age	130	27.885	13.615	300	27.033	11.640

Table 12.2. Regression Results of Business Strategy Impact on Earnings Management.

	(1)	(2)
	Earnings Management	Earnings Management
Variables	Financial Sector	Non-financial Sector
Constant	0.0868*	−0.0391
	(0.022)	(0.575)
Cost leadership	0.0218	0.0560*
	(0.694)	(0.048)
Differentiation	0.0908*	0.00696
	(0.014)	(0.914)
Cash holding	0.0800	0.119**
	(0.053)	(0.009)
ROA	−0.00846	−0.00837*
	(0.084)	(0.019)
Size	−0.0343***	0.00316
	(0.000)	(0.790)
Leverage	0.0296	−0.0122
	(0.180)	(0.472)
Tangibility	−0.0699	−0.0190
	(0.231)	(0.395)
Sales growth	−0.0000510	0.0000317
	(0.901)	(0.933)
Firm age	0.000979	−0.0000276
	(0.065)	(0.962)
Year	Included	Included
Observations	130	300
R^2	0.343	0.1703
Prob	0.000	0.00149
Wald chi^2	75.57	33.40

p-Values in parentheses. $*p < 0.05$, $**p < 0.01$, $***p < 0.001$. Variables definition included in Section 3.

of 17% (R^2). Cost leadership strategy is significantly and positively associated with earnings management practices. Thus, due to the low-profit margins in this sector, the firms tend to manage their earnings to reflect better performance. This result is consistent with the findings of the Chinese listed firms (Wu et al., 2015).

4.3. Robustness Analysis

To address endogeneity concerns, Table 12.3 presents a two-step system of generalized methods of moment (GMM) to produce efficient estimates and address biased estimator issues with a dynamic model of panel data (Blundell & Bond, 1998). The lagged independent variables are used as instruments, and their

Table 12.3. Systems GMM Regression Results of Business Strategy Impact on Earnings Management.

	(1)	(2)
	Earnings Management Financial Sector	Earnings Management Non-financial Sector
L.Cost leadership	−0.0245	0.0210
	(0.505)	(0.345)
L. Differentiation	0.225**	−0.109**
	(0.004)	(0.009)
Cost leadership	−0.111	0.117*
	(0.395)	(0.017)
Differentiation	0.0135	0.137
	(0.873)	(0.138)
Cash holding	−0.388*	0.186***
	(0.012)	(0.000)
ROA	−0.0362***	−0.00759**
	(0.000)	(0.009)
Size	0.0292	−0.0312
	(0.534)	(0.239)
Leverage	0.0810	−0.00464
	(0.144)	(0.887)
Tangibility	0.105	−0.101***
	(0.053)	(0.001)
Sales growth	0.000486	−0.000251
	(0.226)	(0.158)
Firm age	0.00154	−0.00356
	(0.865)	(0.267)
Year	Included	Included
Constant	−0.0859	0.175
	(0.824)	(0.257)
Observations	129	300
Chi^2	818.6	77.73
P	6.65e-164	4.27e-10
AR1	0.035	0.002
AR2	0.550	0.627
Sargan	0.141	0.003
Hansen	0.957	0.129

p-Values in parentheses. $^{*}p < 0.05$, $^{**}p < 0.01$, $^{***}p < 0.001$ variables definition included in Section 3.

validity is confirmed through the autocorrelation test (AR2) and Hansen J test for overidentification. Both tests' null hypotheses cannot be rejected for alternate hypotheses, suggesting that the instruments are valid and consistent. The OLS results obtained for the non-financial sector are confirmed by GMM, as cost leadership is positively and significantly associated with earnings management.

5. CONCLUSION AND RECOMMENDATIONS

This study investigates the impact of business strategies on the financial and non-financial sectors' earnings management practices in Oman. Porter (1980) business strategies typologies cost leadership and differentiation were used in the study. Using a sample of 430 observations for the period 2015–2019, it was observed that the business strategies adopted by the firms in Oman had a significant impact on earnings management practices. The findings of this study suggest that the financial sectors' differentiation strategy and the non-financial sectors' cost leadership strategy impact their EM practices, respectively.

The study has several implications. The regulators can derive information on which strategy is associated with earnings management practices. For the non-financial firms, the results indicate that cost leadership is associated with low-profit margins, and the cost leaders would be under pressure to meet an earnings target. Thus, they are more likely to manage their earnings. Similarly, non-financial firms adopting differentiation strategies are also more likely to adopt earnings management. Thus, regulators are required to monitor such practices and develop rules that would prevent price competitions or cost competitions to deter cost leaders from manipulating earnings.

The study also suffers from certain limitations. The study was conducted for listed firms in Oman before COVID-19. This is a limitation, as during the pandemic there were other challenges due to which companies had to change their strategies for survival. This could have had a different impact on earnings management. The findings of this study can be generalized to other GCC countries but not to other emerging markets, as they differ from economic and social perspectives. Future studies can be extended to cover the pandemic period specifically and other emerging markets.

ACKNOWLEDGMENT

The authors are grateful for the financial support provided by Muscat College for attending this conference.

REFERENCES

Agustia, D., Muhammad, N. P. A., & Permatasari, Y. (2020). Earnings management, business strategy, and bankruptcy risk: Evidence from Indonesia. *Heliyon*, *6*(2), E03317.

Badertscher, B. A. (2011). Overvaluation and the choice of alternative earnings management mechanisms. *The Accounting Review*, *86*(5), 1491–1518.

Bentley, K. A., Omer, T. C., & Sharp, N. Y. (2013). Business strategy, financial reporting irregularities, and audit effort. *Contemporary Accounting Research*, *30*(2), 780–817.

Blundell, R., & Bond, S. (1998). Initial conditions and moment restrictions in dynamic panel data models. *Journal of Econometrics*, *87*(1), 115–143.

Braam, G., Nandy, M., Weitzel, U., & Lodh, S. (2015). Accrual-based and real earnings management and political connections. *The International Journal of Accounting*, *50*(2), 111–141.

Chun, S., & Cho, E. (2017). Differentiation strategy, CSR, and real activities earnings management: Evidence from Korea. *Journal of Applied Business Research*, *33*(4), 669–692.

Cohen, D. A., Dey, A., & Lys, T. Z. (2008). Real and accrual-based earnings management in the pre- and post-Sarbanes–Oxley periods. *The Accounting Review*, *83*(3), 757–787.

Cohen, D. A., & Zarowin, P. (2010). Accrual-based and real earnings management activities around seasoned equity offerings. *Journal of Accounting and Economics*, *50*(1), 2–19.

Dalwai, T., Habib, A. M., Mohammadi, S. S., & Hussainey, K. (2023). Does managerial ability and auditor report readability affect corporate liquidity and cost of debt? *Asian Review of Accounting*, *31*(3), 437–459.

Dalwai, T., & Salehi, M. (2021). Business strategy, intellectual capital, firm performance, and bankruptcy risk: Evidence from Oman's non-financial sector companies. *Asian Review of Accounting*, *29*(3), 474–504.

Dalwai, T., & Sewpersadh, N. S. (2023). Intellectual capital and institutional governance as capital structure determinants in the tourism sector. *Journal of Intellectual Capital*, *24*(2), 430–464.

David, J. S., hwang, Y., Pei, B. K. W., & Reneau, J. H. (2002). The performance effects of congruence between product competitive strategies and purchasing management design. *Management Science*, *48*(7), 866–885.

Dokas, I., Leontidis, C., Eriotis, N., & Hazakis, K. (2021). Earnings management. An overview of the relative literature. *Bulletin of Applied Economics*, *8*(2), 25–55.

Govindarajan, V., & Fisher, J. (1990). Strategy, control systems, and resource sharing: Effects on business-unit performance. *Academy of Management Journal*, *33*(2), 259–285.

Habib, A., & Hasan, M. M. (2021). Business strategy and labor investment efficiency. *International Review of Finance*, *21*(1), 58–96.

Habib, A. M., & Dalwai, T. (2023). Does the efficiency of a firm's intellectual capital and working capital management affect its performance? *Journal of the Knowledge Economy*. Vol. ahead-of-print No. ahead-of-print

Hambrick, D. C. (1983). Some tests of the effectiveness and functional attributes of miles and snow's strategic types. *Academy of Management Journal*, *26*(1), 5–26.

Hambrick, D. C., & Mason, P. A. (1984). Upper Echelons: The organization as a reflection of its top managers. *Academy of Management Review*, *9*(2), 193–206.

Kayed, S., & Meqbel, R. (2022). Earnings management and tone management: Evidence from FTSE 350 Companies. *Journal of Financial Reporting and Accounting*. Vol. ahead-of-print No. ahead-of-print

Kong, D., Yang, X., Liu, C., & Yang, W. (2020). Business strategy and firm efforts on environmental protection: Evidence from China. *Business Strategy and the Environment*, *29*(2), 445–464.

Kothari, S. P., Leone, A. J., & Wasley, C. E. (2005). Performance matched discretionary accrual measures. *Journal of Accounting and Economics*, *39*(1), 163–197.

Magerakis, E., & Habib, A. (2021). Business strategy and environmental inefficiency. *Journal of Cleaner Production*, *302*, 127014.

Maji, S. G., & Goswami, M. (2016). Intellectual capital and firm performance in emerging economies: The case of India. *Review of International Business and Strategy*, *26*(3), 410–430.

Martínez-Ferrero, J., Banerjee, S., & García-Sánchez, I. M. (2016). Corporate social responsibility as a strategic shield against costs of earnings management practices. *Journal of Business Ethics*, *133*, 305–324.

Mathew, D., Brintha, N. C., & Jappes, J. T. W. (2023). Artificial intelligence powered automation for Industry 4.0. In A. Nayyar, M. Naved, & R. Rameshwar (Eds.), *New horizons for Industry 4.0 in modern business* (pp. 1–28). Cham: Springer International Publishing.

Miles, R. E., Snow, C. C., Meyer, A. D., & Coleman, H. J. (1978). Organizational strategy, structure, and process. *The Academy of Management Review*, *3*(3), 546–562.

Miller, D., & Friesen, P. H. (1986). Porter's (1980) generic strategies and performance: An empirical examination with American data: Part I: Testing Porter. *Organization Studies*, *7*(1), 37–55.

Parnell, J. A., & Wright, P. (1993). Generic strategy and performance: An empirical test of the Miles and Snow typology. *British Journal of Management*, *4*(1), 29–36.

Patra, G., & Roy, R. K. (2023). Business sustainability and growth in journey of Industry 4.0 – A case study. In A. Nayyar, M. Naved, & R. Rameshwar (Eds.), *New horizons for Industry 4.0 in modern business* (pp. 29–50). Cham: Springer International Publishing.

Porter, M. E. (1980). *Competitive strategy: Techniques for analyzing industries and competitors* (Vol. 13). New York, NY: Free Press.

Porter, M. E. (1991). Towards a dynamic theory of strategy. *Strategic Management Journal*, *12*(S2), 95–117.

Purba, G. K., Fransisca, C., & Joshi, P. L. (2022). Analyzing earnings management preferences from business strategies. *Journal of Financial Reporting and Accounting*, *20*(5), 979–993.

Scafarto, V., Dalwai, T., Ricci, F., & della Corte, G. (2023). Digitalization and firm financial performance in healthcare: The mediating role of intellectual capital efficiency. *Sustainability*, *15*(5), 4031. doi:10.3390/su15054031

Widuri, R., & Sutanto, J. E. (2019). *Differentiation strategy and market competition as determinants of earnings management*. Dordrecht: Atlantis Press.

Wu, P., Gao, L., & Gu, T. (2015). Business strategy, market competition and earnings management: Evidence from China. *Chinese Management Studies*, *9*(3), 401–424.

Youndt, M. A., & Snell, S. A. (2004). Human resource configurations, intellectual capital, and organizational performance. *Journal of Managerial Issues*, *16*(3), 337–360.

Zang, A. Y. (2012). Evidence on the trade-off between real activities manipulation and accrual-based earnings management. *The Accounting Review*, *87*(2), 675–703.

CHAPTER 13

IMPACT OF FINANCIAL TECHNOLOGY ON FUTURE OF BANKING IN BAHRAIN: OPPORTUNITIES AND CHALLENGES

Shafeeq Ahmed Ali[a], Mujeeb Saif Mohsen Al-Absy[a], Ahmad Yahia Mustafa Al Astal[b] and Ahmad Mohammad Obeid Gharaibeh[a]

[a]*Accounting and Financial Science Department, College of Administrative and Financial Science, Gulf University, Sanad 26489, Kingdom of Bahrain*
[b]*Administrative Science Department, College of Administrative and Financial Science, Gulf University, Sanad, Kingdom of Bahrain*

ABSTRACT

Financial technology (fintech) has emerged as a major player in the global financial system, providing a range of services such as payments, digital currencies, money transfers, loans, crowdsourcing, and insurance. Fintech startups in Arab countries have also gained traction due to economic openness and globalization. However, concerns remain about the safety, durability, and security of traditional financial services, especially with the increasing use of artificial intelligence (AI) and digitization. The Central Bank of Bahrain and other regulatory authorities need to balance risk avoidance with the global trend toward

Digital Technology and Changing Roles in Managerial and Financial Accounting: Theoretical Knowledge and Practical Application
Studies in Managerial and Financial Accounting, Volume 36, 141–153

Published under exclusive licence by Emerald Publishing Limited
ISSN: 1479-3512/doi:10.1108/S1479-351220240000036014

innovation in fintech, as well as ensure that these technologies are not used for fraud, money laundering, piracy, or terrorist financing. The Bahraini government and supervisory authorities must strike a balance between preserving the integrity and robustness of the financial and banking sector and developing innovation. This can be achieved by adjusting the rhythm of comparison, strengthening and enhancing the safety of banks, achieving financial stability, and ensuring compliance with laws and legislation. It is important to address gaps in regulatory rules, information security, and the business environment, and launch financial awareness at the community level before embracing the potential of fintech and its unseen future development at the level of cryptocurrencies and others. The current work examines the impact of Fintech on the Future of banking in Bahrain and the opportunities and challenges.

Keywords: Financial technology; artificial intelligence; electronic cloud; financial cloud; banking in Bahrain; Fintech

1. INTRODUCTION

The third millennium has witnessed rapid progress and boundless cognitive development, as this progress has become the distinguishing feature of this millennium. It is necessary to bring about a revolution in the economic systems so that we create a generation that can deal with what is going on around us in light of economic globalization and can predict and be creative so that future generations will have the skills to deal with these variables, and the economy is one of the most important factors influencing the provision of the requirements of progress and societal development. Therefore, countries have taken it upon themselves to examine their economic systems in search of shortcomings, as it has been generated by countries that traditional systems in light of technological development are no longer able to meet the requirements of economic development plans, and they are working on a radical and comprehensive review of economic systems and the application of modern systems to suit the nature of scientific and technological development (Léon & Zins, 2020).

The trend today is to build financial technology platforms Bahrain Bay and the transformation from traditional industries to knowledge-intensive industries based on distinguished products with added value by merging traditional elements of production with creative ones by investing heavily in human capital capable of creating, disseminating, and exploiting knowledge to become a major source of competition and improving the quality of life by translating Knowledge into practical applications to achieve wealth, well-being, and happiness. Research and generate new ideas and innovations that achieve excellence following international standards, with the establishment of a broad base of knowledge workers with superior skills within a regulatory environment. And the development of the business environment and the infrastructure of information and communication technology, the Kingdom of Bahrain (Gharaibeh, 2015a) is one of the advanced Arab countries moving toward the application of financial technology (financial technology).

Fintech by investing in human capital, developing individual talents and capabilities, as well as providing an appropriate environment for them, and transforming from the traditional economy based on fossils. To a digital economy based on building intellectual capital and working on marketing it to motivate talents and achieve leadership under national will and political leadership that was able to read global economic changes early on through the lofty vision 2030 of His Majesty the King (may God protect him), so plans and strategies were developed, initiatives were put forward, and funding was provided. Partnerships were held and obstacles were overcome by refining capabilities, upgrading skills, setting up systems for innovation, leadership, scientific research, nurturing talented people, providing effective and flexible management characterized by transparency, and moving from centralization to decentralization to allow more freedom for all institutions, in order to build the most important new economic resource, which is knowledge to achieve sustainable development.

2. RESEARCH PROBLEM

Given the tremendous advancements in financial technologies around the world, and despite the huge opportunities associated with this development, some great challenges and risks prevent benefiting from this tremendous development in the field of technology (Farooq & Miah, 2022). Accordingly, this research will study and scrutinize the risks and challenges facing banks and other financial institutions in the Kingdom of Bahrain.

2.1. Research Hypothesis

H1. Financial technology affects the safety and durability of banking in the Kingdom of Bahrain?

H2. Financial technology fosters economic growth.

H3. Financial technology contributes to achieving financial stability and shaping the future of financial transactions.

3. OBJECTIVES OF THE RESEARCH

- Identifying the effects of financial technology on the safety and durability of banking in the Kingdom of Bahrain.
- Find out about the reality of financial technology in Bahrain and learn about its role in fostering economic growth.
- Analyzing the impact of financial technology on achieving financial stability and shaping the future of financial transactions in the Kingdom of Bahrain.

4. SIGNIFICANCE OF THE RESEARCH

The importance of the research stems from the occurrence of a huge development in financial tools in recent years and the development of the field of dealing with financial technology in addition to the development of electronic payment applications and the ease of access to the largest population segment through the virtual world.

5. LIMITATIONS OF THE RESEARCH

- Spatial boundaries: The applied aspect of this research is limited to the banking and financial services sector in the Kingdom of Bahrain.
- Temporal boundaries: Financial technology indicators in the Kingdom of Bahrain will be analyzed and studied, focusing on the period from 2012 to 2022.

6. LITERATURE REVIEW

6.1. The Concept and Dimensions of Financial Technology

The structure of financial services could change as a result of financial technology, making them faster, cheaper, more secure, and more transparent for a wide segment of society, particularly those who do not interface with the banking system. However, the brisk growth of financial technology services and the rise of new businesses offering creative financial solutions that mimic what the banking sector offers and streamline banking and financial procedures present a challenge. They urge the implementation of all preventative steps to ensure the security and stability of the banking industry and in general, the financial industry as a buffer against it (Gharaibeh, 2015b). For banks and other financial organizations, financial technology, and its many uses today bring both opportunities and challenges, which may lead to a significant change in the nature and scope of banking risks due to the increasing reliance on financial technology. It is commonly recognized that financial technology, or "fintech," has seen previously unheard-of advancements in recent years, including improvements in mobile payments, digital currencies, technology lending, and market financing.

The majority of fintech innovations have emerged outside of the conventional banking and financial system, primarily as the result of non-banking organizations like fintech startups and non-traditional service providers like Oracle and Apple. Many more are anticipated to do the same. These non-banking organizations may operate in an unregulated financial environment and frequently concentrate their operations solely on offering a certain range of new banking and financial services. FinTech businesses seek to draw clients with increasingly automated, transparent, and user-friendly goods and services. Aims Financial technology also leads to the application of highly responsive marketing strategies and flexibility in providing new services, reaching a greater number of customers, and reaching people who are less bankable or even people who do not have bank accounts around the world (Vives, 2017).

The acceleration of technological progress and the expansion of smartphone applications, technology, and programs specialized in financial transactions and money transfers create opportunities for companies and banks that can keep pace with modern financial technological changes, and at the same time, it can pose a challenge to traditional banks and traditional financial institutions that follow the traditional business model, as it is expected that financial technology innovations in banks will reach far beyond what most people reach when thinking about banking services via the Internet. Fintech, which refers to any technology tools that offer financial services and products through software like using online banking, including mobile payment applications, or even cryptocurrency, is referred to as a development in banking technology.

Fintech is a broad category that encompasses a range of technologies, but its main objectives are to alter how financial technology is used. Consumer and corporate access to their financial resources and competition with traditional financial services. According to the Federal Deposit Insurance Corporation, traditional financial institutions like banks were successful before the 1990s and the Internet era. From roughly 13,500 commercial bank branches in 1950 to more than 83,000 in 2008, banks have increased significantly. Online financial technology companies like PayPal joined the market in the late 1990s and early 2000s, but until the global financial crisis of 2008, they did not pose a challenge to established infrastructure. Many people around this period began to lose faith in traditional banks as the new millennium generation began to experience free online financial services. As more services move to new technological paradigms, such as using a payment app on a mobile wallet instead of carrying physical credit cards in a physical wallet, today's Fintech solutions are posing a threat to the old financial infrastructure. Several markets have been transformed by financial technology, but the banking, trading, insurance, and risk management sectors have seen the most significant changes. Fintech firms use cutting-edge technologies like big data and AI, and they include major financial institutions as well as startups and technology firms (Arner, Buckley, & Zetzsche, 2018).

6.2. The Benefits and Advantages of Financial Technology

The most prominent benefits of financial technology are embodied in the following. Achieving and improving financial efficiency and increasing productivity: *Because banks and credit unions view financial technology companies as partners in this endeavor, financial technology enhances the quality of conventional financial institutions. Additionally, by delivering enhanced and modernized services, it is certain that the customer retention rate.

6.2.1. Scope of Service

Fintech enables businesses to broaden their service offerings and leverage cutting-edge technologies. FinTech companies can benefit greatly from innovative mobile applications as this expands the population of individuals who can utilize this kind of service as well as improves the quality and convenience of transactions. Can the company has also streamlined its operations with an option for customers to use tablets and smartphones to handle their finances?

6.2.2. Quality of Security

Using the new mobile technology necessitates a sizable security expenditure to guarantee that customer data is safe; critical data, encryption, and data encryption are some of the most recent security solutions employed by businesses in this industry.

6.2.3. Advanced Payment Systems

One of the important benefits of financial technology is that it makes companies more efficient in their work and allows them to collect their liabilities with higher accuracy. This can provide a more professional service and help improve customers' lives, increasing the likelihood that they will return as regular buyers of the company's products.

6.2.4. Convenience for Businesses and Customers

If businesses make good use of mobile connectivity, more people can access the site, improve efficiency and be able to save on conversions. Moreover, the possibility of a company simplifying things with the best overall options may also increase if consumers share many options for managing their finances via smartphones and startups. Additionally, one benefit of businesses in the financial technology sector is that they offer a single platform for payments, like Adyen, which has a long list of clients that includes Netflix, Uber, Microsoft, and others.

6.2.5. Valuable Advice

Many modern systems rely on bot advice to guide people about their finances. It is the fastest and least expensive way to get valuable information about investments.

For the advantages:

The best service: Customers can perform many banking services without going to banks or financial institutions, as they can carry out a large number of financial transactions only by using smart devices and specialized software.

Quick decisions: Financial technology enables banks and institutions to take quick decisions regarding financial transactions, as financial technology provides them with customer data, their financial options, their history, and the speed of access to and completion of financial transactions (Makina, 2019).

An easier way to pay: Customers can pay in easy ways, where customers point their smartphone, card or other RFID or NFC equipped device through the point-of-sale reader. However, contactless payment requires customers to be near the device payment: As for financial technology applications, payment can be made from a place in the store (Arslanian & Fischer, 2019).

5. AI/ELECTRONIC CLOUD/FINANCIAL CLOUD

There are some terms associated with financial technology such as AI, the electronic cloud, and the financial cloud. It can be displayed as follows:

5.1. Artificial Intelligence

I. Emulating human intelligence in machines created to act and think like people is known as AI. Any device that demonstrates traits of the human mind, such as learning and problem-solving, can also be referred to by the phrase. The ideal quality of AI is the capacity to reason and take actions that have the best chance of achieving a particular goal or set of goals. Machine learning is the process by which computer systems automatically adapt to new data and learn from it without human intervention.

II. *Electronic Cloud*: The cloud is anything that exists remotely because the name "cloud" alludes to a network or the internet. The cloud can offer services over any network, including WAN, LAN, VPNs, and virtual private networks, whether it is public or private.

III. *Cloud Finance*: With an ecosystem of interconnected tools for managing accounts, producing financial reports, processing payments, handling payroll, and managing budgets, cloud finance enables enterprises and finance teams to manage an organization's financial planning on the cloud. The data can be viewed whenever and from anywhere because it is connected to the Internet.

6. THE RELATIONSHIP OF FINANCIAL TECHNOLOGY WITH AI

Fintech companies and the broader financial sector can both benefit from AI in a variety of ways. The main benefit of AI is that it allows businesses to save time and money while also solving difficulties. By 2030, financial institutions will be able to cut their operating costs by 22% thanks to AI technology, predicts independent research. The deployment of AI enables the sector to improve the client experience by offering better customer service through a range of various operations. AI is frequently used in business to help organizations examine data in a useful and effective manner (Mohamed, Hamdan, Karolak, Razzaque, & Alareeni, 2021).

Companies, particularly financial institutions, frequently have a deluge of client data, but they rarely do anything with it because it takes effort to navigate and analyze it to extract anything valuable. AI can help with this since it is very good at evaluating enormous volumes of data, making conclusions from it, or suggesting the best course of action. Automated customer support is one of the other use cases for AI. When we browse the Internet, chat boxes are accustomed to appearing at the bottom of our displays. Of course, these are AI bots that are constantly there to assist. Businesses can quickly submit their most commonly asked queries, educate about how to respond, and direct it to refer customers for more complicated problems (Rowan et al., 2018).

7. CYBER SECURITY AND FINANCIAL TECHNOLOGY

The greatest hazards to today's financial services come from cybersecurity threats. According to research, increasing internet and data security is currently financial technology businesses' top concern, and preventing weaknesses in the financial system requires education and awareness of technological solutions. Previous studies indicated that about 70% of European companies lack basic knowledge about their vulnerability to cyberattacks, although four out of five of them suffered from some type of electronic incident in previous periods. The cost of cyberattacks in the banking industry amounted to more than $18 million annually. Successful attacks against banks and other financial institutions are the most expensive for a single organization, both in terms of cash damages and in terms of the decreased user confidence these breaches generate in the financial system. According to research by ImmuniWeb, a multinational business that specializes in application security testing technologies, 98% of international financial companies are exposed to significant cyberattacks, such as phishing, mobile, and online application security threats. The analysis also revealed that web applications, APIs, and other subfields all have at least a few security or privacy vulnerabilities that are common to all fintech organizations. Significant hazards include cross-site scripting (XSS), sensitive data disclosure, and incorrect security configuration. All mobile applications in FinTech are believed to have at least one security vulnerability as this is one of the most important cyber security risks for the FinTech sector these days due to organizations in the industry adopting more computing power and increasing the use of digital services, as it is important to go beyond traditional security models and consider the latest trends and solutions (Mention, 2019).

8. INFLUENCE OF FINANCIAL TECHNOLOGY ON BAHRAIN'S BANKING INDUSTRY PERFORMANCE

The Central Bahrain Bank has formed the "FinTech and Innovation Unit," a specialized unit in financial technology, to perform market research on innovations that occur in the financial sector and to build strategies to profit effectively from emerging technology. This unit was created to keep up with the impact of financial technology on the performance of the banking business. The Regulatory Sandbox Framework was released by the Central Bank of Bahrain in May 2017. As part of this framework, this unit reviews applications to join the experimental regulatory environment for financial technology, manages the regulatory process for applications that have been approved, and studies and analyzes new services and products. Or creative, which is meant to be fostered or given by businesses with Central Bank licenses, or by businesses meant to have Central Bank licenses (Razzaque, Cummings, Karolak, & Hamdan, 2020).

On Thursday, February 21, 2019, the Third Financial Technology Forum for the Middle East and North Africa Region was launched in the Kingdom of Bahrain to show that financial technology is no longer just a technical method for developing financial and banking performance, as a technical option among other options that countries and the financial and banking sector are free to adopt. Whether or not it has become an inevitable necessity for the continued existence and growth of the financial and banking sector and an important element of the competitive environment that it faces. The forum stressed that financial technology is an inevitable and necessary transformation that requires a comprehensive re-engineering of financial and banking engineering in various countries of the world, and a fundamental change in its means and mechanisms by shifting to technological digital systems and platforms to develop its business to keep pace with the new era, the era of the Fourth Industrial Revolution, as well as creating the legislative environment and its appropriate oversight. In other words, it is a new turning point for the financial and banking systems in the world, extending its effects and relationships back and forth to the various economic, logistical, and educational sectors (Kheira, 2021).

The Kingdom of Bahrain, through the noble Vision 2030, has given great attention to embracing and adopting modern technologies in providing digital banking and financial services. Therefore, the Kingdom has taken serious steps in the field of financial technology (fintech) industry by developing a wide range of innovations and initiatives in this field. The Central Bank of Bahrain has launched several distinguished initiatives supporting financial technology, including the Bahrain FinTech Bay It is one of the largest and most prominent financial technology centers in the region. In addition, the Bank has issued policies and regulations related to crowdfunding for conventional and Islamic banking services and other initiatives that will contribute to making a quantum leap in the financial sector in Bahrain (Hassan, Jreisat, Rabbani, & Al-Mohamed, 2022).

9. OPPORTUNITIES AND CHALLENGES FOR THE IMPACT OF FINANCIAL TECHNOLOGY ON THE PERFORMANCE OF BANKING IN THE KINGDOM OF BAHRAIN

The data indicates that the Kingdom of Bahrain has topped the countries of the region in terms of providing the infrastructure for communications, the Internet, and the services that can be provided by communications technology to banks and financial companies. In addition, we find great progress in smart devices through which financial programs and platforms can be dealt with, as there are great opportunities for development in the field of financial technology, and this development may be accompanied by many opportunities as well as many challenges in the Kingdom of Bahrain:

9.1. First: Opportunities Related to Financial Technology

1. *Remote work strategy*: Financial technology firms may not currently be interested in the remote work environment, but in the future, they may find it to be a viable strategy since it can improve employee work-life balance as well. The Kingdom has resorted to remote work due to the corona pandemic. Also, considering the actual fixed expenses that businesses have incurred in the infrastructure for remote work, you may want to give it a try in the long run as well. Financial technology firms use social media to engage with their communities and possible investors, just like the burgeoning technology sector does. Such events will still draw many participants even if they are conducted online through webinars and live "questions and answers," and they may be hosted for very little money (Nicolettie, 2017).

2. *Mobile phone*: There is no doubt that the increase in mobile application payments is one of the biggest opportunities resulting from the current situation in the Kingdom of Bahrain, where most of the population work from home due to the corona pandemic. The decisions of the committee formed to combat corona, whose latest decision was to work from home by 70%. It led to a significant increase in the rate of use of the main cash payment applications, as most financial technology companies are currently working to redirect their resources to take advantage of this and increase the increasing rate of adoption of these applications.
3. *Attracting customers*: In current challenging times, a lot of fintech startups are coming up with ideas to help struggling communities as much as possible. This could signal the beginnings of a new industry trend where the needs of customers and the community are given top priority by these businesses.
4. *The availability of large technological infrastructure in the Kingdom of Bahrain*: The Kingdom of Bahrain is considered the first country in the region in terms of technological infrastructure and communication networks. This large infrastructure opened the way for the development of financial programs, as well as opening the way for international financial companies to invest in the Kingdom and apply financial technology to it.

9.2. Second: Challenges Associated with Financial Technology

1. *Data privacy and security*: Fintech companies typically retain a lot of very sensitive user data, including social security numbers, credit card information, information about earnings and investments, and more. This may be the reason why financial companies are placing more emphasis on application security and data privacy. Hence, the Kingdom of Bahrain faces many cases of fraud and fraud by hackers and information hackers who are constantly trying to obtain citizens' banking data through e-mails or phone calls.
2. *Failure to comply with regulatory requirements and laws*: Due to the delicate services they offer, fintech companies are particularly exposed to regulatory constraints, fulfillment, and legal duties. About two-thirds of financial technology companies fail the General Data Protection Regulation (GDPR) standards. Given what the Kingdom of Bahrain and the world are going through from circumstances resulting from the Corona pandemic. It has become more difficult for financial technology companies to meet such regulatory requirements during the pandemic, which exposes them to penalties and fines. Fintech companies lag behind traditional banks in terms of establishing a process-simplified organization because they lack resources like established regulatory processes and skilled people.
3. *Maintaining the human touch*: The coronavirus crisis has personally impacted fintech users. Although there is a chance to demonstrate digital capabilities, fintech companies face challenges due to the absence of direct consumer touch. People are concerned about their jobs, market circumstances are unpredictable, and the capital is experiencing a crisis. Clients would undoubtedly feel

eased in these situations if they can communicate with their financial advisors in person. Many FinTech businesses in Bahrain are employing straightforward yet efficient strategies to address this problem, such as making check-in calls, sending personalized messages, and holding video lectures.

4. *Economic changes*: The continuous economic slowdown and the sharp decline in interest rates have forced financial technology companies to rethink revenue and expenditure management as well as adjust or expand their resources. Many companies have adopted strategies to reduce costs, such as reducing the number of employees and reducing wages, to withstand the economic pressures.
5. *Harmonization between the educational system and the needs of the labor market*: The attempt to reconcile and harmonize between the educational outputs and the needs of the labor market necessarily leads to the preparation of specialized cadres of Bahraini competencies that may contribute to supporting the financial technology environment, as it is one of the most growing sectors in the Kingdom.

10. CONCLUSIONS AND RECOMMENDATIONS

- Technological progress and the increasing development of programs and technological structure had a significant impact on the development of financial technology work.
- Financial technology has great advantages in terms of facilitating customers by providing banking services to them and implementing them on smart devices and tablets without the need to go to financial institutions or banks, and this is evidenced by the Benefit Pay application, which provided a lot and facilitated many banking operations, transfers, bill payments, and even the least transactions money transfers are made possible through this application.
- Financial technology helps create new opportunities for the flow of money transfers between customers through banking operations facilitated by financial technology, saving time, and effort.
- Those who are unable to catch up with financial technology have fewer opportunities for their financial institutions to continue in the future, as it has become clear that the next stage will be AI as well as financial technology in the field of banking.
- Although financial technology contributes greatly to the facilitation and relief of customers, there are some negatives related to privacy and the possibility of penetration of sensitive data of customers, as well as the possibility of canceling some jobs, which leads to an increase in unemployment.
- By encouraging a more consumer-centric and interactive approach to banking and financial services, Fintech innovation is transforming customer experience and expectations.
- Fintech innovation is increasingly giving a larger portion of the global population access to liquidity, financial, and banking services, as the wide spread of data networks and smartphones is taken advantage of.

For the recommendations:

- Establish knowledge and innovation centers that act as points of contact for emerging technology companies to exchange common views.
- Adopting distinctive models in digital transformation and innovative ideas in this field in a way that supports the developmental orientations of countries, which will facilitate and accelerate business through a comprehensive system of electronic services, which will enhance its attractive elements for investment, and the importance of bridging the "digital divide" by expanding access to information technology and communications.
- Establishing a legal, regulatory, and oversight framework that permits the creation and use of financial technology besides AI in business models that allow regulatory and oversight bodies to lower risks and create chances for growth in a market that is competitive.

ACKNOWLEDGMENTS

The authors wish to thank Gulf University for funding this research.

REFERENCES

Arner, D. W., Buckley, R. P., & Zetzsche, D. A. (2018). *Fintech for financial inclusion: A framework for digital financial transformation*. UNSW Law Research Paper No. 18-87. University Of Luxembourg Law Working Paper.

Arslanian, H., & Fischer, F. (2019). *The future of finance: The impact of Fintech, AI, and crypto on financial services*. Berlin: Springer.

Farooq, M. O., & Miah, M. D. (2022). Fintech, Technomania, and persistent socio-civilizational challenges. In *Digital transformation in Islamic finance* (pp. 64–79). Abington: Routledge.

Gharaibeh, A. (2015a). The determinants of common share prices: New empirical evidence from Kuwait. *EPRA International Journal of Economic and Business Review*, *3*, 18–40.

Gharaibeh, A. M. O. (2015b). Empirical evidence of the determinants of commercial banks profitability in Bahrain. *Journal of Emerging Trends in Economics and Management Sciences*, *6*(5), 299–314.

Hassan, M. K., Jreisat, A., Rabbani, M. R., & Al-Mohamed, S. (2022). Islamic Fintech and Bahrain: An opportunity for global financial services. In M. K. Hassan, M. R. Rabbani, & M. Rashid (Eds.), *Fintech in Islamic financial institutions: Scope, challenges, and implications in Islamic finance* (pp. 65–87). Palgrave Macmillan, Cham. https://doi.org/10.1007/978-3-031-14941-2_4

Kheira, T. (2021). Financial technology prospects in the Middle East and Africa. *Journal of Economic Growth*, *4*(3), 14–25.

Léon, F., & Zins, A. (2020). Regional Foreign Banks and financial inclusion: Evidence from Africa. *Economic Modelling*, *84*, 102–116.

Makina, D. (2019). *Extending financial inclusion in Africa*. Cambridge, MA: Academic Press.

Mention, A.-L. (2019). *The future of Fintech* (Vol. 62, pp. 59–63). Oxfordshire: Taylor & Francis.

Mohamed, H. Y., Hamdan, A., Karolak, M., Razzaque, A., & Alareeni, B. (2021). *Fintech in Bahrain: The role of Fintech in empowering women*. Paper presented at the importance of new technologies and entrepreneurship in business development: In the context of economic diversity in developing countries.

Nicolettie, B. (2017). *The future of Fin Tech: Integrating finance and technology in finance services*. Berlin: Springer.

Razzaque, A., Cummings, R. T., Karolak, M., & Hamdan, A. (2020). The propensity to use Fintech: Input from bankers in the Kingdom of Bahrain. *Journal of Information & Knowledge Management*, *19*(1), 2040025.

Rowan, P., Garvey, K., Zhang, B. Z., Soriano, M., Umer, Z., Cloud, K., ... Ahimbisibwe, D. (2018). *Fintech in Uganda: Implications for regulation*. Retrieved from SSRN 3621272.

Vives, X. (2017). The impact of Fintech on banking. *European Economy*, *2*, 97–105.

CHAPTER 14

THE MANAGEMENT OF ELECTRONIC CUSTOMER RELATIONSHIPS THROUGH APPLYING 5IS MODEL ON THE MENTAL IMAGE OF UMNIAH MOBILE NETWORK OPERATOR COMPANY'S CUSTOMERS IN AMMAN CITY

Khaled Tawfiq Al-Assaf

Faculty of Economics and Business Administrative Sciences, Zarqa University, Zarqa, Jordan

ABSTRACT

This research sought to determine the impact of the management of electronic customer relationships through applying 5IS model on the mental image of Umniah Mobile Network Operator Company's customers in Amman City. To fulfill the goals of the study, the researcher adopted the descriptive, analytic method. He developed an instrument to collect the data through a questionnaire, which was distributed through the simple, random sampling method over 700 customers of Umniah Company, in the City of Amman, out of which 400 analyzable questionnaires were retrieved. The researcher further employed the convenient statistical methods applying SPSS 22 Program for data analysis.

Digital Technology and Changing Roles in Managerial and Financial Accounting: Theoretical Knowledge and Practical Application
Studies in Managerial and Financial Accounting, Volume 36, 155–166

ISSN: 1479-3512/doi:10.1108/S1479-351220240000036015

The study concluded many results such as there is statistically significant impact at the significance level ($\alpha < 0.05$) for the administration of consumer relationships through the use of 5IS model on the mental image of the provided services of Umniah Mobile Network Operator Company in Amman city. In this concern, the integration component is the most influential in the mental image with the customers of Umniah Company. Therefore, the study recommended the need Umniah Telecom Company has to search for the best means to positively influence shaping the mental image of its products, especially the means through which it can provide more information about its services.

Keywords: Identification; individualization; interaction; integration; integrity; mental image; customer relationships

1. INTRODUCTION

The development of the customer relationship management concept did not suddenly appear in a short time but rather proceeded for a relatively long period. This came as a result of the competition expansion at the local and international levels, the tremendous technological developments, and the development of modern and sophisticated means of communication, which enabled customers to have a growing interest in interacting with their environment. Also, at the time of seeking individual assistance, there is an increase in the interest in exchanging information about products and services, which had a significant impact on business organizations adopting a new marketing philosophy. Accordingly, this was reflected in the formulation of new marketing strategies based on developing the relationship between the organization and its customers to achieve profitable relationships (Mateias & Brettel, 2016).

As a consequence, companies have an opportunity to achieve a competitive advantage by focusing on individual customers, knowing their needs, and dealing with each request individually as if this product was specifically made for that customer (Ramani & Kumar, 2008). And so, there is an impact of information technology, which is a key factor in building and managing a direct connection between businesses and their clients. Meanwhile, a framework is presented for developing the infrastructure required for an effective and sustainable relationship between the customer and the organization. Thus, through the use of modern IT tools as input to collect useful data from customers. After that, the data is collected and the required operations are performed in the organizations' customer relations department. This matter leads to achieve an improved relationship with customers and sustainable competitive advantages as well as reduces the costs of the organization, which is one requirement of the customer relationship management requirements (Al-Momani, & Al Assaf, 2020; Hashem, 2012).

Therefore, the interaction with customers has the impact of one individual on another individual, and since the influences between individuals are related to their tendencies and directions, consequently, the way individuals think usually influence each other, namely, the influence of one mind in another mind, this means the substitution of a good idea about the organization ability on influencing and persuading (Khaled, 2012). And so, technological progress has helped in the formation of modern means of communication capability of achieving interactive, reciprocal communication, which means controlling the flow of the contents of the communication process, which achieves the change that the organization wants through its interaction with its customers (Al Assaf, Tawfeq, Al-Momani, & Musa, 2020).

Recently, there has been increased interest in the mental image issue as well as its importance for societies and organizations due to the effective value it plays in shaping opinions, forming self-impressions, and creating positive behavior for individuals toward it. However, the formation of a good image has become a primary goal sought by most organizations that seek success. And so, organizations have realized the importance of studying and shaping the mental image formed in the minds of their target audience in order to build their plans and strategies that are concerned with improving the impressions and mental knowledge of this audience, thus creating an appropriate environment to achieve the organization's various activities in all its administrative and marketing fields.

Additionally, since the process of changing the mental image is very difficult in some cases, the individuals refuse to change the typical image that was formed based on the accumulations of previous knowledge and experiences that formed this image, so they resist this change because their subconscious mind rejects the idea of changing a previous solid image. This study came to identify the impact of electronic customer relationship management through 5IS model (identification, individualization, interaction, integration, and integrity) based on the customers' mental image of Umniah Mobile Network Operator Company.

2. THEORETICAL FRAMEWORK

Several studies have addressed customer relationship management (CRM) for telecommunications companies in Jordan, a developing market. These studies looked at how a sample of customers from Jordanian telecoms firms responded to various CRM success factors. Notably, the results showed that the sample had a positive attitude toward the study variables (profitability, knowledge, loyalty, behavior, and satisfaction) on enhancing the mental image (Almarshad, Al-Nawafah, & Tahrawi, 2020).

On the other hand, traditional CRM focused on transitional exchange to manage customer interactions. Whereas, true CRM can only be achieved by incorporating it with KM platforms to develop knowledge-enabled CRM procedures that enable businesses to assess important business metrics like client satisfaction, client profitability, or client loyalty to support business choices. Instead of using an entire generalization of client attributes, these technologies will assist marketers in meeting consumer wants based on what marketers know about their customers. This study suggested using knowledge management technology to propose an integrated framework for CRM. As a result, the framework can serve as the foundation for improving development of the relationship with customers (Bose & Sugumaran, 2003).

Taking into account the results of a study conducted on the Mobilis Corporation (Jijel Agency) concluded that there is an impact between managing the customer's connection at Mobilis Corporation (Jijel Agency) and the mental image formed by its customers. It also concluded that the customer is the real capital of the company, and the good management of the relationship with him allows it to reduce marketing costs (Zabat & Bougriga, 2020).

First of all, identification is intended to recognize the characteristics of customers in detail so that the organization can conduct a dialogue with them. Whereas individualization is tailoring the output of the organization to the size of the customer and providing an advantage to the customer based on his individual needs and desires. In addition to that the product provided by the organization was specifically designed for him and not for anyone else. As for interaction, it is the adoption of a continuous dialogue to understand the needs of customers and build value for them. While integration, in the sense that integration must extend in the relationship and knowledge between the customer and the organization. Finally, integrity, which refers to the concept that relationships are built on trust (Mahmoud, Dima, Ihab, Al-Yazuri, 2020).

In terms of the development occurred in technology and the significant emergence of social networking sites, the study concluded that truthful information social networking websites has an effect on the perception of and the attitudes of the study sample toward products (Arora & Agrawal, 2020).

3. STUDY HYPOTHESES

H0. There is no statistically significant impact at the significance level ($\alpha < 0.05$) for customer relationship management through the use of 5IS model on the mental image of the provided services of Umniah Mobile Network Operator Company in Amman City.

Out of this hypothesis the following supporting hypotheses:

H01. There is no statistically significant impact at the significance level ($\alpha < 0.05$) for customer relationship management through the use of identification on the mental image of the provided services of Umniah Mobile Network Operator Company in Amman City.

H02. There is no statistically significant impact at the significance level ($\alpha < 0.05$) for customer relationship management through the use of individualization on the mental image of the provided services of Umniah Mobile Network Operator Company in Amman City.

H03. There is no statistically significant impact at the significance level ($\alpha < 0.05$) for customer relationship management through the use of interaction on the mental image of the provided services of Umniah Mobile Network Operator Company in Amman City.

H04. There is no statistically significant impact at the significance level ($\alpha < 0.05$) for customer relationship management through the use of integration on the mental image of the provided services of Umniah Mobile Network Operator Company in Amman City.

H05. There is no statistically significant impact at the significance level ($\alpha < 0.05$) for customer relationship management through the use of integrity on the mental image of the provided services of Umniah Mobile Network Operator Company in Amman City.

The researcher relied on the study problem based on Almarshad et al. (2020), Mateias and Brettel (2016), and Mahmoud et al. (2020).

4. RESEARCH METHODOLOGY

4.1. The Approach of Description and Analysis

To review the most important related literature to the elements of electronic CRM and the mental image. In addition, to refer to the previous studies with certain analyses and comparisons, whenever possible, to cover the theoretical aspect of the study.

4.1.1. Field Research Method

It was used to cover the applied aspect of this study, through which it attempts to test the validity of its hypotheses, answer its questions, and extract its results through reliance on a questionnaire that was specially designed to the purposes of this study according to the applicable practical procedures.

4.1.2. Study Population and Sample

The study population consisted of customers of Umniah Company in the Hashemite Kingdom of Jordan, who are related to the company. Due to the wide volume of the study population, which may exceed one million subscribers, and according to Robert Mason Equation (Mason, Gunst, & Hess, 2003), the required size of the sample to represent the study population is 385 respondents. Because of the huge number the population's size and geographic distribution, the researchers chose the straightforward random sampling approach. Accordingly, 700 questionnaires were distributed over the study sample, electronically; 175 questionnaires were disqualified due to lack of complete filling, and 125 questionnaires were also disqualified due to lack of seriousness in their data, which was clear of the respondent's selection of the same response for all the items. As a result, 400 questionnaires were adopted to analyze and extract the results for the purposes of this current study.

4.1.3. Study Sample and Description

To achieve the study objectives, and following the revision of previous studies the study instrument was constructed to measure the effect of the CRM on the mental image of the services of the Jordanian communication companies. The instrument consisted of three major axes, as shown in Table 14.1.

Table 14.1. Study Instrument.

	Items Sequence	Scale
First Axis: Personal Information	Three Items	Multiple Choice
Second axis: Electronic customer relationship management	1–21	1–5
Identification	1–5	1–5
Individualization	6–9	1–5
Interaction	10–12	1–5
Integration	14–17	1–5
Integrity	18–21	1–5
Third axis: Mental image of the company's services	22–31	1–5
Total	34	

The sample participants were asked to response to the instrument items and were told that the data contained in it will be confidentially treated and are for the scientific research only. The responses were classified according to Likert 5-point scale, which were defined as follows: (strongly agree, agree, neutral, disagree, or strongly disagree).

5. RESULTS OF THE STUDY QUESTIONS AND TEST OF ITS HYPOTHESES

5.1. What Impact Does Electronic Customer Relationship Management Have on Creating a Mental Image? Of the Services of Umniah Telecom Company?

The answer to this question lies in testing the main hypothesis of the study:

5.1.1. Main Hypothesis (H0)

There is no statistically significant impact at the significance level ($\alpha < 0.05$) for CRM through the use of 5IS model on the mental image of the provided services of Umniah Mobile Network Operator Company in Amman City.

To test this hypothesis, the researcher used the multiple linear regression test, and Table 14.2 explains the test results.

Table 14.2 shows that F value is 238.944 and it has a significance level of 0.00, which is lower than the significance threshold of 0.05. This indicates that the rejection of the nihilism hypothesis that "There is no statistically significant

Table 14.2. Multiple Linear Regression Analysis.

Dependent Variable	R	R^2	F	Sign.	Independent Variable	B	T	Sign.
The Mental Image of Umniah Telecom Company Services	0.867	0.752	238.944	0.00	Identification	0.088	2.195	0.029
					Individualization	0.005	−0.12	0.904
					Interaction	0.171	4.187	0.000
					Integration	0.334	7.714	0.000
					Integrity	0.305	7.375	0.000

impact at the significance level ($\alpha < 0.05$) for CRM through the use of 5IS model on the mental image of the provided services of Umniah Mobile Network Operator Company in Amman city." Rather, we acceptance of the alternative theory "There is statistically significant impact at the significance level ($\alpha < 0.05$) for customer relationship management through the use of 5IS model on the mental image of the provided services of Umniah Mobile Network Operator Company in Amman city." We can also conclude that there is an effect of the dimensions of the independent variable (for CRM through the use of 5IS model) collectively, on the dependent variable (the mental image of the services of Umniah Telecom Company). These dimensions explained that 75.2% of the changes occurred in the mental image of Umniah Telecom Company's services.

5.1.2. First Sub-Hypothesis (H01)

There is no statistically significant impact at the significance level ($\alpha < 0.05$) for CRM through the use of identification on the mental image of the provided services of Umniah Mobile Network Operator Company in Amman City.

To test this hypothesis, the researcher used the simple linear regression test, as indicated in Table 14.3.

Table 14.3 shows that *T* value is 20.614, and its significance level is 0.00, which is less than 0.05 significance level; which means a statistically significant effect of the identification in shaping the mental image of services of Umniah Telecom Company. Therefore, we reject the nihilism hypothesis that "There is no statistically significant impact at the significance level ($\alpha < 0.05$) for customer relationship management through the use of identification on the mental image of the provided services of Umniah Mobile Network Operator Company in Amman city." Rather, we accept the alternative hypothesis that "There is statistically significant impact at the significance level ($\alpha < 0.05$) for customer relationship management through the use of identification on the mental image of the provided services of Umniah Mobile Network Operator Company in Amman city." Moreover, there is a direct relationship between the Identification and the mental image of the services of Umniah Telecom Company, as the correlation value between them is 0.719. The Identification in the electronic CRM (51%) of the changes taking place in the mental image of the services of Umniah Telecom Company.

5.1.3. Second Sub-hypothesis (H02)

There is no statistically significant impact at the significance level ($\alpha < 0.05$) for CRM through the use of individualization on the mental image of the provided services of Umniah Mobile Network Operator Company in Amman city.

Table 14.3. First Sub-hypothesis Simple Linear Regression.

Dependent Variable	*R*	R^2	Independent Variable	*B*	*T*	Sign.
The mental image of Umniah Telecom Company Services	0.719	0.516	Identification	0.65	20.614	0.00

Table 14.4. Simple Linear Regression of the Second Sub-hypothesis.

Dependent Variable	*R*	R^2	Independent Variable	*B*	*T*	Sign.
The mental image of Umniah Telecom Company Services	0.703	0.494	Individualization	0.623	19.726	0.00

The researcher relied on the simple linear regression test to test this hypothesis as shown in Table 14.4.

Table 14.4 shows that *T* value is 19.726, and it has a significance level of 0.00, which is lower than the significance threshold of 0.05; this indicates individualization's statistically significant contribution to shaping the mental image of services of Umniah Telecom Company. As a result, we disagree with the nihilism hypothesis "There is no statistically significant impact at the significance level ($\alpha < 0.05$) for customer relationship management through the use of individualization on the mental image of the provided services of Umniah Mobile Network Operator Company in Amman city." Rather, we acknowledge the alternate theory that "There is statistically significant impact at the significance level ($\alpha < 0.05$) for customer relationship management through the use of individualization on the mental image of the provided services of Umniah Mobile Network Operator Company in Amman city." Moreover, there is a direct relationship between the individualization and the mental image of the services of Umniah Telecom Company, as the correlation value between them is 0.703. The individualization in the CRM (49%) of the changes taking place in the mental image of the services of Umniah Telecom Company.

5.1.4. Third Sub-hypothesis (H03)

There is no statistically significant impact at the significance level ($\alpha < 0.05$) for CRM through the use of interaction on the mental image of the provided services of Umniah Mobile Network Operator Company in Amman city.

To test this hypothesis, the researchers used the simple linear regression test, as shown in Table 14.5.

Table 14.5 shows that *T* value is 23.856. The entertainment had a statistically significant impact on how people perceived the services of Umniah Telecom Company, as indicated by its significance level of 0.00, which is less than 0.05 significance level. In light of this, we disagree with the nihilism hypothesis "There is no statistically significant impact at the significance level ($\alpha < 0.05$) for customer

Table 14.5. Third Sub-hypothesis Simple Linear Regression.

Dependent Variable	*R*	R^2	Independent Variable	*B*	*T*	Sign.
The mental image of Umniah Telecom Company Services	0.767	0.585	Interaction	0.658	23.856	0.00

relationship management through the use of interaction on the mental image of the provided services of Umniah Mobile Network Operator Company in Amman city." Rather, we accept the alternative theory "There is statistically significant impact at the significance level ($\alpha < 0.05$) for customer relationship management through the use of interaction on the mental image of the provided services of Umniah Mobile Network Operator Company in Amman city." Moreover, there is a direct relationship between the interaction and the mental image of the services of Umniah Telecom Company, as the correlation value between them is 0.767. The interaction in the CRM (58%) of the changes takes place in the mental image of the services of Umniah Telecom Company.

5.1.5. Fourth Sub-hypothesis (H04)

There is no statistically significant impact at the significance level ($\alpha < 0.05$) for customer relationship management through the use of integration on the mental image of the provided services of Umniah Mobile Network Operator Company in Amman City.

To test this hypothesis, the researchers used the simple linear regression test, as shown in Table 14.6.

Table 14.6 shows that *T* value is 24.489. The fact that its significance level is 0.00, which is lower than 0.05, indicates that the incentives had a statistically significant impact on how people perceived the services provided by Umniah Telecom Company. Therefore, we reject the nihilism hypothesis that "There is no statistically significant impact at the significance level ($\alpha < 0.05$) for customer relationship management through the use of integration on the mental image of the provided services of Umniah Mobile Network Operator Company in Amman city." Rather, we accept the alternative theory "There is statistically significant impact at the significance level ($\alpha < 0.05$) for customer relationship management through the use of integration on the mental image of the provided services of Umniah Mobile Network Operator Company in Amman city." Moreover, there is a direct relationship between the Integration and the mental image of the services of Umniah Telecom Company, as the correlation value between them is 0.819. The integration in the CRM (67%) of the changes takes place in the mental image of the services of Umniah Telecom Company.

5.1.6. Fifth Sub-hypothesis (H05)

There is no statistically significant impact at the significance level ($\alpha < 0.05$) for CRM through the use of integrity on the mental image of the provided services of Umniah Mobile Network Operator Company in Amman City.

Table 14.6. Fourth Sub-hypothesis Simple Linear Regression.

Dependent Variable	*R*	R^2	Independent Variable	*B*	*T*	Sign.
The mental image of Umniah Telecom Company Services	0.819	0.671	Integration	0.720	24.489	0.00

Table 14.7. Fifth Sub-hypothesis Simple Linear Regression.

Dependent Variable	*R*	R^2	Independent Variable	*B*	*T*	Sign.
The mental image of Umniah Telecom Company Services	0.767	0.589	Integrity	0.809	23.873	0.00

To test this hypothesis, the researchers used the simple linear regression test, as shown in Table 14.7.

Table 14.6 shows that *T* value is 23.873, and its significance level is 0.00, which is lower than the 0.05 significance level, indicating that the convenience has a statistically significant impact on how people perceive the services provided by Umniah Telecom Company. As a result, we disagree with the nihilism hypothesis "There is no statistically significant impact at the significance level ($\alpha < 0.05$) for customer relationship management through the use of integrity on the mental image of the provided services of Umniah Mobile Network Operator Company in Amman city." Rather, we accept the alternative hypothesis that "There is statistically significant impact at the significance level ($\alpha < 0.05$) for customer relationship management through the use of integrity on the mental image of the provided services of Umniah Mobile Network Operator Company in Amman city." Moreover, there is a direct relationship between the integrity and the mental image of the services of Umniah Telecom Company, as the correlation value between them is 0.767. The integrity in the CRM (58%) of the changes takes place in the mental image of the services of Umniah Telecom Company.

5.1.7. Stepwise Linear Regression Analysis

Following the response to the study questions and testing its hypotheses, the researchers carried out the gradual linear regression analysis for the purpose of identifying the most interpretive independent variables to the changes taking place in the dependent variable and arranging them in a descending order. The results are shown in Table 14.8.

Through Table 14.8, we find that the results of the gradual linear regression test showed that four examples that explain the changes occurring in the dependent variable are arranged to the strongest influence of the independent variable.

Table 14.8. Stepwise Linear Regression Analysis.

Example	Independent Variable	*B*	*R*	R^2	*F*	Sign.
1	Integration	0.72	0.819	0.671	811.612	0.00
2	Integration	0.489	0.853	0.728	530.469	0.00
	Integrity	0.375				
3	Integration	0.353	0.865	0.749	393.406	0.00
	Integrity	0.321				
	Interaction	0.209				
4	Integration	0.332	0.867	0.752	299.423	0.00
	Integrity	0.304				
	Interaction	0.170				
	Identification	0.087				

Results of Example 1 showed that the integration interpret (67.1%) of the changes occurring in shaping the according mental image of Umniah Telecom Company services. Example 2 added the integrity variable so that the volume of explaining the changes in the dependent variable became 72.8%; and, by adding the interaction variable to Example 3, the explanation size became 74.9%. Finally, by adding the identification variable to Example 4, the explanation size became 75.2%. On the other hand, the individualization variable was disqualified as the program considered it less interpretive of the dependent variable. Nonetheless, this does not mean that there is no effect of CRM through the use of individualization in shaping the mental image of the services of Umniah Telecom Company, which was proven in the simple regression equation, but the effect of this variable becomes weak in the shade of the existence of other variables.

6. DISCUSSION

The study's findings indicated that the independent variable, "The Management of Electronic Customer Relationships Through Applying 5IS Model," had an overall impact on the dependent variable, "The mental image" of Umniah Telecom Company's services, as it was able to account for 75.2% of the changes in the mental image. Further analysis of the results revealed a statistically significant influence of the 5IS model, which is used to manage electronic customer relationships, on how people perceive the services provided by Umniah Telecom Company.

7. RECOMMENDATIONS

In the light of the results of the study, the researchers recommend the following:

The need for Umniah Telecom to pay attention to the mental image formed by individuals for CRM through the use of 5IS model, especially for the integration and integrity variables because of their great influence in shaping the mental image. And the need for Umniah Telecom to pay attention to the individualization, as the results showed weakness of this variable as compared to the other variables in the CRM of the company. In addition, Umniah Telecom Company has to search for the best means to positively influence shaping the mental image of its products, especially the means through which it can provide more information about its services

REFERENCES

Al Assaf, D., Tawfeq, K., Al-Momani, D., & Musa, M. (2020). The influence of e-marketing technology and website features on attracting students to private universities in Jordan (case study: Zarqa university). *International Journal of Management*, *11*(9), 1261–1267.

Al-Momani, M. M., & Al Assaf, K. T. (2020). The impact of marketing information systems on decision-making systems at Islamic international Arab bank in Jordan. *Journal of Management Information & Decision Sciences*, *23*(S1), 387–396.

Almarshad, M., Al-Nawafah, S., & Tahrawi, M. (2020). The role of customer relationship management success factors on enhancing the mental image of telecommunications companies in Jordan. *Management Science Letters*, *10*(15), 3155–3206.

Arora, T., & Agarwal, B. (2020). An empirical study on determining the effectiveness of social media advertising: A case on Indian millennials. *International Journal of E-Business Research*, *16*(2), 47–68.

Bose, R., & Sugumaran, V. (2003). Application of knowledge management technology in customer relationship management. *Knowledge and Process Management*, *10*(1), 3–17.

Hashem, T. N. (2012). The impact of customer relationship marketing on costumers' image for Jordanian five star hotels. *Economics, Management, and Financial Markets*, *7*(4), 716–725.

Khaled, A. (2012). The tourists assessment of the services provided in the tourist sites in Jordan from the Jordanian tourists point of view. *Dirasat: Human and Social Sciences*, *46*(3), 257–269.

Mahmoud, S., Dima, D., Ihab, Q., & Al-Yazuri, D. (2014). *Customer relationship management* (1st ed.). Abingdon: Routledge.

Mason, R. L., Gunst, R. F., & Hess, J. L. (2003). *Statistical design and analysis of experiments: With applications to engineering and science*. Hoboken, NJ: John Wiley & Sons.

Mateias, M., & Brettel, M. (2016). Going the extra mile: Customer Interaction orientation, customer satisfaction, and firm performance. *AMA Summer Academic Conference Proceedings*, *27*, 42–44.

Ramani, G., & Kumar, V. (2008). Interaction orientation and firm performance. *Journal of Marketing*, *72*(1), 27–45.

Zabat, S., & Bougriga., R. (2020). Customer relationship management as a tool to enhace the mental image of the service foundation (case of Mobilis company-Jigel Agency). *El-Bahith Review*, *20*, 653–666.

CHAPTER 15

FINANCIAL STATEMENTS AND FINANCIAL REPORTING – A NARRATIVE EMBEDDED IN NUMBERS, A TWO PRONG PHILOSOPHY – GRAMEEN BANK & ISLAMI BANK BANGLADESH LIMITED (IBBL)

Hafizur Rahman

Rahman Foundation Inc, Alumnus (166th), Franklin Fellows- US Department of State, Silver Spring, Maryland, USA

ABSTRACT

Today's financial reporting inherits its origin in money, numbers and accounting dated back 7,000 years in Mesopotamia. The Italian Luca Pacioli, "first person to publish a work on double-entry bookkeeping"[1] *is regarded as the father of accounting and bookkeeping. In USA, SEC issued its first Accounting Series Release which appeared to be Commission's views on auditing and accounting, later, in 1982 has become known as Financial Reporting Releases. Today more than 100 countries permit publicly held companies to use International Financial Reporting Standards. This meteoric rise for use of financial reporting was due to a worldwide demand from regulators, lenders, trade partners, businesses, investors and policy makers. "The Companies Act of 1994 mandates*

Digital Technology and Changing Roles in Managerial and Financial Accounting: Theoretical Knowledge and Practical Application
Studies in Managerial and Financial Accounting, Volume 36, 167–180

Published under exclusive licence by Emerald Publishing Limited
ISSN: 1479-3512/doi:10.1108/S1479-351220240000036016

requirement for financial reporting by all companies in Bangladesh."[2] *Banks' reporting formats and disclosures in Bangladesh based on BAS 30 is similar to the requirements of the Companies Act of 1994. The research depicts how the two banking institutions of Bangladesh – Islami Bank Bangladesh Limited (IBBL) and Grameen Bank having two philosophical objectives – uniquely present their results of operation under a uniform financial reporting system and how they differ in their financial operations.*

Keywords: Financial statements; *p*-value; relationships; reporting; compliance; accountability; Silicon Valley Bank (SVB)

1. INTRODUCTION

Financial reporting is the mechanism that provides its users the best tool to examine the magic word accountability. It is the "process of producing financial statements that discloses an organization's financial status to stakeholders, including management. Investors, creditors and regulatory agencies" as one of the definitions reflects very vividly. It is used essentially for both external and internal reporting.

2. REVIEWS OF THE RELATED LITERATURE AND PROPOSED RELATIONSHIPS IN THE CONCEPTUAL MODEL

In the paper "Does Sharia compliance affect financial reporting quality? An evidence from Muslim majority countries" author Gokberk Can (College of Business Administration, American University of the Middle East, Kuwait, Kuwait) based on sample of 2,300 companies constructed from 15 Muslim majority countries found that "Sharia compliance increases the financial reporting quality by decreasing the discretionary accruals and audit aggressiveness."

Posted in IMF Blog – April 6, 2015 authors Mohamed Norat, Marco Pinon, and Zeine Zeidane in their article "The Promise of Islamic Finance: Further Inclusion with Stability" concluded that

> Islamic finance has an important potential to act as an engine of stability and inclusion. Since investors are required to bear losses that may arise on loans. There is therefore less leverage, and greater incentive to exercise strong risk management. These risk-sharing features also serve to help ensure the soundness of individual financial institutions and help discourage the types of lending booms and real estate bubbles that were the precursors of the global financial crisis.

In the research publication (May 2011) titled "Deposit Assessment in Bangladesh" commissioned by the International Finance Corporation, the authors observed that Islami Bank's Mudaraba saving scheme popularly called MSS where clients make monthly recurring deposits accounts "27% of Islami Bank's deposit base." In their paper "Aspects of Microfinance System of Grameen Bank of Bangladesh" J. N. Islam, H. Mohajan, and R. Datta remarked

> The microfinance system of Grameen Bank is a revolutionary tool to eradicate poverty of the rural people especially the women of Bangladesh .... It provides loans to assetless and landless poor people whom no commercial bank give loan. Microcredit is the most useful and popular financial system in the world to face financial crisis of the poor people.

Columbia Business School distinguished authors in their paper "Grameen Bank: Taking Capitalism to the Poor" portrayed Grameen Bank as

> From these humble efforts emerged a new industry: microcredit – the extension of small loans and other financial and business services to entrepreneurs too poor to qualify for traditional bank loans. Microcredit has since proven to be an effective tool for alleviating poverty and, in addition to creating wealth, generating positive externalities, such as better education and improved health.

3. METHODOLOGY, DESIGN OF THE STUDY, AND DATA COLLECTION PROCEDURE

The study is based on secondary historical data primarily of Financial Statements of Grameen Bank and IBBL, Bangladesh Bank's (Central Bank of Bangladesh) policy guidelines, International Accounting Standards, that is, GAAP and IFRS, Bureau of the Fiscal Services, United States Government, author's personal experiences and reputable websites. The large body of data has been taken in order to verify data integrity for comparison and underlying analysis. A p-value is used using T-test whether or not there are enough evidence to reject the null hypothesis. It is used to see how likely different sets of data related to financial reporting of IBBL and Grameen Bank (GB) would have occurred under the null hypothesis ("there is no difference between certain characteristics of a population") of the statistical test or rejects the null hypothesis that relationships are significant (p-value being less than 0.05). Excel Software was employed to calculate p-value and other statistical results throughout this paper.

4. OBJECTIVES OF FINANCIAL REPORTING[3]

- "Financial reporting should assist in fulfilling the entity's duty to be accountable for monies raised through issuing shares and other means and for their expenditure in accordance with the shareholders assertion. Financial reporting should provide information that helps the reader to determine how resources have been obtained and used and whether their acquisition and use were in accordance with the legal authorization."
- "Financial reporting should assist report users in evaluating the service efforts, costs, and accomplishments of the reporting entity; the manner in which these efforts and accomplishments have been financed; and the management of the entity's assets and liabilities."
- "Financial reporting should assist report users in assessing the impact on the country of the entity's operations and investments for the period and how, as

a result, the governments and the nation's financial condition has changed and may change in the future."

- "Financial reporting should assist report users in understanding whether financial management systems and internal accounting and administrative controls are adequate to ensure that assets are properly safeguarded to deter fraud, waste, and abuse; and performance measurement information is adequately supported."

5. RESULTS AND DATA ANALYSIS

5.1. Core Components of Financial Reporting

The body of financial statements generally and for the same reasons, financial reporting consists of the following:

1. Business Organizations:
   a. Balance Sheet
   b. Income Statement (Profit & Loss Account)
   c. Statement of Cashflows

2. Government Operations (US Federal Systems):
   a. Balance Sheet
   b. Statement of Net Cost
   c. Statements of Operations & Changes in Net Position[4]
   d. Statement of Budgetary Resources

It should be borne in mind that audited financial statements do contain notes (disclosures vary from some to several hundred depending the size and complexity of the organizational operations). They accompany the financial statements and considered the integral part of the financial report.

6. CHARACTERISTICS DIFFERENTIALS OF ISLAMI BANKING AND MICRO FINANCING

Table 15.1 shows the distinguishing characteristics of IBBL and GB.

6.1. How Financial Reporting Is Embedded in a Balance sheet – A Comparative Historical Exposures of Some of the Selected Items – Grameen Bank and Bangladesh Limited – IBBL

A balance sheet shows the book value of an entity as of a specific date. It portrays resources available, how they are financed. It conveys information about an entity's type of assets, liabilities and owners' equity meaning the amount invested by the owners. It is a "reference document" for investors and stockholders and

Table 15.1. Characteristics Differentials of Islami Banking and Micro Financing.

Islami Banking	Micro Financing (Non-Islamic)
Shariah compliant: Interest is forbidden	
Wealth must be generated from legitimate trade and asset-based investments	Lack access to conventional banking
Investment should also have and an ethical benefit to wider society beyond pure return	Micro credit, the provision of small loans to poor
Risks should be shared	Promote economic development, employment and growth through the support of small businesses
All harmful activities (haram) should be avoided	Often financed without any collateral

displays the financial health of an entity. As a result users and shareholders can compare current assets and liabilities, liquidity and can calculate the rate of return. It is worth mentioning that Sharia compliance itself implies that compliant institution "operates not only under regulations but also to the restrictions and permission of Islam." They include the following, that is:

- Bans interest.
- Bans gambling, short-sales.
- Requires fair treatment.
- Institutes sanctity of contracts.
- Lenders should share in both the risks and rewards of the projects and loan they finance.

6.1.1. Assets

6.1.1.1. Cash. *t*-Test: Two-sample assuming unequal variances cash in hand – Grameen Bank and Islami Bank Bangladesh Limit.

Table 15.2. Cash in Hand – In US Dollar.

Year	Grameen Bank (GB)	Islami Bank Bangladesh Ltd. (IBBL)
2011	$36,822	$76,831,633
2012	$25,457	$88,079,792
2013	$27,535	$105,145,848
2014	$23,510	$99,275,699
2015	$27,848	$117,342,775
2016	$69,729	$147,542,592
2017	$21,002	$188,518,813
2018	$42,821	$207,138,589
2019	$1,448	$150,405,525
2020	$4,597	$187,679,659
Average 2011–2020	$28,077	$136,796,092

	Variable 1	Variable 2
Mean	28,076.8413	136,796,092.5
Variance	374,149,394	2.14112E+15
Observations	10	10
Hypothesized mean difference	0	
df	9	
t-Stat	−9.346815	
$p\ (T \leq t)$ one-tail	3.13E−06	
t Critical one-tail	1.83311293	
$p\ (T \leq t)$ two-tail	6.26E−06	
t Critical two-tail	2.26215716	

Fig. 15.1. t-Test: Two-Sample Assuming Unequal Variances Cash in Hand – Grameen Bank & Islami Bank Bangladesh Limited.

6.1.2. Analysis

In Fig. 15.1, a p-value in the hypothesis tests (t-test results above) reveals that relationship of cash managed between IBBL and GB were statistically very significant. Over the period 2011–2020 GB with a cash balance of average $28,077 compared to $136,796,092 (Table 15.2) of Islamic Bank Bangladesh shows how both the organizations managed their banking operation. This phenomenal difference is primarily due to the characteristics of their modus operandi. A Shariah-based commercial bank like IBBL requires critical liquidity balance for daily operation. GB is a micro financing institution where higher balance is not required for its daily operation. Despite these operational distinct characteristics, both the banks are to maintain a required reserve balance with Bangladesh Bank (Central Bank of Bangladesh) which represents uniformity in financial reporting.

6.1.3. Total Assets

6.1.3.1. Total Assets at a Glance

Table 15.3. Islami Bank Bangladesh Limited & Grameen Bank at December 31, 2020 in US$.

Description	Grameen Bank	Islami Bank Bangladesh Limited
Cash in hand	$4,597	$187,679,659
Balance with Bangladesh Bank (Central Bank)	$59,839	$1,952,518,007
Balance with other banks	$1,198,439,117	$615,004,497
Investments & loans & advances	$1,558,577,323	$11,106,169,929
Fixed assets including premises, furniture, & fixture	$14,610,594	$178,295.112
Investment property	$766,956	
Other assets	$133,737,557	$144,220,261
Total assets	$2,906,195,981	$14,183,887,287

6.1.4. Analysis

Balance sheet in both the organizations (Table 15.3) did not separate between current and non-current balances of assets, displayed major items as above (distinctly different from other commercial entities). For financial reporting purposes, a classification between current and non-current assets provides a ready reference for analysts to conduct multiple analysis. However, the current formats serve some useful purpose of comparison between these two banks. In GB balance with other banks was its fixed deposits ($1,198,439,117) – a good source for interest income. When combined with investments (loans advances) it totaled $2,757,080,875, equivalent to 95% of the total assets as of December 31, 2020. IBBL maintained 14% of its total assets with the central bank of the country. Both the banks dedicated 1% of their total assets to the fixed assets like premises, fixture, and furniture by both the banks in 2020, a challenging historic period of mankind, impacted by COVID 2019. With the assets composition as shown above both the banks appeared to meet financial reporting requirements meticulously.

6.1.5. Liabilities

Table 15.4. As of December 31, 2020 Total Liabilities in US$.

	Grameen Bank	Islami Bank
Borrowing/placement from banks and other institutions	$9,695,147	$445,182,884
Deposits and other funds	$2,502,205,707	$11,807,753,295
Bonds	$	$260,286,315
Other liabilities	$145,670,535	$1,037,760,925
Deferred liabilities	$	$16,096.562
Total	$2,657,571,389	$13,567,079,980

6.1.6. Analysis

Changes in total liabilities although did vary from year to year due to operational requirements and practices. The balance sheet in its line-item presentation for the year 2020 (Table 15.4) showed that deposits and other funds accounted 94% of the total liabilities in GB while the share of deposits and other funds was 87% of the total liabilities in IBBL. However, other liabilities in Islami Bank Bangladesh accounted 8% of the total liabilities as of December 31, 2020 primarily consisted of provision for bad debt $482 million and Suspense compensation $260 million. On the other hand primarily provision for bad debt in the GB was reported to be $109 million as of December 31, 2020. With all the notes to the financial statements both the banks appeared to show a fair presentation of their total liabilities in their financial reporting useful to their users.

7. SHAREHOLDERS' EQUITY

Table 15.5. Breakdown of Shareholders' Equity (US$) – Grameen Bank & Islami Bank Bangladesh Ltd as of December 31, 2020.

Descriptions	Grameen Bank	Islami Bank Bangladesh Ltd
Paid up capital	$9,620,783	$161,176,361
Statutory reserve/general reserve	$139,693,663	$197,571,992
Other reserves	$32,396,999	$241,941,318
Capital	$37,700,619	$
Retained earnings	$29 212,528	$16,117,636
Total shareholders' equity	$248,624,592	$616,807,307

7.1. Analysis

Shareholders' equity is the last sub section of the balance sheet in a financial reporting scenario. Total liabilities and shareholders' equity together equal total assets in an entity in the Islami Bank Bangladesh Ltd. With 2.48 times larger in equity than GB, IBBL did operate its operations in 2020 with five times larger load of liabilities and five times asset acceleration (refer Table 15.5).

8. INCOME STATEMENT (PROFIT AND LOSS ACCOUNT)

Income statement in financial reporting perspective provides information about financial results of a business over a period of time (typically one year). It reflects how much revenue is generated and what costs are incurred in generating the revenue and the gains or losses accrue from the operation. With other two key statements – balance sheet and cash flow statement – it displays entity's financial performance.

8.1. Operating Income in US$

Table 15.6. Sources of Operating Income for the Period Ending December 31, 2020 – Grameen Bank & Islami Bank Bangladesh Limited in US$.

Description	Grameen Bank	Islami Bank Bangladesh Ltd.
Interest income	$408,164,971	$
Investment income	$	$743,871,606
Dividend income from investments	$292,318	–
Income from shares and securities	$	$19,948,028
Commission exchange and brokerage income	$	$47,261,025
Other income	$23,654,740	$34,783,662
Total	$432,112,030	$845,864,321

8.2. Analysis

Table 15.6 reveals that during 2020 share of interest income that GB profited by maintaining fixed deposits with other bank was 94% of its total operating income for the year. During the same period, Islami Bank earned 88% of its total income from its investment in the several sectors including garment industry. Islami bank's income coming from commission exchange and brokerage income accounted 6% of its total income. Income generating from deposits with other bank although considered a passive income, GB management classified it as operating income for their financial reporting. One of the major differences, although Islami Bank operates on Shariah principle, generating income by being an active partner of the national economic activities was its significant contribution in Bangladesh's economic growth.

9. COMPOSITION OF TOTAL EXPENSES (US$) FOR THE YEAR ENDED DECEMBER 31, 2020 – GRAMEEN BANK AND ISLAMI BANK BANGLADESH LTD –

9.1. Analysis

A breakdown of the costs structure in Table 15.7 above also indicates that during 2020 total costs was proportionately lower in Islami Bank Bangladesh Ltd. (167%) of Grameen Bank although GB did not have any zakat expenses nor taxes payable to the treasury. GB is exempted from corporate tax expenses while Islami

Table 15.7. Classifications of Expenses in US$.

Description	Grameen Bank	Islami Bank Bangladesh Ltd
Salary and allowances	$123,257,850	$165,948,313
Rent, taxes, insurance, electricity, etc.	$2,721,551	$12,336,696
Legal expenses/professional fees	$4,151,008	$98,848
Postages, stamps, and telecommunications	$511,684	$749,249
Stationery, printing, and advertisements	$845,151	$2,567,235.5
Chief executive's salary and fees		$143,358
Director's fees and expenses	$10,549	$62,148
Shariah supervisory committee's fees and expenses		$21,903
Auditors' fees	$15,830	$34,538
Depreciation and repairs	$1,293,189	$14,879,913
Zakat expense		$8,183,979
Other expenses	$22,499,542.7	$44,329,710
Total provision	$55,520,888	$41,136,552
Total expenses before taxes	$210,827,243	$290,492,442
Taxes	0	$62,169,433
Total expenses including taxes	$210,827,243	$352,661,875

Bank taxes to the treasury was $62.1 million (18% of the total expenses of this Shariah-based bank). Zakat expenses in the **IBBL** for the year 2020 was $8.2 million (2.32% of its total expenses). Zakat in the Islami Bank Bangladesh Ltd. was the share of the poor people, an indispensable obligation of the Shariah-based banking, profoundly distinct than GB. It is said that GB brought capitalism to the poor.

It was a distinguishing characteristic of **IBBL** operations that it contributed to the State exchequer $870 million during the period 2011–2020 an average of $87 million per annum (Table 15.9) while GB has been exempted from taxes. Taxes of over three-fourth of a billion dollar in a decade both proves the efficacy of corporate taxation system in Bangladesh as well as the fiscal discipline of **IBBL**.

9.2. Net Profit in US$ – Grameen Bank & Islami Bank Bangladesh Ltd.

Table 15.8. Net Profit in US$- Grameen Bank & Islami Bank Bangladesh Ltd.

Year	Grameen Bank	Islami Bank Bangladesh Ltd.
2011	$11,279,931	$76,313,427
2012	$20,313,532	$78,424,371
2013	$17,132,375	$64,978,948
2014	$5,623,775	$51,172,667
2015	$331,079	$42,856,302
2016	$20,307,961	$65,305,997
2017	$29,945,974	$88,611,378
2018	$48,724,849	$88,218,694
2019	$47,284,433	$53,342,618
2020	$34,907,898	$45,259,866
Average Profit 2011–2020	$23,585,181	$65,448,427

9.3. Analysis

Table 15.8 indicates that during the 2011–2020 the net profits of Grameen and Islami Bangladesh Limited were $23.6 million and $65.4 million, respectively (Islami Bank having approximately 300% higher than GB although GB's average net profit on average equity was 13% compared to 11% in Islami Bank Bangladesh Ltd.; refer Chart 15.1).

10. STATEMENTS OF CASH FLOWS

The statement of cash flow states "cash inflow and cash outflows during the same time interval" as the loss and profit account shows. It also reports all cash outflows that "pay for business activities and investments" during the same period. Thus statement of cash flows enables its users to extract important financial data about the financial health of an entity.

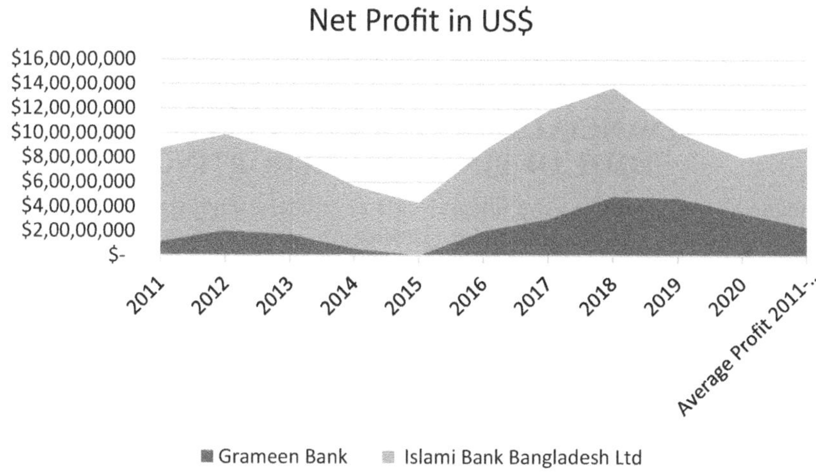

Chart 15.1. Net Profit – Grameen Bank & Islami Bank Bangladesh Ltd.

10.1. Summary of Cash Flow Statement

Table 15.9. Summary of Cash Flow Statement for the Period Ended December 31, 2020 – Grameen Bank & Islami Bank Bangladesh Ltd.

	Grameen Bank	Islami Bank Bangladesh Ltd.
Cash flows from operating activities	$164,014,382	$1,328,114,605
Net cash flows from investing activities	$136,119,028	$228,650,748
Net cash flows from financing activities	$22,231,115	$33,937,424
Net increase or decrease	$5,664,238	$1,133,401,281
Cash & cash equivalent at-beginning of the year	$17,230,215	$1,621,683,110
Cash & cash equivalent at the end of the year	$22,894,453	$2,755,201,985

10.2. Analysis

Table 15.9 indicates that at December 31, 2020 Cash & Cash equivalent balance was $22.9 million in GB compared to $2.8 billion in Islami Bangladesh Limited (Islami Bank having approximately 120 higher than GB). Islami Bank posted a net cash inflow of $1.1 billion primarily from operating activities as being a full-fledged commercial bank and with $228.6 million outflow in investment activities. GB posted a net cash flow of $5.6 million broken into as net from operating activities $164 million, $136 million net cash outflow from investing activities and net outflow of cash $22.2 million on financing activities. Both the banks maintained good liquidity balances as warranted by the operating practices, provided an adequate insight for a good financial reporting in the area of cash in and out.

11. FINANCIAL DISCLOSURE – AN EFFECTIVE TOOL OF FINANCIAL REPORTING

Financial disclosures are the integral part of modern-day financial statements. The disclosures provide additional information of an entity's financial operations. Usually large business organizations often use disclosures. Also government operations nowadays increasingly incorporate the disclosures in their financial statements ensuring greater accountability to the public. Thus, financial reporting system both in the private and public sector does recognize the importance of financial disclosure in their financial statements. Some of the items that usually included are accounting changes, accounting errors, asset retirement, insurance contract modifications, voluntary disclosures, and any other important subject, managements deem necessary to convey better clarity to their financial positions. In the following discussions, attempts have been made to examine the comparative analysis on certain financial disclosures of IBBL and GB:

11.1. Analysis

IBBL is the largest private bank operating under the guidelines of the central bank (Bangladesh Bank). It is also an Islami bank that runs its business under Sharia compliant guidelines. For financial reporting purposes it follows GAAP internal standards. A disclosure in the 2021 audited financial statements stated under note 17.1 the following:

> (*) as on 31 December 2021 provision of Tk. 24,902.75 million against Ananda Shipyard & Slipways Ltd., writ clients, rescheduled clients & restructured clients (considering qualitative judgment) is included in the specific provision (Bad & Loss) of Tk. 35,894.68 million against Tk. 23,572.03 million as on 31 December 2020. Adequate provision for the investments, off-balance sheet items and other assets have been made as per the relevant circulars issued by Bangladesh Bank as well as decision taken in tripartite meeting amongst Bangladesh Bank Inspection Team, External Auditors and the Management of Islami Bank Bangladesh Limited and subsequent Bangladesh Bank Letter No.DBI-6/51(1)/2022-308 dated 20 April 2022.

$249.2 million out of total accumulated provision balance (47% of the total) in 2021 was attributable to client Ananda Shipyard & Slipways Ltd. The continuation of such a significant balance from 2020 is considered a red light for the purpose of good governance. Cautious regulatory and adequate management prudence appeared seriously lacking. The disclosures warrant effective public scrutiny for good corporate governance and increased accountability.

12. LIMITATIONS

Although sound financial reporting is a good instrument to measure and monitor the financial health of an organization, the recent trend in the banking sectors indicates that corporate governance and appropriate monetary policy implications are nonetheless very important even in the very highly developed economies like USA where demise of a 200 billion 16th largest USA bank – Silicon Valley Bank (SVB) was witnessed by the world (March 10, 2023).

13. INTERESTING FACTS & FINDINGS

Financial reporting layouts, presentations of the line items in the main body of financial statements, and underlying notes disclosures therein are structured in consistent with professional standards, for both the banks under study – GB and IBBL. Chief executive salary and fees under Table 15.7 is a unique line-item presentation by the IBBL absent in the GB. Provision of bad debt and non-collection of receivables is a serious concern. Mere disclosure as IBBL did in its notes to the financial statements is not sufficient. It remains an outstanding actionable item for IBBL.

14. RECOMMENDATIONS

Given the special nature of the objectives and operations of GB and IBBL, an independent monitoring body designated by the central bank should be formed. This should comprise subject-matter experts, reputable economists, business representatives, and executive from non-profit organizations (both from national and international communities) to evaluate, monitor, recommend, and follow-up necessary insights for policy implications and effective execution regularly.

15. CONCLUSION

All the tables, charts, and analyses mentioned earlier show that although IBBL and GB are two pronged financial institutions, IBBL being Shariah compliant and GB, a collateral-free microfinance, they follow uniform principles in their financial reporting. The process is transactional and conforms to the Generally Accepted Accounting Principles (GAAP) as well as standards of prominent International authorities (such as IFRS). The underlying message it does convey is the financial accountability. Also, customers' sovereignty is intensely integrated and is based on the simple rule – choosing the quality product at the cheapest price (Be it IBBL product or GBs). Economists call it market mechanism, a free economy – doctrine. Competition in essence is its governing gift. This way, a financial reporting process is the instrument through which financial performance is evaluated both quantitively and qualitatively. The basis of the evaluation is always embedded in the financial statements. To the business world, financial reporting is its economic barometer, to an accountant, it is the beginning of an end.

NOTES

1. Financial accounting – Wikipedia.
2. Bangladesh (iasplus.com).
3. Descriptions in this section are taken primarily from: FASAB Handbook of Federal Accounting Standards and Other Pronouncements, as Amended.

4. "These statements report the results of government operations (net operating costs). They include non-exchange revenues, which are generated from transactions that do not require a government entity to give value directly in exchange for the inflow of resources. The government does not "earn" the non-exchange revenue. These are generated principally by the government's sovereign power to tax, levy duties, and assess fines and penalties. These statements also include the net cost reported in the Statements of Net Cost. They further include certain adjustments and unmatched transactions and balances that affect the net position." – Source Financial Statements of the United States Government for the Fiscal Years Ended September 30, 2021, and 2020 – Bureau of the Fiscal Service>Financial Report of the United States Government>Financial Statements.

REFERENCES

FASAB handbook of federal accounting standards and other pronouncements, as amended.

Financial Report of the United States Government – Financial Statements of the United States Government for the Fiscal Years Ended September 30, 2021, and 2020 (treasury.gov)

Fordyce, J., & Murray, A. A Nobel prize-winning economist debunks 3 misconceptions about SVB's collapse – And explains what really went wrong (msn.com)

Islam, J., Mohajan, H., & Datta, R. (2012). Aspects of microfinance system of Grameen Bank of Bangladesh. *International Journal of Economics and Research*, *3*(4), 76–96.

Mainsah, E., Heuer, S. R., Zhang, Q., & Kalra, R. (2004). Grameen bank: Taking capitalism to the poor. *Chazen Web Journal of International Business*.

Mawla, A. H. M. R., & Khanam, F. A. Performance evaluation of Islamic banks in Bangladesh – A statistical analysis. *European Journal of Business and Management*, *10*(36).

Quiggle, J. *Cathie Wood makes a big prediction on the future of banks*.

Silicon Valley Bank collapse puts new spotlight on Trump banking law (msn.com) – Silicon Valley Bank collapse puts new spotlight on Trump banking law – Story by Sahil Kapur and Julia Jester and Scott. Retrieved from https://www.msn.com/en-us/money/markets/banking-crisis-president-joe-biden-says-taxpayer-money-won-t-be-used-to-bail-out-svb-signature-bank/ar-AA18ySm1?ocid=msedgdhp&pc=U531&cvid=596d424e1e744a7cb22629d298cf7e65& – Banking crisis: President Joe Biden says taxpayer money won't be used to bail out SVB, Signature Bank – Story by Francesca Chambers, USA TODAY.

Silicon Valley Bank: Why did it collapse and is this the start of a banking crisis? *The Guardian*.

The Companies (Bangladesh) Act, 1994 (icsi.edu) Recent reviews and pronouncements of monetary policy Monetary Policy Statement (January–June 2023) Bangladesh Bank (bb.org.bd)

The promise of Islamic finance: Further inclusion with stability (imf.org)

CHAPTER 16

A STUDY ON BEHAVIOURAL FINANCE INVESTMENT DECISIONS OF INVESTORS IN BANGALORE

M. Chandrakala and Raja Kamal Ch

Kristu Jayanti College, Bangalore, India

ABSTRACT

The field of behavioural finance analyses the effects of mental factors on financial decisions including risk. If you want to know how people think about money and investments, you need to study behavioural finance. People's attitudes about investing were uncovered through this study. Hence, their views on financial investing. Overconfidence, perception, representative, anchoring cognitive dissonance, regret aversion, limited framing, and mental accounting are only few of the behavioural finance concepts that are discussed in this article, along with their effects on stock market investor decision making. In order to poll 181 Bangalore investors, we employed a conventional questionnaire. The primary focus was on learning how behavioural financing influences investors and their investment choices. Our secondary objective was to study behavioural finance and investor psychology.

Keywords: Behavioural finance; psychological factors; mental accounting; investor decision making; emotions on financial decisions; foresee future market movements

Digital Technology and Changing Roles in Managerial and Financial Accounting: Theoretical Knowledge and Practical Application
Studies in Managerial and Financial Accounting, Volume 36, 181–190

ISSN: 1479-3512/doi:10.1108/S1479-351220240000036017

1. INTRODUCTION

Decisions about investing, working capital, dividends, and the distribution of funds go under the purview of finance, whereas questions of what, how, and for whom to produce fall under the purview of economics. In addition, behavioural finance considers hard choices. Numerous concepts have been created in the fields of economics and finance, yet they still fail to account for why people often make foolish choices with their money. The field of finance seeks to provide explanations and evidence for the actions of market participants and the decisions made by investors. They explain the processes and guidelines for making investments. Common sense recommendations are difficult for investors to follow. Investors overtrade, make poor timing decisions, let their emotions get the better of them, and grossly underestimate the odds of success because of inefficient rules.

The Behavioural finance theory put out by psychologists has failed to gain traction in the financial world. Those who came first in the field of behavioural finance were reviled. Popularity of behavioural finance increased as research revealed the influence of psychology and emotions on financial decisions. The 2002 Nobel Prize in economics shared by psychologist Daniel Kahneman (2013) and experimental economist Vernon Smith (2013) provided validation for the field of behavioural finance.

2. TRADITIONAL FINANCE VERSUS BEHAVIOURAL FINANCE

The key difference between the traditional finance and Behavioural finance is as follows:

2.1. Traditional Finance

- That people are rough and proper with data.
- That people make decisions based on the potential benefits and costs.
- Believe people possess sound reasoning and independence.
- Asserts that because markets are efficient, the value of a security's price is a fair reflection of its intrinsic worth.

2.2. Behavioural Finance

- It acknowledges that humans use flawed processing rules.
- It acknowledges that emotions and intuition influence choices.
- It implies that issue framing affects risk and return perceptions.
- Behavioural biases and mistakes, frame-dependent effects, emotions, and social factors frequently explain market pricing discrepancies.
- Investors drive prices to unsustainable heights both ways.

The area of Behavioural Economics' offshoot, Behavioural Finance, offers psychologically grounded explanations for stock market oddities such unexpectedly large price increases or decreases. The goal is to discover and comprehend the factors that influence individuals' monetary decisions. Behavioural finance operates on the hypothesis that investors' choices and market results are systematically impacted by factors such as market structure and participant characteristics.

3. BEHAVIOURAL FINANCE CONCEPTS

3.1. Heuristic Driven Biases

3.1.1. Overconfidence

Overconfident individuals tend to place too much stock in their own prognostications. The mistaken belief that one is knowledgeable contributes to overconfidence. The human brain may be wired to glean as much information as possible from any given set of circumstances, but it often lacks the context to realize when its collected data is insufficient for making a reliable prediction (refer Fig. 16.1).

3.1.2. Anchoring

People are notoriously resistant to altering their previously held beliefs, even when confronted with compelling new evidence to the contrary. Let's pretend that investors believe A company's long-term profits prospects are better than average. A sudden reveal much lower than anticipated profits.

3.1.3. Familiarity

People tend to feel most at ease with things that are already well-known to them. The human brain typically takes the shortcut of familiarity while making financial decisions. In fact, trust is built via regular interaction. That's why a lot of individuals put their money into their own firm, the companies around them, and the ones that are based in the country.

3.1.4. Conformation Bias

Information that runs counter to one's beliefs is often disregarded in favour of data that supports those beliefs. Sometimes shareholders only hear the news that they want to hear. They are more concerned with finding evidence in favour of their ideas than against them.

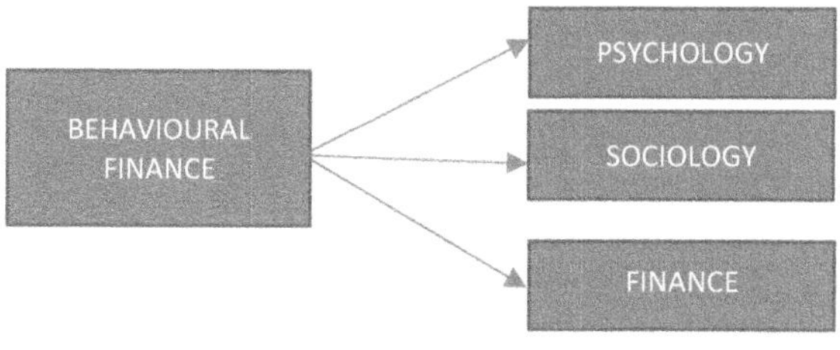

Fig. 16.1. Determinants of Behavioural Finance.
Source: Constructed by researcher.

3.1.5. Innumeracy

Many people struggle with mathematics. The difference between nominal and actual changes is often misunderstood. This phenomenon is known as money illusion in the field of economics. People have a hard time estimating probability accurately. To rephrase, it's likely that they are unaware that they are unaware. Big numbers get more attention, whereas little ones get less.

3.2. Frame Dependence

3.2.1. Prospect Theory

By providing an alternate account of how individuals frame and evaluate a choice with uncertainty, prospect theory, proposed by Kahneman and Tversky (1979), is possibly the most fundamental notion of Behavioural finance. Instead, then basing utility on the total amount of money, as is done in more conventional theories, this one looks at how wealth has changed through time. When considering gains, the utility function concave.

3.2.2. Mental Accounting

According to the tenets of conventional financial theory, wealth and money must be seen as interchangeable, and each financial choice must be grounded in a careful analysis of how it will affect one's net worth. However, in practice, individuals lack the cognitive abilities and self-control to analyze decisions based on their potential influence on societal wealth.

3.2.3. Narrow Framing

In a perfect world, investors would keep tabs on their net worth. When investors narrow their focus on just one investment at a time, rather than the portfolio, they are engaging in cross-sectional framing. As a result, they care more about the performance of certain equities than the performance of their portfolio.

3.2.4. Shadow of the Past

People are more inclined to take chances when they've had some success. When novice gamblers win money, they often don't completely accept it as their own and are motivated to keep betting. That's what we call the house money effect in the gambling world. People become more risk averse after experiencing a setback. The snake bite effect is another name for this phenomenon. A setback is like being bitten by a snake; it makes you more careful in the future.

3.3. Emotional and Social Influences

3.3.1. Emotional Effect

Risk tolerance is affected by feelings, and feelings in turn affect which investments are chosen for a portfolio. Investors experience a range of feelings as they weigh their options, determine how much risk to take, watch their selections play out, evaluate if the original plan requires change, and eventually discover how close they have come to attaining their financial goals.

3.3.2. Heard Instincts/Information Cascade
Humans have an innate need to feel like they belong to a community. Consequently, groups form naturally. However, conforming to the herd just amplifies the existing prejudices. It encourages people to make choices based on what the majority thinks rather than after doing their own thorough research. When making a choice in a situation with a lot of unknowns, this pattern tends to become more pronounced.

4. LITERATURE REVIEW

Nichlas Barberis (2017):The theory of behavioural finance proposes that certain financial events may be adequately explained by models in which some participants are not entirely rational. The two pillars of the field are the concept of limits to arbitrage, which argues that skilled traders may struggle to fix the disruptions caused by less rational traders, and the field of psychology, which provides a catalogue of the different types of deviations from complete rationality that we can expect to see.

Birău (2018): An innovative approach to the analysis of the financial markets is presented here: Behavioural Finance. Behavioural finance studies how people's thoughts and feelings have influenced the evolution of the financial sector.

Andrea Masini (2020): A growing number of people are seeking to invest in renewable energy technology as a method to kickstart economic activity and hasten the process of getting back on one's feet following the recent financial crisis.

Mangee (2021): In this article, econometric evidence is provided to support the idea that investor mood plays a major impact in market fluctuations. In order to do so, a slew of multivariate empirical studies using data from Bloomberg News' end-of-day stock market reports are applied to the Net Psychology Index, a novel measure of stock market mood.

Kevin Brady (2022): News events don't always precede or coincide with large stock market fluctuations. Then, other from these numbers, what else do buyers and sellers think about when making pricing decisions? The authors found that investors use both industry standards and personal information signals while making decisions.

5. RESEARCH OBJECTIVES

5.1. Primary Objective

To identify the role that behavioural financing in investors' choices.

5.2. Secondary Objectives

- To examine the elements that affect investors.
- To investigate the mental processes and tendencies of financial backers.
- To get insight into people's investment preferences.

5.3. Scope of Study

- The research is confined to the Indian city of Bangalore.
- Investors of all ages fall within the sphere of interest.
- The research was restricted to certain hypotheses.

5.4. Research Design

The research strategy used in this research is descriptive design since its primary function is to provide an account of the examined population or phenomenon.

5.5. Data Collection Sources

5.5.1. Primary Data

Schedules, questionnaires, interviews, and observations are all employed to gather information for this study.

5.5.2. Secondary Data

We have mostly relied on secondary sources for our study, such as the Internet, books, newspapers, articles, magazines, and blogs.

5.6. Sampling Plan

- Population: People of Bangalore
- Sampling frame: Investors
- Sampling method: Convenience
- Sampling size: 181 investors

5.7. Expected Contribution

Behavioural finance is important and may be used to choose where to put your money. The study's findings will improve our understanding of both conventional and behavioural finance. This study has potential use for future researchers.

6. DATA ANALYSIS: BI-VARIANT ANALYSIS

The correlation between schooling and arrogance was investigated (Table 16.1). Therefore, those with more education tend to have more faith in their capacity to foresee future market movements.

Emotional and gender biases were used as analogies (see Table 16.2), so when it comes to investing, women are more likely to go with their gut instincts. Emotional prejudice is more common among women than men.

Table 16.1. Education Cross-tabulation.

Cross-tabulation	Education						Total
	Undergraduate	Graduate	Postgraduate	Professional	PhD	Others	
How confident are you that you have enough?	5	43	42	8	2	5	105
Understanding of it?	7	26	32	8	2	1	76
Total	12	69	74	16	4	6	181

Source: Compiled by the researcher.

Table 16.2. Intuitions and Gut Feelings – Gender Cross-tabulation.

Cross-tabulation		Gender		Total
		Female	Male	
You put less thought on rational analysis and analysis of data while making financial investing choices	Yes	44	59	103
	No	31	47	78
Total		75	106	181

Source: Compiled by the researcher.

This study found no correlation between conformation bias and investor age (Table 16.3). Investors of any age might experience conformation bias.

In this article, we investigate how profession is related to the trying to break-even effect. The striving to break-even effect may be shown to have a greater impact on those in business and the self-employed than it does on those in retirement (refer to Table 16.4). Those in the business world and those who work for themselves take more risks than the average worker.

Table 16.3. Positive News Related With Age Cross-Tabulation.

		Age						Total
		18–25	25–35	35–45	45–55	55–65	>65	
You've recently invested in shares of, in which case you'll be more interested in hearing good news about the company	Yes	19	27	54	41	6	7	154
	No	3	8	6	6	1	3	27
Total		22	35	60	47	7	10	181

Source: Compiled by the researcher.

Table 16.4. Recovering the Loss With Occupation.

Cross-tabulation		Age					
		Service	Business	Self-employed	Retired	Home maker	Total
Will you keep holding if your investment is losing money?	Yes	58	22	15	5	19	119
	No	28	8	8	6	12	62
Total		86	30	23	11	31	181

Source: Compiled by the researcher.

7. HYPOTHESIS TESTING

H0. There is no influence of Behavioural finance on investment decisions.

H1. There is influence of Behavioural finance on investment decisions. According to the data presented in Table 16.5, behavioural finance is a valid financial theory.

H1. is accepted, there is influence of Behavioural financing n investment decisions on investors.

8. FINDINGS

- The average level of overconfidence indicates that more individuals have opted for the yes option, indicating that they are susceptible to overconfidence bias.
- If the average rating of financial advisor returns factors including experience, familiarity, objectives, and investment research is more than 3, it indicates that these factors are considered by investors.

Table 16.5. Influencing Factors of Behavioural Bias.

Behavioural Bias	Percentage
Overconfidence	64
Trying to break even effect	69
Emotional effect	57
Mental accounting	57
Familiarity with investment	67
Confidence bias	90
The shadow of the past	61
Anchoring theory	48
Prospect theory	70
Herd instinct/information cascade	57
Innumeracy bias	38
Narrow framing	23

Source: Compiled by the researcher.

- The average answer to the innumeracy question is 1.6, indicating that individuals prefer larger numbers to those with a higher calculative return, lending credence to the hypothesis of innumeracy.
- The mean score of 1.4 on the conformation bias question indicates that opinions are very evenly split.
- The average response to the familiarity question was 1.3, indicating that investors choose comfort with their investment above increased potential return.
- The mean score of 1.5 on the conformation bias survey indicates that the frequency of positive and negative responses is nearly equal and that most respondents are indifferent.
- The average response to the question concerning previous experiences was 3, indicating that respondents did not have a strong opinion one way or the other.
- The mean score of 1.3 on the question about breaking even indicates that the break-even point bias has a considerable impact on respondents.
- The average response to the question on emotional bias was 1.4, indicating that emotional factors have a significant role in how individuals ultimately decide how much to spend.

9. CONCLUSIONS

The research team in Bangalore wanted to see whether the Behavioural Finance theories still hold water and if the typical investor in the city's investment market is always acting rationally. This article primarily focuses on the following behavioural biases: overconfidence, anchoring, familiarity, conformation bias, innumeracy, prospect theory, mental accounting, limited framing, shadow of the past, emotional bias, and information or heard instinct.

The impact of these prejudices on the investment choices made by residents of Bangalore was investigated. The data was gathered by questionnaire, and 181 individual investors participated. According to the research, investors are not rational, and the aforementioned biases always have some degree of influence on their investing decisions.

REFERENCES

Barberis, N., Huang, M., & Santos, T. (2001). Prospect theory and asset prices. *The Quarterly Journal of Economics*, *116*(1), 1–53.

Birau, M. M. (2018). It is easy to do the right thing: Avoiding the backfiring effects of advertisements that blame consumers for waste. *Journal of Business Research*, *87*, 102–117.

Brady, K. (2022). The use of alternative social networking sites in higher educational settings: A case study of the e-learning benefits of Ning in education. *Journal of Interactive Online Learning*, *9*(2), 151–170.

Kahneman, D. (2013). Prospect theory: An analysis of decision under risk. In L. C. MacLean & W. T. Ziemba (Eds.), *Handbook of the fundamentals of financial decision making: Part I* (pp. 99–127). Hackensack: World Scientific Publishing.

Kahneman, D., & Tversky, A. (1979). Prospect theory: An analysis of decision under risk. *Econometrica, Econometric Society*, *47*(2), 263–291.

Mangee, N. (2017). New evidence on psychology and stock returns. *Journal of Behavioral Finance*, *18*(4), 417–426.

Masini, A. (2021). Contracting for technology improvement: The effect of asymmetric bargaining power and investment uncertainty. *European Journal of Operational Research*, *293*(2), 481–494.

Smith, V. G. (2013). Critical thinking: More than test scores. *International Journal of Educational Leadership Preparation*, *8*(2), 16–25.

PART III

DIGITAL TECHNOLOGIES, STAKEHOLDER ENGAGEMENT, AND SUSTAINABLE REPORTING PRACTICES

CHAPTER 17

FIRM SIZE, FIRM PERFORMANCE, AND ENVIRONMENTAL INFORMATION DISCLOSURE QUALITY: EVIDENCE FROM LISTED A-SHARES COMPANIES IN CHINA'S SHANGHAI AND SHENZHEN STOCK EXCHANGES

Xiaobin Luo, Junainah Jaidi* and Debbra Toria Nipo

Universiti Malaysia Sabah, Sabah, Malaysia

ABSTRACT

This study examines the impact of corporate performance and corporate size on corporate environmental information disclosure of A-share listed enterprises in Shanghai and Shenzhen during the period 2008–2017. In this study, corporate size (size) is represented by total assets, and corporate performance (Jzc) is represented by return on net assets. Environmental information disclosure quality (EID) is measured by the Environmental Information Disclosure Index (EIDI). Non-balanced panel data models are used. In order to eliminate the influence of unobservable factors during the sample period, year fixed effects and industry fixed effects are included. The results show that corporate size and performance both promote the improvement of EID quality. Measures

Digital Technology and Changing Roles in Managerial and Financial Accounting: Theoretical Knowledge and Practical Application
Studies in Managerial and Financial Accounting, Volume 36, 193–201

ISSN: 1479-3512/doi:10.1108/S1479-351220240000036018

such as improving corporate management efficiency and setting clear environmental performance indicators can help improve corporate competitiveness and core values, thus providing important support for improving EID quality. Future research is recommended to focus on the influence of internal corporate characteristics such as corporate nature (state-owned or not), equity structure, and executive background on EID quality.

Keywords: Company size; company performance; environmental information disclosure quality; listed companies; environmental information disclosure index (EIDI); environmental responsibilities

1. INTRODUCTION

In recent years, EID has received extensive attention from the international community, and many countries have issued their own guidelines for corporate EID. According to the "2018 China Corporate Green Transparency Report," from 2014 to 2016, 64 countries issued mandatory corporate EID regulations. Corporate EID is a social responsibility that can eliminate market failures caused by information asymmetry, play a role in social supervision, and promote the construction of a modern environmental governance system. EID is also an important way for enterprises to fulfill their environmental responsibilities and a significant channel for the government to promote a modern environmental governance system. Currently, there are mainly four methods for measuring the quality of corporate EID: EID indices, report guideline evaluation, content analysis, and survey questionnaire methods. Because EID indices collect and analyze corporate EID data and transform it into indices for performance comparison and ranking, it is a widely used method. Commonly used EID indices include the Dow Jones Sustainability Index, FTSE4Good, and MSCI ESG.

In the study of the internal influencing factors on corporate EID quality, factors such as internal management (Chen, Luo, & Yuan, 2010), culture and values (Bi, Gu, & Zhang, 2015), resource constraints, corporate governance structure (Shu, 2010), and business conditions can all affect their EID, as well as corporate size and performance.

The main factors affecting the impact of firm size on EID are multifaceted. Generally speaking, larger firms may place greater emphasis on EID because their environmental impact is greater, they face stricter environmental pressures and regulations, and they need to disclose information to reduce environmental risks and gain social recognition (Brammer & Pavelin, 2010). Moreover, larger firms often have more resources and expertise to conduct EID.

The impact of corporate performance on EID is mainly influenced by the following factors.

1.1. Corporate Reputation and Image

The performance and EID of a company directly affect its image and reputation in the public and investors' minds. Some companies, while pursuing profit maximization, also need to pay attention to their own image and reputation and therefore may be more proactive in disclosing environmental information. Chang (2015) used unbalanced panel data from China's heavily polluting industries to test the correlation between EID and financial performance and found that EID has a significant impact on the image and social reputation of listed companies.

1.2. The Influence of Policy and Regulations

The formulation of policies and regulations can affect both corporate performance and EID. Some countries and regions may take measures to promote the improvement of corporate EID, such as the enactment of environmental protection regulations and strengthened supervision. Zhu Xinling and Li Na (2017) believe that there are significant differences in the level of EID among different industries, and the reasons for these differences are the different government pressures, social pressures, and internal monitoring faced by different industries.

1.3. Investor Demand

Investors are increasingly concerned about a company's environmental performance, and they want to understand a company's environmental information in order to better assess its long-term value. Therefore, companies may be more proactive in disclosing environmental information to meet the needs of investors.

On the other hand, different evidence has been presented in some literature regarding the relationship between small businesses and EID. Freedman and Jaggi (1982) argued that there is no correlation between economic performance and pollution disclosure for smaller companies. Similarly, Ingram and Frazier (1980) found no relationship between corporate performance and EID.

The relationship between company size, performance, and the quality of EID is an important issue that has attracted the attention of many scholars. However, to date, there is no consensus among scholars regarding the relationship between company performance and the quality of EID. What is the relationship between company performance and its EID quality? Does firm size promote the governance of EID for listed companies as a whole?

Given that most empirical studies have focused on heavily polluting industries and have rarely covered the entire A-share listed companies, the measures of firm size, performance, and EID quality used in different studies vary. Therefore, this study aims to fill these gaps by investigating the effects of firm size and performance on the quality of EID.

2. LITERATURE REVIEW

Academics have two main viewpoints regarding the impact of company size and performance on environmental accounting information. Scholars generally believe that larger companies with better performance are more likely to prefer disclosing environmental accounting information to reduce the negative impact of information asymmetry on stakeholders.

Mak (2003) studied the impact of internal governance on EID among companies listed on the Singapore Stock Exchange at the end of 1995 and found that larger firms and firms with lower debt had greater disclosure. Zhang et al. (2008) analyzed the impact of corporate governance factors on voluntary EID from a financial accounting perspective among listed companies in the Chinese chemical industry from 2003 to 2005 and found that larger and more profitable companies were more likely to disclose environmental accounting information, but the overall level of voluntary disclosure was low. Tian and Hong (2010) conducted an empirical study using a sample of 112 listed companies in Shanghai and Shenzhen and found that firm size had a significant impact on EID behavior. Brammer and Pavelin (2010) studied the pattern of voluntary EID among large UK companies and found that larger, less leveraged, and more widely held firms were significantly more likely to disclose such information, and the quality of disclosure was positively correlated with firm size and environmental impact. Lu and Li (2010) studied the disclosure status of environmental information among A-share manufacturing companies listed in the Shanghai Stock Exchange in 2007 and 2008 and found that firm size and ownership structure had a significant impact on EID behavior. Zheng and Xiang (2013) conducted an empirical study on 170 listed companies in heavily polluted industries in Shanghai and found that firm size and debt level had a significant impact on their EID. Xiong (2015) found that most of the environmental information disclosed by listed companies in China was qualitative rather than quantitative, and the disclosure was subjective, incomplete, and lacked comparability. Empirical studies have shown that larger, more profitable, and state-owned listed companies are more willing to disclose environmental accounting information.

Some scholars also argue that there is no traditional linear relationship between them. The most representative research on this issue is represented by Freedman and Jaggi (1982), who found that for the association between economic performance and pollution disclosure, the subset of large under-performing companies provided the most detailed pollution information, while there was no association between economic performance and pollution disclosure for smaller companies. Their study on the relationship between pollution disclosure and pollution performance in high-polluting industries found that there is no association between them. Gray, Javad, Power, and Sinclair (2001) also expanded the literature by considering more classification specifications of social and EID and adopting detailed time-series datasets, finding two possible explanations for uncertainty: any relationship between company characteristics and disclosure depends on the type of disclosure, and any such relationship is not stable over time. This study attempts to provide empirical evidence by examining the important links between company size, performance, and EID quality using A-share listed companies in the Shanghai and Shenzhen stock exchanges as a sample.

3. DATA AND METHODOLOGY

This article used annual data to study all A-share listed companies from 2008 to 2017 as the initial research sample. The sample was screened to exclude the financial industry and outliers. Finally, a non-balanced panel data of 28,602 "annual observations of corporate" was obtained, which has a large sample size and guarantees the reliability of research conclusions. Data used in this article were from the CSMAR database. Winsorization was conducted to trim extreme values, and clustering was used to eliminate possible clustering characteristics. Data analysis was performed using Stata 17.0 software.

To eliminate the influence of unobservable factors during the sample period, this study includes year fixed effects and industry fixed effects. Regression analysis is conducted according to the following model:

$$EID_{it} = a_0 + a_1 Size + a_2\text{Lev} + a_3\text{Growth} + a_4\text{CFO} + a_5\text{SOE} + a_6\sum\text{ind} + a_7\sum\text{year} + e1 \quad (1)$$

$$EID_{it} = a_0 + a_1 Jzc + a_2\text{Lev} + a_3\text{Growth} + a_4\text{CFO} + a_5\text{SOE} + a_6\sum\text{ind} + a_7\sum\text{year} + e2 \quad (2)$$

where EID is the EID index, Size and Jzc are the independent variables, a_0 is the constant term, $a_1 \sim a_7$ is the regression coefficient, and e_1, e_2 is the disturbance term.

4. RESULTS AND DISCUSSION

4.1. Descriptive Statistics

In order to gain a preliminary understanding of the characteristics of the variables, this section provides a detailed description of the sample size, mean, standard deviation, minimum value, median, and maximum value of each variable.

From Table 17.1, it can be seen that the mean of the EID index (lnEID) is 1.4132, with a maximum value of 3.3673 and a minimum value of 0.0000. The large difference between the minimum and maximum values indicates a significant difference in the quality of EID among different companies. The mean of 1.4132

Table 17.1. Descriptive Statistics.

	Count	Mean	SD	Min	p50	Max
lnEID	28,602	1.4132	0.9691	0.0000	1.3863	3.3673
Size	28,602	22.1239	1.3001	19.3502	21.9363	26.8060
Jzc	28,542	0.0561	0.1537	−1.8862	0.0688	0.3689
Lev	28,602	0.4335	0.2076	0.0310	0.4283	0.9246
Growth	28,602	0.1767	0.4364	−0.6718	0.1083	4.3095
CFO	28,602	0.0460	0.0719	−0.2218	0.0454	0.2904
SOE	28,602	0.3889	0.4875	0.0000	0.0000	1.0000

and the median of 1.3863 are almost equal, indicating a relatively symmetrical distribution of data on EID quality.

The mean of corporate size (Size) is 22.1239, with a maximum value of 26.8060 and a minimum value of 19.3502. The large difference between the minimum and maximum values indicates a significant difference in the number of technological innovations among different companies. The mean of 22.1239 is not much different from the median of 21.9363, indicating a relatively symmetrical distribution of data on the number of technological innovations.

The mean of corporate performance (Jzc) is 0.0561, with a maximum value of 0.3689 and a minimum value of −1.8862. The large difference between the minimum and maximum values indicates a significant difference in the quality of technological innovation among different corporate. The mean of 0.0561 is not much different from the median of 0.0588, indicating a relatively symmetrical distribution of data on the quality of technological innovation.

The descriptive statistics results show that all variables have reasonable statistical characteristics.

4.2. Correlation Analysis

This section uses Pearson and Spearman coefficients to test the correlation between variables, and the results are shown in Table 17.2, where the lower left corner shows the results of the Pearson correlation coefficient test and the upper right corner shows the results of the Spearman correlation coefficient test.

Usually, when the absolute value of the correlation coefficient between variables is greater than 0.75, it means that the variables are highly correlated, and there may be a serious problem of multicollinearity, which will ultimately lead to a certain bias in the empirical results. From the results of the correlation analysis, it can be seen that the absolute values of the correlation coefficients between the variables used in this study do not exceed 0.75. This indicates that there is no problem of multicollinearity between the variables, and the empirical regression model in this study is reliable.

4.3. Regression Results

Table 17.3 presents the regression results of models 1 and 2, with overall goodness of fit measures of 0.336 and 0.252, respectively, indicating strong explanatory

Table 17.2. Correlation Analysis.

	lnEID	Size	Jzc	Lev	Growth	CFO	SOE
lnEID	1.0000	0.3826***	0.0691***	0.0987***	−0.0256***	0.1383***	0.1265***
Size	0.4038***	1.0000	0.1319***	0.4897***	0.0381***	0.0564***	0.3234***
Jzc	0.0590***	0.0958***	1.0000	−0.0754***	0.3529***	0.3649***	−0.0487***
Lev	0.0946***	0.4829***	−0.1731***	1.0000	−0.0003	−0.1433***	0.2969***
Growth	−0.0505***	0.0416***	0.1947***	0.0294***	1.0000	0.0491***	−0.0889***
CFO	0.1329***	0.0540***	0.2465***	−0.1544***	0.0080	1.0000	0.0212***
SOE	0.1290***	0.3311***	−0.0074	0.2966***	−0.0644***	0.0189***	1.0000

*$p < 0.1$, **$p < 0.05$, ***$p < 0.01$.

Table 17.3. Regression Analysis Results.

	lnEID	lnEID
Size	0.2903***	
	(31.44)	
Jzc		0.5696***
		(12.25)
Lev	−0.1538***	0.7082***
	(−2.76)	(11.77)
Growth	−0.0930***	−0.0968***
	(−8.37)	(−8.09)
CFO	0.8047***	1.1008***
	(8.05)	(10.04)
SOE	0.1517***	0.3040***
	(5.71)	(10.76)
_cons	−5.5282***	0.1066
	(−28.48)	(1.19)
Industry	Yes	Yes
Year	Yes	Yes
N	28,602	28,542
R^2	0.336	0.252
Adj. R^2	0.336	0.251
F	173.0686	119.0784

t statistics in parentheses.
*$p < 0.1$, **$p < 0.05$, ***$p < 0.01$.

power of the selected independent variables. The *F*-values for the models are 173.0686 and 119.0784, respectively, and are significant at the 1% level, indicating a good overall fit of the models.

The regression results of models 1 and 2 with fixed effects on industry and year are shown in Table 17.3. The regression results in Column 1 indicate that Size has a positive and significant effect on lnEID at the 1% level. The regression results in Column 2 indicate that Jzc also has a positive and significant effect on lnEID at the 1% level.

These results are consistent with previous studies by Brammer and Pavelin (2010), Zheng and Xiang (2013), and Xiong (2015), which show that firm size and performance have a strong positive impact on improving the quality of EID. On the one hand, larger firms tend to have higher standards for EID, possibly due to advantages in resources, brand value, regulatory pressure, and market demand. On the other hand, firms that pursue good performance typically need to pay more attention to sustainable development and environmental responsibility, thus being more likely to proactively disclose their environmental information to enhance transparency and build trust.

5. CONCLUSION AND RECOMMENDATION

The empirical evidence found in this study strongly supports the hypothesis of a positive relationship between firm size and performance and the quality of EID. Notably, among all the indicators tested in this study, firm performance (Jzc) had the greatest impact on the quality of EID because of its relatively large coefficient. This finding further suggests that ensuring stable improvement in firm performance is an important mechanism for enhancing the quality of EID and can be achieved by improving internal recycling management within companies.

Some policy implications and recommendations can be drawn.

Regulatory and guidance measures for EID in companies should be strengthened, especially for smaller and poorly performing companies, to improve their EID quality and promote their main responsibility for environmental protection.

Encouragement and support for companies to improve the quality and transparency of EID, especially in larger and better-performing companies, can enhance their social image and sense of social responsibility.

Companies need to develop clear environmental performance indicators based on their actual situations and incorporate them into their performance evaluation systems. By quantitatively assessing environmental performance, employees can be effectively motivated to engage in environmental protection work and improve the quality of EID.

However, several limitations of this study should be noted. First, to simplify data and models in measuring firm performance, this study used only one representative data point. Future consideration of firm performance can be more diverse.

Second, this study focused primarily on firm size and performance and did not compare with other internal characteristics of companies.

REFERENCES

Bi, Q., Gu, L., & Zhang, J. (2015). Traditional culture, environmental institutions, and corporate environmental information disclosure. *Accounting Research*, *3*, 8.

Brammer, S., & Pavelin, S. (2010). Voluntary environmental disclosures by large UK companies. *Journal of Business Finance & Accounting*, *33*(7–8), 1168-1188.

Chang, K. (2015). Does environmental information disclosure affect financial performance? Empirical analysis based on cross-sectional data of China's heavy polluting industries. *Journal of Finance and Economics*, *190*(1), 71.

Chen, X., Luo, F., & Yuan, D. (2010). Public pressure, social trust, and the quality of environmental information disclosure. *Contemporary Economy*, *8*, 11.

Freedman, M., & Jaggi, B. (1982). Pollution disclosures, pollution performance and economic performance. *Omega*, *10*(2), 167–176.

Gray, R., Javad, M., Power, D. M., & Sinclair, C. D. (2001). Social and environmental disclosure and corporate characteristics: A research note and extension. *Journal of Business Finance & Accounting*, *28*(3–4), 327–356.

Ingram, R. W., & Frazier, K. B. (1980). Environmental performance and corporate disclosure. *Journal of Accounting Research*, *18*, 614–622.

Lu, X., & Li, J. (2010). Research on the current situation of environmental information disclosure of Chinese listed companies: A case study of A-share manufacturing listed companies in Shanghai Stock Exchange in 2007 and 2008. *Audit and Economic Research*, *3*, 8.

Mak, L. (2003). Corporate governance and voluntary disclosure. *Journal of Accounting and Public Policy*, *22*(4), 325–345.

Shu, Y. (2010). An empirical study on the impact of corporate governance structure on environmental information disclosure: Evidence from listed companies on the Shanghai Stock Exchange in 2008. *Accounting Research*, *1*, 4.

Tian, Y., & Hong, P. (2010). Empirical study on influencing factors of environmental information disclosure of listed companies. *Accounting Friend*, *3*, 66–69.

Xinling, Z., & Na, L. (2017). Research on industry differences in corporate environmental information disclosure: Empirical evidence from heavy pollution industries. *Enterprise Economy*, *36*(8), 23–29.

Xiong, J. (2015). The current status and influencing factors of environmental accounting information disclosure in China's listed companies: Empirical evidence from listed companies in heavily polluting industries. *Southern Finance*, *12*, 7.

Zhang, J., Guo, H., Jia, Z., & Liu, D. (2008). A study on the influencing factors of corporate environmental accounting information disclosure: Empirical evidence from Chinese chemical industry-listed companies. *Statistical and Information Forum*, *23*(5), 7.

Zheng, C., & Xiang, C. (2013). Research on influencing factors of environmental information disclosure of listed companies in China: An empirical study based on 170 listed companies in Shanghai Stock Exchange. *Science and Technology Progress and Policy*, *30*(12), 5.

CHAPTER 18

THE EXTENT OF ACCOUNTING GRADUATES' ABILITIES (AGAS) IN JORDAN TO USE MODERN INFORMATION TECHNOLOGY SYSTEMS (MITSs) TO MAKE OPTIMAL FINANCIAL DECISIONS (OFDs)

Thaer Faisal Abdelrahim Qushtom[a] and Sami Sobhi Saleem Waked[b]

[a]*Zarqa University, Zarqa, Jordan*
[b]*Northern Border University, Arar, Saudi Arabia*

ABSTRACT

The current study aimed to explore the extent of accounting graduates' abilities (AGAs) in Jordan to use modern information technology systems (MITSs) to make optimal financial decisions (OFDs). To carry out this study, the descriptive analytical approach was used to collect and analyze data. Accordingly, an electronic questionnaire was designed and distributed to 5,000 students in 30 universities in Jordan. However, only 1,067 questionnaires were valid for analysis, which constituted the sample of study. To test the research hypotheses, the descriptive analysis and multivariate regression test were used. The results

Digital Technology and Changing Roles in Managerial and Financial Accounting: Theoretical Knowledge and Practical Application
Studies in Managerial and Financial Accounting, Volume 36, 203–213

ISSN: 1479-3512/doi:10.1108/S1479-351220240000036019

indicated that the majority of accounting graduates (AGs) in Jordanian universities (JUs) do not realize the importance role of MITSs to make OFDs. In addition, the biggest challenge face AGs in JUs is the weakness of current accounting curricula in JUs in terms of not including materials related to MITSs and the role of these systems in performing accounting tasks. Finally, the study found that the current abilities of AGs in JUs moderate negatively and significantly the positive relationship between the use of MITSs and making OFDs. Accordingly, the study recommended that JUs work on developing accounting curricula through including modern courses related to the use of MITSs in performing accounting tasks.

Keywords: Modern information technology systems (MITSs); cloud computing; artificial intelligence; Internet of things; big data; blockchain; Jordanian Universities (JUs); accounting graduates (AGs); financial decisions (FDs)

1. INTRODUCTION

AGs play a crucial role in ensuring that FDs made by organizations are accurate and reliable (Carnegie, Parker, & Tsahuridu, 2021). As technology continues to evolve rapidly, it is important that AGs keep up with the latest trends and innovations to ensure they can effectively utilize technology to make OFDs (Parashar, Sharma, Rana, & Balaji, 2023; Yoon, 2020). This is particularly important in countries like Jordan, where technology adoption is increasing rapidly, and organizations need to stay competitive by utilizing modern information technology (Luffi, 2021; Shaqqour et al., 2021; Parashar, Sharma, Rana, & Balaji, 2023).

In this context, this paper aims to investigate the extent to which AGs in Jordan are equipped with the skills and knowledge necessary to invest MITSs to make OFDs. The study explores the current level of awareness and adoption of technology among AGs, the challenges they face in using MITSs, and the moderating effect of AGAs on the relationship between using technology and financial decision making in organizations.

Several studies have highlighted the importance of technology adoption in accounting and financial decision making, including the use of big data analytics, artificial intelligence, and blockchain technology (Al-Rowais, Al-Faouri, & Al-Karaghouli, 2021; Shaqqour et al., 2021; Yousef et al., 2021; Al-Tamimi, 2020; Parashar et al., 2023; Yoon, 2020). However, there is limited research that examines the ability of AGs to utilize modern information technology in Jordan specifically.

By investigating these aspects, this study will contribute to a better understanding of the current state of technology importance realization among AGs in Jordan and provide indications of the challenges face AGs in using MITSs in financial decision-making processes.

Since MITSs are the dominant features of the future, AGs should be able to invest these technologies to provide the best performance in their jobs. Hence, the current study raises the following questions:

1. What is the current level of awareness and understanding of MITSs among AGs in Jordan?
2. What are the key challenges face AGs in Jordan when it comes to use MITSs for financial decision making?
3. What role can universities and educational institutions play in enhancing the ability of AGs in Jordan to use MITSs for financial decision making?
4. What is the expected effect for using MITSs on making OFDs in light of the current abilities of AGs in Jordan?

Next section provides a review of the related literature findings, followed by building the theoretical framework and hypotheses development. Then, the methodology of study, data analysis, and results are presented, and finally, the conclusion of study.

2. LITERATURE REVIEW

The accounting profession has been evolving rapidly due to the increasing use of MITSs (Mosteanu & Faccia, 2020). AGs must have the necessary skills and knowledge to use MITSs to make OFDs for their organizations.

Several studies have been conducted to investigate the use of modern technology in the accounting profession in Jordan. Mousa and Al-Zu'bi (2019) found that Jordanian accountants have a moderate level of knowledge and skills in using modern technology, and their use of technology is mainly limited to basic tasks such as data entry and record-keeping. Al-Rowais et al. (2021) investigated the impact of blockchain technology on accounting information systems in Jordan and found that the technology has the potential to improve the quality and reliability of financial information.

Big data analytics is another modern technology that can enhance financial decision-making processes. Al-Tamimi (2020) found that big data analytics has a positive impact on financial performance in the Jordanian banking sector. Al-Smadi, Al-Dmour, and Al-Tarawneh (2021) investigated the role of big data analytics in enhancing financial performance in Jordanian banks and found that it can improve risk management and decision-making processes.

Accounting information systems (AIS) are also important in enhancing financial decision-making processes. In this regard, Al-Htaybat and Al-Maani (2020) investigated the role of information technology in enhancing the performance of AIS in Jordanian banks and found that it can improve the quality and timeliness of financial information. Obeidat and Abdallah (2019) found that AIS have a positive impact on the performance of Jordanian commercial banks.

Artificial intelligence (AI) is another modern technology that can improve financial decision-making processes. In this context, Yoon (2020) investigated the impact of AI on financial performance in the Jordanian banking sector and found that it can improve efficiency and accuracy in decision-making processes.

Accordingly, it can be concluded that the literature suggests that AGs in Jordan have a moderate level of knowledge and skills in using MITSs. However, the use of MITSs in financial decision-making processes can have a positive impact on financial performance (Yousef et al., 2021). Therefore, AGs in Jordan need to be trained to utilize MITSs to make OFDs for their organizations. This study can contribute to enhancing the ability of AGs in Jordan to invest in modern information technology for financial decision making.

3. THEORETICAL FRAMEWORK AND HYPOTHESES DEVELOPMENT

The theoretical framework for this study is based on the technology acceptance model (TAM) and the contingency theory in IT. As the TAM is a theoretical framework that describes the factors that influence an individual's acceptance and use of technology. The TAM posits that an individual's perceived usefulness and ease of use of technology are the key determinants of their acceptance and use of that technology (Makmor, Abd Aziz, & Alam, 2019). In the context of this study, TAM can be used to understand the factors that influence AGs' ability to invest modern information technology to make the OFDs. While the contingency theory in IT explains that the main purpose of modern information technologies is to help and facilitate the implementation of operations to enhance the efficiency of these operations in attaining the optimal performance (Araral, 2020). In the context of this study, the contingency theory in IT can be used to understand the expected effect of using modern information technology on making OFDs.

According to the aforementioned theoretical discussion, the present study introduces the following hypotheses:

H1. AGs in Jordan realize the importance of using MITSs in carrying out the tasks related to accounting profession.

H2. AGs in Jordan face a set of challenges related to using MITSs to make OFDs.

H3. Universities and educational institutions can play an important role in enhancing the ability of AGs in Jordan to use MITSs to make OFDs.

H4. There is an expected statistically significant effect for using MITSs in making OFDs in light of the current abilities of AGs in Jordan.

3.1. Model of Study

Relying on the prior-mentioned theoretical framework and hypotheses, Fig. 18.1 shows the model of present study that shows the hypothesized relationships between the variables of study:

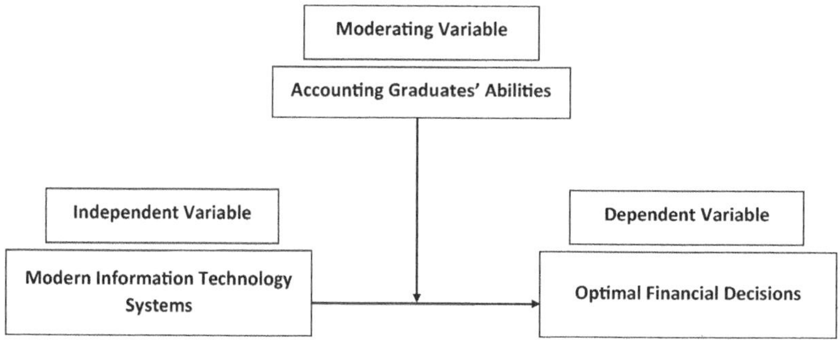

Fig. 18.1. Model of Study.

4. METHODOLOGY, DATA ANALYSIS, AND RESULTS

To answer the current research questions, the current study used the qualitative approach to collect, test, and analyze data.

For collecting data, an electronic questionnaire developed by the researchers was used. The questionnaire comprised two main sections; the first section contained five questions focused on the demographic data of respondents, in addition to three closed-ended questions to determine the extent to which AGs realize the importance of using MITSs to carry out accounting tasks. As well as the challenges face AGs regarding the use of MITSs to make OFDs. Finally, the role of universities and educational institutions in enhancing the ability of AGs to use MITSs to make OFDs. While the second section contained 13 questions explored the background and perspective of AGs on MITSs. Further, it included 12 questions focused on the abilities of AGs and their skills in using the MITSs in carrying out accounting operations in general. Finally, it included 18 questions focused on the possibility of exploiting the skills of AGs in using MITSs to make OFDs.

The population of study consisted of all accounting students in JUs who are in the penultimate and graduation semesters, and their number is estimated to be between 4,000 and 7,000 students. Based on that, the electronic questionnaire was distributed to 5,000 students in 30 universities in Jordan. Consequently, 1,187 questionnaires were retrieved, of which 1,067 were valid for analysis.

As for the data analysis process, it included four stages. Initially, Cronbach alpha test was implemented to ensure the reliability of questionnaire. In this context, the result of Cronbach alpha test was 0.692, which can be considered acceptable. Then, the normal distribution of questionnaires was tested by Skewness and Kurtosis measures. In this vein, the values of Skewness and Kurtosis ranged between −0.78 and 1.95, which indicate that the questionnaires were normally distributed. After that, the descriptive analyses were performed to answer the first four questions of the current study. Finally, the regression analysis was implemented to answer the fifth question of this study.

4.1. Descriptive Analysis Results

To test the first three hypotheses of the current study, the researchers used descriptive analysis. The descriptive statistics used to measure hypotheses are mean, median, and standard deviation. Table 18.1 shows the descriptive results.

The results of the descriptive analysis showed that 43% of accounting students graduates in JUs realize the importance of using MITSs in carrying out tasks related to the accounting profession. While 57% are ignorant of the role of various MITSs in improving and developing the performance of accounting tasks.

As for the challenges face AGs in Jordan related to use MITSs to make OFDs, 96% of students indicated that the weakness of current accounting curricula and the failure to update them in line with modern technological developments is the biggest challenge they face, as it limits their knowledge of the nature and effects of these technological developments on the accounting profession and the mechanisms for using these systems to improve the performance of accounting tasks. In same vein, 83% of the students indicated that keeping up with the pace of technological change is a big challenge for them, as information technology systems are characterized by rapid change and development, and the accounting curricula in JUs do not keep pace with these changes. In addition, 74% of the students indicated that the lack of knowledge of the role and function of each modern technological system prevents them from realizing the mechanism for achieving integration between different systems to perform accounting tasks. As well as, 46% of the students indicated that their lack of knowledge of data security systems in light of the modern digital revolution limits their ability to use these technologies efficiently and effectively. Likewise, 38% of the students pointed out that the lack of understanding of the working mechanism of MITSs limits their ability to monitor the outputs of these systems.

Regarding the role of universities and educational institutions in enhancing the ability of AGs to use MITSs to make OFDs, 98% of accounting students indicated that universities and educational institutions can play a crucial role in enhancing the abilities of AGs through developing accounting curricula, providing software and modern technological systems for practical application and simulation, conducting seminars, courses, and workshops focus on technological developments in the field of accounting profession.

4.2. Regression Analysis Test

In order to explore the relationship between using MITSs and making OFDs, the expected moderating effect of AGAs on this relationship the study used the regression analysis test. Accordingly, two regression models were developed and tested.

First Regression Model: Tests the direct relationship between using modern information technologies systems and making OFDs:

$$\text{OFDs (InvD; FinD; OpeD; BudD; RMD; TPD)} = a0 + a1\ \text{MITSs} + ei$$

Table 18.1. Descriptive Analysis Results.

First Section of Questionnaire: Demographic Data of Respondents (Valid No. 1067)					
1. Gender	Male			Female	
	754			313	
2. Graduation semester	Last semester			Penultimate semester	
	487			580	
3. Accounting experience (years)	None	<3	3–5	5–7	>7
	716	186	84	54	27
4. Age (years)	21–23		24–26	27–30	More 30
	492		380	102	93
5. Level of computer skills	1–3.3 (Weak)		3.4–6.7 (Med)	6.8–10 (Strong)	
	87		713	269	

The extent to which AGs in Jordan realize the importance of using modern information technology in carrying out accounting tasks									
Question: Do you know the role of each of the following IT systems and how they help in performing accounting tasks?									
Modern Information Technologies									
Cloud Computing (CC)		Artificial Intelligence (AI)		Internet of Things (IoT)		Big Data (BD)		Blockchain (Bc)	
Yes	No	Yes	No	Yes	No	Yes	No	Yes	No
511	556	617	450	349	718	427	640	407	660
Yes = 43%					No = 57%				

Challenges face AGs regarding the use of modern information technology to make OFDs		
Determine which of the following challenges face AGs to use modern information technology to make OFDs		
Challenge	Answers	Percentage
1. The weakness of current accounting curricula	1,024	96
2. Keeping up with the pace of technological change	886	83
3. The lack of knowledge of the role and function of each modern technological system	790	74
4. The lack of knowledge of data security systems	491	46
5. The lack of understanding of the working mechanism of MITSs	405	38

The role of universities in enhancing the ability of AGs to invest modern information technology to make OFDs			
Do you think that universities can play a role in enhancing the ability of AGs to invest the modern information technology to make OFDs? If yes, how?			
Yes		No	
Number of answers	Percentage	Number of answers	Percentage
1,047	98	21	2
1. Developing accounting curricula (98%)			
2. Providing software and modern technological systems for practical application and simulation (79%)			
3. Conducting seminars, courses and workshops focus on technological developments in the field of accounting profession (66%)			

Note: Developing the questionnaire relied on Al-Tamimi (2020), Al-Smadi et al. (2021), Araral (2020), Carnegie et al. (2021), Gibran (2022), Mousa and Al-Zu'bi (2019), and Mosteanu and Faccia (2020).

Second Regression Model: Tests the expected moderating effect of the AGAs on the relationship between using MITSs and making OFDs:

$$\text{OFDs (InvD; FinD; OpeD; BudD; RMD; TPD)} = b0 + b1\ \text{MITSs*AGAs} + \epsilon i$$

where,

OFDs = optimal financial decisions
InvD = investment decisions
FinD = financing decisions
OpeD = operational decisions
BudD = budgeting decisions
RMD = risk management decisions
TPD = tax planning decisions
MITSs = modern information technology systems
AGAs = accounting graduates' abilities
$a0$, $a1$, $b0$, $b1$ = constants of equations
ei, ϵi = error terms

Table 18.2 shows the results of testing the aforementioned regression models.

The regression analysis results in Table 18.2 show that there is a significant positive relationship between using MITSs and making OFDs at the significance level of 0.01. On the other hand, the results show that the current AGAs have a significant negative moderating effect on the relationship between using MITSs and making OFDs at the significance level of 0.01. These results imply that the current abilities of AGs in JUs have a significant negative moderating effect on the relationship between using MITSs and making OFDs. So, the *H4* of the current study is accepted.

Table 18.2. Regression Analysis Results ($N = 1{,}068$).

Variables	Dep. V	First Regression	Second Regression
		OFDs	OFDs
Ind. V		Coefficient Estimate	Coefficient Estimate
Constants		0.000 (0.972)	0.000 (0.129)
MITSs		0.637** (0.001)	0.112** (0.000)
MITSs_AGAs			−0.717** (0.000)
R^2		0.81	0.94
Adj. R^2		0.80	0.90
F-value		3,665.42	2,119.27
Sig. level		0.000	0.000

p-value (sig. level) is reported in parentheses.
**p*-value is significant at level 0.05; ***p*-value is significant at level 0.01.

5. CONCLUSION

Based on the descriptive analysis results, only 43% of AGs in JUs realize the importance role of MITSs to make OFDs, while the majority of AGs (57%) do not realize that. The researchers believe that the reason behind this is the lack of knowledge of AGs in JUs about the nature of MITSs and the role played by each system. This belief is confirmed by the other results of the current study, as the results indicated that the biggest challenge facing the vast majority of AGs in JUs (96%) is the weakness of current accounting curricula in JUs in terms of not including materials related to MITSs and the role of these systems in performing accounting tasks. This result justifies the lack of awareness of AGs in JUs of the importance of the role of MITSs in the field of accounting. In this regard, Al-Qadash and Al-Hawari (2019) and Carnegie et al. (2021) pointed out that the extent to which individuals are aware of a particular subject depends on the amount of knowledge they receive about this subject. Alshdifat (2022) also explained that the responsibility for individuals' lack of awareness of the importance of certain issues rests with the bodies that take care of these individuals. Therefore, the researchers believe that the lack of awareness of AGs of the importance of MITSs in performing accounting tasks is a result of the weakness of accounting curricula in terms of their inclusion of materials related to this modern technology. In addition, the results showed that 98% of AGs think that universities and educational institutions can play a significant role in enhancing the ability of AGs to invest the modern information technology to make OFDs. In this vein, Al-Khawaldeh and Al-Rawashdeh (2019) and Gibran (2022) pointed out that students are inputs to educational systems, so the outputs of these systems are the results of the processing processes that occur for these inputs. Finally, finding that the current abilities of AGs in JUs moderate negatively and significantly the positive relationship between the use of MITSs and making OFDs can be attributed to the fact that the current knowledge of AGs about MITSs does not help them to use this technology correctly and effectively (Alshdifat, 2022; Bawadi & Abu-Madi, 2019; Yoon, 2020).

The current results imply that the level of awareness of AGs of the importance of MITSs to perform accounting tasks is low. Therefore, JUs have to work on raising the level of awareness of AGs by developing accounting curricula and including them various and modern materials on MITSs and how to benefit from these systems to perform accounting tasks in addition to conducting seminars, courses, and workshops to enhance the level of students' knowledge about these systems.

Based on the current results, the study recommends that JUs work on developing accounting curricula and courses through including modern courses related to the use of MITSs in performing accounting tasks. As well as, providing and equipping the necessary technological infrastructure (hardware, software, laboratories, simulators, etc.) to keep pace with the continuous technological development. Finally, the study recommends that AGs in Jordan be keen to continuously develop their accounting and related technological skills to ensure keeping pace with the continuous technological change and obtaining better job opportunities in the market.

It should be noted that there are some limitations surround the current study, namely the current study is limited to the JUs. So, the results cannot be generalized to other universities in other countries. In addition, the data was collected in the period from 3-2023 to 5-2023. Thus, data and results may vary over time depending on changes and updates that may occur in accounting curricula and programs in JUs. Accordingly, there is an opportunity for researchers in other countries to carry out similar studies to explore the extent of AGAs in that countries to use the modern information technologies in performing accounting tasks.

REFERENCES

Al-Htaybat, K., & Al-Maani, M. (2020). The role of information technology in enhancing performance of accounting information systems in Jordanian banks. *Journal of Applied Accounting Research*, *21*(2), 220–237.

Al-Khawaldeh, S., & Al-Rawashdeh, S. (2019). The role of accounting information systems in enhancing the efficiency of financial performance: Evidence from Jordan. *International Journal of Accounting and Finance*, *9*(1), 75–93.

Al-Qadash, M. A., & Al-Hawari, A. M. (2019). The impact of information technology on the performance of Jordanian Industrial Companies: An empirical study. *Academy of Accounting and Financial Studies Journal*, *23*, 1–18.

Al-Rowais, N. A., Al-Faouri, R., & Al-Karaghouli, W. (2021). The impact of blockchain technology on accounting information systems: Evidence from Jordan. *Journal of Accounting and Finance*, *21*(2), 37–52.

Al-Smadi, M. O., Al-Dmour, R. H., & Al-Tarawneh, H. (2021). The role of big data analytics in enhancing financial performance: Evidence from Jordanian Banks. *Academy of Strategic Management Journal*, *20*(3), 1–14.

Al-Tamimi, H. A. H. (2020). The impact of big data analytics on financial performance in the Jordanian banking sector. *Journal of Accounting and Finance*, *20*(1), 23–38.

Alshdifat, R. A. (2022). Obstacles facing the application of distance learning during the corona pandemic, from the viewpoint of students of Hail University in the Kingdom of Saudi Arabia. *Zarqa Journal for Research and Studies in Humanities*, *22*(2), 228–239. doi:10.12816/0061208

Araral, E. (2020). Why do cities adopt smart technologies? Contingency theory and evidence from the United States. *Cities*, *106*, 1–13. https://doi.org/10.1016/j.cities.2020.102873

Bawadi, H. A., & Abu-Madi, M. K. (2019). The impact of information technology and accounting information systems on the performance of the Jordanian industrial sector. *Academy of Accounting and Financial Studies Journal*, *23*, 1–17.

Carnegie, G., Parker, L., & Tsahuridu, E. (2021). It's 2020: What is accounting today? *Australian Accounting Review*, *31*(96), 65–73.

Gibran, A. M. (2022). Education development in higher education institutions: Transition to qualitative teaching. *International Journal for Quality Assurance*, *5*(1), 46–56.

Lutfi, A. (2021). Understanding cloud based enterprise resource planning adoption among SMEs in Jordan. *Journal of Theoretical and Applied Information Technology*, *99*(24), 5944–5953.

Makmor, N., Abd Aziz, N., & Shah Alam, S. (2019). Social commerce an extended technology acceptance model: The mediating effect of perceived ease of use and perceived usefulness. *Malaysian Journal of Consumer and Family Economics*, *22*, 119–136.

Mosteanu, N. R., & Faccia, A. (2020). Digital systems and new challenges of financial management – FinTech, XBRL, blockchain and cryptocurrencies. *Journal of Management Systems*, *21*(174), 159–166.

Mousa, B., & Al-Zu'bi, Z. (2019). The extent of the use of modern technology in the accounting profession: A field study on Jordanian accountants. *International Journal of Managerial and Financial Accounting*, *11*(3), 268–292.

Obeidat, B. Y., & Abdallah, A. B. (2019). The effect of accounting information systems on the performance of Jordanian commercial banks. *Journal of Applied Accounting Research*, *20*(3), 267–286.

Parashar, B., Sharma, R., Rana, G., & Balaji, R. D. (2023). Foundation concepts for Industry 4.0. In A. Nayyar, M. Naved, & R. Rameshwar (Eds.), *New horizons for Industry 4.0 in modern business. Contributions to environmental sciences & innovative business technology*. Cham: Springer. https://doi.org/10.1007/978-3-031-20443-2_3

Shaqqour, O. F., Alkabbji, R. F., & Masoud, A. A. (2021). The impact of appling cloud accounting on the financial fraud at Jordanian companies. In *22nd International Arab conference on information technology*, Muscat (pp. 1–6).

Yousef, M., Al-Badareen, R., & Almomani, H. (2021). Artificial intelligence and financial performance in the Jordanian banking sector. *International Journal of Business and Economics Research*, *10*(1), 1–13.

Yoon, S. (2020). A study on the transformation of accounting based on new technologies: Evidence from Korea. *Sustainability*, *12*(20), 1–22. https://doi.org/10.3390/su12208669

CHAPTER 19

ENSURING COMPETITIVE ADVANTAGES OF THE BANKING SECTOR OF UKRAINE IN THE CONTEXT OF GLOBAL DIGITAL TRANSFORMATION

Anna Slobodianyk[a], Anna Maryna[a], Halyna Kosovets[b], Liudmyla Tsiukalo[c] and George Abuselidze[d]

[a]*National Aviation University, Kyiv, Ukraine*
[b]*Institute Independent, Kyiv, Ukraine*
[c]*Taras Shevchenko National University of Kyiv, Kyiv, Ukraine*
[d]*Batumi Shota Rustaveli State University, Batumi, Georgia*

ABSTRACT

This chapter considers aspects of ensuring competitive advantages of the banking sector of Ukraine in the context of global digital transformation. It is proved that operations that previously required a large amount of resources and time can now be carried out automatically using software solutions and artificial intelligence (AI). Companies like FinTech and BigTech that combine financial technology with their core services pose a serious threat to traditional banks. The authors noted that digital technologies make it possible to provide faster and more efficient customer service and improve the security of operations and reduce costs. The emphasis is placed on the fact that the use of AI in the banking sector will contribute to improving the efficiency and accuracy

Digital Technology and Changing Roles in Managerial and Financial Accounting: Theoretical Knowledge and Practical Application
Studies in Managerial and Financial Accounting, Volume 36, 215–227

Published under exclusive licence by Emerald Publishing Limited
ISSN: 1479-3512/doi:10.1108/S1479-351220240000036020

of banks, reducing risks and costs, and also contributes to the selection of personalized approaches to their customers. It has been proven that, thanks to AI, banking companies can improve the efficiency of their work, reduce costs, and improve interaction with their customers, thereby gaining competitive advantages in the market.

Keywords: Digital banking; competitiveness; market; digital technologies; banking sector; Fintech; BigTech; artificial intelligence

1. INTRODUCTION

In today's world, where digital technologies are entering all spheres of life, the banking sector is no exception. Ukrainian banks also face the need to adapt to the new technological challenges that have emerged in recent years. Global digital transformation is currently one of the main trends in the global economy, and banks that are not ready for it may lose their competitive advantage in the market. In addition, digital technologies allow banks to increase the efficiency of their activities and reduce costs. Operations that previously required a large amount of resources and time can now be carried out automatically using software solutions and AI. This allows banks to focus on developing new products and services that meet the needs of customers and provide them with a competitive advantage in the market. However, along with the benefits of digital transformation, banks face new challenges and threats. The most tangible of them are cybersecurity and competition. Competition in the banking services market has grown significantly in recent years. New players have emerged offering innovative and convenient products and services. Companies like FinTech and BigTech that combine financial technology with their core services pose a serious threat to traditional banks. Therefore, banks must adapt to the new realities and focus on the development of innovative technologies and products that will provide a competitive advantage in the market.

The theoretical foundations of the economic efficiency of innovative activity of banking institutions, the essence, types and types of banking innovations, and the organization of innovation processes are studied in the works of such scientists-economists: Ziemnowicz (1942), Carlsson (2007), Drucker (2014), Porter and Sölvell (2008), Porter (2008), Abuselidze (2021, 2023), Abuselidze and Kizinidze (2019), Miller (2018, 2020, 2021), Frame and White (2004), Agolla, Makara, and Monametsi (2018), Frame, Wall, and White (2018), and Wilson (2023). Contemporaries, exploring the development and implementation of innovative technologies in the banking sector, focus on the globalization of this issue within the framework of the informatization of the economy. Among these authors is necessary to allocate: Onetti, Zucchella, Jones, and McDougall-Covin (2012), Porter (2000), Abuselidze and Mamaladze (2021), Acs, Desai, and Hessels (2008), Abuselidze, Ostapchuk, Talavyrya, and Lutsiak (2022), Gomber, Kauffman, Parker, and Weber (2018), Goyal and Joshi (2011), Kniazieva, Maryna, Shevchenko, Shvets, and Goncharenko (2022). At the same time, some applied aspects that take into account the specifics of the introduction of new types of banking products and services remain unexplored and need to be finalized. However, many aspects of this problem remain insufficiently investigated. In particular, they need in-depth study of theoretical and practical issues of ensuring competitive advantages of the banking sector of Ukraine in the context of global digital transformation.

The purpose of the scientific article is to deepen the theoretical and methodological principles of ensuring the competitive advantages of the banking sector of Ukraine in the context of global digital transformation. This, in turn, is the result of evaluating the economic efficiency of innovative activity of Ukrainian banks and developing scientific and practical recommendations for its improvement, taking into account the risk-oriented approach and the possibilities of virtualization of banking business.

2. METHODS

The following methods were used to perform the study: dialectical cognition: for outlining, analyzing, and explaining the topic of the investigation; for clarifying and assembling a categorical conceptual apparatus in the chosen study path, abstraction, and morphological analysis; philosophical and historical analysis are used to examine how general marketing theory concepts have evolved, and an abstract-logical technique is used to theoretically generalize study data and generate intermediate and final conclusions.

3. RESULTS AND DISCUSSION

The modern stage of digitalization has been marked not only by advantages but also disadvantages. The latest developments play an important role in the efficiency of state and economic management through the development and implementation of radio electronics, telecommunications, and computer science. Digitalization also plays an important role in creating new types of social elevators, namely, bridging the digital gap between segments of the population and reducing the poverty of the population itself.

The change in the economic vision of the world due to digitalization has contributed to a change in the public vision of the development of digital processes. Information, ideas, knowledge, and innovations from which a continuous stream of data is formed contribute to the development of digitalization of economic systems and have carried out the industrialization of developed countries through the introduction of automation and the use of digital platforms and AI. Despite the fact that digitalization was characterized by the development of society, the question arose whether it violated human rights to anonymity and privacy?! (Slobodianyk & Abuselidze, 2021).

According to research by the analytical company Juniper Research, the number of digital banking users in the world will reach 3.6 billion by 2024. For comparison, this figure at the beginning of 2020, coinciding with the beginning of the global COVID-19 pandemic, was about 1.8 billion. Such a significant pace of digital banking promotion will occur mainly at the expense of users born since the 1980s of the last century called generations Y and Z. During the formation of these generations, there is an active development of mobile communications, the World Wide Web, computer technologies, social networks, digital media, and the evolution of devices (Slobodianyk et al., 2022).

In 2021, investments in the FinTech industry increased by 96% compared to 2020 and their total amount exceeded 90 billion US dollars. The largest funding was received by the sphere of making payments of almost 52 billion US dollars. The second position is occupied by the spheres of blockchain and crypto currencies with investments of more than 30 billion US dollars. Completing the top three is an equally important area of cyber security with an investment of 5.5 billion US dollars. 2022 also maintains a trend of investment growth, which is partly explained by previously planned modernization initiatives, but it has also been accelerated by an increase in demand for digital financial services and e-commerce amid the COVID-19 pandemic and military aggression of the Russian Federation (Abuselidze & Slobodianyk, 2020; Shpachuk et al., 2023).

Analyzing the banking sector as a whole for digitalization and the introduction of FinTech, it should be noted that the following banks are recognized as world leaders: BBVA Banking Group, Bank of America, JPMorgan Chase, N26, Revolut, Bunq, and Yuh. These are, relatively speaking, the best options for new banks when it comes to combining financial control and insurance packages in a single whole (Slobodianyk & Mohylevska, 2022).

Juniper Research recently conducted a study "Retail Banking: Digital Transformation & Disruptor Opportunities 2020–2024" and the data show that by 2024 the number of digital banking users in the world could reach 3.6 billion, which is 50% more than in 2020 (Table 19.1).

According to the forecast report of the European Retail Banking Radar, about 20% of European residents will start using the services of fully digital banks in the next five years. According to the forecast of Mordor Intelligence, the assessment of global AI in the financial technology market may increase to $26.67 billion in 2026 (*AI in Fintech Market – Growth, Trends, Covid-19 Impact, and Forecasts (2023–2028)*). KPMG's forecast shows that by 2030 all banks

Table 19.1. The Number of Active Users of Digital Banking in the World in 2020 and With a Forecast Until 2024, by Region, Million.

	2020	2021	2022	2023	2024
Latin America	109	126.4	146.7	170.4	198
Europe	361.7	379.9	398.1	416.4	435
North America	240.1	250.5	261.4	272.7	279.6
The Far East and China	805.1	844.4	885.6	928.9	974.3
The rest of the world	387.3	441.8	504.9	578.5	664.9
Total	1,903.2	2,043	2,196.7	2,366.9	2,551.8

Note: Compiled by the authors according to *Retail Banking: Digital Transformation & Disruptor Opportunities 2020–2024*.

will move completely into the "digital world" and will be available to customers electronically as various services, personal assistants, or various applications. According to the conclusions of KPMG Global experts in the framework of the report "The Future of Digital Banking," the main changes in the banking sector by 2030 will be presented: personalization using AI technologies, interaction with each client will be carried out using a voice assistant and biometrics. Banks will create digital platforms on which they will offer their customers all kinds of third-party services (*Banking and Capital Markets*). An important role will be played by the issue of users' confidence in the protection of their personal data and the targeted use of data, a high-quality cyber security system using AI to protect data.

If we take into account the banking sector of Ukraine and the pace of introduction of FinTech, then domestic banks have a fairly low level of participation in the capital of FinTech companies, unlike global ones. According to the international auditing company Ernst & Young, which conducted research within the framework of the USAID Project "Transformation of the Financial Sector" in cooperation with the Ministry of Social Policy of Ukraine during 2016–2020, only no more than 15% of banks have shares in FinTech companies. According to the international auditing company Ernst & Young, which conducted research within the framework of the USAID Project "Transformation of the Financial Sector" in cooperation with the Ministry of Social Policy of Ukraine during 2016–2020, only no more than 15% of banks have shares in FinTech companies (Slobodianyk et al., 2022).

However, despite extraneous factors, this direction still remains one of the most dynamic and opens for investment in Ukraine. The primary direction of digital transformation is the development of a strategy for the introduction of financial technologies, which includes remote identification, digitalization of back-office operations, automation of operational processes, blockchain, development of electronic payment technology, the use of predictive analytics, and the introduction of a comprehensive customer service system with the integration of digital signatures on cloud technologies.

Today, FinTech is one of the main drivers of the digital transformation of banking. The state does not stay away from this process and contributes to digitalization in every possible way. So, at the beginning of March 2022, the National Bank of Ukraine allowed banks to provide services for the period of martial law plus two consecutive years, using cloud services using equipment on the territory of the states of the European Union, Great Britain, the United States of America, and Canada.

Banks have been raising issues of deeper use of cloud technologies for a long time and now they are conditionally independent of critical infrastructure within the country. The use of blockchain technology, remote identification, electronic payments, etc. is already real for the domestic banking system. The experience of their practical implementation in the banking system is associated with the possibility of improving the transmission of information.

The introduction of new types of banking products and services is an innovative activity that has the characteristics of remoteness in time, riskiness, loss of liquidity and subordination to the main operational activity, which are traditional for this type of activity. It remains clear that with the inefficient introduction of new types of banking products and services, systematic investment risks of income shortfall and loss of invested capital will lead to critical problems with the profitability indicators of the bank's operating activities.

Taking into account the peculiarity of the work of banks, the concept of income and expenses should be considered in the context of their activities (Fig. 19.1).

Profit generation, administrative, and other operating expenses have a steady tendency to increase with the growth of the customer base, the expansion of the market for banking services. However, the introduction of new types of banking products also entails a reduction in variable costs, including staff working hours. Optimization of administrative expenses, on the composition and structure of which the bank's profit before taxation depends, is one of the main advantages of introducing the latest technologies. The introduction of new types of banking products and services is the key to supporting the competitiveness of the bank in the modern world of information technology.

At a time when financial boundaries are blurring and the distribution and redistribution of financial resources acquires a global scale, lagging behind competitors can lead to a loss of position in the market and a loss in competition.

One of the ways to ensure the competitive advantage of Ukrainian banks is to create their own innovative products. To do this, it is necessary to have its own innovative potential based on knowledge and technical resources. Banks can use internal and external resources to develop innovations, such as startups, scientific research, development of new technologies, and market research (Fig. 19.2).

Digital technologies allow us to provide faster and more efficient customer service, improve the security of operations, and reduce costs as indicated in Fig. 19.2. These technologies help banks improve operational efficiency, improve customer interaction, and reduce costs. However, along with the growth of the use of digital technologies, the threat of abuse and cyber-attacks also manifests itself. Therefore, banks should pay sufficient attention to the protection of their systems and data to ensure the security of customers and information confidentiality. In addition, competition in the banking services market has increased significantly in recent years. New players have emerged offering innovative and convenient products and services. Companies such as FinTech and BigTech that combine financial technology with their core services can become a serious threat to traditional banks. Therefore, banks must adapt to the new realities and focus on the development of innovative technologies and products that will provide a competitive advantage in the market. In particular, Capital One Bank uses AI for automatic text recognition on photo checks and automatic processing of customer transactions. Thus, the bank can ensure fast processing of transactions and avoid human error. JP Morgan Chase Bank uses machine learning and neural network technologies to analyze large amounts of data in order to identify suspicious transactions and prevent financial fraud. Santander Bank also uses AI to analyze customer behavior and provide customized product and service offerings. These are just a few examples of how banks can use AI.

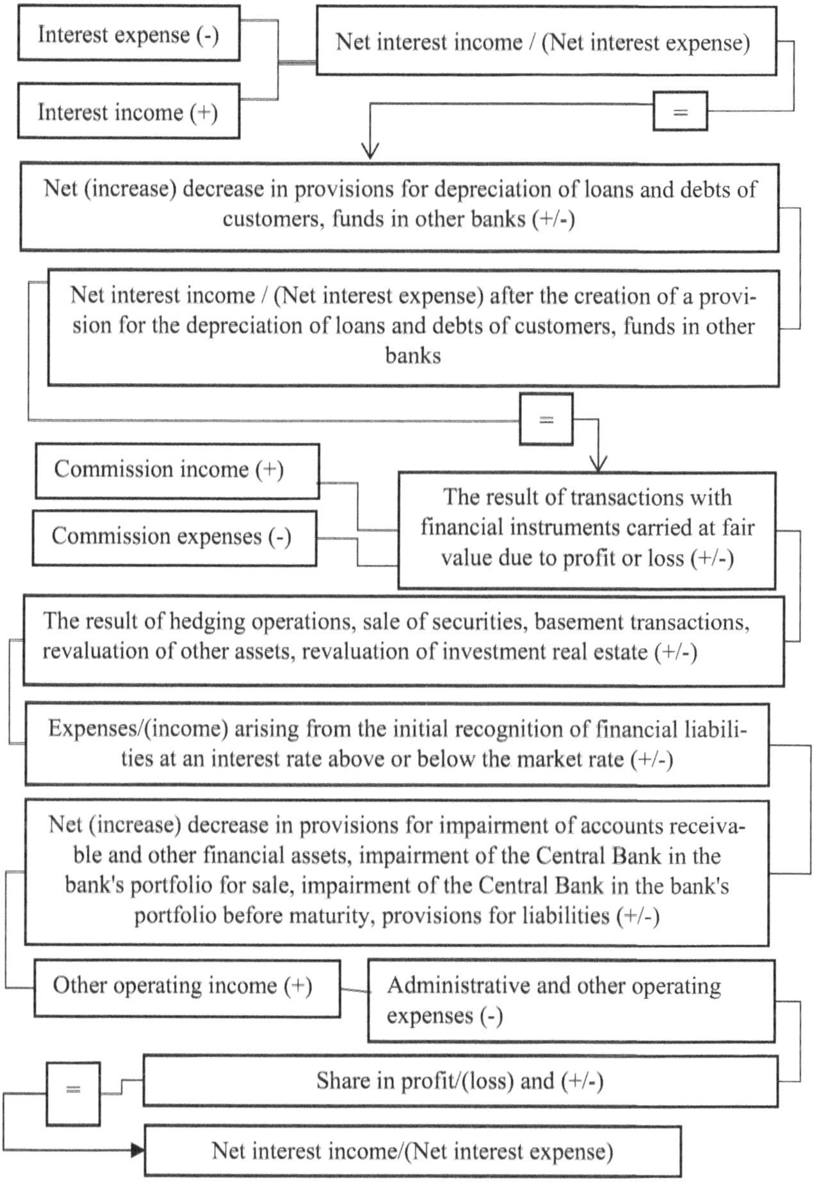

Fig. 19.1. The Process of Forming the Bank's Profit Taking into Account the Introduction of the Latest Digital Banking Products and Services.
Note: Compiled by the authors according to the data.

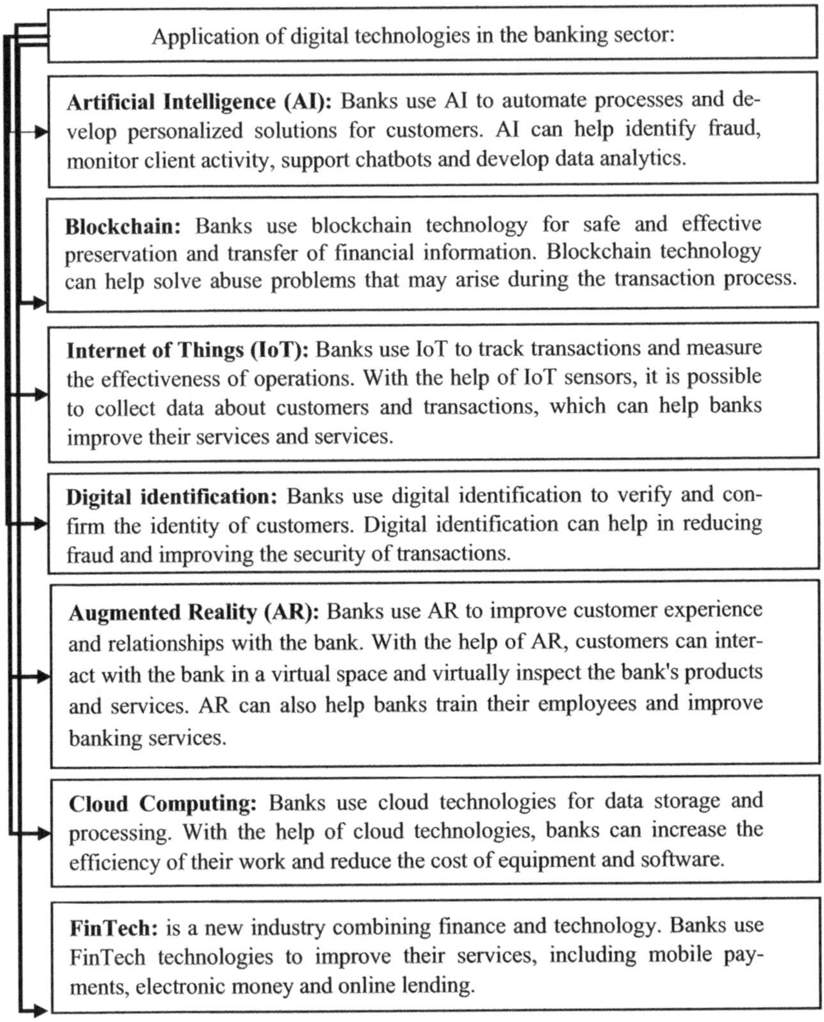

Fig. 19.2. The Latest Digital Technologies Used in the Banking Sector.
Note: Compiled by the authors based on the generalization of research.

AI is a very powerful technology that can provide significant competitive advantages for the banking sector, in particular:

- *Speed and efficiency*: AI can process and analyze large amounts of data in real time, which allows banks to make decisions quickly and efficiently and respond to changes in the market.

- *Improved accuracy*: AI can provide higher accuracy in data processing and solutions, which reduces the risk of errors and improves the quality of customer service.
- *Improved personalization*: AI can help banks make more personalized offers and services for customers, which ensures improved customer satisfaction and loyalty.
- *Minimizing costs*: AI can reduce the costs of working with data and processes, in particular for processing documents and responding to customer requests.
- *Increased security*: AI can help banks detect and prevent financial crimes, such as fraud, using analytical technologies and machine learning.

The use of AI in the banking sector can provide significant benefits for banks and their customers. This allows banks to be more efficient, accurate, and personalized in their activities and ensure greater security and customer satisfaction. In addition, the use of AI can help banks reduce costs and improve their competitiveness in the market. In general, the use of AI in the banking sector will contribute to improve the efficiency and accuracy of banks, reduce risks and costs, and also contribute to the selection of personalized approaches to their customers. The use of AI in the banking sector is a necessary step to achieve success and ensure the competitiveness of the bank in the market.

Thanks to AI, banking companies can improve the efficiency of their work, reduce costs, and improve interaction with their customers, thereby gaining competitive advantages in the market, in particular: improving the work of the banking sector; providing more efficient and secure operations; improving the quality of customer service and reducing the cost of working with data and processes. At the same time, the use of AI must be carried out in compliance with the requirements for data protection and customer confidentiality, which is very important for the banking industry (Fig. 19.3).

So, we can say that AI is an important tool for the banking industry to improve the quality of customer service and the efficiency of banks. However, it is important to ensure the protection of customer data and privacy by using AI with appropriate attention to these issues.

The use of AI in the banking sector has great potential and helps banks to improve the efficiency of their work, ensure the accuracy and security of operations, reduce risks and costs, and provide a personalized approach to customers. The realization of the opportunities provided by AI gives banks the opportunity to compete in the market and provide high-quality service to their customers. In a world where dynamism and speed of action are key success factors, the use of AI to automate banking processes is becoming a necessity.

4. CONCLUSIONS

So, the use of AI is another top trend in the field of FinTech, which has taken root in Ukraine. It has a direct impact on the development of the industry and, as various experts note, will continue to do so in the coming years.

Risk Analysis - Banks use machine learning systems to analyze large amounts of data and identify risks in accordance with customer behavior. For example, AI can be used to analyze a customer's credit history and their ability to repay a loan.

Document Processing – AI can help banks automate the document processing process. For example, character recognition applications can recognize and classify documents using example learning.

Customer Support – Banks can use chatbot systems that interact with customers using natural language and AI. This allows customers to get quick and effective answers to questions and problems.

Useful Tips – Banks can use AI systems to provide clients with useful financial management and investment advice.

Marketing Research – Banks can use AI to analyze customer data and identify market trends. This can help banks make better decisions on marketing strategies and forecasting demand for various products and services.

Automatic Credit Line Assignment – AI can be used to automatically assign credit lines to customers based on their credit rating and financial transaction history.

Processing large–scale transactions - Banks can use AI to automatically process large-scale transactions, such as mortgage transactions, which usually require a lot of time and effort from bank employees.

Market Analysis – AI can be used to analyze data from conventional sources, such as social networks and news portals, to determine market sentiment and trends. This allows banks to make better investment decisions and develop new products.

Fraud Detection – AI can be used to detect fraud and prevent it in the banking sector. Machine learning programs can analyze data from many sources, including internal and external data, to identify suspicious transactions and prevent financial crimes.

Customer Behavior Analysis – AI can be used to analyze customer behavior and predict their needs. Banks can use this data to support their customers and develop personalized offers and services that better meet their needs.

Customer Support – AI can be used to support customers 24/7, which allows banks to keep in touch with their customers at any time. This can be implemented through the use of chatbots and other forms of automated communication with customers.

Investment Recommendations – AI can be used for investment recommendations, helping clients make better decisions on their investments. AI can analyze the client's history and behavior to determine their level of risk and recommend investment products that meet their needs and goals.

Image and Signature Recognition – AI can be used to automatically recognize images and signatures on documents. This allows banks to reduce the time for processing documents and store them in digital format, which ensures the safety of information and ensures its security.

Network Data Analysis – AI can be used to analyze large amounts of network data, such as transactional data, helping banks identify suspicious transactions and prevent financial fraud.

Fig. 19.3. Ways of Using AI by Ukrainian Banks in Order to Ensure Competitive Advantages. *Note*: Compiled by the authors based on the generalization of the study.

AI is able to create patterns that humans cannot track. He can be a reliable consultant (even in matters of investment). Today, AI for FinTech is the key to obtaining loyalty and trust from consumers. For its part, this allows you to attract more funding, get higher profits, develop faster, and create new bright products.

AI and machine learning have benefited banks and financial technologies because they can process huge amounts of customer information. Then these data and information are compared to get the results of timely services/ products that customer's need, which, in fact, helped in the development of customer relationships.

Ensuring the competitive advantages of the Ukrainian banking sector in the global conditions of digital transformation is the most important task for the further development of the industry. To achieve this goal, banks must actively implement digital technologies and innovative solutions that allow them to compete more effectively in the market and provide high-quality customer service.

One of the key components of the successful development of the banking industry is the use of AI and machine learning to automate routine processes, data analysis, and risk forecasting. Thanks to this, banks can increase the efficiency of their work, ensure the accuracy and safety of operations, reduce risks and costs, and provide a personalized approach to customers.

Also, to ensure competitiveness in the market, the banking sector should actively introduce digital channels of communication with customers and expand the range of online services that allow financial transactions and interaction with the bank without visiting the office.

In addition, banks should actively cooperate with FinTech startups and other technology companies in order to introduce innovative solutions and develop new products and services that meet the needs of customers and meet the requirements of the modern digital world.

REFERENCES

Abuselidze, G. (2021). The impact of banking competition on economic growth and financial stability: An empirical investigation. *European Journal of Sustainable Development*, *10*(1), 203–220. https://doi.org/10.14207/ejsd.2021.v10n1p203

Abuselidze, G. (2023). Analysis and forecasts of the impact of non-performing loans on the economy in pandemic conditions. *Lecture Notes in Networks and Systems*, *620*, 129–143. https://doi.org/10.1007/978-3-031-26953-0_14

Abuselidze, G., & Kizinidze, M. (2019). Influence of central bank regulations on interbank competition in association with EU. *E3S Web of Conferences*, *135*, 04037. https://doi.org/10.1051/e3sconf/201913504037

Abuselidze, G., & Mamaladze, L. (2021). The impact of artificial intelligence on employment before and during pandemic: A comparative analysis. *Journal of Physics: Conference Series*, *1840*, 012040. https://doi.org/10.1088/1742-6596/1840/1/012040

Abuselidze, G., Ostapchuk, A., Talavyrya, M., & Lutsiak, V. (2022). Theoretical and methodological aspects of attracting speculative capital on the exchange market. *AIP conference proceedings*, *2656*, 020005. https://doi.org/10.1063/5.0106277

Abuselidze, G., & Slobodianyk, A. (2020). Social responsibility of business and government in the conditions of the COVID-19 pandemic. *E3S Web of Conferences*, *210*, 15016. doi:10.1051/e3sconf/202021015016

Acs, Z. J., Desai, S., & Hessels, J. (2008). Entrepreneurship, economic development and institutions. *Small Business Economics*, *31*, 219-234.

Agolla, J. E., Makara, T., & Monametsi, G. (2018). Impact of banking innovations on customer attraction, satisfaction and retention: The case of commercial banks in Botswana. *International Journal of Electronic Banking*, *1*(2), 150–170.

AI in Fintech Market – Growth, Trends, Covid-19 Impact, and Forecasts (2023–2028). Report. Retrieved from https://www.mordorintelligence.com/industry-reports/ai-in-fintech-market.

Banking and Capital Markets. Retrieved from https://kpmg.com/xx/en/home/services.html

Carlsson, B. (2007). Innovation systems: A survey of the literature from a Schumpeterian perspective. *Elgar Companion to Neo-Schumpeterian Economics*, 857–871.

Drucker, P. (2014). *Innovation and entrepreneurship*. Abingdon: Routledge.

Frame, W. S., Wall, L. D., & White, L. J. (2018). Technological change and financial innovation in banking: Some implications for Fintech. In A. N. Berger, P. Molyneux, & J. O. S. Wilson (Eds.), The Oxford handbook of banking (3rd ed., pp. 262–284). Oxford: Oxford University Press.

Frame, W. S., & White, L. J. (2004). Empirical studies of financial innovation: Lots of talk, little action? *Journal of Economic Literature*, *42*(1), 116–144.

Gomber, P., Kauffman, R. J., Parker, C., & Weber, B. W. (2018). On the fintech revolution: Interpreting the forces of innovation, disruption, and transformation in financial services. *Journal of Management Information Systems*, *35*(1), 220–265.

Goyal, K. A., & Joshi, V. (2011). A study of social and ethical issues in banking industry. *International Journal of Economics and Research*, *2*(5), 49–57.

Kniazieva, T. V., Maryna, A. S., Shevchenko, A. V., Shvets, K., & Goncharenko, M. (2022). Issues of competitiveness estimation of financial institutions. *Review of Economics and Finance*, 2022, *20*, 917–925.

Miller, M. (2018). Cross-border banking and monetary independence. In P. Hartmann, H. Huang, & D. Schoenmaker (Eds.), *The changing fortunes of central banking* (p. 276). Cambridge: Cambridge University Press.

Miller, M. (2021). Choosing the narrative: The shadow banking crisis in light of Covid. *Open Economies Review*, *32*(2), 291–310.

Miller, S. M. (2020). Empirical analysis of production economics: Applications to banking. In S. C. Ray, R. G. Chambers, & S. C. Kumbhakar (Eds.), *Handbook of production economics* (pp. 1–27). Berlin: Springer.

Onetti, A., Zucchella, A., Jones, M. V., & McDougall-Covin, P. P. (2012). Internationalization, innovation and entrepreneurship: Business models for new technology-based firms. *Journal of Management & Governance*, *16*, 337–368. https://doi.org/10.1007/s10997-010-9154-1

Porter, M. (2008, January 22). Clusters, innovation, and competitiveness: New findings and implications for policy. In Presentation given at the European Presidency conference on innovation and clusters in Stockholm, Stockholm (p. 23).

Porter, M. E. (2000). Location, competition, and economic development: Local clusters in a global economy. *Economic Development Quarterly*, *14*(1), 15–34.

Porter, M. E., & Sölvell, Ö. (1998). The role of geography in the process of innovation and the sustainable competitive advantage of firms. In A. Chandler, P. Hagström, & Ö. Sölvell (Eds.), *The dynamic firm: The role of technology, strategy, organization, and regions* (pp. 440–457). Oxford: Oxford University Press.

Retail Banking: Digital Transformation & Disruptor Opportunities 2020–2024. Retrieved from https://www.juniperresearch.com/researchstore/fintech-payments/digital-banking-trends-report

Shpachuk, V., Hornyk, V., Kravchenko, S., Vizirov, B., Aleinikova, O., & Abuselidze, G. (2023). State policy of cooperation between countries and global institutions: Condition and prospects. *E3S Web of Conferences*, *371*, 05004. doi:10.1051/e3sconf/202337105004

Slobodianyk, A., & Abuselidze, G. (2021). Influence of speculative operations on the investment capital: An empirical analysis of capital markets. *E3S Web of Conferences*, *234*, 00084. doi:10.1051/e3sconf/202123400084

Slobodianyk, A., Abuselidze, G., Buriak, R., Muzychenko, A., Momot, O., & Romanova, L. (2022). Stock trading indices: A mechanism for attracting speculative capital. *Lecture Notes in Networks and Systems*, *246*, 897–905. doi:10.1007/978-3-030-81619-3_100

Slobodianyk, A., & Mohylevska, O. (2022). Peculiarities of speculative operations on the capital market in Ukraine. *International Science Journal of Management, Economics & Finance*, *1*(2), 8–14. Retrieved from https://isg-journal.com/isjmef/article/view/9

Srivastava, S. (2023). Prospective application of blockchain in mutual fund industry. In A. Nayyar, M. Naved, & R. Rameshwar (Eds.), *New horizons for industry 4.0 in modern business. contributions to environmental sciences & innovative business technology* (pp. 121–148). Cham: Springer. https://doi.org/10.1007/978-3-031-20443-2_6

Ziemnowicz, C. (1942). Joseph A. Schumpeter and innovation. *Socialism and Democracy*, *2*(1), 2–4.

CHAPTER 20

CULTURE AND BUSINESS PERFORMANCE OF MICROENTERPRISES IN THE ANCASH REGION – PERU

Nilda Barrutia-Montoya[a], Elia Ramirez-Asis[b], K. P. Jaheer Mukthar[d], Mercedes Huerta-Soto[b], Robert Concepción-Lázaro[a] and Juan Villanueva-Calderón[c]

[a]*Universidad Cesar Vallejo, Lima, Peru*
[b]*Universidad Nacional Santiago Antunez de Mayolo, Huaraz, Peru*
[c]*Universidad Señor de Sipán, Chiclayo, Perú*
[d]*Kristu Jayanti College, Autonomous, Bengaluru, India*

ABSTRACT

Many scholars and practitioners in the fields of business and management have recently published theoretical and empirical studies on the subject of business culture and its impact on its growth and effectiveness; yet, there has been a dearth of research on the topic of how organizational culture affects productivity. Moreover, there are hardly any theoretical or empirical research that examines these two concepts within the context of a micro-enterprise. This chapter uses a sample of 279 Ancash Region microenterprises to investigate the effect of local entrepreneurial culture on businesses' overall performance. Among the four types of entrepreneurial cultures studied, only the Hierarchical culture was shown to have no effect on the degree of performance of the micro-enterprises. There is evidence of a significant causal relationship between the

Digital Technology and Changing Roles in Managerial and Financial Accounting: Theoretical Knowledge and Practical Application
Studies in Managerial and Financial Accounting, Volume 36, 229–239

Published under exclusive licence by Emerald Publishing Limited
ISSN: 1479-3512/doi:10.1108/S1479-351220240000036021

variables studied, the coefficient of determination was; business performance ($r^2 = 0.796$), with an SRMR of 0.037, the confirmatory model is relevant within its range of accuracy, while market culture has the greatest impact on business performance.

Keywords: Adhocratic culture; business performance; clan culture; entrepreneurial culture; hierarchical culture; microenterprises

INTRODUCTION

Business and management experts have spent the better part of the last two decades studying the impact of company culture on productivity at work (Ortega-Verdugo, 2020). However, prevalent practice in academic circles to find multiple articles stating that corporate culture significantly improves business performance (BP), but relatively few publications have focused on demonstrating that different types of corporate culture also have a direct and indirect relationship with BP (Pérez, 2019), There has to be more research done to back up the theory that there is a correlation between corporate culture and business success.

In this sense, multiple studies published in the business literature have found inconsistencies in the relationship between corporate culture and firm performance (Melgarejo & Simon-Elorz, 2019); furthermore, business culture and company performance have been proven to have a favorable and substantial association in another research as well (Koontz, Weihrich, & Cannice, 2020; Rajagopal et al., 2022). But then, how can corporate culture be defined? There are as many definitions published in the current literature as there are authors who have written on this important topic, but one of the most widely used by authors is the one given by Cordero-Olivares (2020) who states that corporate culture can be defined as "the general constellation of beliefs, customs, values, behavioral norms and forms that characterize firms and make them unique and different from one another."

Similarly, corporate culture has generally been considered as one of the most important elements that impact on the working dynamics of organizations, yet this basic construct has always been the subject of study among researchers, academics, and practitioners in business and management sciences (Coso-Paucarchuco & Quiroz, 2021), especially in the impact that is manifested in the existing differences between two systematic elements within organizations, while investigating the connection between company culture and output, which can have a positive or negative influence on companies, primarily in small and medium-sized enterprises (microenterprises) (Barrios et al., 2020).

Of course, there are cultural similarities between companies with equal or close partnerships, which are generally strongly influenced by aspects of work and values, as well as containing important elements related to the organizations themselves, such as the type of culture they are implementing (David, 2017). It is also important to consider in the study of business culture the relationship between the leader and the employees and workers of the organization, which is why it is not convenient to overlook this important element in organizations (Casares, 2022), especially in the business culture of microenterprises (Hinojosa-Gómez, Limón-Villegas, & Navarrete-Cova, 2020).

Therefore, as consider, the best way to measure firm performance is constantly being studied through the development of theories focused on firm culture, which has given rise to a diversity of models and theories that have been published in the literature. Hence, a large number of ideas on the influence of entrepreneurial culture on firm performance are currently considered, but there is relatively a dearth of studies in the existing literature that have related these two constructs (Koontz et al., 2020), and even fewer that have focused on analyzing the impact of entrepreneurial culture on the performance of microenterprises.

In this context, entrepreneurial culture has been studied and analyzed by researchers, academics, and practitioners from different perspectives, and theoretical and more recent empirical research has centered on quantifying the link between entrepreneurial culture and outcomes like productivity, organizational structure, leadership styles, efficiency, and effectiveness, but there are few studies that have focused on analyzing the effects and influence that entrepreneurial culture has on firm performance (Pardo-Quezada & Malla-Alvarado, 2022).

LITERATURE REVIEW

Business culture plays a fundamental role both in creating the values and behavior of employees and workers in firms, as well as in achieving firm performance since according to Demuner-Flores, Saavedra-García, and Cortes Castillo (2022), firm performance is strongly associated with the development of the organizational culture that firms have. Also, Pallathadka et al. (2023) concluded that the success of firms depends to a large extent on the appropriate fit between firm strategies and culture. Therefore Shaikh et al. (2022) corporate culture may greatly enhance BP since culture can be seen as an integrative process that governs organizational behavior (Chiavenato & González, 2017).

However, found typically in the business science literature that despite the fact that corporate culture plays an essential role in the behavior of workers in the organization, there is a lack of consistency between corporate culture and BP, according to research that have presented both theoretical and empirical data, especially in the case of microenterprises (Ferrer Abella-Garcés, and Maza, 2019). Thus, for example, studies that have found a strong positive and significant association between corporate culture and firm performance are those by Thommandru et al. (2021), among more studies.

In addition, other research shows a negative association between corporate culture and firm performance, such as the study by Pelekais and Carvajalino (2020) who concluded that not all businesses or organizations find cultural considerations to be of importance have a cultural development that can generate a positive influence on corporate performance. Providing evidence in this regard,

Findyartini. Greviana, Felaza, Faruqi, Zahratul Afifah, and Auliya Firdausy (2022) found in their study that organizational culture development has little or no effect on BP. In a later study, Ramirez-Asis, Maguina, Infantes, and Naranjo-Toro (2020) concluded that corporate culture is an essential predictor only when accordance with established theories of business success, these findings provide more evidence that the culture of an organization significantly affects how well it operates.

In addition, advocates of the association between business culture and corporate performance have recently provided further theoretical and empirical evidence confirming a strong influence and high power between these two constructs (Cuevas-Vargas et al., 2020). Thus, Yating et al. (2022) concluded that corporate culture has positive effects on corporate performance. Likewise, Misigo et al. (2019) considered that when corporate culture is proactive and aligned to business strategies, it is more likely to have a positive influence on BP. Obviously, if the corporate culture is consistent with the values of employees and workers, then the organization will perform better (Chiavenato & González, 2017; Rajagopal et al., 2022).

Cheng, Dai, Lin, and Ye (2021) found significant empirical evidence in their study with a sample of 34 companies representing 25 different types of industries and using two indices: work organization and decision making, which were found to have a strong correlation with the financial performance of the companies. In addition, these researchers also found that corporate culture can be a predictor of corporate performance in the short term, especially when performance is considered with indicators such as investment, capital, and sales, leading to more and better results for firms as well.

In addition, Demuner-Flores et al. (2022) presented a model that looked at the impact of corporate culture on firm effectiveness, whose components fully related corporate culture to organizational involvement, adaptability, consistency, and mission, with mission and involvement being the two components more associated with effectiveness and profitability than the other components. Furthermore, Shaikh et al., 2022) concluded that corporate culture is strongly associated with BP, especially when the firm has a humanistic orientation that is characterized by cooperation between different members of the organization such as teamwork, employee upgrading and empowerment.

Similarly, Yating et al. (2022) concluded as shown in their research that corporate culture has a significant impact on various firm outcomes, including firm performance, as employee involvement is very effective in motivating employees and workers in the organization, and these in turn have a close relationship with the results achieved by the firm. Furthermore, Thommandru et al. (2021) considered that not only business strategies and organizational culture must be aligned to achieve a higher level of BP but also that both elements would have to be compatible with the business environment since when the business environment changes drastically, the business culture has to adapt to achieve higher performance.

Pallathadka et al. (2023) analyzed the relationship between the four cultural dimensions of the value competitiveness model (group culture, developed culture, Hierarchical culture, and rational culture) and the four types of BP (innovation in product and process quality, product and process innovation, and overall product quality). The data were analyzed across 194 small and medium-sized firms in Australia who were consistently engaged in knowledge management practices related to quality and innovation issues and found a positive association between corporate culture and firm performance, mainly through developed culture which was the strongest predictor of the four dimensions and product quality.

In the same way, the organizational culture that companies have is a basic point that has to be evaluated (Solarte, Solarte, & Barahona, 2020) because it usually leads to a result on company performance, which can be not so reliable because it is not known in detail how the internal status or the level of influence exerted by the organizational culture is (Cuevas-Vargas et al., 2020). Therefore, organizational culture will always be influenced by the relationship between the company's employees and workers (Cheng et al., 2021), so it is important that all staff in the organization know and share the company's values, and work as a team to achieve a better level of BP.

Finally, each organizational culture has its own potential value that is reflected in the traits of the firms themselves, especially those firms that have a developing culture (Koontz et al., 2020). It is also important that firms, especially MSEs, assess their own risks from the effects of their competition (Rodríguez, Pumarejo, & Hernández, 2023), from the effects of the uncertain business environment (Casares, 2022), and from their own characteristics and values (Pardo-Quezada & Malla-Alvarado, 2022). Ultimately, organizational culture has always been considered a cornerstone of any company (Findyartini et al., 2022), which is why it has high positive and significant effects on the achievement of goals and, above all, on the attainment of BP (Solarte et al., 2020).

METHODOLOGY

Due to the study variables such as entrepreneurial culture and BP, which are important for microenterprises in the Ancash Region, qualitative research was carried out in a first stage, which was evaluated through a "Business Panel" with the participation of representatives of microenterprises, federal and state government, and financial institution support managers. Analysis and discourse were the primary goals of this qualitative study of the data collection instrument that would be used later, as well as qualitative information that would allow for a deeper and more detailed knowledge of the business culture and performance of microenterprises in the Ancash Region.

Likewise, for the development of this work, the Business Directory 2020 of the Peruvian Business Information System (SIEP) of the Ancash Region was taken as a reference for 8,661 companies. The research process only included companies with between 5 and 50 employees, leaving a sample of 1,128 companies. The original sample for this study consisted of 600 companies. A straight application of the survey was made to the managers of micro-companies between September and December 2022, through a sample of 500 companies, finally receiving 385 surveys, of which six had to be invalidated because they did not meet the requirements established by the survey itself, thus validating 279 surveys and finally registering an 80% response rate.

RESULTS

In addition, the model proposed by Misigo et al. (2019), which clearly identifies four types of company culture: Clan, Adhocratic, Market, and Hierarchical, was used to measure company culture. For the measurement of the performance variable, the model proposed by Findyartini et al. (2022) was used, which includes 12 items (three items for each of the four models) and four models: Models of Human Relations, Rational Decision-Making, Open Systems, and Internal Procedures, on a scale from 1 (Strongly Disagree) to 5 (Strongly Agree), where 1 is the most extreme and 5 is the mildest.

To further examine the performance scale's dependability and validity, a confirmatory factor analysis (CFA) was run using the maximum likelihood approach in SPSS v26 (Supo & Zacarias, 2020). Therefore, we used Cronbach's alpha and the composite dependability index (CFI) to measure dependability, proposed by Sarstedt and Cheah (2019), obtaining results that show a good fit of the data (S-BX2 = 171.854; df = 48; $p = 0.000$; NFI = 0.973; NNFI = 0. 981; CFI = 0.979; and RMSEA = 0.061), in addition to the fact that the values of Cronbachs alpha and CFI are above 0.7 which indicates that there is evidence of good reliability, thus justifying the use of the performance scale (Richter, Schubring, Hauff, Ringle, & Sarstedt, 2020).

Additionally, the recommendations made by Hair et al. (2021) were considered in this empirical study to improve the correctness of the statistics when normality of the performance scale variables is assumed to be present, and robust statistics were employed to give stronger proof that the performance scale was statistically appropriate (Sarstedt & Cheah, 2019). Also, all associated factor items are significant ($p = 0.01$) in the CFA, demonstrating convergent validity, the size of all standardized factor loadings are greater than 0.60 (Richter et al., 2020), and the index of variance extracted of each pair of constructs of the performance model is greater than 0.5 (Afthanorhan, Ghazali, & Rashid, 2021), indicating that the performance model has a good fit to the data and has a good level of validity as can be seen in Fig. 20.1.

As far as discriminant validity is concerned, the measurement of the performance model was carried out by means of two tests: the confidence interval test and the variance extracted test. Regarding the first test, with a 95% confidence interval none of the latent factor elements of the correlation matrix contains the value of 1.0 (Supo & Zacarias, 2020). For the second test, the EVI between any two constructs is larger than the EVI between any single build (Hair et al., 2021). Therefore, based on these criteria it is possible to conclude that the different measures performed in this empirical study show proof of validity, reliability, and capacity to discriminate.

To answer the hypotheses of the empirical study, structural equation modeling (SEM) was used with EQS 6.1 software (Sarstedt & Cheah, 2019). With respect

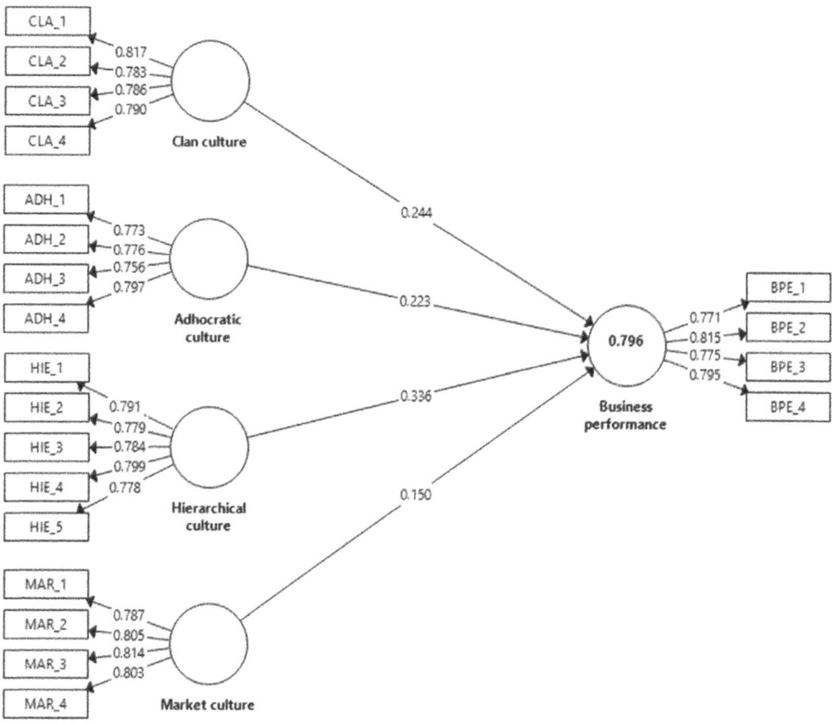

Fig. 20.1. Research Model.
Source: Own elaboration.

to the nomological validity of the business culture and performance model, results from the measurement model were compared to those from the theoretical model, and there was no statistically significant difference found. This allows us to account for the correlations we see between the two models' latent variable constructions (Hair et al., 2021). The results obtained by means of SEM can be better appreciated in Table 20.1.

The results obtained in Table 20.1 allow us to establish that with respect to the *H1*, $\beta = 0.224$, 4.746, and 0.000, $p < 0.001$, respectively, indicate that Clan culture has a positive and significant influence on the four types of BP. For the case of the *H2* stated, $\beta = 0.223$, 3.443, and 0.001, $p < 0.01$, respectively, indicate that also Adhocratic culture has a positive and significant influence on the four types of BP. However, for the *H3* posed, $\beta = 0.336$, 6.099, and 0.000, $p < 0.001$, respectively, clearly show that hierarchical culture has a positive influence on the four types of BP. Finally, with respect to the *H4* stated, $\beta = 0.150$, 2.193, and 0.001, $p < 0.01$, respectively, prove that the market culture affects business success in a good way.

In summary, of the four types of entrepreneurial culture that every organization has, it stands out that the Clan, Adhocratic, and Market cultures are present

Table 20.1. Testing the Hypotheses.

Hypothesis		Standardized Path Coefficient (β)	D.E.	Boots Trapping	*p*-Value
Hip 1	Clan culture → BP	0.224	0.051	4.746	0.000
Hip 2	Adhocratic culture → BP	0.223	0.065	3.443	0.001
Hip 3	Hierarchical culture → BP	0.336	0.055	6.099	0.000
Hip 4	Market culture → BP	0.150	0.068	2.193	0.001

Source: Own elaboration.

in the microenterprises of the Ancash Region and have a positive and significant influence on BP, but even though the Hierarchical culture is also present in the microenterprises, it does not have a significant positive influence on the performance of the enterprises. This allows us to establish that when the managers of the microenterprises establish a hierarchy in the organization, and when they do not allow employees and workers to break the hierarchical rules established within the enterprise, then business activities do not have a strong influence on the performance of the enterprise.

DISCUSSION

Based on the findings of this empirical investigation, two main points may be drawn. Firstly, the Clan, Adhocratic, and Market cultures present in the microenterprises generate in the employees and workers of the enterprises a series of entrepreneurial activities that have a positive impact on the level of performance of the enterprises. In this sense, the culture established in the microenterprises of the Ancash Region (Clan, Adhocratic, and Market), which determines both the values and the behaviors of employees, workers, and managers of the organization, has become today not only a business strategy but rather a fundamental tool to significantly improve the level of performance of enterprises (Misigo et al., 2019).

Secondly, the Hierarchical culture that is present in various microenterprises established in the Ancash Region does not generate any significant positive influence on the performance of the companies, which is why the managers of the microenterprises that have this type of culture generally establish very rigid rules for the behavior of employees and workers and institute a hierarchy in the organization's decision making. This slows down or inhibits workers and employees from contributing possible solutions to the main problems of the company, thus generating apathy and disinterest in participating in the various activities carried out by the authorities of the microenterprises, which has a negative impact on the level of BP (Findyartini et al., 2022).

On the other hand, these results also have a series of implications for both the enterprises and the managers of the MSEs. Thus, for the case of the enterprises it will be of utmost importance that if they want to significantly increase their BP then they will have to adopt and implement a Clan, Adhocratic, or Market type of organizational culture, as any of these three types of enterprise culture generates a significant increase in the level of performance in the enterprises. Therefore, the enterprise culture is fundamental in the organization if it is looking for alternatives in order to boost its efficiency; therefore the microenterprises of the Ancash Region, like any other enterprise in Peru or in any other country, have the possibility to increase their enterprise performance by improving their enterprise culture.

In this sense, the managers of microenterprises have in their hands the important decision of deciding what type of business culture they will adopt and implement in their business, considering that a high percentage will depend on this in order to facilitate the generation of a higher level of BP. Likewise, managers will have to implement a series of values among workers and employees, seeking at all times that the staff participate in the achievement of these values as well as in the definition of these values because it will depend on this that the culture that is defined in the organization is understood and accepted by employees, workers, and managers of the microenterprises; in addition, it will allow the company to have greater possibilities of achieving a better BP than other companies.

Finally, managers who have decided to implement a hierarchical business culture in their organizations should think about changing this culture if they want to drastically raise the BP levels of their companies. Otherwise, various obstacles or challenges will prevent microenterprises from improving their performance and could turn into serious difficulties for their permanence in the market. One of the ways in which microenterprises can remain competitive is by adopting and implementing a certain business culture. However, it is important for managers to realize that only three of the four organizational cultures discussed by Ferrer et al. (2019) have a significant impact on BP.

CONCLUSIONS

From the results we can conclude that Clan culture has a positive and substantial impact on all four categories of entrepreneurial performance. The results of the alternative hypothesis tests show that adhocratic culture also has a positive and substantial impact on the four dimensions of BP mentioned above. The results of *H3*, however, show that Hierarchical culture does have an insignificant effect on the four measures of entrepreneurial growth. Finally, the results of *H4* indicate that market culture positively influences entrepreneurial performance.

Clan, adhocratic, and market cultures are the most notable of the four forms of entrepreneurial culture that every firm possesses, which are particularly prevalent in microenterprises in the Ancash Region and have a positive and significant impact on BP. However, Hierarchical culture is also present in microenterprises in the Ancash Region, although with less impact on BP.

REFERENCES

Afthanorhan, A., Ghazali, P. L., & Rashid, N. (2021). Discriminant validity: A comparison of CBSEM and consistent PLS using Fornell & Larcker and HTMT approaches. *Journal of Physics: Conference Series*, *1874*(1), 012085. https://doi.org/10.1088/1742-6596/1874/1/012085

Barrios, D., Restrepo-Escobar, F. J., & Cerón-Muñoz, M. (2020). Desempeño empresarial en la industria lechera. *Suma de Negocios*, *11*(25), 180–185. https://doi.org/10.14349/sumneg/2020.v11.n25.a9

Casares, C. A. (2022). Hacia una cultura empresarial que incorpore la salud mental. *Capital Humano: Revista Para la Integración y Desarrollo de Los Recursos Humanos*, *379*, 25. Retrieved from https://dialnet.unirioja.es/servlet/articulo?codigo=8589212

Cordero-Olivares, R. A. (2020). Impacto del microcrédito en las condiciones de vida (ingreso y cultura empresarial) de mujeres tabasqueñas. *Caso Compartamos Banco Hitos de Ciencias Económico Administrativas*, *26*(75), 127–138. https://doi.org/10.19136/hitos.a26n75.3978

Coso-Paucarchuco, K. M., & Quiroz, M. A. (2021). Implementación de la cultura empresarial para el mejoramiento del desempeño laboral. *E-IDEA Journal of Business Sciences*, *3*(11), 25–35. https://doi.org/10.53734/eidea.vol3.id90

Cuevas-Vargas, H., Parga-Montoya, N., & Estrada, S. (2020). Incidencia de la innovación en marketing en el rendimiento empresarial: Una aplicación basada en modelamiento con ecuaciones estructurales. *Estudios Gerenciales*, *36*(154), 66–79. https://doi.org/10.18046/j.estger.2020.154.3475

Cheng, J., Dai, Y., Lin, S., & Ye, H. (2021). Clan culture and family ownership concentration: Evidence from China. *China Economic Review*, *70*, 101692. https://doi.org/10.1016/j.chieco.2021.101692

Chiavenato, I., & González, E. A. (2017). *Comportamiento organizacional: la Dinámica del éxito en las organizaciones*. México DF: McGraw-Hill.

David, F. (2017). *Conceptos de administración estratégica*. México, DF: Pearson.

Demuner-Flores, M. D. R., Saavedra-García, M. L., & Cortes Castillo, M. D. R. (2022). Rendimiento empresarial, resilencia e innovación en PYMES. *Investigación Administrativa*, *51*(130). https://doi.org/10.35426/iav51n130.01

Ferrer, J. R., Abella-Garcés, S., & Maza, M. T. (2019). Spanish wine cooperatives' business performance: Innovation capabilities and Miles and Snow strategies. *Journal of Wine Economics*, *14*(4), 409–416. https://doi.org/10.1017/jwe.2019.36

Findyartini, A., Greviana, N., Felaza, E., Faruqi, M., Zahratul Afifah, T., & Auliya Firdausy, M. (2022). Professional identity formation of medical students: A mixed-methods study in a hierarchical and collectivist culture. *BMC Medical Education*, *22*(1), 443.

Hair, J. F., Hult, G. T., Ringle, C. M., Sarstedt, M., Danks, N. P., & Ray, S. (2021). *Partial least squares structural equation modeling (PLS-SEM) using R: A workbook*. https://doi.org/10.1007/978-3-030-80519-7

Hinojosa-Gómez, C. A., Limón-Villegas, E. S., & Navarrete-Cova, C. (2020). Cultura empresarial en las pymes del municipio de Tamazula de Gordiano, Jalisco (México). *Ánfora*, *27*(49), 143–172. https://doi.org/10.30854/anf.v27.n49.2020.743

Koontz, H., Weihrich, H., & Cannice, M. V. (2020). *Essentials of management – An international, innovation and leadership perspective* (11th ed.). New Delhi: McGraw-Hill Education.

Melgarejo, Z., & Simon-Elorz, K. (2019). Desempeño empresarial y ciclo económico en la industria de alimentos y bebidas colombiana: Una aproximación no paramétrica. *Estudios Gerenciales*, *35*(151), 190–202. https://doi.org/10.18046/j.estger.2019.151.3162

Misigo, G. K., Were, S., & Odhiambo, R. (2019). Influence of adhocracy culture on performance of public water companies in Kenya. *International Academic Journal of Human Resource and Business Administration*, *3*(5), 84–103. Retrieved from https://www.iajournals.org/index.php/8-articles/529-iajhrba-v3-i5-84-103

Ortega-Verdugo, F. J. (2020). *Resultado, rentabilidad y caja*. Ortega Verdugo: ESIC Editorial.

Pallathadka, H., Wenda, A., Ramirez-Asís, E., Asís-López, M., Flores-Albornoz, J., & Pha-sinam, K. (2023). Classification and prediction of student performance data using various machine learning algorithms. *Materials Today: Proceedings*, *80*, 3782–3785. https://doi.org/10.1016/j.matpr.2021.07.382

Pardo-Quezada, S. L., & Malla-Alvarado, F. Y. (2022). La cultura empresarial y su relación con la dirección de las orquestas sinfónicas del Ecuador en el periodo 2018–2020. *Ciencia Latina Revista Científica Multidisciplinar*, *6*(4), 482–524. https://doi.org/10.37811/cl_rcm.v6i4.2601

Pelekais, E. A., & Carvajalino, D. V. (2020). Rendimiento empresarial sostenible para las micro, pequeñas y medianas empresas en Colombia. *Revista Internacional de Cooperación y Desarrollo*, *2*(7), 104–118. Retrieved from https://revistas.usb.edu.co/index.php/Cooperacion/article/view/4955

Pérez, J. B. (2019). *Cultural empresarial*. Málaga: Editorial Elearning.

Rajagopal, N. K., Qureshi, N. I., Durga, S., Ramirez Asis, E. H., Huerta Soto, R. M., Gupta, S. K., & Deepak, S. (2022). Future of business culture: An artificial intelligence-driven digital framework for organization decision-making process. *Complexity*, 1–14. https://doi.org/10.1155/2022/7796507

Ramirez-Asis, E., Maguina, M. E., Infantes, S. E., & Naranjo-Toro, M. (2020). Emotional intelligence, competencies and performance of the university professor: Using the SEM-PLS partial least squares technique. *Revista Electrónica Interuniversitaria de Formación Profesorado*, *23*, 99–114. https://doi.org/10.6018/reifop.428261

Richter, N. F., Schubring, S., Hauff, S., Ringle, C. M., & Sarstedt, M. (2020). When predictors of outcomes are necessary: Guidelines for the combined use of PLS-SEM and NCA. *Industrial Management & Data Systems*, *120*(12), 2243–2267. https://doi.org/10.1108/IMDS-11-2019-0638

Rodríguez, J. C. C., Pumarejo, J. R. B., & Hernández, V. V. (2023). Innovación y desempeño empresarial: Estudio bibliométrico. *Revista Venezolana de Gerencia: RVG*, *28*(102), 888–908. https://doi.org/10.52080/rvgluz.28.102.27

Sarstedt, M., & Cheah, J. H. (2019). Partial least squares structural equation modeling using SmartPLS: A software review. *Journal of Marketing Analytics*, *7*(3), 162–202. https://doi.org/10.1057/s41270-019-00058-3

Shaikh, A. A., Lakshmi, K. S., Tongkachok, K., Alanya-Beltran, J., Ramirez-Asis, E., & Perez-Falcon, J. (2022). Empirical analysis in analysing the major factors of machine learning in enhancing the e-business through structural equation modelling (SEM) approach. *International Journal of System Assurance Engineering and Management*, *13*(Suppl 1), 681–689. https://doi.org/10.1007/s13198-021-01590-1

Solarte, C. M., Solarte, M. L., & Barahona, J. F. (2020). Cultura organizacional e innovación en la orientación al mercado de empresas familiares de Pasto (Colombia). *Contaduría y Administración*, *65*(1), 1–25. https://doi.org/10.22201/fca.24488410e.2019.1725

Supo, J., & Zacarias, H. (2020). *Metodología de la investigación científica: Para las ciencias de la salud y las ciencias sociales*. Peru: Sincie.

Thommandru, A., Espinoza-Maguiña, M., Ramirez-Asis, E., Ray, S., Naved, M., & Guzman-Avalos, M. (2021). Role of tourism and hospitality business in economic development. *Materials Today: Proceedings*, *80*(3), 2901–2904. https://doi.org/10.1016/j.matpr.2021.07.059

Yating, Y., Mughal, N., Wen, J., Ngan, T. T., Ramirez-Asis, E., & Maneengam, A. (2022). Economic performance and natural resources commodity prices volatility: Evidence from global data. *Resources Policy*, *78*, 102879. https://doi.org/10.1016/j.resourpol.2022.102879

CHAPTER 21

CUSTOMER SATISFACTION OF SMALL FINANCE BANKS IN INDIA

N. M. Vipulkumar, Cherian Thomas and Ibha Rani

Kristu Jayanti College (Autonomous), Bengaluru, Karnataka, India

ABSTRACT

Any banking institution's success depends heavily on customer satisfaction. Understanding and evaluating customer satisfaction has become crucial with the rise of small finance banks (SFBs) in India, which serve the underserved and unbanking segments of society. In the context of SFBs in India, this chapter aims to examine the variables affecting customer satisfaction as well as how it affects these banks' overall performance and sustainability. This study will help us better understand the dynamics of customer satisfaction in the Indian financial landscape by examining the particular difficulties and opportunities that SFBs face.

Keywords: Small finance bank; SFBs customer satisfaction; banking in India; banks in India; banking system in India; financial inclusion; micro finance; types of banking

1. INTRODUCTION

SFBs are a category of banks in India that have been established to provide basic banking services and financial inclusion to underserved and unbanked sections of society. SFBs were introduced by the Reserve Bank of India (RBI) in 2015 as part of its efforts to promote financial inclusion and expand access to formal banking

Digital Technology and Changing Roles in Managerial and Financial Accounting: Theoretical Knowledge and Practical Application
Studies in Managerial and Financial Accounting, Volume 36, 241–246

Published under exclusive licence by Emerald Publishing Limited
ISSN: 1479-3512/doi:10.1108/S1479-351220240000036022

services in rural and semi-urban areas. SFBs have been a prominent player in the Indian banking industry in recent years, offering financial services to underprivileged groups in society. Small enterprises, farmers, low-income households, and others with little access to banking services are the main beneficiaries of these institutions' attention. Customer satisfaction grows in importance as SFBs work to increase financial inclusion, which is crucial for their long-term sustainability. Customer satisfaction is widely acknowledged as a key determinant of a bank's effectiveness, profitability, and client loyalty. Customers who are happy with their banks typically maintain longer relationships with them, carry out repeated transactions, and offer favorable word-of-mouth recommendations, all of which benefit the bank's reputation and efforts to attract new clients. Understanding the elements that affect customer satisfaction in the particular setting of SFBs is important.

The purpose of this research study is to look into the factors that affect customer satisfaction in India's Small Finance banking industry. The study will examine a number of variables that affect consumer satisfaction, including product offerings, interest rates, trust and transparency, customer service quality, accessibility and ease of banking channels, and financial literacy programmes run by SFBs. Insights into the aspects that affect customer satisfaction will be revealed by looking at these elements, and SFBs will be able to pinpoint areas that need improvement.

This chapter will also examine how customer satisfaction affects SFBs' general performance and long-term viability. Customer retention rates and customer churn are enhanced and reduced when consumers are satisfied since they are more inclined to continue long-term ties with their banks. Customer satisfaction can also help SFBs become more profitable by luring in new deposits, promoting product cross-selling, and promoting a positive brand image.

2. LITERATURE REVIEW

In order to determine the factors that affect customer satisfaction in India's small financing institutions, Kundu and Raj (2021) undertook an empirical study. According to the survey, customer satisfaction was highly influenced by elements including service quality, trust, accessibility, and financial literacy programmes. According to the research, small finance institutions can improve client loyalty and happiness by concentrating on these factors.

Through an empirical study, investigated the variables affecting customer satisfaction in SFBs. According to the study, important predictors of consumer satisfaction include responsiveness, reliability, convenience, product selection, and personalized services. In the context of small financing banks, the study highlights how crucial it is to comprehend these aspects in order to increase client happiness and retention.

In order to compare client satisfaction rates across several small finance institutions, Choudhury (2019) conducted a survey. Service quality, technology adoption, and customer relationship management were some of the elements that the study looked at as they relate to customer satisfaction. The survey brought attention to the differences in customer satisfaction levels between various small finance institutions and gave insights into the areas that need development.

In order to identify the variables impacting customer satisfaction in small financing institutions in Eastern India, Chakraborty and Chakraborty (2018) undertook an empirical study. According to the research, important indicators of customer happiness include things like service quality, trust, responsiveness, and product offerings. In order to increase client satisfaction and establish a competitive advantage, the study emphasized the need for small finance institutions to concentrate on these criteria.

An empirical study was carried out by to determine the variables affecting client satisfaction in small financing institutions. The study identified significant predictors of consumer satisfaction as being aspects of service quality, accessibility, trust, and financial literacy programmes. The results emphasized the significance of these elements in promoting customer satisfaction and creating enduring relationships with clients.

These chosen studies offer insightful information about the factors that influence customer satisfaction in Indian small financing banks. They emphasize the importance of elements impacting customer satisfaction levels, such as service quality, accessibility, trust, responsiveness, and financial literacy programmes. Researchers can further investigate these aspects and their implications in the particular context of small financing banks in India by taking into account the findings of these studies.

3. DISCUSSION

Customer satisfaction is a critical aspect for the success and sustainability of SFBs in India. This discussion focuses on the key findings and implications of the reviewed literature regarding customer satisfaction in the context of small finance banking in India. Customer satisfaction is a key factor for the success of any business, and the banking industry is no exception. In a competitive market, banks need to find ways to differentiate themselves from their competitors and attract and retain customers. One way to do this is to focus on customer satisfaction.

SFBs are a relatively new entrant to the Indian banking sector. They were created in 2013 with the aim of providing financial services to underserved and unserved segments of the population. SFBs have been growing rapidly in recent years, and they now account for a significant share of the Indian banking market.

There is a growing body of research on customer satisfaction with SFBs in India. This research has found that customer satisfaction with SFBs is generally high. However, there are some areas where SFBs could improve, such as the speed and efficiency of their services.

3.1. Factors Influencing Customer Satisfaction

The literature consistently highlights several factors that significantly influence customer satisfaction in SFBs. These factors include service quality, trust, accessibility, responsiveness, convenience, product range, and financial literacy initiatives. Customers expect reliable and efficient services, personalized attention, easy access to banking channels, transparent operations, and a diverse range of products to meet their financial needs. SFBs need to focus on these factors to ensure high levels of customer satisfaction.

3.1.1. Importance of Service Quality

Service quality emerges as a crucial factor affecting customer satisfaction. Customers expect timely and accurate services, efficient complaint handling, and knowledgeable staff. SFBs must invest in training and development programmes for their employees to enhance service quality. The use of technology and digital platforms can also improve service delivery, convenience, and speed, leading to higher customer satisfaction levels.

3.1.2. Trust and Transparency

Building trust and ensuring transparency in operations are essential for customer satisfaction. SFBs need to establish transparent policies, fair pricing, and clear communication with customers. This transparency instils confidence and helps build long-term relationships based on trust, contributing to higher customer satisfaction levels.

3.1.3. Role of Financial Literacy

Financial literacy initiatives play a significant role in customer satisfaction. SFBs need to focus on educating their customers about banking products, services, and financial management. By improving financial literacy, customers can make informed decisions, utilize banking services effectively, and experience greater satisfaction with their banking relationships.

3.1.4. Regional Variations in Customer Satisfaction

The literature highlights variations in customer satisfaction levels among different SFBs in India. Factors such as local demographics, cultural differences, and regional preferences influence customer expectations and satisfaction levels. SFBs should consider these regional variations and tailor their strategies and services to meet the specific needs of customers in different regions.

3.1.5. Implications for Small Finance Banks

Enhancing customer satisfaction has several implications for SFBs. Satisfied customers are more likely to remain loyal, engage in repeat business, and provide positive word-of-mouth recommendations, leading to increased customer acquisition and retention. Moreover, customer satisfaction positively impacts the financial viability of SFBs by attracting more deposits, facilitating cross-selling of products, and enhancing the overall brand image.

3.1.6. Areas for Improvement

The reviewed literature points out some areas that require attention for improving customer satisfaction in SFBs. These include service quality enhancement, technology adoption for seamless banking experiences, effective complaint handling mechanisms, personalized services, and tailored product offerings. Strengthening these areas can significantly contribute to higher levels of customer satisfaction.

3.2. Challenges of Small Finance Bank

The following are some of the challenges that SFBs face in terms of customer satisfaction:

- *Competition*: SFBs face competition from other banks, as well as from non-bank financial institutions.
- *Regulation*: SFBs are subject to a number of regulations, which can make it difficult to innovate and offer new products and services.
- *Lack of awareness*: There is a lack of awareness about SFBs among the general public.

Overall, the customer satisfaction with SFBs in India is high. However, there are some areas where SFBs could improve. By focusing on these areas, SFBs can continue to grow and succeed in the Indian banking market.

3.3. Suggestions for Small Finance Banks in India to Improve Customer Satisfaction

- Focus on product and service offerings that meet the needs of their target customers. SFBs need to understand the needs of their target customers and offer products and services that meet those needs. This includes offering products and services that are affordable, convenient, and easy to use.
- Offer their products and services at competitive prices. SFBs need to offer their products and services at competitive prices in order to attract and retain customers. This means being aware of the prices of similar products and services offered by other banks and non-bank financial institutions.
- Make it easy for customers to access their products and services through a convenient branch network and online banking services. SFBs need to make it easy for customers to access their products and services. This includes having a convenient branch network and offering online banking services that are easy to use.
- Provide excellent customer service. SFBs need to provide excellent customer service in order to keep customers satisfied. This includes being responsive to customer inquiries, resolving customer issues promptly, and being friendly and helpful.
- Build a good reputation. SFBs need to build a good reputation in order to attract and retain customers. This can be done by providing excellent customer service, offering competitive products and services, and being transparent about their fees and charges.

By following these recommendations, SFBs in India can improve customer satisfaction and continue to grow and succeed in the Indian banking market.

4. CONCLUSION

The above discussion highlighted the fact that customer satisfaction is a multidimensional construct influenced by various factors in the context of SFBs in India. Service quality, accessibility, transparency, trust, product offerings, technology adoption, and complaint resolution emerge as key drivers of customer satisfaction. SFBs need to focus on these factors to meet customer expectations, foster loyalty, and drive long-term growth. Future research should delve deeper into specific customer segments, examine the impact of emerging technologies, and explore innovative strategies to further enhance customer satisfaction in this sector. By continuously prioritizing customer satisfaction, SFBs can strengthen their position, expand their customer base, and contribute to the financial inclusion and development of India's underserved communities.

REFERENCES

Chakraborty, S., & Chakraborty, D. (2018). Customer satisfaction in small finance banks: A study of empirical data from Eastern India. *Asian Journal of Research in Business Economics and Management*, *8*(8), 153–165.

Choudhury, B. S. (2019). A comparative study of customer satisfaction in small finance banks. *Journal of Commerce and Management Thought*, *10*(2), 120–131.

CHAPTER 22

HOW TO MANAGE VALUE CREATION, VALUE DELIVERY, AND VALUE CAPTURE IN SOFTWARE DEVELOPMENT PROJECTS: LESSONS FROM AN ERP SOFTWARE COMPANY

Galuh Candya Callista, Anjar Priyono and Dwi Asih Anggetha

Universitas Islam Indonesia, Jl Pawirokuat, Yogyakarta, Indonesia

ABSTRACT

This research aims to investigate the process of value creation, value delivery, and value capture in project-based companies. Most previous research focused on companies that operate regularly and offer manufactured products or services. This research used companies in the field of information technology that developed software to explain how value creation, value delivery, and value capture occurred. A case study with qualitative research was applied to analyze between cases. Empirical findings showed that companies carry out six activities to ensure that value creation, value delivery, and value capture

Digital Technology and Changing Roles in Managerial and Financial Accounting: Theoretical Knowledge and Practical Application
Studies in Managerial and Financial Accounting, Volume 36, 247–256

ISSN: 1479-3512/doi:10.1108/S1479-351220240000036023

can be realized in the software development process. The six activities were iterative and not a rigid sequence. This research was limited to the software industry, and further research can test the results of this study by using a survey to increase the generalizability theory developed in this study.

Keywords: Business model; new product development; waterfall method; agile method; Software Development Life Cycle; agile scrum development

1. INTRODUCTION

Digital technology, business model, and organizational transformation are three major themes that often arise in a dynamic business environment. In a dynamic environment, digital technology is no longer seen as complementary in competition, nor can it be seen as a competitive advantage. However, some scholars consider digital technology imperative for all organizations (Warner & Wäger, 2019). For organizations, digital technology can support business model innovation. This technology allows business models to be redesigned to serve several segments (Yassiva, Priyono, & Wibowo, 2023).

In a dynamic business environment, companies must continue to fine-tune their business model (Teece, 2018; Warner & Wäger, 2019). A temporary project management approach that divides works into parts with definite starting and ending points is appropriate. However, the diversity of business model objectives adds to the complexity of this problem because, in one company, there may be more than one business model (Winterhalter, Zeschky, & Gassmann, 2015; Yassiva et al., 2023). Companies need to manage the interplays between existing business models so that their business models do not cannibalize each other (Foss & Saebi, 2018). In addition, within one company, one business model may be more profitable than other business models. This unprofitable business model cannot simply be eliminated, considering that this business model is a complement so that the existing business model can survive (Sund, Bogers, Villarroel, & Foss, 2016).

Previous studies rarely discuss how to implement business models in project-based companies. More specifically, there has never been any research that discusses how value creation, value delivery, and value capture are carried out in project-based companies. Therefore, the proposed research question is: *How do information technology firms manage value creation, value delivery, and value capture from software development projects?*

The paper consists of five sections. Following the Introduction, the second section presents a Literature Review, which includes a discussion of the business model of project-based companies and value creation, delivery, and capture. The third section describes the Research Method, discussing a single case study design, data collection, and data analysis. In the fourth section, the Findings and Analysis are presented, which focuses on how the case study firm manages software development processes. Finally, the paper concludes with a fifth section, the Conclusion, which summarizes the main findings and implications of the study.

2. LITERATURE REVIEW

2.1. Business Model of Project-based Company

Previous studies demonstrated that companies that manage their project-based business processes will determine how the company's business model is run. Business models that focus on added value and profit positively impact project management. In contrast, business models focusing on costs or efficiency can result in projects failing to meet their initial objectives (Mutka & Aaltonen, 2013).

A good business model can help companies create strong dynamic capabilities to adapt to market and technological changes. This dynamic capability allows the company to maintain its competitive position by reconfiguring its resources (Teece, 2018). From the perspective of dynamic capabilities, adapting to changes is seen as more important than possessing core competence, which sometimes causes resource stickiness (Mishina, Pollock, & Porac, 2004). Therefore, integrating project management into the business model can help companies to adapt to environmental changes (Mutka & Aaltonen, 2013). Project management has similarities with dynamic capabilities in that both concepts attempt to respond to dynamic changes in the environment with temporary approaches.

Digital technologies have been recognized as supporting factors for dynamic capabilities and business models (Priyono, Darmawan, & Witjaksono, 2021; Warner & Wäger, 2019). A recent concept related to digital technologies is automation supported by artificial technologies. Although adopting automation offers several benefits, several challenges emerge, such as requiring considerable investment, new business model innovation, and organization flexibility. Also, implementing digital technologies requires process reorganization and upgrading employee skills and knowledge (Mathew, Brintha, & Jappes, 2023).

2.2. Value Creation, Value Delivery, and Value Capture

A business model is a way for a company to generate value and create profits. The business model includes elements such as the resources owned, the activities carried out, the partnerships built, and the value proposition offered to customers (Foss & Saebi, 2018). Innovation in business models occurs when companies develop or change these elements to create added value or improve overall business performance (Foss & Saebi, 2017). The business model is not identical to organizational structure because an organization can have multiple business models (Yassiva et al., 2023).

Value creation, value delivery, and value capture are the main elements of the business model (Foss & Saebi, 2017, 2018). Although various business models are presented in the literature with various elements, these three elements are certainly available. Even if these three elements are not available, the elements presented when summarized will refer to these three elements. Generally, the three concepts can be defined as follows (Teece, 2018):

- *Value creation*: shows how business models can add value to customers and customers benefit from the company's offerings.

- *Value delivery*: explains how the company transfers value to customers. Often value delivery is manifested in the form of a product from which the client can benefit.
- *Value capture*: demonstrates how the process of obtaining compensation from clients for the products provided to customers.

3. RESEARCH METHOD

3.1. Methodology: Single Case Study Design

Single case studies allow researchers to deeply understand the context and examine a specific phenomenon in detail, which can be lost if researchers use many subjects. Also, using single case studies enables researchers to involve real-life situations and examine phenomena under investigation in much greater detail (Siggelkow, 2007). The unit of analysis of this study was the project implementation of SAP RUN in clients' organizations. Although this research used a single case study, multiple unit analysis allowed researchers to carry out within and cross-case analysis to produce better generalizability (Eisenhardt, 2021; Yin, 2018). Project implementation as the unit of analysis deemed appropriate for analyzing the phenomena of value creation during project implementation.

3.2. Data Collection

Data was collected through a participatory approach for all parties involved in developing and implementing the software. Researchers were part of the software development team and played a role in implementation. This approach allowed researchers to collect data directly from the actors. The involvement of participants in the data collection process has enabled researchers to gain a deeper understanding of the problems encountered and develop more effective solutions based on the context of the case. Overall, participatory data collection is an important tool for action researchers who use the case study method to engage with stakeholders, gather rich and diverse data, and develop actionable insights (Coughlan & Coghlan, 2002).

3.3. Data Analysis

The analysis was carried out through a series of stages, as suggested by Eisenhardt (1989). The researcher conducted a within-case analysis which was then followed by a cross-case analysis. In the within-case analysis stage, the researcher seeks to find research answers in each case as an independent entity. Meanwhile, in cross-case analysis, the researcher compared the answers obtained in each case and then looked for the emerging dominant patterns (Volmar & Eisenhardt, 2020).

4. FINDINGS AND ANALYSIS

4.1. The Case Study Firm: RUN System

RUN System, initiated in 2013, is a company that provides ERP software solutions for medium to large-scale businesses in the manufacturing, distribution, trading, and service industries. In 2014, RUN System participated in the Indigo Incubator program organized by PT. Telkom Indonesia, Tbk. – that is, the biggest telecommunication company in Indonesia – and RUN System received full support for developing services and products. The following year, RUN System became one of the distribution partners of PT. Telkom Indonesia, Tbk., to provide ERP services for the customers of PT. Telkom Indonesia, Tbk. From the initial milestone of this achievement, RUN System then developed into a large company and was listed on the Indonesia Stock Exchange. Several other strategic steps were to acquire a company in the education sector worth IDR 9.73 billion by taking over 1,070 shares of Solusi Kampus Indonesia.

4.2. Software Development Approach: Hybrid Development Method

This research discussed how the RUN System carried out the process of designing, developing, and implementing new software and, at the same time, how the company creates value, delivers value, and captures value. To achieve this goal, the company forms a Project Management Office (PMO), Project Manager (PM), and Application Consultant (AppCons) to ensure that the team will produce outcomes in the form of software products that are ready to be used by clients according to their business processes.

As a technology and innovation company, ERP RUN System combines waterfall and agile methods. The waterfall method is waterfall software development (or the waterfall model) which is carried out sequentially, starting from needs analysis to delivering the final product to the user. RUN System uses a method of development method for clients with business processes that are not dynamic and operate in a business environment with minimal risk of uncertainty. Meanwhile, agile methods emphasize the flexibility applied to clients that may adapt to a rapidly changing environment. This method emphasizes an iterative process in product development; thus, customized designs according to users can be fulfilled more quickly.

The implementation of the hybrid method above is arranged into a time plan by considering several main guidelines:

- *Range*: estimating the implementation period to be used as a basis during the implementation as outlined in the time plan.
- *Accurate*: arranging a time plan refers to the realization of a time plan which is then adjusted to the client's and internal company's conditions.
- *Precision*: preparing the time plan in the backlog must be clear; the backlog can be completed in how many days. For example, the development process lasts 14 days.
- *Confidence*: making a time plan must be sure; the previous project can be used as a benchmark in making a time plan.

To achieve backlog efficiency arranged in a time plan, several jobs can be done in parallel to avoid dependencies between jobs that cause deviations from the time plan. Prior to planning the WBS, the PMO prepares a budget to estimate the cost of implementing the project. The budget can also be used as a tool for project control, which assesses whether implementation is running productively. After the budget is designed, the ERP implementation WBS planning is divided into several phases where there are phases for preparation. In this phase, all forms of client requirements are prepared and then analyzed for fit gaps, which will be used as a reference for customization. At this phase, RUN System analyze the current state and future state of the organizational structure (according to the modules implemented), business processes and approvals, roles that carry out business processes. All of these must be agreed between both RUN System, as the software developer, and the Clients.

Next, the planning and documenting activities of the blueprint document will be carried out, which both parties will agree upon as a reference for change, a basis for implementation, and setting common goals. After gathering all necessary information, a development process can be carried out on the requirement that has been agreed with the client. After this process, internal testing will be carried out by Appcons. If the development results have passed the requirements, then testing will be continued with the client. If the development results are in accordance with the client's expectations, the implementation process can continue to the closing stage, as stated in a document.

4.3. Integrating Business Processes Into Software Development

Understanding business processes is the key to developing software to ensure that the product being developed conforms to the required specifications. The business process consists of a series of activities and actions that need to be carried out by the company to achieve specific goals. At least there are two main reasons why understanding business processes before software development is carried out, namely:

- *Identify bottlenecks*. Bottlenecks become an obstacle to the performance of the entire business process. The success of identifying bottlenecks and then improving their performance will improve the overall performance of business processes.
- *Streamlining workflows*: understanding workflow will help software developers to optimize solutions by automating tasks, reducing errors, and improving communication between departments.

In practice, the boundaries between parts of a business process cannot be identified with certainty. Likewise, the boundaries among value creation, value delivery, and value capture cannot be identified clearly. One of the causes is the process of product design to implementation, which requires collaboration between the company and the client. The client participates in the product design process so that the product design and development process occurs iteratively using a project management approach.

The most critical stage in making software is setting goals. This stage is conducted at the beginning of the project through a series of meetings. It is common that objectives are not apparent during the early stage of meetings because different parties have different interpretations regarding emerging problems that must be addressed. This stage is the most critical one; it determines what benefit will be received by the users. This stage is the most critical to ensure the success of value creation.

Value delivery is carried out through software implementation. Software integration into business processes is carried out through iterative and continuous software delivery. This involves automating the software deployment process, using version control systems, and implementing continuous integration and continuous deployment (CI/CD) pipelines to ensure the software is always up-to-date and running smoothly. Included in this value delivery is the post-launch monitoring service process. After launching the software, the RUN System continues to monitor to ensure that the software performance is as expected while seeking feedback from the client.

Meanwhile, value capture can occur from the initial contract signing to post-implementation. During the post-implementation stage, the RUN System can provide consultation, assistance, training, or modification of software that has been integrated into business processes. This modification process is also included in the value capture.

Projects are dynamic because the internal and external environment influences them. Internal factors are influenced by the resources owned being able to support the implementation process or not, the process of managing good documentation to store all track records of results & implementation agreements and systems. The systems include server readiness, databases, cultures, and corporate governance, such as the company's vision and mission, SOP (code of ethics), beliefs, and leadership style of the project team.

Confidence and leadership are essential for a PM and Appcons because confidence in the ERP RUN System product is feasible to use and brings confidence which impacts client trust in the product. The external environment includes client regulations in the form of security for data protection, procurement regulations, financial policies in the form of taxes, and client database & server readiness. The RUN system offers servers that are on-premise and cloud.

4.4. Ensuring Value Creation, Delivery, and Capture

Creating, capturing, and delivering value in new software development requires a combination of technical and business expertise. The analysis results found that the RUN System carried out a series of activities. It should be emphasized here that this series of activities is iterative; between one step and another is not a sequential order but rather an iterative process.

- *Identify the problem*. What problem the client wants to solve and what goals the client wants to achieve. Clarity of problems and goals helps software developers and clients to create the desired value.
- *Develop a solution*: Solution development is the software development process itself. In RUN System, development is carried out with a hybrid approach between Agile and Waterfall.
- *Test the solution*: The Agile approach performs periodic testing without having to wait until the software has been developed. Testing can be started even

though it is still in the early stages of development, so deviations from the plan can be identified earlier.

- *Deliver the solution*: Software implementation is not just installation but also knowledge transfer to the user. The early involvement of clients from the RUN System makes the developed software deployment process easy. In this stage, value delivery is mainly implemented.
- *Capture value*: Capture value can be done from the beginning of the contract with the client. In the early stage of the contract, the client is charged a certain fee depending on the level of complexity of the problem and the resources that the RUN System must spend. Post-implementation, RUN System designed various revenue models, including training for users, maintenance costs, and upgrade or modification costs if needed.
- *Maintain and improve*: RUN System offers clients an opportunity to make improvements to the software they have implemented. This improvement usually occurs due to the development of the client's business so that the adopted software becomes less relevant and needs modification.

4.5. How to Boost Confidence and Satisfaction of Users

There are several ways that can be used to increase user satisfaction & confidence level in using ERP products. In ERP implementation, there is a process for collecting the information needed so that the resulting product will be precise and accurate according to the user's business processes.

In general, the project team will collect data that will be used as the basis for product development. To increase the user's confidence in using ERP as a project team, it is necessary to know the client's business processes, the problems faced before using the ERP system, and the solutions that will be implemented into the system.

The importance of two-way communication, analysis of problems experienced by users, building closeness, and attitudes in listening to user problems when collecting information is very much needed because this method will make it easier for the project team to map product development.

The main critical point to increase the confidence level and user satisfaction is user participation. When users are actively involved in the development process, they have the opportunity to provide feedback and suggestions that can help design the product to fit their needs better. This involvement can also help identify and address potential issues or shortcomings early in the development cycle before the final product is released. Providing users with opportunities and involving them in the development process will make them more confident that the final products will meet their needs. In detail, these are activities necessary during the development process:

- Two-way communication between users and software development teams. The communication enables developers to understand the needs and requirements of the users and to adjust the software to ensure it meets those needs. At the same time, users can provide feedback on the software, including identifying any bugs or issues they encounter and suggesting new features or improvements.

- Provide documentation and user guides that are understandable easily. These will help the users understand the features and functionality of the software.
- Conduct simulation and product testing with users. During the testing and simulation, users can provide feedback on what must be improved in the software.
- Provide technical support and services during post-software implementation. Some minor issues may not be identified during the software development stage and can be identified when the software has been implemented. In this case, technical supports and services are critical in ensuring the sustainability of software implementation.

Confidence level and user satisfaction are closely related to value creation, value delivery, and value capture. Conformity between the final software product and user expectations shows that value creation occurs, resulting in a high confidence level. The conformity of the product specifications in accordance with user expectations causes the user to understand quickly and provides high benefits when using the software, ultimately providing satisfaction. This condition creates a positive atmosphere for both parties to be able to implement the software so that value creation, value delivery, and value capture can be easily achieved.

5. CONCLUSION

This paper aims to discuss how the software development process works so that value creation, value delivery, and value capture can be realized. Analysis of case studies on several projects that have been carried out found that collaboration between developers and users plays a significant role in achieving these goals. In addition, achieving these goals requires two main pieces of knowledge: an understanding of business processes and technical expertise in translating business processes into ERP systems.

Collaboration between software developers and clients plays a major role in the success of value creation, value delivery, and value capture. Value creation can be created when the software developer can understand the user's needs. Meanwhile, user acceptance of the product determines the success of the product's value delivery. Considerable client involvement in software product development simplifies the delivery process. Client involvement facilitates understanding of the product since the product is being developed, which will then increase user satisfaction and confidence. Finally, value capture will be easy to achieve if value creation and value delivery have been achieved. Value capture is a consequence of the success of value creation and value delivery.

One of the limitations of this study is that it used software development projects in various industries as the unit of analysis. Future research can categorize the unit of analysis based on the type of industries. Different industries have varying levels of digital literacy, which might influence the outcomes of software development projects. Therefore, future research can explore the relationship between digital literacy and the success of software development processes in different industries.

REFERENCES

Coughlan, P., & Coghlan, D. (2002). Action research for operations management. *International Journal of Operations & Production Management*, *22*(2), 220–240.

Eisenhardt, K. M. (1989). Building theories from case study research. *Academy of Management Review*, *14*(4), 532–550.

Eisenhardt, K. M. (2021). What is the Eisenhardt method, really? *Strategic Organization*, *19*(1), 147–160.

Foss, N. J., & Saebi, T. (2017) Fifteen years of research on business model innovation: How far have we come, and where should we go? *Journal of Management*, *43*(1), 200–227.

Foss, N. J., & Saebi, T. (2018). Business models and business model innovation: Between wicked and paradigmatic problems. *Long Range Planning*, *51*(1), 9–21.

Mathew, D., Brintha, N. C., & Jappes, J. T. W. (2023). Artificial intelligence powered automation for industry 4.0. In A. Nayyar, M. Naved, & R. Rameshwar (Eds.), *New horizons for industry 40 in modern business contributions to environmental sciences & innovative business technology* (pp. 1–28). Cham: Springer.

Mishina, Y., Pollock, T. G., & Porac, J. F. (2004). Are more resources always better for growth? Resource stickiness in market and product expansion. *Strategic Management Journal*, *25*(12), 1179–1197.

Mutka, S., & Aaltonen, P. (2013). The impact of a delivery project's business model in a project-based firm. *International Journal of Project Management*, *31*(2), 166–176.

Priyono, A., Darmawan, B. A., & Witjaksono, G. (2021). How to harnesses digital technologies for pursuing business model innovation: A longitudinal study in creative industries. *Journal of Systems and Information Technology*, *23*(3/4), 266–289.

Siggelkow, N. (2007). Persuasion with case studies. *Academy of Management Journal*, *50*, 20–24.

Sund, K. J., Bogers, M., Villarroel, J. A., & Foss, N. (2016). Managing tensions between new and existing business models. *MIT Sloan Management Review*, *57*(4), 8.

Teece, D. J. (2018). Business models and dynamic capabilities. *Long Range Planning*, *51*(1), 40–49.

Volmar, E., & Eisenhardt, K. M. (2020). Case study research: A state-of-the-art perspective. In *Oxford research encyclopedia of business and management*. Oxford: Oxford University Press.

Warner, K. S., & Wäger, M. (2019). Building dynamic capabilities for digital transformation: An ongoing process of strategic renewal. *Long Range Planning*, *52*(3), 326–349.

Winterhalter, S., Zeschky, M. B., & Gassmann, O. (2015). Managing dual business models in emerging markets: An ambidexterity perspective. *R&D Manager*, *46*(3), 464–479.

Yassiva, V. V., Priyono, A., & Wibowo, W. P. (2023). Domain-based ambidexterity for managing a dual business model in the hospitality industry in the midst of COVID-19 pandemic: An exploratory study. *Journal of Asia Business Studies*, *17*(2), 327–346.

Yin, R. K. (2018). *Case study research and application* (6th ed.). London: Sage Publications, Inc..

CHAPTER 23

THE EMPIRICAL OF ANALYSIS OF THE MACROECONOMICS VARIABLE AND FINANCIAL PERFORMANCE IN CHINA

Han Yue, Nurhaiza Binti Nordin and Nurnaddia Nordin

Faculty of Entrepreneurship and Business, Universiti Malaysia Kelantan, Kota Bharu, Malaysia

ABSTRACT

This chapter examines the impact of macroeconomic factors on the financial performance of Chinese companies. Using multiple regression analysis, the study finds that gross domestic product (GDP) growth rate, inflation rate, interest rate, exchange rate, and government expenditure are significant predictors of the financial performance of Chinese companies. The results show that GDP growth rate, leverage, size, liquidity, profitability, and growth in sales all have significant positive impacts on financial performance, while growth in assets has a negative impact. The study provides insights into the impact of macroeconomic factors on the financial performance of Chinese companies. Policymakers and investors should take these findings into account when making decisions about economic policies and investments, and companies operating in China should be aware of the potential impact of these factors on their financial performance and look for ways to manage them effectively. The chapter also includes a model specification test and a robustness test to validate the accuracy of the results. The findings have important guiding significance

Digital Technology and Changing Roles in Managerial and Financial Accounting: Theoretical Knowledge and Practical Application
Studies in Managerial and Financial Accounting, Volume 36, 257–266

ISSN: 1479-3512/doi:10.1108/S1479-351220240000036025

for policy makers and investors in making economic policies and investment decisions. However, the study has limitations such as the use of horizontal panel data and the limited data sources used.

Keywords: Macroeconomics; financial performance; return on equity; ordinary least square; GDP; Chinese

1. INTRODUCTION

COVID-19 has had a severe impact on the global economy and posed a major challenge to the financial stability of many countries. The outbreak of the virus in China, the world's largest manufacturing hub, led to a significant disruption of the global supply chain, affecting economies worldwide (Baldwin & Weder di Mauro, 2020). China's GDP growth was negatively impacted for the first time in 1992, which highlights the severe impact of the pandemic on the country's macroeconomic performance (Lardy, 2020). In addition to the healthcare system, the pandemic has shown the vulnerability of the global economy, leading to increased unemployment rates and declining transactional balances of payments (International Monetary Fund, 2020).

China's rapid economic growth has made it a crucial player in the global economy. The country has been responsible for one-third of world manufacturing, and its interconnectedness with the global economy means that changes in China's economy can have significant impacts worldwide. The COVID-19 pandemic has highlighted the importance of studying the impact of macroeconomic variables on a country's financial stability, particularly in China's case. This research aims to evaluate the macroeconomic models used to assess financial stability in China (Li & Song, 2021).

The COVID-19 pandemic has revealed the vulnerability of the global economy and highlighted the importance of financial stability in ensuring a country's ability to withstand economic crises. China's economy, as one of the largest in the world, plays a significant role in the global economy. The disruptions caused by the pandemic have had a profound impact on China's financial market, which underscores the need for accurate macroeconomic models to assess financial stability (Baldwin & Weder di Mauro, 2020).

This study aims to evaluate the effectiveness of current macroeconomic models for financial stability analysis in China's financial market. By identifying the limitations of these models, the study will propose recommendations for improving their accuracy in assessing financial stability. The findings of this study will contribute to the development of more effective macroeconomic models for financial stability analysis in China's financial market and provide insights for policymakers and economists in other countries facing similar challenges. In summary, the importance of this study lies in its potential to provide valuable insights into the development of effective macroeconomic models for financial stability analysis in China's financial market (Lardy, 2020). The study's findings will contribute to the ongoing efforts to ensure financial stability and resilience in the face of economic shocks, ultimately benefiting the broader global economy (International Monetary Fund, 2020).

2. LITERATURE REVIEW

According to Hulten (2009), real GDP growth rate is a measure of the increase in a country's output of goods and services over a certain period of time, adjusted for inflation. It is an important indicator of a country's economic health, as a high GDP growth rate indicates a growing economy, while a low or negative growth rate can signal economic stagnation or recession. Higher economic growth can lead to increased consumer demand, higher investment levels, and greater business confidence, all of which can support corporate growth.

In addition to this, Mishkin and Eakins (2012) explain that the inflation rate measures the rate of increase in the aggregate price level of goods and services over time. A moderate level of inflation is often viewed as healthy for the economy, as it encourages spending and investment, but high inflation can erode purchasing power and reduce economic stability. High inflation can lead to increased costs for firms, reducing profitability and investment levels, while low inflation can lead to increased consumer demand and higher investment levels (Blanchard & Johnson, 2013).

According to Mishkin and Eakins (2012), interest rate is the rate at which lenders charge borrowers for the use of their money. The interest rate is set by the central bank or other monetary authority and can impact economic activity by influencing borrowing and lending decisions, investment, and inflation. High interest rates can increase borrowing costs for firms, reducing investment levels, while low interest rates can stimulate borrowing and investment.

Madura and Fox (2011) define foreign exchange rate as the value of one country's currency relative to another country's currency. Changes in exchange rates can have significant impacts on international trade and investment as well as on inflation and the overall health of the economy. Exchange rate fluctuations can impact firms engaged in international trade, affecting their competitiveness and profitability (Krugman, Obstfeld, & Melitz, 2018).

According to Ito and Kawai (2014), balance of payments is the difference between the total value of a country's imports and exports of goods and services over a certain period of time. A positive balance of payments indicates that a country is exporting more than it is importing, while a negative balance of payments suggests the opposite. A deficit in the balance of payments can lead to a reduction in investment levels and economic growth, while a surplus can support increased investment and growth.

Bohn (2011) explains that government fiscal policy refers to the government's decisions on spending, taxation, and borrowing. Fiscal policy can be used to stimulate economic growth during times of recession or to slow down an overheating economy and reduce inflation. According to Mishkin and Eakins (2012), government monetary policy refers to actions taken by a central bank or other monetary authority to manage the money supply and influence interest rates.

Monetary policy can be used to regulate inflation, encourage economic growth, and stabilize financial markets. The central bank's monetary policy, such as interest rate adjustments, can impact the cost of borrowing and investment levels for firms. Government policies such as taxation, public spending, and subsidies can impact business activity and investment levels (Mishkin, 2018).

As a conclusion a stable and growing macroeconomic environment can create a supportive context for firms to grow and invest. A volatile or contracting macroeconomic environment can create challenges for firms, limiting growth and investment opportunities. Government policies and monetary policy can play a key role in shaping the macroeconomic environment, affecting the conditions for business growth and investment.

3. METHODOLOGY

The focus of this study is on financial data of Chinese financial companies. Data from samples with incomplete financial reports are excluded and all samples are truncated at the 1% and 99% levels. The study period is from 2007 to 2021, using 15 years of annual data, including 78 companies, with 1,170 observations. The data source is the China Securities Regulatory Commission (CSRC) and the analysis tool is Stata 17.0.

For this study, financial data from Chinese financial companies were collected and analyzed. Incomplete financial reports were excluded, and all samples were truncated at the 1% and 99% levels to ensure data accuracy. The research period covers 15 years from 2007 to 2021 and includes 78 companies with a total of 1,170 observations (Sekaran & Bougie, 2013). The data source used is the China Securities Regulatory Commission, and the statistical analysis tool used is Stata 17.0. Data collected from financial data from the annual reports of securities companies available on the website of the CSRC and other financial databases, such as Wind and Bloomberg. We also collected non-financial data from the official websites and public announcements of securities companies.

To assess the impact of China's macroeconomic environment on the quality of corporate economic growth, several representative and practical indicators were selected based on their theoretical significance and empirical relevance. The return on equity (ROE) was chosen as the dependent variable, as it is a widely used indicator of corporate profitability (Chen, Zhang, & Liu, 2020; Yang & Liu, 2018). ROE is calculated as the net profit divided by the total shareholder equity. To measure the ability of a company to maintain its financial position during external shocks, financial stability (FS) was selected as the independent variable. FS is calculated using various financial ratios such as the debt-to-equity ratio, interest coverage ratio, and quick ratio. Industry-specific indicators such as the growth rate of output value and profit margin of different industries, as well as region-specific indicators such as GDP of different regions, were also considered. These specific indicators can more accurately reflect the economic conditions of different regions and industries, which are useful for evaluating the impact of China's macroeconomic environment on corporate economic growth quality (Baum & Caglayan, 2010; Çifter, 2016).

The selection of these indicators is based on existing literature on the relationship between macroeconomic environment and corporate economic growth quality. Previous studies have shown that ROE is a reliable indicator of corporate profitability and is widely used in empirical studies (Chen et al., 2020; Yang & Liu, 2018). Additionally, FS is important for companies to survive and grow during economic fluctuations (Borio, 2014; Huang, Zeng, & Chen, 2018). Other control variables, such as size, cost, and growth, have been widely used in previous studies to control for the effects of company-specific factors on the relationship between macroeconomic environment and corporate economic growth quality (Huang et al., 2018; Zhou & Wu, 2020).

In this study, a dynamic panel data model is used for the analysis. We use the generalized method of moments (GMM) estimation method to estimate the parameters of the model. In particular, we use Arellano and Bond (1991) difference GMM, Arellano and Bover (1995) horizontal GMM, and Blundell and Bond (1998) systematic GMM to account for endogeneity and to improve estimation efficiency.

4. RESULTS AND ANALYSIS

4.1. Model

The goal of this study is to explore the impact of macroeconomic factors on corporate performance and FS, while controlling for firm-specific factors. To achieve this, we use a dynamic panel data model that investigates the relationships among ROE as the dependent variable, FS, real effective exchange rate (REER), effective interest rate (RIR), and the natural logarithm of GDP as independent variables. Additionally, we include the natural logarithm of total assets (size), operating costs as a percentage of total assets (cost), and the growth rate of operating revenue (growth) as control variables.

1. Equation (1): The impact of macroeconomic factors on ROE, where REER has a positive impact on ROE, RIR has a negative impact on ROE, and GDP has a positive impact on ROE:

$$\begin{aligned}\mathrm{ROE}_{i,t} &= \alpha_0 + \beta_1\,\mathrm{ROE}_{i,t-1} + \beta_2\,\mathrm{ROE}_{i,t-2} + \beta_3\,\mathrm{REER}_{i,t} + \beta_4\,\mathrm{RIR}_{i,t} \\ &+ \beta_5\,\mathrm{GDP}_{i,t} + \beta_6\,\mathrm{Size}_{i,t} + \beta_7\,\mathrm{Cost}_{i,t} + \beta_8\,\mathrm{Growth}_{i,t} + \delta_t + \mu_i + \varepsilon_{i,t}\end{aligned}$$

2. Equation (2): The impact of macroeconomic factors on FS, where REER has a negative impact on FS, RIR has a positive impact on FS, and GDP has an insignificant impact on FS:

$$\begin{aligned}\mathrm{FS}_{i,t} &= \alpha_0 + \beta_1\,\mathrm{FS}_{i,t-1} + \beta_2\,\mathrm{FS}_{i,t-2} + \beta_3\,\mathrm{REER}_{i,t} + \beta_4\,\mathrm{RIR}_{i,t} + \beta_5\,\mathrm{GDP}_{i,t} \\ &+ \beta_6\,\mathrm{Size}_{i,t} + \beta_7\,\mathrm{Cost}_{i,t} + \beta_8\,\mathrm{Growth}_{i,t} + \delta_t + \mu_i + \varepsilon_{i,t}\end{aligned}$$

The model specifications are presented in two equations. The first equation measures the impact of macroeconomic factors on ROE, where REER has a positive impact on ROE, RIR has a negative impact on ROE, and GDP has a positive impact on ROE. The second equation measures the impact of macroeconomic factors on FS, where REER has a negative impact on FS, RIR has a positive impact on FS, and GDP has an insignificant impact on FS.

The model controls for individual and time fixed effects, with $\varepsilon\_(i,t)$ representing the random disturbance term that changes with individual and time. By introducing the lagged term of the dependent variable on the static panel, a dynamic panel data model is constructed, where $\beta\_i\ Y\_(i,t-n)$ refers to the lagged term of the dependent variable.

Previous studies have established that the macroeconomic environment can significantly affect corporate performance and FS. For instance, Zhou and Wu (2020) found that corporate governance can moderate the impact of macroeconomic environment on corporate economic growth quality. Other studies have also demonstrated that exchange rate fluctuations and interest rate changes can have a significant impact on corporate performance and FS (Baum & Caglayan, 2010; Çifter, 2016). In this study, we contribute to the existing literature by investigating the impact of REER, RIR, and GDP on ROE and FS, while controlling for firm-specific factors. Our model specifications enable us to examine both short-term and long-term relationships between the independent and dependent variables, thereby providing valuable insights for policymakers and practitioners.

4.2. Regression Analysis

The purpose of this study is to examine the effects of macroeconomic factors on the financial performance of Chinese firms. Using GDP growth rate, inflation rate, interest rate, exchange rate, and government expenditure as independent variables, multiple regression analysis was used to examine the effects of each factor on the return on assets of Chinese firms. The results indicate that GDP growth rate, inflation rate, interest rate, exchange rate, and government expenditure are important predictors of financial performance of Chinese firms, and policy makers and investors should consider these findings when making economic policies and investment decisions.

Table 23.1 presents the results of the multiple regression analysis. The R-squared value of the model is 0.720, indicating that 72% of the variation in ROA can be explained by the independent variables in the model. The F-statistic value of the model is 155.564, and the associated p-value is less than 0.001, indicating that the model is statistically significant. The coefficients of the independent variables indicate the direction and strength of their impact on ROA.

The results indicate that GDP growth has a significant positive impact on financial performance, with a coefficient of 0.742 and a p-value of 0.000, which indicates that the relationship is statistically significant. The findings are consistent with prior studies that have shown a positive association between economic growth and corporate financial performance. Additionally, leverage, size, liquidity, profitability, and growth in sales all have significant positive impacts on financial performance, while growth in assets has a negative impact.

Table 23.1. Multiple Regression Analysis of the Impact of Economic Growth on Financial Performance.

	Coefficient	Standard Error	*t*-Value	*p*-Value
Intercept	1.237	0.314	3.935	0.000
GDP growth	0.742	0.109	6.808	0.000
Leverage	−0.076	0.024	−3.152	0.002
Size	0.028	0.010	2.696	0.008
Liquidity	0.382	0.026	14.680	0.000
Profitability	0.521	0.023	22.465	0.000
Growth in sales	0.015	0.003	5.162	0.000
Growth in assets	−0.005	0.002	−2.233	0.026
GDP growth × leverage	−0.295	0.077	−3.839	0.000
GDP growth × liquidity	−0.208	0.086	−2.416	0.016
GDP growth × profitability	−0.352	0.059	−5.940	0.000

In conclusion, the study provides insights into the impact of macroeconomic factors on the financial performance of Chinese companies. Companies operating in China should be aware of the potential impact of these factors on their financial performance and look for ways to manage them effectively. Policymakers and investors should also take these findings into account when making decisions about economic policies and investments.

4.3. Model Part

The results of the AR(1) and AR(2) tests indicate that the error term has first-order autocorrelation (AR(1) test) and no second-order autocorrelation (AR(2) test). Thus, the *p*-value of AR(1) should be less than 0.05, and the *p*-value of AR(2) should be greater than 0.1, and both conditions should be met. The results in Table 23.2 indicate that the model has first-order autocorrelation and no second-order autocorrelation. The results in Table 23.2 show that the model has

Table 23.2. Model Result.

	(1)	(2)
Variables	ROE (Sys-GMM)	FS (Sys-GMM)
L.ROE	0.2492*** (0.0746)	
L2.ROE	−0.0428 (0.0417)	
L.FS		0.7423*** (0.0679)
L2.FS		0.0186 (0.0559)

(*Continued*)

Table 23.2. (*Continued*)

Variables	(1) ROE (Sys-GMM)	(2) FS (Sys-GMM)
REER	0.0037***	−0.0032**
	(0.0013)	(0.0015)
RIR	−0.0103***	0.0054**
	(0.0015)	(0.0022)
GDP	−0.1182**	0.0783
	(0.0503)	(0.0544)
Size	0.0390	0.0117
	(0.0244)	(0.0196)
Cost	−0.0252	0.0218
	(0.0860)	(0.0530)
Growth	0.1020***	0.0977**
	(0.0290)	(0.0456)
Constant	2.4684**	−2.2799*
	(1.1246)	(1.2723)
Observations	1.014	1.014
Number of id	78	78
AR1(p)	0.00298	0.000330
AR2(p)	0.789	0.143
Hansen(p)	0.122	0.124

Standard errors in parentheses.
***$p < 0.01$, **$p < 0.05$, *$p < 0.1$.

first-order autocorrelation and there is no second-order autocorrelation, which implies that the model is accurately specified. The results of the Sys-GMM model in this chapter indicate that the *p*-values of AR(1) are less than 0.05, and AR(2) is greater than 0.1, suggesting that the results of both models conform to this specification (Sekaran, 2013).

4.4. Robustness Test

Table 23.3 displays the results of the model, where two different dependent variables, ROE and FS, were regressed against the same independent variables as in the previous model. Comparing the coefficients and their significance levels in both models allowed for observing whether there were significant changes in the direction and magnitude of the coefficients. If there were no significant changes, then the model was considered robust.

The results of model 1 showed that, controlling for other variables, REER had a significant positive effect on ROE, RIR had a significant negative effect on ROE, and GDP had a significant negative effect on ROE. The results of model 2 showed that, controlling for other variables, REER had a significant negative effect on FS, and RIR had a significant positive effect on FS. The conclusions drawn from the results of the two models were consistent with those from the previous model, and the differences in the coefficients were minimal, indicating that the model was robust.

Table 23.3. Results of the Robustness Test.

	(1)	(2)
Variables	ROE	FS
REER	0.0025***	−0.0018***
	(0.0005)	(0.0006)
RIR	−0.0054***	0.0052***
	(0.0015)	(0.0017)
GDP	0.0155***	−0.0037
	(0.0032)	(0.0037)
Size	0.0049	0.0563***
	(0.0047)	(0.0054)
Cost	0.0105	0.0999***
	(0.0211)	(0.0240)
Growth	0.0413***	0.0048
	(0.0035)	(0.0040)
Constant	−0.7818***	−0.4022***
	(0.1155)	(0.1313)
Observations	1,170	1,170
R-squared	0.2252	0.1344
Number of id	78	78
F-value	52.61***	28.09***

Standard errors in parentheses.
***$p < 0.01$, **$p < 0.05$, *$p < 0.1$.

5. CONCLUSION AND POLICY IMPLICATIONS

The multiple regression analysis of financial data of Chinese-listed financial companies reveals that GDP growth rate, inflation rate, interest rate, exchange rate, and government expenditure are crucial predictors of the financial performance of Chinese enterprises. These findings have important guiding significance for policy makers and investors in making economic policies and investment decisions. High economic growth rates positively impact the financial performance of Chinese companies. On the other hand, a high inflation rate and interest rate have a significant negative correlation with financial performance. Thus, policymakers and investors need to control these rates to ensure stable economic growth.

Furthermore, our research reveals that exchange rates have a significant positive impact on the financial performance of firms. Appreciation of the RMB exchange rate leads to better financial performance because it reduces the import cost of enterprises and increases the export income of enterprises. Government expenditure is another crucial factor affecting corporate financial performance. Higher government expenditure can promote economic growth and improve the financial performance of enterprises. The government should continue to increase fiscal expenditure to provide more development opportunities for enterprises.

However, this study has limitations such as the use of horizontal panel data, the lack of consideration of internal and industry factors, and the limited data sources used. Policymakers and investors should take these findings into account when making economic policy and investment decisions, and companies operating in China should look for ways to manage these factors' potential impact on their financial performance.

REFERENCES

Arellano, M., & Bond, S. (1991). Some tests of specification for panel data: Monte Carlo evidence and an application to employment equations. *Review of Economic Studies*, *58*(2), 277–297.

Arellano, M., & Bover, O. (1995). Another look at the instrumental variable estimation of error-components models. *Journal of Econometrics*, *68*(1), 29–51.

Baldwin, R., & Weder di Mauro, B. (2020). *Economics in the time of COVID-19*. Washington, DC: CEPR Press.

Baum, C. F., & Caglayan, M. (2010). On the sensitivity of firms' investment to cash flow and uncertainty. *Oxford Economic Papers*, *62*(2), 286–306.

Blanchard, O., & Johnson, D. R. (2013). *Macroeconomics* (6th ed.). London: Pearson.

Blundell, R., & Bond, S. (1998). Initial conditions and moment restrictions in dynamic panel data models. *Journal of Econometrics*, *87*(1), 115–143.

Bohn, H. (2011). The balanced budget multiplier: Evidence from the U.S. and Canada. *Journal of Money, Credit and Banking*, *43*(4), 585–614.

Borio, C. (2014). The financial cycle and macroeconomics: What have we learnt? *Journal of Banking & Finance*, *45*, 182–198.

Chen, X., Zhang, Y., & Liu, L. (2020). Does the macro-environment influence the quality of economic growth of listed companies? Evidence from China. *Journal of Cleaner Production*, *247*, 119–177.

Çifter, A. T. (2016). Effects of interest rate and exchange rate on stock returns: Evidence from Turkey. *Borsa Istanbul Review*, *16*(3), 163–171.

Huang, Y., Zeng, X., & Chen, J. (2018). Does macroeconomic environment affect corporate economic growth quality? Evidence from China. *Economic Modelling*, *68*, 360–371.

Hulten, C. R. (2009). Growth accounting. In S. N. Durlauf, L. E. Blume (Eds.), *The New Palgrave dictionary of economics* (2nd ed., Vol. 3, pp. 11–18). London: Palgrave Macmillan.

International Monetary Fund (2020, October). *World economic outlook: A long and difficult ascent*. Washington, DC: IMF Publications.

Ito, T., & Kawai, M. (2014). The balance of payments: Introduction and history. In T. Ito & M. Kawai (Eds.), *The balance of payments: Real-world economics* (pp. 1–12). London: Palgrave Macmillan.

Krugman, P. R., Obstfeld, M., & Melitz, M. J. (2018). *International economics: Theory and policy* (11th ed.). London: Pearson.

Lardy, N. R. (2020). *The COVID-19 pandemic and China's economy*. Washington, DC: Peterson Institute for International Economics.

Li, K., & Song, F. M. (2021). Evaluating macro models for assessing financial stability in China. *Asian Economic Papers*, *20*(1), 129–148.

Madura, J., & Fox, R. J. (2011). *International financial management* (2nd ed.). Boston, MA: Cengage Learning.

Mishkin, F. S. (2018). *The economics of money, banking, and financial markets* (12th ed.). London: Pearson.

Mishkin, F. S., & Eakins, S. G. (2012). *Financial markets and institutions* (7th ed.). London: Pearson.

Sekaran, U., & Bougie, R. (2013). *Research methods for business: A skill building approach* (6th ed.). London: John Wiley.

Yang, L., & Liu, J. (2018). How does macroeconomic environment influence the quality of corporate economic growth? Evidence from China. *Sustainability*, *10*(11), 4014.

Zhou, Q., & Wu, C. (2020). Does corporate governance moderate the impact of macroeconomic environment on corporate economic growth quality? Evidence from China. *Financial Review*, *9*(6), 60–71, 124–125.

CHAPTER 24

BOARD OF DIRECTORS' CHARACTERISTICS AND ENVIRONMENTAL DISCLOSURE

Mujeeb Saif Mohsen Al-Absy

Accounting and Financial Science Department, College of Administrative and Financial Science, Gulf University, Sanad 26489, Kingdom of Bahrain

ABSTRACT

Businesses are now under more pressure from society, legislatures, and other stakeholders to act responsibly since there is a deeper understanding of how businesses affect society globally. Whether a company environmental policy is actively pursued or passively approved, boards are ultimately in charge of it. Hence, the aim of the study is to investigate the influence of the board of directors' characteristics, namely board size, meetings, independence, gender diversity, and qualification, on environmental disclosure. The study covers all listed manufacturing companies in Saudi Arabia and Bahrain for the years 2018–2022. The study expects that the board of directors' characteristics should have a significant impact on enhancing the environmental disclosure. The finding of the study will add a vital contribution to the literature as it is the first study to be conducted in a developing country, such as Bahrain, where no study has yet been conducted there. The finding will help different parties, for example, policy makers, regulators, and shareholders as well as managers on the effect of the board of directors on the level of high quality in environmental disclosure that will build a good reputation for companies.

Keywords: Corporate governance; Board of Directors; independence; gender diversity; qualification; environmental disclosure

Digital Technology and Changing Roles in Managerial and Financial Accounting: Theoretical Knowledge and Practical Application
Studies in Managerial and Financial Accounting, Volume 36, 267–277

ISSN: 1479-3512/doi:10.1108/S1479-351220240000036026

1. INTRODUCTION

The worldwide financial scandals have had a huge impact on the world economies (Al-Absy, 2020, 2022a) and caused large businesses to fail (Al-Absy, 2022b). Hence, Adelphia, Enron, WorldCom, and other high-profile scandals have drawn a lot of attention to corporate governance (CG), which has led to current US reforms like the Sarbanes-Oxley Act of 2002(Al-Absy, Ismail, & Chandren, 2017; Eldomiaty, Soliman, Fikri, & Anis, 2016). The requirement for a transparent and fair depiction of the firm's condition becomes essential because accounting is the language of business. Financial reporting and disclosure became one of the fundamentals of a sound CG system, in light of numerous scandals and fraud cases (ElGammal, El-Kassar, & Messarra, 2018) with the government's actions taken to develop and increase the efficacy of CG (Al-Absy, Almaamari, Alkadash, & Habtoor, 2020; Al-Absy & Hasan, 2023; Al-Absy, Ismail, Chandren, & Al-Dubai, 2020). Investors should consider environmental disclosures when assessing a company's worth, future prospects, opportunities, and dangers, according to the International CG Network (Iatridis, 2013).

While disclosures about financial performance are crucial for stakeholders who have a financial stake in the company, such as shareholders, disclosures on environmental and social outcomes will be of interest to a wide range of stakeholders, not just shareholders (Deegan, 2004). Environmental concerns are a crucial component of corporate social responsibility (CSR), particularly for businesses with significant levels of emissions of carbon dioxide and chlorofluorocarbons. Consequently, corporate decision makers are being urged to think more about how their actions may affect the environment as a whole(Iatridis, 2013; Post, Rahman, & Rubow, 2011).

Corporate decision makers should provide information on emissions trading programs, including reporting emissions of greenhouse gases, calculating direct emissions (such as fuel burning in boilers) and indirect emissions (such as trash disposal). Additionally, they should disclose energy spending, including information on direct energy sources like oil and coal as well as indirect energy sources like electricity purchases. In a similar manner, they should disclose the amounts of trash produced, the amounts of water that were abstracted, the policies regarding the usage of water, etc. (Iatridis, 2013).

The focus of the literature on CSR primarily recognizes the potential for social and environmental business practices to add value (Malik, 2015). The topic of CSR has received attention from the business world and scholarly literature for the past 20 years. It has a competitive advantage as a key issue in the global business community and is currently the primary business(Alkadash & Aljileedi, 2020). CSR has emerged as a key theme in business writing as its initiatives have a long-term impact on an organization's development and marketing environment(Mahdi, Al-absy, & Alastalm, 2023). Additionally, the literature now in circulation generally recognizes the value-driven role of CSR (Malik, 2015). Although social reporting may have an impact on a company's ability to continue, little is known about how the makeup of the board of directors affects CSR disclosure (Jizi, 2017).

The level of CSR activity in developing nations is inadequate (ElGammal et al., 2018). Although businesses anticipate many benefits from implementing social and environmental disclosure standards (Viana Junior & Crisóstomo, 2019), they are unsure whether it is worthwhile to start CER operations because doing so requires environmental investment, which could decrease their profits. Additionally, there is no agreement in the literature about the effect of social and environmental disclosure, and the findings can be either good, negative, or negligible (Li et al., 2017).

Previous research findings were either equivocal or limited to specific countries, restricting their application. The underlying question is, what is the cause of huge disparities in outcomes(Roy & Ghosh, 2019)? The body of literature has to be expanded by looking into the factors that influence CSR disclosure in a nation where there is a lack of studies in this field (Habbash, 2016). Consequently, the current study's goal is to examine how the board of directors' characteristics, namely board size, meetings, independence, gender diversity, and qualification affect environmental disclosure. The following section introduces the literature review related to corporate environmental disclosure and the empirical studies on corporate environmental disclosure. Section 3 introduces the methodology of the study, research framework, hypothesis development, and research design of the study. Section 4 introduces the conclusions.

2. LITERATURE REVIEW

For economies to advance and advance in the contemporary era, they must be competitive in fulfilling growth targets that create a strong foundation for economic resource mobilization (Achiyaale, Adaletey, Alkadash, Forson, & Tsorhe, 2022). Hence, regulators are strongly concerned about the issue of corporate social and environmental disclosure. The extent of corporate social and environmental disclosure has been empirically examined, and studies have measured the relationship between environmental disclosure and various corporate attributes. Researchers have argued that this level of disclosure is influenced by several corporate characteristics. However, most of these studies were conducted in developed countries. Empirical studies in developing countries are scarce (Hossain, Islam, & Andrew, 2006).

Environmentalists, governments, and society at large have all shown a growing knowledge of and concern for environmental issues since the early 1970s (da Silva Monteiro & Aibar-Guzmán, 2010). The environmental situation has gotten worse and worse due to the economy's rapid growth and the industrialization and urbanization processes (Jinfeng & Huifeng, 2009). Over the past two decades, corporate environmental disclosures by bigger corporations have progressively grown in size and complexity (Jinfeng & Huifeng, 2009).

Concerns about the enterprises' environmental protection efforts have grown among the public at large and other stakeholders, who want the businesses to publicize more environmental information so that they can assess the company's sustainable development and the management's performance in terms of operations (Jinfeng & Huifeng, 2009). As a result, the various CG mechanisms, including boards of directors, audit committees, and auditors, oversee keeping an eye on and reining managers' choices and business operations that have an impact on all stakeholders, including society.

This could show a link between the efficiency of CG systems and the caliber of CSR disclosure. CG refers to the extensive ties that an organization has with its stakeholders or with society (Liu & Zhang, 2017). High standards of CG could protect the rights of stakeholders and promote social awareness (Liu & Zhang, 2017). In order for a CG system to be effective, transparency and accountability in general, and the disclosure of significant actions that have an impact on society and the environment in particular, are likely to be priorities (Habbash, 2016). One method of publishing or disclosing a company's CSR activity is through corporate social reporting. By informing the stakeholders about the firm's operations or by making further disclosures, one approach to close the communication gaps between both the company and its stakeholders (Said, Zainuddin, & Haron, 2009).

The board of directors and other CG mechanisms are crucial in adopting stakeholder engagement policies, excellent CSR practices, and procedures to ensure comprehensive transparency (Frias-Aceituno, Rodriguez-Ariza, & Garcia-Sanchez, 2013). Hence, CG is the determining factor of corporate social and environmental disclosures (Roy & Ghosh, 2019) where the percentage of environmental reporting in annual reports does seem to be impacted by excellent CG (Rao, Tilt, & Lester, 2012).

2.1. Corporate Environmental Disclosure

Businesses are being held more and more responsible for their environmental and social repercussions. It is therefore not surprising that raising literature has developed that analyses the trends in, the drivers behind, and the effects of voluntary social and environmental disclosures. Further, much of this literature focuses on either the frequency or the content of annual corporate reports as well as the separate environmental and social reports (Brammer & Pavelin, 2006).

Corporate environmental responsibility has been the subject of heated discussion for at least 25 years (Roy & Ghosh, 2019). According to Fuente, García-Sanchez & Lozano (2017), firms most typically employ disclosure of information on the practice of CSR to help stakeholders better understand an organization's social and environmental performance. The public is growing more conscious of environmental challenges and sustainable development, and it wants businesses to take action (Fuente et al., 2017).

Business managers now face a variety of environmental, ethical, racial, and social challenges in addition to productivity growth. Corporate environmental reporting (CER), along with these modifications, has grown in significance since the 1980s (Alipour, Ghanbari, Jamshidinavid, & Taherabadi, 2019). The need to produce environmental reports is being pushed by several stakeholders, primarily the government and foreign funding organizations. Practices in environmental reporting and disclosure let an organization inform its stakeholders about the effects of its actions on the environment.

Financial or non-financial reporting may be used for the reporting (Chaklader & Gulati, 2015). Mandatory disclosure improves the information set of financial analysts, as measured by their forecast consensus and overall uncertainty (Cormier, Lapointe-Antunes, & Magnan, 2015). In the decade of 1980, the focus switched over to corporate disclosure of environmental information instead of corporate social disclosure, and the trend sustained till now (Hossain et al., 2006).

The amount of social responsibility data being disclosed by publicly traded companies in sectors with high levels of pollution is falling. Several CG variables influence the level of disclosure of social responsibility information of publicly traded companies in high-pollution industries. A high level of CG is often advantageous for managing legitimacy and disclosing information about social responsibility (Liu & Zhang, 2017).

According to Viana Junior and Crisóstomo (Viana Junior & Crisóstomo, 2019), the companies included in the ISE index actually exhibit a better level of social and environmental disclosure than the competition. The findings stand up to both parametric and non-parametric analysis. The same is true for businesses operating in environmentally dangerous sectors, which disclose more social and environmental data in their financial reports than do those that aren't thought to pose a threat to the environment.

According to a study by Eldomiaty et al. (2016), highly rated businesses in terms of social and governance factors are classified financially as follows: high fixed asset turnover that is predominantly financed by debt and enhanced accounts receivables collection and customer trust results in benefits to the company's liquidity and profitability.

According to the study of Iatridis (2013), environmental disclosure is favorably related to environmental performance. Environmental disclosure quality is positively associated with company qualities such as significant size, the demand for capital, profitability, and capital investment. High-quality environmental disclosures demonstrate excellent company governance and are more likely to have easier access to capital markets. They are typically audited by one of the Big Four auditors or cross-listed on foreign stock exchanges, and they have large levels of managerial and institutional ownership. Environmental disclosures of high quality add value and improve investor views.

2.2. Empirical Studies on Corporate Environmental Disclosure

Several studies contacted to investigate the factors that influence environmental disclosure. The variable used are various where some of them are related to company characteristics and some others are related to CG characteristics. Table 24.1 illustrates some of the previous studies that investigate the factors that influence environmental disclosure.

Table 24.1. Empirical Studies on Corporate Environmental Disclosure.

Authors	Sample	Dependent Variable	Independent Variable	Measurement	Results
Chaklader and Gulati (2015)	50 Indian Profit-making companies (non-banking, non-insurance and non-financial institution companies); period from 2009 to 2012	EDI (environment disclosure index)	ROA	Net profits before tax divided by total assets	S+ (only in 2011)
			FSIZE	Log of total assets	S+
			INDUS	Dummy: 1 given to manufacturing company, 0 otherwise	Ins-
			Environment Certification	Dummy: 1 if it is certified, 0 otherwise	S+
			MNC	Dummy for multinational: 1 if multinational, 0 otherwise	Ins+
			LEV	Total debt/total assets	Ins+
Hossain et al. (2006)	107 Non-financial for the year 2002–2003 listed on the Dhaka Stock Exchange	SEDI (Social environment disclosure index)	International link of auditing firms	International link of auditing firms	Ins-
			FSIZE	Total amount of assets	Ins+
			Net profit margin	Net profit margin	S+
			ROA	% of return on total assets	Ins-
			MNC	Multinationality of companies	Ins-
			Sales	Total assets	
			DEBENTURE	% of public debenture	S+
			AFEES	Audit fees	Ins+
			INDUS	Industry type	S+
Rao et al. (2012)	96 Listed Australian firms in 2008,	Environmental disclosure	BIND	% of independent directors	S+
			BSIZE	Directors on board	S+
			WOB	% of female directors	S+
			FSIZE	- Total assets - Market capitalization - Operating revenue	Ins-
			ROA	Return on asset	S+
			INDUS	Dummy of industry classification	
			INSOWN	Institution ownership	S+

Viana Junior and Crisóstomo (2019)	1,252 Annual observations of 252 Malaysian's companies in the period 2010–2014	SEDI (0.1266)	CONCOWN	Three measurements have been used: Total of voting capital held by biggest shareholder, the two largest shareholders, and the three largest shareholders	S+
			D_10165	Dummy: 1 if the company belongs to environmentally risky industry, 0 otherwise	S+
			D_ISE	Dummy: 1 if firm related to theoretical portfolio (B3 Corporate Sustainability Index (ISE), 0 otherwise	S+
			ROA	Return-on-assets	S+
			FSIZE	Logarithm of total assets	Ins+
Akbas (2016)	Turkish listed firms in 2011	Environmental disclosure (total number of words related to the environmental issues in the annual report of the company) mean (623.952)	BSIZE	Directors on board	S+
			BIND	% of independent directors	Ins−
			WOB	%of female directors	Ins+
			ACIND	% of independent directors on the audit committee	Ins-
			FSIZE	Natural logarithm of total assets	S+
			ROA	Net profit after tax to total assets	Ins−
			INDUS	1 if the firm works in an environmentally sensitive industry, 0 otherwise	S+
Uwuigbe, Egbide, and Ayokunle (2011)	40 Nigeria listed firms both in the financial and non-financial sectors for period 2006–2010	Corporate environmental disclosure (CED)	BSIZE	Directors on board	S−
			BIND	% of non-executive directors	S+
Post et al. (2011)	78 Electronics for 2006 and chemical for 2007 firms list of Fortune 1,000 companies.	ESCR	BIND	% of outside directors	S+
			WOB	Women on the board	S+
			INDUS	Dummy variable (0 = electronics, 1 = chemicals)	S+
			CEO duality	Dummy: 1 if CEO is chairman, 0 otherwise	Ins
			BSIZE	Number of directors	Ins
Brammer and Pavelin (2006)	447 Companies listed in FTSE All-Share Index, London.	Environmental disclosures	FSIZE	Logarithm of total assets	S+
			LEV	Total debt to total assets	S−
			ROA	Pre-tax profits before interest and tax to total assets	Ins
			OWNCON	Largest significant shareholding	S−

S, significant; Ins, insignificant; +, positive; −, negative.

3. METHODOLOGY

3.1. Research Framework and Hypothesis Development

According to agency theory, the BOD's principal purpose is to oversee the decisions of agents to protect the interests of owners. Furthermore, the resource dependence theory suggests that BOD must do more than reduce uncertainty by demonstrating their skill and understanding in internal decision making, as they have worked in other organizations. Hence, BOD plays a major role in an organization. Therefore, the aim of the study is to investigate the influence of the board of directors' characteristics, namely board size, meetings, independence, gender diversity, and qualification, on environmental disclosure. The measurement of variables will rely on the previous literature review. The theoretical basis of this investigation is depicted schematically in Fig. 24.1.

Based on the agency and resource dependence theories, the study expected the following hypotheses:

H1. Board size has a significant positive impact on environmental disclosure.

H2. Board meetings have a significant positive impact on environmental disclosure.

H3. Board independence has a significant positive impact on environmental disclosure.

H4. Board gender diversity has a significant positive impact on environmental disclosure.

H5. Board member qualification has a significant positive impact on environmental disclosure.

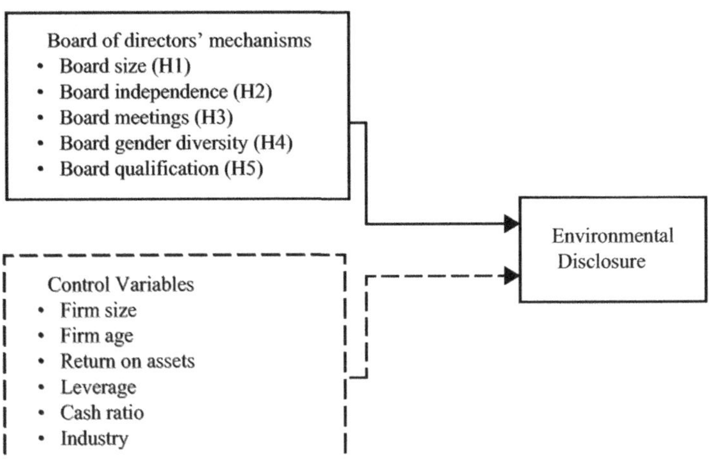

Fig. 24.1. Theoretical Representation of Relationships.

3.2. Research Design

This is a quantitative study using secondary data where the author manually collects data on BOD mechanisms from the annual report of companies published or posted on the website of companies. The study covers all listed manufacturing companies in Saudi Arabia and Bahrain for the years 2018–2022. This study used suitable regression to investigate the influence of the board of directors' characteristics, namely board size, meetings, independence, gender diversity, and qualification, on environmental disclosure. To assess the extent of each variable's impact on environmental disclosure, the following regression models were used:

$$\text{ED} = \beta_0 + \beta_1\,\text{BSIZE} + \beta_2\,\text{BMEET} + \beta_3\,\text{IND} + \beta_4\,\text{BGEN} + \beta_5\,\text{BQ} \\ + \beta_6\,\text{FAGE} + \beta_7\,\text{ROA} + \beta_8\,\text{LEV} + \beta_9\,\text{CR} + \beta_{10}\,\text{INDUS} + \varepsilon$$

where ED being environmental disclosure, BSIZE is board size, BMEET is board meeting, BIND is board independence, BGEN is board gender diversity, BQ is board qualification, FAGE is firm age, ROA is a return on assets, LEV is leverage, CR is cash ratio, and INDUS is industry.

4. CONCLUSION

Businesses have been considered responsible for the environmental effects of their actions as the main driver of economic development. Many stakeholders, for example, governments and regulators, investors, employees, and society have all paid close attention to how businesses affect the environment, including greenhouse gas emissions, carbon footprints, and the disposal of toxic waste. The aim of the study is to investigate the influence of the board of directors' characteristics, namely board size, meetings, independence, gender diversity, and qualification, on environmental disclosure. The study expected that the board of directors' characteristics should have a significant impact on enhancing environmental disclosure.

The study's findings will make an important contribution to the literature because it is the first study to be undertaken in a developing country, such as Bahrain, where no study has previously been conducted. The findings will assist many parties, including policy makers, regulators, shareholders, and managers, in determining the impact of will governance on the level of high quality in environmental disclosure, which will help companies develop a good reputation.

The study has some limitations where it is covering only listed manufacturing companies in Saudi Arabia and Bahrain. Further, it selects only variables related to BOD characteristics. Future studies may cover more countries and some other variables that not including in the current study.

REFERENCES

Achiyaale, R. A., Adaletey, J. E., Alkadash, T. M., Forson, J. A., & Tsorhe, D. K. (2022). Financial markets development and economic competitiveness growth in ECOWAS. *Specialusis Ugdymas*, *1*(43), 282–299.

Akbas, H. E. (2016). The relationship between board characteristics and environmental disclosure: Evidence from Turkish listed companies. *South East European Journal of Economics and Business*, *11*(2), 7–19.

Alipour, M., Ghanbari, M., Jamshidinavid, B., & Taherabadi, A. (2019). Does Board Independence moderate the relationship between environmental disclosure quality and performance? Evidence from static and dynamic panel data. *Corporate Governance: The International Journal of Business in Society*, *19*(3), 580–610.

Al-Absy, M. S. M. (2020). The Board Chairman's characteristics and financial stability of Malaysian-listed firms. *Cogent Business & Management*, *7*(1), 1823586.

Al-Absy, M. S. M. (2022a). Board Chairman characteristics and real earnings management. *Sustainability*, *14*(22), 15025.

Al-Absy, M. S. M. (2022b). Impactful Women Directors and earnings management. *Cogent Business & Management*, *9*(1), 2148873.

Al-Absy, M. S. M., Almaamari, Q., Alkadash, T., & Habtoor, A. (2020). Gender diversity and financial stability: Evidence from Malaysian listed firms. *The Journal of Asian Finance, Economics and Business*, *7*(12), 181–193.

Al-Absy, M., & Hasan, M. (2023). Impact of the Board of Directors' characteristics on firm performance: A case of Bahraini listed firms. *Problems and Perspectives in Management*, *21*(1), 291–301.

Al-Absy, M. S. M., Ismail, K. N. I. K., & Chandren, S. (2017, November 2). Board Chairmen's involvement in Audit Committees and earnings management practices (pp. 1–26). Retrieved from https://ssrn.com/abstract=3063845.

Al-Absy, M. S. M., Ismail, K. N. I. K., Chandren, S., & Al-Dubai, S. A. A. (2020). Involvement of Board Chairmen in Audit Committees and earnings management: Evidence from Malaysia. *The Journal of Asian Finance, Economics and Business*, *7*(8), 233–246.

Alkadash, T. M., & Aljileedi, S. M. (2020). Corporate social responsibility, and employee commitment in Libyan. *International Journal of Intellectual Human Resource Management*, *1*(1), 28–40.

Brammer, S., & Pavelin, S. (2006). Voluntary environmental disclosures by large UK companies. *Journal of Business Finance & Accounting*, *33*(7–8), 1168–1188.

Chaklader, B., & Gulati, P. A. (2015). A study of corporate environmental disclosure practices of companies doing business In India. *Global Business Review*, *16*(2), 321–335.

Cormier, D., Lapointe-Antunes, P., & Magnan, M. (2015). Does corporate governance enhance the appreciation of mandatory environmental disclosure by financial markets? *Journal of Management & Governance*, *19*(4), 897–925.

Da Silva Monteiro, S. M., & Aibar-Guzmán, B. (2010). Determinants of environmental disclosure in the annual reports of large companies operating in Portugal. *Corporate Social Responsibility and Environmental Management*, *17*(4), 185–204.

Deegan, C. (2004). Environmental disclosures and share prices – A discussion about efforts to study this relationship. In *Accounting Forum* (Vol. 28(1), PP. 87–97). Oxfordshire: Taylor & Francis.

Eldomiaty, T., Soliman, A., Fikri, A., & Anis, M. (2016). The financial aspects of the Corporate Responsibility Index in Egypt. *International Journal of Social Economics*, *43*(3), 284–307.

Elgammal, W., El-Kassar, A.-N., & Messarra, L. C. (2018). Corporate ethics, governance and social responsibility in MENA countries. *Management Decision*, *56*(1), 273–291.

Frias-Aceituno, J. V., Rodriguez-Ariza, L., & Garcia-Sanchez, I. M. (2013). The role of the board in the dissemination of integrated corporate social reporting. *Corporate Social Responsibility and Environmental Management*, *20*(4), 219–233.

Fuente, J. A., García-Sanchez, I. M., & Lozano, M. B. (2017). The role of the Board of Directors in the adoption of GRI guidelines for the disclosure of CSR information. *Journal of Cleaner Production*, *141*, 737–750.

Habbash, M. (2016). Corporate governance and corporate social responsibility disclosure: Evidence from Saudi Arabia. *Social Responsibility Journal*, *12*(4), 740–754.

Hossain, M., Islam, K., & Andrew, J. (2006, October). Corporate social and environmental disclosure in developing countries: Evidence from Bangladesh. In *Proceedings of the Asian Pacific Conference on International Accounting Issues*, Maui, HI.

Iatridis, G. E. (2013). Environmental disclosure quality: Evidence on environmental performance, corporate governance and value relevance. *Emerging Markets Review*, *14*, 55–75.

Jinfeng, Z., & Huifeng, X. (2009). Empirical research on factors influencing level of environmental protection information disclosure in annual reports by listed companies. *Chinese Journal of Population Resources and Environment*, *7*(1), 15–22.

Jizi, M. (2017). The influence of board composition on sustainable development disclosure. *Business Strategy and the Environment*, *26*(5), 640–655.

Li, D., Cao, C., Zhang, L., Chen, X., Ren, S., & Zhao, Y. (2017). Effects of corporate environmental responsibility on financial performance: The moderating role of government regulation and organizational slack. *Journal of Cleaner Production*, *166*, 1323–1334.

Liu, X., & Zhang, C. (2017). Corporate governance, social responsibility information disclosure, and enterprise value in China. *Journal of Cleaner Production*, *142*, 1075–1084.

Mahdi, S. M. A., Al-Absy, M. S. M., & Alastalm, A. Y. (2023). Corporate social responsibility and firm's performance: Evidence from Bahrain. In *International conference on business and technology*, Berlin.

Malik, M. (2015). Value-enhancing capabilities of CSR: A brief review of contemporary literature. *Journal of Business Ethics*, *127*(2), 419–438.

Post, C., Rahman, N., & Rubow, E. (2011). Green Governance: Boards of Directors' composition and environmental corporate social responsibility. *Business & Society*, *50*(1), 189–223.

Rao, K. K., Tilt, C. A., & Lester, L. H. (2012). Corporate governance and environmental reporting: An Australian study. *Corporate Governance: The International Journal of Business in Society*, *12*(2), 143–163.

Roy, A., & Ghosh, S. K. (2019). Determinants of corporate environmental disclosure from an Asian perspective. *IIM Kozhikode Society & Management Review*, *8*(2), 171–189.

Said, R., Zainuddin, Y. H., & Haron, H. (2009). The relationship between corporate social responsibility disclosure and corporate governance characteristics in Malaysian public listed companies. *Social Responsibility Journal*, *5*(2), 212–226.

Uwuigbe, U. N., Egbide, B.-C., & Ayokunle, A. M. (2011). The effect of board size and board composition on firms corporate environmental disclosure: A study of selected firms in Nigeria. *Acta Universitatis Danubius. Œconomica*, *7*(5), 164–176.

Viana Junior, D. B. C., & Crisóstomo, V. L. (2019). The effects of voting ownership concentration on social and environmental disclosure: Empirical Evidence from Brazil. *Revista Brasileira de Gestão de Negócios*, *21*(4), 906–927.

PART IV

SUSTAINABILITY, BIG DATA AND FINANCIAL MANAGEMENT

CHAPTER 25

TECHNOLOGIES IN SUSTAINABLE SUPPLY CHAIN: INSIGHTS FROM A SYSTEMATIC LITERATURE REVIEW

Nitha Mary Siju[a,b] and Avinash Shivdas[a]

[a]*Amrita School of Business, Kollam, Kerala, India*
[b]*Department of Business and Accounting, Muscat College, Muscat, Oman*

ABSTRACT

Sustainability has become the topic of the era, and the world is moving toward a circular economy. As part of it, companies are also integrating sustainability in supply chain management. Therefore, this study conducts a technology-empowered systematic literature review to examine the state of the literature on the technologies in the sustainable supply chain. The review reveals that limited studies have been conducted in the area. There is still scope for the researchers to explore new innovative technologies, many clusters in author collaboration, and involve more sectors in the study. Future studies can enrich the field by employing other methodologies like meta-analysis review.

Keywords: Supply chain; technology; sustainability; systematic literature review; SPAR-4-SLR; 5W1H framework

Digital Technology and Changing Roles in Managerial and Financial Accounting: Theoretical Knowledge and Practical Application
Studies in Managerial and Financial Accounting, Volume 36, 281–304

ISSN: 1479-3512/doi:10.1108/S1479-351220240000036027

1. INTRODUCTION

Sustainability is now a matter of concern for most organizations. A research report from McKinsey & Company showcased that those organizations who have ratings for environmental, social and governance at a high level have a low cost of debt and equity and are not performing in a long-term supply chains have a major impact on society, environment, and financial performance (Bonini & Swartz, 2014). Companies are facing a growing chorus of demands to make a sustainable supply chain. Customers are also putting pressure and are interested to know the way the products have been made. According to Chopra (2019), the supply chain comprises financial, information, and product flows, and proper management of the above components can impact achieving competitive advantage. Production and technological advancements are the results of globalization. Due to these advancements, the organization needs a more dynamic supply chain (Defee & Fugate, 2010). Appropriate technologies can assist in creating and encouraging sustainability. The uncertainty in the global value chain might endanger the financial feasibility by causing supply sources disruptions (Jajja, Chatha, & Farooq, 2018). Supply chain risks might originate from various sources, such as volatility in price natural disasters (Pettit, Croxton, & Fiksel, 2013) and scandals related to sustainability (Villena & Gioia, 2020). COVID-19 pandemic was the recent supply chain risk the organizations have dealt with.

However, the COVID-19 pandemic has impacted all supply chain elements, unlike other disasters the world has witnessed. This led to disruption in the flow of the supply chain. It has been reported that freight and shipping account for around 3% of carbon emissions (Ivanov, 2021; Panday, 2020). The quarantines and lockdown have impacted all the elements like production, transportation, supplies, and caused uncertainties in demand and supply. Academics have started exploring the devasting effects of COVID-19 in the supply chain. Various studies have proposed that technology is a significant element in deciding the success or failure of the company during the pandemic. They have suggested that multiple technologies like artificial intelligence (AI) and blockchain technology can assist in making the supply chain more resilient (Goel, Saunoris, & Goel, 2020; Hinge, Muksor, Goyal, Goyal, & Goyal, 2020; Ivanov & Dolgui, 2020; Ranney, Griffeth, & Jha, 2020; Sharma, Adhikary, & Borah, 2020). Various other researchers have focused on the role of technologies in the sustainability of the supply chain (Alnuaimi, Khan, & Ajmal, 2021; Umar, Khan, Zia-ul-haq, Yusliza, & Farooq, 2022).

The researchers and practitioners believe that supply chain digitization has the potential to increase visibility and collaboration along the supply chain. According to Agrawal, Narain, and Ullah (2019), very few companies have adopted their supply chain integration technologies. Only 5% of firms have analyzed the importance of doing so (Dougados & Felgendreher, 2016). Hence, the current research focuses on a systematic literature review of the technologies adopted by various sectors in the sustainable supply chain. This can be a realization for various other sectors to apply the digitization for an improvement in the supply chain performance.

2. PROBLEM DESCRIPTION AND RESEARCH QUESTIONS

Nowadays, much attention has been given to sustainability for organizations and their supply chain. Various studies can be observed in the sustainability, digitization, and integration in the supply chain; however, the essential aspects have received less attention in those studies. The studies related to these areas were conducted in separate ways. Various studies have identified the positive and negative factors of using technology in a sustainable supply chain (Berkhout, Muskens, & Velthuijsen, 2000; Sarkis, 2019). The combination of digital technologies and sustainability issues were addressed (Büyüközkan & Göçer, 2018). The drivers and effects of sustainable supply chain practices have been explored (Akhtar, 2019). According to Friedman and Ormiston (2021), minimal studies have been published to analyze technology's role in sustainable supply chain development critically. Several articles have been published focusing on a particular technology in a sustainable supply chain for a specific sector (Di Vaio & Varriale, 2020; Diniz et al., 2021). Hence there is a lack of articles integrating the various technologies used in sustainable supply chain and identifying the sectors where they were employed. Therefore, the authors feel the importance of creating a common cluster in the research domain from various articles related to technologies published until now. Motivated by the above gaps in the literature, the current study provides a systematic literature review regarding the research trends in the area of study, analyzes the various technologies prevalent in the sustainable supply chain and identifies the sectors that rely on these technologies for sustainability. Thus, this study provides a comprehensive view of sustainable supply chain management technologies using a systematic literature review. The study seeks to achieve the following objectives:

1. What are the characteristics of publication trends in sustainable supply chain technologies?
2. What are the various technologies used in the sustainable supply chain?
3. Which sectors are using these technologies in the sustainability of the supply chain?
4. What are the different methodologies used in the research?
5. What are the thematic breakouts and future research directions in technology in a sustainable supply chain?

This chapter is structured into nine sections: (1) Introduction, (2) Current problem description and objectives, (3) Related works and motivations, (4) The methodology section, which describes the article selection, categorization and the inclusion criteria, (5) Findings section which analyzes the results according to the research objectives framed, (6) Practical Implications, and (7) Conclusion.

3. RELATED WORK AND MOTIVATIONS

The concept of sustainability has been introduced in recent years in management and in technology-related fields and supply chains. The organizations are focusing more on environmental strategies. One of the major environmental strategies that the organization aims for is supply chain management. A sustainable supply chain becomes an important strategy that helps organizations to gain a competitive advantage. SSCM strategy is still unclear and can result in both positive and negative impacts. Hence, various research studies have been conducted to identify the advantages and barriers of a sustainable supply chain. The managing process involved in the supply chain management activities for environmental, economic and social issues for the enhancement of economic gals which are long term.

According to Gonzálvez-Gallego, Molina-Castillo, Soto-Acosta, Varajao, and Trigo (2015) and Lai, Hsu, and Chen (2012), it is stated that the technologies increase the business performance of the supply chain. IT can become more sustainable, and at the same time, sustainability can be enhanced by IT (Piotrowicz & Cuthbertson, 2009). Melville (2010) states that environmental sustainability can be improved by IT. The future of the Green supply chain can also be enhanced by Srivastava (2007). The technology can be applied in different parts of the supply chain. Most research papers have focused on the forward flow of the supply chain. Quite a few research papers have also discussed the supply chain's reverse flow. The supply chain's forward flow mainly focuses on transportation and its environmental impacts, and the reverse flow focuses on reuse and recycling. Sourirajan et al. (2009) focused on the IT planning tools for calculating carbon emissions. Schiller (2012) highlighted that various companies could make their warehouses larger and shorten the distance for travel too. Lacob, van Sinderen, Steenwijk, and Verkroost (2013) proposed a method to calculate the carbon calculation of transportation. Vehicle routing is another improvement by using technology to achieve sustainability in the supply chain. The social network can be used to solve the delivery issues, thereby reducing the delay in the delivery (Suh, Smith, & Linhoff, 2012). The Indian agricultural value chain was improved by technology (Verma & Chaudhuri, 2009). The efficiency can be enhanced by technology.

The web-based systems were used for information exchange Edwards, Lyons, and Kehoe (2004) and are used in reverse logistics. SMART containers, SMART warehousing, SMART ports, SMART shelves and SMART manufacturing result from integration technology in the supply chain. The above innovations have led to an increase in efficiency, visibility and control, thereby decreasing the downtime, waste and defects. According to Chaopaisarn and Woschank (2019), apart from eliminating unnecessary waste, the sustainable supply chain leads the way for the agile supply chain. Automation of warehouses, smart vehicles and SMART logistics planning are a few advantages of using technologies in the supply chain (Brettel, Friederichsen, Keller, & Rosenberg, 2014). Various technologies were listed by Mittal, Khan, Romero, and Wuest (2019). The authors have clustered this technology into 11 groups. The technologies include big data, visual technology, intelligent control systems, energy-saving technology, smart products, cloud computing, cybersecurity, Internet of things, Cyber-Physical Systems, Additive printing, Advanced Manufacturing and IT-based production Management.

4. METHODOLOGY

Systematic literature reviews are used to summarize the research findings and the literature in a systematic and organized way (Davis, Mengersen, Bennett, & Mazerolle, 2014). In the current study, the systematic literature review is used to analyze the types of technologies used in sustainable supply chains and identify the most used sectors. Thus, the review can be classified as a domain-based review. According to the domain-based review, focus is on the advancement in a particular area. In the current research, the area of sustainable supply chain and the topic of technology in the sustainable supply chain are taken for review. In the category of domain-based review, the current study can be further classified as a framework-based review. The review that depends on an established framework to guide the domain review is known as framework-based review. According to Lim, Ahmad, Rasul, and Parvez (2021), systematic literature reviews rely on review protocols in the past. However, in the systematic literature review in social sciences, especially in entrepreneurship and business, new review protocols have been developed by researchers such as Scientific Procedures and Rationales for Systematic Literature Reviews (SPAR-4-SLR).

The current study relied on the SPAR 4SLR model as represented in Fig. 25.1, consisting of three stages and six sub-stages, as the model's insights can be logically justified. The SPAR4 SLR is used in the research instead of PRISMA protocol which was developed by Moher et al. (2009), as PRISMA protocol will permit the researchers to only categorize the reviews orderly and transparently rather than analysing logically.

4.1. Assembling

The first stage in SPAR4SLR includes assembling, which identifies and acquires the literature that is the non-synthesized form (Paul et al., 2021). According to Kumar, Paul, and Unnithan (2022), the identification stage sets out the scope for the review. With regard to the identification stage, this literature review tries to identify the publications relating to the domain "Technologies in the sustainable supply chain" and will be helpful in sorting the research questions (RQ1 to RQ4). This review has concentrated on journal publications (Source Type) indexed in Scopus (Source Quality). Journal articles are concentrated as it is peer-reviewed compared to book chapters. The Scopus has been included in the source quality based on the database's stringent quality criteria in indexing. The decisions taken are consistent with the guideline published by Paul et al. (2021).

The second substage includes acquisition, highlighting the searching and material acquisition mechanism. Scopus database is used for the acquisition of data. According to Donthu, Kumar, Paul, Pattnaik, and Strong (2021), all the bibliometric information regarding the database can be achieved by Scopus. Similarly, Scopus provides more high-quality journal publications than other prominent databases (Paul et al., 2021). The search words "Technology" AND "Sustainable" AND in AND "Supply" AND "chain" for the title, abstracts and keywords. The search terms generated 3,104 documents. Further filtering was done on the year of publication. The research articles published between the year 2015 and 2022 in Scopus were selected for the study as the research domain is relevant to technology, a dynamic concept vulnerable to updating and changes. Hence the five to seven years seems to be appropriate for the study. The subject

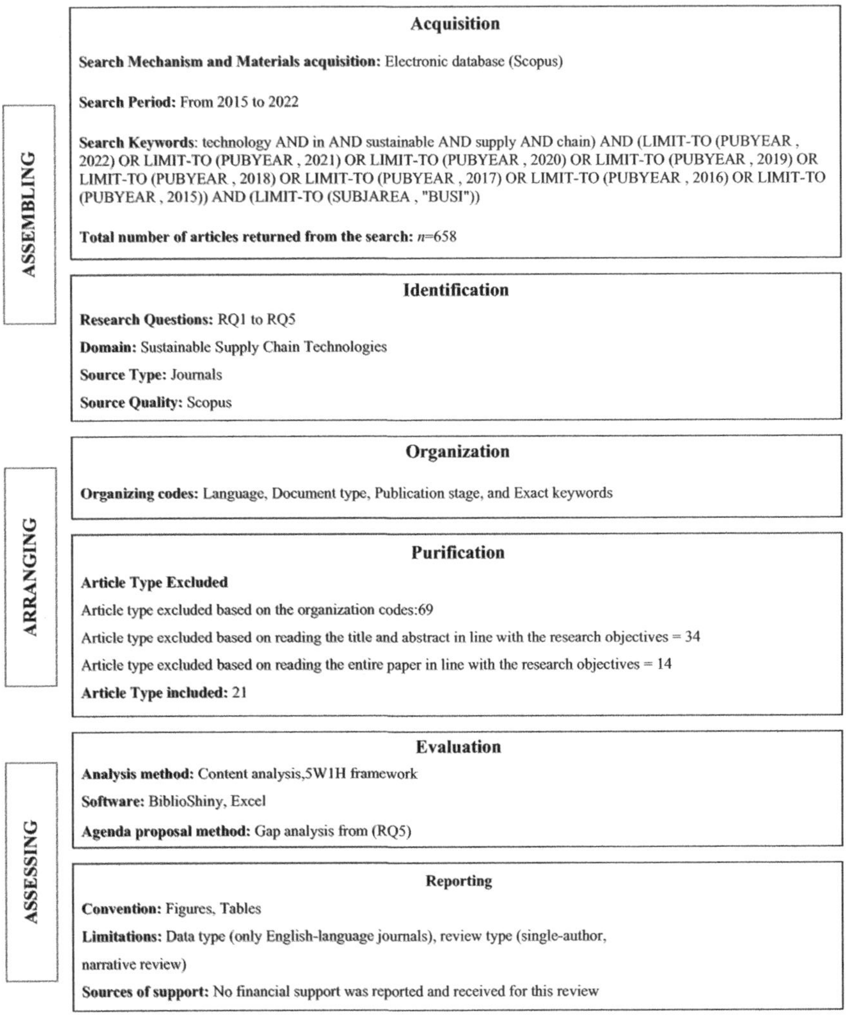

Fig. 25.1. Implementation of Systematic Literature Review According to SPAR-4-SLR Protocol (Paul, Lim, O'Cass, Hao, & Bresciani, 2021).

area is chosen as Business, Management and Accounting. Hence the search term has been revised to **technology AND in AND sustainable AND supply AND chain) AND (LIMIT-TO (PUBYEAR, 2022) OR LIMIT-TO (PUBYEAR, 2021) OR LIMIT-TO (PUBYEAR, 2020) OR LIMIT-TO (PUBYEAR, 2019) OR LIMIT-TO (PUBYEAR, 2018) OR LIMIT-TO (PUBYEAR, 2017) OR LIMIT-TO (PUBYEAR, 2016) OR LIMIT-TO (PUBYEAR, 2015)) AND (LIMIT-TO (SUBJAREA, "BUSI"))**. In total, 658 articles were screened to the arranging stage.

4.2. Arranging

The arranging stage also includes two stages organization and purification. Categorical filters were used in the organization stage, such as language, document type, publication stage, and exact keywords. The abovementioned is used as organization codes which is consistent with the guidelines proposed by Paul et al. (2021).

The purification stage utilizes specifically mention the exclusion and inclusion criteria. The purification considered the inclusion criteria of language taken as English in the case of the current article. The author of the current study is proficient in English. Then the document type which is the article, publication stage, which is final and the exact keywords as "Sustainable Development," "Supply Chains," "Supply Chain Management," "Sustainability," "Industry 4.0," "Sustainable Supply Chains," "Block-chain," "Supply Chain," "Sustainable Supply Chain," "Internet Of Things," "Technology," "Artificial Intelligence" and "Sustainable Food Supply Chain" which have reduced the number of literature to 69.

In the second stage of purification, the articles were further screened based on the title and abstract in line with the research objective, which narrowed down the inclusion criteria to 34 and then reading the full research paper, it was further reduced to 21.

4.3. Assessing

Evaluation and reporting of the literature review are included in the last stage of assessing (Paul et al., 2021). Content analysis and thematic analysis: content analysis is used to determine the theme. 5W1H.5W1H is an interrogative framework that includes What, Why, Where, When, Who and How (Lim, 2020). Paul et al. (2021) recommend the use of the 5W1H framework for structuring the literature review as it provides clarity and coverage of reviews at a high level. The 5W1H framework for the current study is shown in Fig. 25.2. To delineate the research trend and the top articles in the domain (RQ1), to identify the types of technologies used (RQ2) and to analyze the future research directions in the field of technology (RQ5) in the sustainable supply chain, the interrogative framework of "What" is utilized. The reason for using the top technologies derived from (RQ2) can be analyzed from the "Why framework." Other characteristics of RQ1, such as identifying the top authors' "How," is being utilized. The RQ3 and the top countries where the research has been done regarding the domain (RQ1) is analyzed using the "Where" from the framework. To identify the advantages of using these technologies, "How" has been utilized.

Reporting has been done using tables (Biblioshiny) and figures (network visualization, word cloud) and words (narratives). The current study did not have any external funding and is solely based on the accuracy and completeness of information available in Scopus (Donthu et al., 2021).

5. FINDINGS

The current research is regarding the technologies in a sustainable supply chain. The results have been developed out of 21 articles filtered through the SPAR4SLR model. The word cloud developed from the Nvivo as shown in

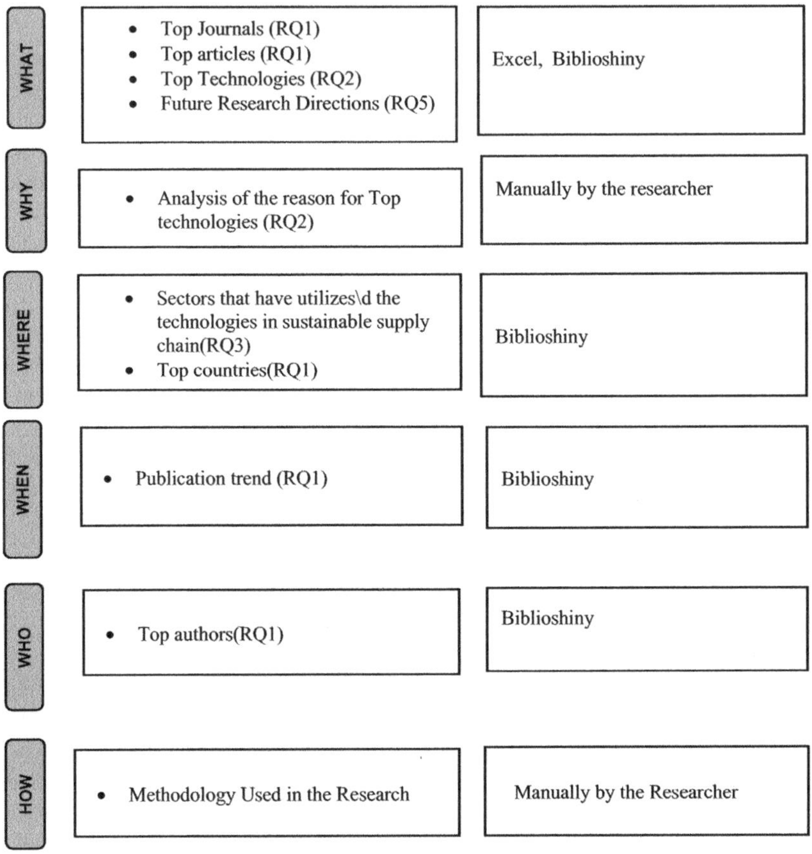

Fig. 25.2. 5W1H Framework Used in the Research.

Fig. 25.3 shows that articles filtered are closely related to the area selected for the review. The highlighted words, including "technology, sustainable supply chain, blockchain, management, supply information," are the central themes of most articles. The results in this section are arranged according to the research questions using the 5W1H framework. This is evidence for the validity of the review being conducted.

5.1. Characteristics of the Nature of Research Trend in the Domain

The features of the research trend are further categorized into the following clusters:

- *Publication Trend*

The publication trend in technologies in the supply chain is depicted in Fig. 25.4 and Table 25.1. The figure shows that research in the high-quality journals has

Fig. 25.3. Word Cloud Exported from Nvivo Deriving the Theme of the Articles.

shown an increasing trend in 2021. 2015 can be considered a starting stage in the domain as only one article relevant to the area of study was published in 2015. In the years 2016–2018, there has been negligible contribution in the research related to the current research. A minimum of three articles can be seen published relevant to the study's objectives from 2019 onwards. The publication trend clearly indicates that there are still areas relevant to be explored in the case of the domain in the current study.

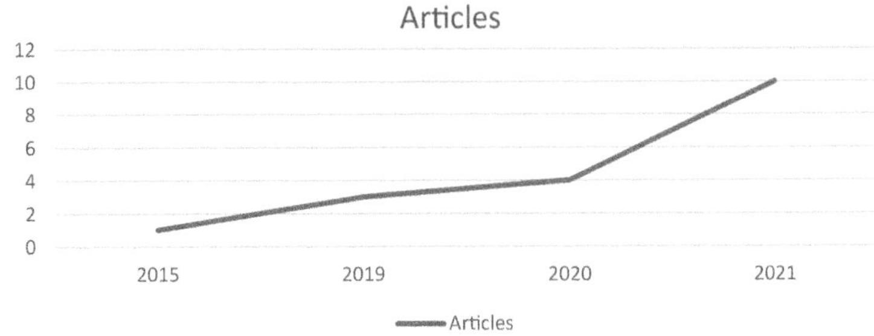

Fig. 25.4. Publication Trend Derived from Biblioshiny Based on Table 25.1.

Table 25.1. Publication Trend of Technologies in Sustainable Supply Chain.

Year	Articles
2015	1
2019	3
2020	4
2021	10
2022	3

Note: Source of data = Scopus. Period of coverage = 2015 to 2022. Total publications = 21.

- *Top Journals*

The top articles that published the technologies in the sustainable supply chain are given in Table 25.2.

Table 25.2 and Fig. 25.5 indicate that the "*Journal of Cleaner Production* has published six articles." Three have been published each by the *International Journal of Production Economics* and Technological forecasting and social change. In a holistic view, the list of journals from the above table suggests that journals focusing on social aspects as well as in engineering and management are publishing the major articles related to technology in sustainable supply chain.

- *Top Articles*

The top articles can be analyzed based on global citations and local citations. According to Donthu et al. (2021), the number of citations received by a Scopus indexed article by other Scopus indexed articles is known as global citations. Table 25.3 shows that the paper titled "Modeling the blockchain-enabled traceability in the agriculture supply chain" by S. S. Kamble (2020) is top in the list with 175 citations, followed by the article titled "Blockchain technology and the sustainable supply chain: Theoretically exploring adoption barriers" by M. Kouhizadeh (2021) with 129 citations. It is noteworthy that all the articles have technology as their central theme.

Table 25.2. Journals for Technologies in Sustainable Supply Chain.

Sources	Articles
Journal of Cleaner Production	6
International Journal of Production Economics	3
Technological Forecasting and Social Change	3
Industrial Management and Data Systems	2
International Journal of Information Management	2
IEEE Engineering Management Review	1
IEEE Transactions on Engineering Management	1
Journal of Global Information Management	1
TQM Journal	1
Transportation Research Part E: Logistics and Transportation Review	1

Note: Source of data = Scopus. Period of coverage = 2015 to 2022. Total publications = 21.

Fig. 25.5. Most Relevant Sources Based on Table 25.2.

Table 25.3. Top Articles Technologies in Sustainable Supply Chain.

Paper	Total Citations	TC per Year
KAMBLE SS, 2020,	175	58.33
KOUHIZADEH M, 2021,	129	64.50
LI Y, 2020,	88	29.33
DI VAIO A, 2020,	77	25.67
GNTHER HO, 2015,	61	7.62
ALLAOUI H, 2019,	59	14.75
KHLER S, 2020,	44	14.67
FETANAT A, 2019,	38	9.50
SHARMA M, 2021,	33	16.50
SARKIS J, 2021,	15	7.50
ROY M, 2019,	14	3.50
MANGLA SK, 2021,	12	6.00
YU Y, 2021,	7	3.50
UNIYAL S, 2021,	7	3.50
QUAYSON M, 2021,	5	2.50
DINIZ EH, 2021,	5	2.50
ALNUAIMI BK, 2021,	3	1.50
UMAR M, 2022,	1	1.00
SUN J, 2021,	1	0.50
YOUSEFI S, 2022,	0	0.00

Note: Source of data = Scopus. Period of coverage = 2015 to 2022. Total publications = 21.

Local citation means the number of citations an article receives in the corpus from other corpus articles (Donuthu et al., 2021). Table 25.4 shows that none of the articles received a local citation. Hence it is important to analyze the local citation for the purpose of determining the extent of in-field influence and the bibliometric review value.

Table 25.4. Articles With Top Local Citations in Technologies in Sustainable Supply Chain.

Document	DOI	Year	Local.Citations	Global.Citations
GNTHER HO, 2015,	NA	2015	0	61
ALLAOUI H, 2019,	NA	2019	0	59
LI Y, 2020,	NA	2020	0	88
DI VAIO A, 2020,	NA	2020	0	77
KAMBLE SS, 2020,	NA	2020	0	175
KOUHIZADEH M, 2021,	NA	2021	0	129

Note: Source of data = Scopus. Period of coverage = 2015 to 2022. Total publications = 21.

Table 25.5. Statistics of Countries Related to the Top Countries.

Region	Freq
China	12
USA	10
India	7
France	5
Iran	4
Finland	3
Turkey	3
Brazil	2
Italy	2
Morocco	2
UK	2
Canada	1
Denmark	1
Germany	1
Malaysia	1
Netherlands	1
Pakistan	1
South Korea	1
Taiwan	1

Note: Source of data = Scopus. Period of coverage = 2015 to 2022. Total publications = 21.

- *Top Countries*

The statistics of the country regarding the 21 articles, as shown in Table 25.5, highlights that the top five countries publishing in the field are China (12), the USA (10), India (7), France (5) and Iran (4). The above statistics may result from cross-country author collaboration, that is, authors from multiple countries working on a single article (refer Fig. 25.6).

To have a more detailed analysis on this, the co-author's countries' have been taken into account and the collaboration has been shown in Table 25.6. SCP shows the intra country collaboration, and MCP offers intercountry collaboration. According to Kwiek (2020), the collaboration will provide prestige, recognition and more chances of getting research funding as well.

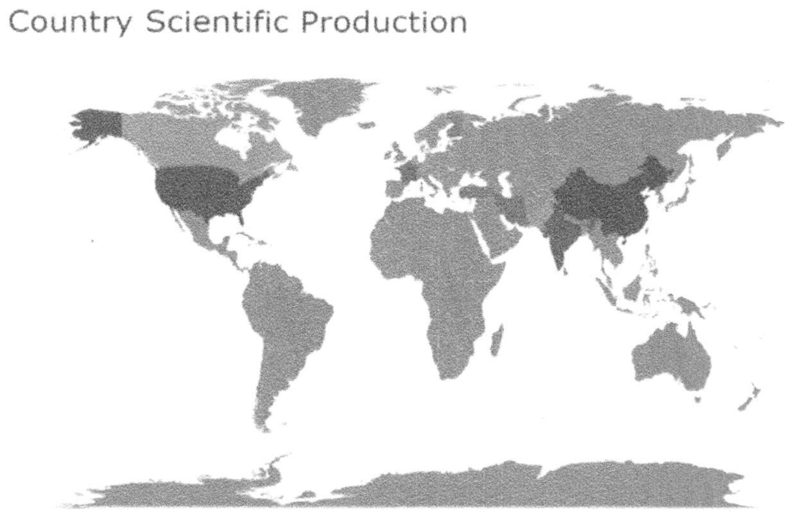

Fig. 25.6. Geographic Map Exported From Biblioshiny Related to the Country-specific Production of Articles.

Table 25.6. Statistics of Country Collaboration.

Country	Articles	Freq	SCP	MCP
China	6	0.30	2	4
USA	3	0.15	2	1
Brazil	1	0.05	1	0
Canada	1	0.05	1	0
Denmark	1	0.05	1	0
Iran	1	0.05	1	0
Italy	1	0.05	1	0
France	3	0.15	0	3
Finland	1	0.05	0	1
India	1	0.05	0	1
Korea	1	0.05	0	1

Note: Source of data = Scopus. Period of coverage = 2015 to 2022. Total publications = 21.

In the case of China, the intercountry collaboration (4) between the authors is found to be high than the intracountry collaboration (2). The trend is similar for France, Finland, India and Korea. However, the trend is vice versa in the case of the USA, Brazil, Canada, Denmark, Iran and Italy. It can be concluded that the trend of intercountry and intracountry collaboration is there in the research study of Technologies in Sustainable supply chain. However, the numbers are found to be low in both cases, which can be improved in future by the researchers.

Collaboration between different countries has also been developed, as shown in Fig. 25.7. Two clusters can be seen in the figure. USA and China seem to be

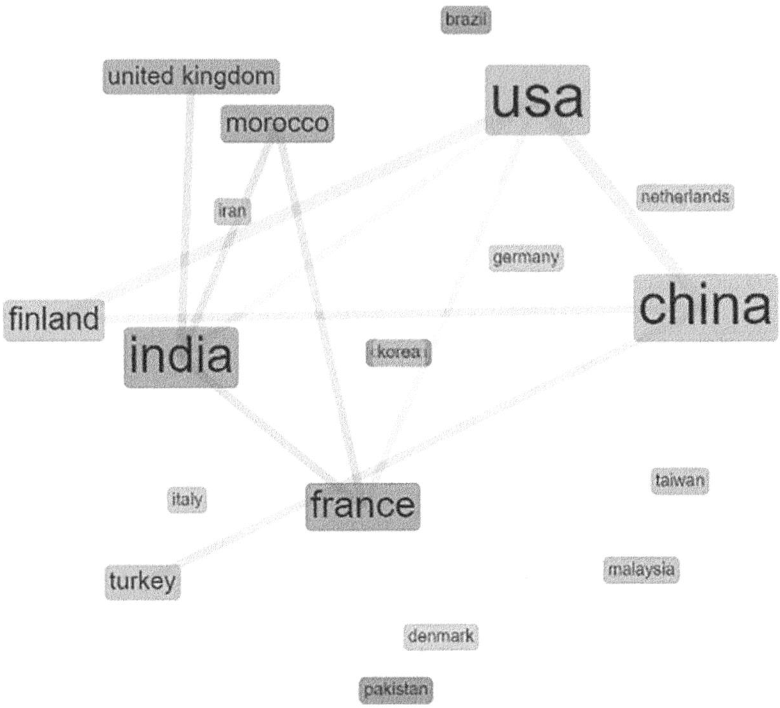

Fig. 25.7. Country Collaboration in Sustainable Supply Chain Management Technologies.

the heart of one cluster which have cross collaborations with Finland and Turkey. Similarly, India is the heart of another cluster with cross collaborations with the United Kingdom and Morrocco. Hence it is evident that these collaborations identified can be nurtured to grow further in having more research with new countries not involved currently in this area of the domain and also developing more research with the existing countries. Thus the researchers need to focus on increasing the depth and breadth of the geographical networks.

- Top Authors

Table 25.7 depicts the top authors in the domain of technologies in the sustainable supply chain. The table shows that Sarkis J is the author who has four articles in the domain area, followed by Belhadi, Gunasekaran, Kamble, Kazancogluy, Kouhizadeh, Mangla, Mani and Sharma, each with two articles. The remaining authors in the list have published one article each. It is found that four is the maximum number of articles with the top author; hence there is more opportunity and room to develop research in the field of study.

Table 25.8 shows that blockchain technology is referred to by most of the authors for sustainable supply chain, which is of frequency nine followed

Table 25.7. Top Authors in Sustainable Supply Chain Management Technologies.

Authors	Articles	Authors-Frac	Articles Fractionalized
Sarkis J	4	SARKIS J	1.333
Belhadi A	2	KOUHIZADEH M	0.667
Gunasekaran AA	2	DI VAIO A	0.5
Kamble SS	2	GUNASEKARAN AA	0.5
Kazancoglu V	2	KAMBLE SS	0.5
Kouhizadeh M	2	KHLER S	0.5
Mangla SK	2	MOHAMADPOUR TOSARKANI	0.5
Mani V	2	PIZZOL M	0.5
Sharma V	2	ROY A	0.5
Ajmal MM	1	ROY M	0.5
Algo AS	1	SHARMA V	0.5
Allaoui H	1	VARRIALE L	0.5
Alnuaimi BK	1	YOUSEFI S	0.5
Autenrieb N	1	KAZANCOGLU V	0.417
Bai C	1	MANGLA SK	0.367
Cao Y	1	AJMAL MM	0.333
Carvalho M	1	ALLAOUI H	0.333
Cui L	1	ALNUAIMI BK	0.333
Dai J	1	AUTENRIEB N	0.333
Di Vaio A	1	BAI C	0.333

Table 25.8. Top Technologies Refereed in the Articles.

Types of Technologies	Frequency
Blockchain technology	9
Internet of things	3
Big data	2
Artificial intelligence	1
Cloud computing	1
Quantum computing	1
Information technology	1
Artificial intelligence	1
RFID	1
Information and communication technology	1

by Internet of Things (3) and Big Data (2). AI, Cloud Computing, Quantum Computing, Information and Communication Technology, and RFID are also referred to as the technology for the sustainable supply chain. It should also be noted that few articles have referred to more than one technology, and specific papers have discussed one technology in detail.

5.2. Top Technologies Used in the Sustainable Supply Chain and the Reason Behind It

There is still a scope to explore more types of technologies like Additive Manufacturing, Drones, Robotics, and Smart Plastics. As the technology is volatile and is undergoing profound changes, there is still scope for the researchers to analyze the innovative technologies in a sustainable supply chain. The reason for using the above technologies in sustainable supply chain operations, as stated in the articles, have been summarized in Table 25.9.

Table 25.9. Advantages of Sustainable Supply Chain Technologies.

Technology	Reasons
Blockchain technology	Broader participation of stakeholders, lower transaction costs, reduced lead times resulting in increased efficiency
	Waste reduction and management in circular fashion (Zhang & Zhu, 2019)
	Information asymmetries can be reduced (Charlebois, 2018)
	Reduction in unethical, corrupt and counterfeit practices (O'Dair, 2016)
	Product tracking and tracking of greenhouse gas emissions and securing the sharing of sensitive information improve internal efficiency and sustainability and maintain effective communication with partners in the supply chain (Hofmann, Strewe, & Bosia, 2018)
	Stakeholders in the supply chain can access real-time data information
	The products and processes are recorded clearly through traceability which enables the purchase to be made from ethical sources (Saberi, Kouhizadeh, & Sarkis, 2019)
	Improvement in operational efficiencies can be achieved, which results in a productivity improvement (Irani et al., 2018)
	Provides a platform for resource sharing
	Renewable energy resources distribution and payment is supported using decentralized energy management (Li, Li, & Sun, 2019)
Internet of things	To track blockchain-enabled emissions and carbon trading (Fu, Shu, & Liu, 2018; Manupati et al., 2019)
	Visualize and track products in the supply chain
	IoT devices can monitor material and product sources
	Evaluate the conditions of storage and other environmental conditions associated with procurement (Agarwal, Sharma, & Pughat, 2019; Manavalan & Jayakrishna, 2019; Tsang, Zhu, Sarkis, & Chiu, 2018)
	Supply chain speed and environmental performance can be tracked
	Green Production smart facility can be designed that provides minimal greenhouse gas emissions
	A smart transportation system can be developed which will help the companies to plan shipments and delivery on time by making product location in real-time (Li, 2011)
Quantum computing	Climate change concerns can be addressed
	Address by using environment models to predict the climate change
	Energy usage in the supply chain can be optimized with which the organizations and supply chains can measure the utility and usage of resources (Ajagekar & You, 2019)
	Dynamic routing and scheduling (Sanjeev, 2019)
	Simulate scenarios for the optimal process that maximize the usability, reusability and life cycle of products
Big data	The information related to procurement functions can be gathered (Chidambaram, Evans, & Etheredge, 2015)
	Contribution in the case of the price of raw materials, lead time, environment and visibility of procurement

Table 25.9. *(Continued)*

Technology	Reasons
	Detecting problems, monitoring the behaviour of suppliers, and measurement of cash flow, lead times and cost (Hickey, 2018)
	Predictive analysis of the procurement process is possible (Moretto, Ronchi, & Patrucco, 2017)
Cloud computing	Improve efficiency and productivity by condensing the resources used for manufacturing into an open network
ICT	Cost savings and waste reduction can be made by optimizing the resources and through communication between the members (Goodrum, Miller, Sweany, & Alruwaythi, 2016)
AI	Traffic flow improvement, increase in information exchange and decision support tools improvement (Chang et al., 2001; Groppe, Pagliari, & Harris, 2009)
	When integrated with manufacturing technology, AI can create a knowledge-driven framework for decision making. This paves the way for SMART manufacturing
RFID	The tagged objects can be traced, and the unique identification can be realized, resulting in fewer shrinkages and higher visibility of the supply chain. Out of stock can be reduced (Szmerekovsky & Zhang, 2008) and improve transportation efficiency (Lee, Palekar, & Qualls, 2011)

Some of the repeated benefits have been excluded before compiling the advantages. Hence, the Table 25.9 shows that technology effectively amplifies sustainability in the supply chain. From the advantages listed above, it can be understood that integrating more than one technology can further enhance the outcome.

5.3. Top Sectors That Are Using These Technologies in the Sustainability in Supply Chain

Table 25.10 depicts various sectors involved in research in the domain of study. The articles selected for review has conducted the research related to Manufacturing firms (5) followed by Food sector (4) and Agriculture (3), Energy (2) and Automobile (2). Only one research has been conducted in Telecommunication, Retail, Petrochemicals, IT, Banking and Airport. It is being found that the articles have been concentrated on particular sectors like Manufacturing, Food and Agriculture, as it is feasible to obtain the visibility of result in the application of technological tools in their supply chain. However, the author feels that there is still a deficiency in the sectors chosen for the study in the domain. As Government and customers are pushing pressures on the organization, the supply chain management sustainability has been forced rather than a choice for the organizations. Hence the researchers can explore and conduct the study with more relevant sectors. Service sectors like Education, Hospitals and hotels need to be explored as they contribute more to the economy post-COVID. The right technologies need to be identified for the above sectors is one of the steps that the organization have to check when in the future to adopt the technology as a sustainable tool.

Table 25.10. Top Sectors Referred to in the Articles.

Sectors	Frequency
Manufacturing	5
Food	4
Agriculture	3
Energy/power	2
Automobile/automotive	2
Telecommunication	1
Retail	1
Petrochemicals	1
IT	1
Banking	1
Airport	1

Table 25.11. Methodology Used in the Articles.

Methodology	Frequency
Quantitative	7
Meta-analysis Literature Review	5
Systematic Literature Review	4
Qualitative	3
Mixed method	2

5.4. Methodologies Used in the Research

The researchers followed various methodologies in the articles selected for the study as depicted in Table 25.11. However, the studies have been majorly concentered on the quantitative and metanalysis review. This may be because of the nature of the sectors and the technology selected for the study. However, most of the methods were adopted by the researchers in the articles.

5.5. Thematic Breakouts and Future Research Directions

The authors' keywords and interconnections are taken into clusters to generate themes. Density and centrality are the major properties of thematic analysis. Fig. 25.8 provides a thematic map in the domain. This is divided into four quadrants (Q1–Q4).

Motor themes are found in Quadrant 1 which are central and developed AI and digital supply chain are themes in this cluster. The second quadrant shows basic and transversal themes which are central and underdeveloped. The cluster in the niche theme consists of Information Management, Disruptive Technology and Internet of Things. The highly developed and isolated themes are shown in Quadrant 3. Basic themes are merged in to a cluster with sustainable development, supply chains and supply chain management. Emerging and declining themes are shown in Quadrant 4 and are merged into a cluster greenhouse gases, industrial research and finance.

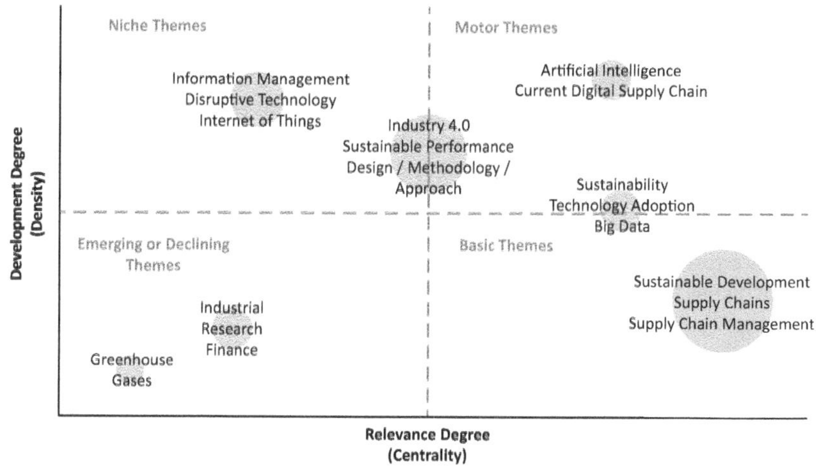

Fig. 25.8. Thematic Map Emerged by Biblioshiny.

5.6. Future Research Directions in the Field of Technology in Sustainable Supply Chain

The articles selected for review paved the way for future research directions based on the limitations explored from each research. Apart from exploring the other geographical areas, sectors and technologies for future research, the following are the summary of recommendations for future research:

1. The combined effect of I4 capabilities, Digital Business Transformation, organizational ambidexterity and circular business models at the supply chain level can be explored.
2. The relationship between digital technologies for Industry 4.0 and sustainable performance can be explored.
3. New digital technologies can be explored.
4. Longitudinal studies can be conducted to trace the adoption effect of blockchain in developing efficiency, transparency and traceability of sustainable supply chains.
5. Methods used for analysis like optimization models PLS-SEM can be explored in the future studies.
6. Reliability and uncertainty concepts can be used to identify the weight of the relationships.
7. More tiers of upstream suppliers can be included in the study rather than only focusing on the focal organization in the sectors.
8. The impact on human resource practices in adopting digital technologies can be studied in relation to a sustainable supply chain.
9. Impact of cultural and social variables that affect the benefit of blockchai technology in SCM for the sustainability.

6. PRACTICAL IMPLICATIONS

The current study can be used as a reference by the organizations in various sectors, specifically the manufacturing and the food sector, as they can provide insight into the type of technologies they can implement to achieve sustainability in the supply chain. The study will help the researchers to identify the areas that are still yet to be explored. From the review, it is evident that there is still scope to explore both in-depth and breadth in various aspects of the domain. Hence this can be an eye-opener for the researchers to explore the opportunities to come with more research. The Government can use this study to understand the feasibility of using technologies in various sectors and can think of ways to promote the sectors that have not yet taken the opportunity to use technology to support sustainability in the supply chain. Academicians can use this study to understand the scope of practical implementation in technology in sustainability as sustainability is a part of all the academic disciplines.

7. CONCLUSION

This systematic literature review on technologies in the sustainable supply chain using the online scientific database from Scopus that has been analyzed using bibliometric software (Biblioshiny) has delivered its research objectives and the specific research questions. It is worthy to note that this review has shed light on the publication trend based on five aspects (RQ1), various technologies used in the sustainable supply chain (RQ2), sectors that are using these technologies in the sustainability of the supply chain (RQ3), different methodologies used in the research (RQ4) and future research directions in technologies in the sustainable supply chain (RQ5). From the findings from the above perspectives, it is evident that the research on the area still needs to be explored in breadth and depth. There are still many sectors that have not been explored to analyze the role of technology in a sustainable supply chain. Similarly, as pandemic has paved the way for a technology-dependent world, technological innovations have been evolving on a minute basis in the nook and corner of the world. Hence the review is an eye-opener for the researcher to explore this opportunity to analyze the new innovative technologies in sustainable supply chain.

Apart from the contributions and insights made by the research, the research has the following limitations, which can be addressed in future research. The database used for the review is limited to Scopus, Google scholar, web of science, and other databases that can be further explored in future research where alternative measures of quality can also be input in this regard. This review provides a bird's eye view of the topic. However, this review accomplishes what is expected from the systematic literature reviews. It is noteworthy that a meta-analysis review can also be conducted in this domain in future. Similarly, future studies can only focus on cluster-specific reviews. Various clusters identified from the current review, such as the geographic clusters and author-specific clusters, can be taken for further reviews. A quantitative or qualitative sector-specific study on the topic can also be explored in the future. Various other sectors which are not explored in the study can be taken for further analysis.

New technologies like additive manufacturing and SMART Manufacturing, combining any two existing technologies can also be adopted in the new studies.

REFERENCES

Agarwal, S., Sharma, V., & Pughat, A. (2019). Supplier selection problem in IoT solutions. *International Journal of Pervasive Computing and Communications*, *15*(1), 16–19.

Ajagekar, A., & You, F. (2019). Quantum computing for energy systems optimization: Challenges and opportunities. *Energy*, *179*, 76–89.

Akhtar, P. (2019). Warsaw School of Economics Drivers of green supply chain initiatives and their impact on economic performance of firms: Evidence from Pakistan's manufacturing sector. *Journal of Competitiveness*, *11*, 5–18.

Alnuaimi, B. K., Khan, M., & Ajmal, M. M. (2021). The role of big data analytics capabilities in greening e-procurement: A higher order PLS-SEM analysis. *Technological Forecasting and Social Change*, *169*, 120808.

Berkhout, P. H., Muskens, J. C., & Velthuijsen, J. W. (2000). Defining the rebound effect. *Energy Policy*, *28*, (6–7), 425–432.

Bonini, S., & Swartz, S. (2014). *Profits with purpose: How organizing for sustainability can benefit the bottom line*. New York, NY: McKinsey & Company.

Brettel, M., Friederichsen, N., Keller, M., & Rosenberg, M. (2014). How virtualization, decentralization and network building change the manufacturing landscape: An industry 4.0 perspective. *International Journal of Information and Communication Engineering*, *8*(1), 37–44.

Büyüközkan, G., & Göçer, F. (2018). Digital supply chain: Literature review and a proposed framework for future research. *Computers in Industry*, *97*, 157–177.

Chang, K., Howard, K., Oiesen, R., Shisler, L., Tanino, M., & Wambsganss, M. C. (2001). Enhancements to the FAA ground-delay program under collaborative decision making. *Interfaces*, *31*(1), 57–76. https://doi.org/10.1287/inte.31.1.57.9689

Chaopaisarn, P., & Woschank, M. (2019, March). Requirement analysis for SMART supply chain management for SMEs. In *Proceedings of the international conference on industrial engineering and operations management*, Bangkok (pp. 5–7).

Charlebois, S. (2018). *How blockchain technology could transform the food industry*. Toronto: Retail Insider.

Chidambaram, V., Evans, H., & Etheredge, K. (2015). Big data: Is the energy industry starting to see real applications? *Supply Chain Management Review*, *19*(1), 62–64. Retrieved from http://search.ebscohost.com/login.aspx?direct=true&db=bsu&AN=101388010&site=ehost-live

Chopra, S. (2019). *Supply chain management: Strategy, planning, and operation*. Prentice-Hall: Pearson Education.

Davis, J., Mengersen, K., Bennett, S., & Mazerolle, L. (2014). Viewing systematic reviews and metaanalysis in social research through different lenses. *SpringerPlus*, *3*(511), 1–9.

Defee, C. C., & Fugate, B. S. (2010). Changing perspective of capabilities in the dynamic supply chain era. *The International Journal of Logistics Management*, *21*(2), 180–206.

Di Vaio, A., & Varriale, L. (2020). Blockchain technology in supply chain management for sustainable performance: Evidence from the airport industry. *International Journal of Information Management*, *52*, 102014.

Diniz, E. H., Yamaguchi, J. A., dos Santos, T. R., de Carvalho, A. P., Alego, A. S., & Carvalho, M. (2021). Greening inventories: Blockchain to improve the GHG Protocol Program in scope 2. *Journal of Cleaner Production*, *291*, 125900.

Donthu, N., Kumar, S., Paul, J., Pattnaik, D., & Strong, C. (2021). A retrospective of the *Journal of Strategic Marketing* from 1993 to 2019 using bibliometric analysis. *Journal of Strategic Marketing*, *30*(1), 1–21.

Dougados, M., & Felgendreher, B. (2016). The current and future state of digital supply chain transformation. Retrieved from https://www.supplychainquarterly.com/ext/resources/files/pdfs/white-papers/gtexus_digital_transformation.pdf?

Edwards, J., Lyons, A., & Kehoe, D. (2004). A web-based demand planning system (DPS) to enable coordinated re-manufacture of automotive components. *International Journal of Internet and Enterprise Management*, *2*(4), 366–382.

Friedman, N., & Ormiston, J. (2022). Blockchain as a sustainability-oriented innovation? Opportunities for and resistance to blockchain technology as a driver of sustainability in global food supply chains. *Technological Forecasting and Social Change*, *175*, 121403.

Fu, B., Shu, Z., & Liu, X. (2018). Blockchain enhanced emission trading framework in fashion apparel manufacturing industry. *Sustainability*, *10*(4), 1105.

Goel, R. K., Saunoris, J. W., & Goel, S. S. (2020). *Supply chain reliability and international economic growth: Impacts of disruptions like COVID-19*. CESifo Working Paper 2020 No. 8294. Retrieved from https://ssrn.com/abstract=3603829

Gonzálvez-Gallego, N., Molina-Castillo, F.-J., Soto-Acosta, P., Varajao, J., & Trigo, A. (2015). Using integrated information systems in supply chain management. *Enterprise Information Systems*, *9*(2), 210–232. doi:10.1080/17517575.2013.879209

Goodrum, P. M., Miller, J., Sweany, J., & Alruwaythi, O. (2016). Influence of the format of engineering information and spatial cognition on craft-worker performance. *Journal of Construction Engineering and Management*, *142*(9), 04016043. doi:10.1061/(ASCE)CO.1943-7862.0001157

Groppe, M., Pagliari, R., & Harris, D. (2009). Applying cognitive work analysis to study airport collaborative decision making design. In *Proceedings of the ENRI international workshop on ATM/CNS* (EIWAC2009), Tokyo, Japan (pp. 77–88).

Hickey, R. (2018). Big data analytics – The impact on procurement. Retrieved from https://softco.com/blog/big-data-analytics-procurement/

Hinge, G., Muksor, A., Goyal, M. K., Goyal, R. K., & Goyal, M. (2020). Integrated risk of virus outbreaks. In *Integrated risk of pandemic: COVID-19 impacts, resilience and recommendations. Disaster resilience and green growth; Indian Institute of Technology, National Institute of Disaster Management*. Singapore: Springer.

Hofmann, E., Strewe, U. M., & Bosia, N. (2018). *Conclusion – What can we learn from blockchain-driven supply chain finance? Supply chain finance and blockchain technology* (pp. 89–91). Cham: Springer.

Irani, Z., Sharif, A. M., Lee, H., Aktas, E., Topalo˘glu, Z., Van't Wout, T., & Huda, S. (2018). Managing food security through food waste and loss: Small data to big data. *Computers & Operations Research*, *98*, 367–383.

Ivanov, D. (2021). Lean resilience: AURA (Active Usage of Resilience Assets) framework for post-COVID-19 supply chain management. *The International Journal of Logistics Management*, *33*, 1196–1217.

Ivanov, D., & Dolgui, A. (2020). A digital supply chain twin for managing the disruption risks and resilience in the era of Industry 4.0. *Production Planning and Control*, *32*, 1–14.

Jajja, M. S. S., Chatha, K. A., & Farooq, S. (2018). Impact of supply chain risk on agility performance: Mediating role of supply chain integration. *International Journal of Production Economics*, *205*, 118–138.

Khanra, S., Dhir, A., Kaur, P., & Mäntymäaki, M. (2021). Bibliometric analysis and literature review of ecotourism: Toward sustainable development. *Tourism Management Perspectives*, *37*, 100777. https://doi.org/10.1016/j.tmp.2020.100777.nalysis

Kumar, A., Paul, J., & Unnithan, A. B. (2020). "Masstige" marketing: A review, synthesis and research agenda. *Journal of Business Research*, *113*, 384–398.

Kwiek, M. (2020). Internationalists and locals: International research collaboration in a resource-poor system. *Scientometrics 124*, 57–105. https://doi.org/10.1007/s11192-020-03460-2

Lacob, M. E., van Sinderen, M. J., Steenwijk, M., & Verkroost, P. (2013). Towards a reference architecture for fuel-based carbon management systems in the logistics industry. *Information Systems Frontiers*, *15*(5), 725–745.

Lai, R. S. Q., Hsu, L.-L., & Chen, J. C. H. (2012). Green SCM systems: A case study in the textile industry. *Human Systems Management*, *31*(2), 111–121. doi:10.3233/HSM-2012-0765

Lee, J., Palekar, U. S., & Qualls, W. (2011). Supply chain efficiency and security: Coordination for collaborative investment in technology. *European Journal of Operational Research*, *210*(3), 568e578.

Li, G., Li, L., & Sun, J. (2019). Pricing and service effort strategy in a dual-channel supply chain with showrooming effect. *Transportation Research Part E: Logistics and Transportation Review*, *126*, 32–48.

Li, L. (2011). Application of the internet of thing in green agricultural products supply chain management. In *4th International conference on intelligent computation technology and automation*, Washington, DC.

Lim, W. M. (2020). Challenger marketing. *Industrial Marketing Management, 84*, 342–345. https://doi.org/10.1016/j.indmarman.2019.08.009

Lim, W. M., Ahmad, A., Rasul, T., & Parvez, M. O. (2021). Challenging the mainstream assumption of social media influence on destination choice. *Tourism Recreation Research, 46*, 137–140. https://doi.org/10.1080/02508 281.2020.1814521

Manavalan, E., & Jayakrishna, K. (2019). A review of Internet of Things (IoT) embedded sustainable supply chain for industry 4.0 requirements. *Computers and Industrial Engineering, 127*, 925–953.

Manupati, V. K., Schoenherr, T., Ramkumar, M., Wagner, S. M., Pabba, S. K., & Inder Raj Singh, R. (2019). A blockchain-based approach for a multi-echelon sustainable supply chain. *International Journal of Production Research, 58*(7), 1–20.

Melville, N. P. (2010). Information systems innovation for environmental sustainability. *MIS Quarterly, 34*(1), 1–21.

Mittal, S., Khan, M. A., Romero, D., & Wuest, T. (2019). Smart manufacturing: Characteristics, technologies and enabling factors. *Proceedings of the Institution of Mechanical Engineers, Part B: Journal of Engineering Manufacture, 233*(5), 1342–1361.

Moher, D., Shamseer, L., Clarke, M., Ghersi, D., Liberati, A., Petticrew, M., Shekelle, P., & Stewart, L. A. (2015). Preferred reporting items for systematic review and meta-analysis protocols (PRISMA-P) 2015 statement. *Systematic Reviews, 4*(1), 1. https://doi.org/10.1186/2046-4053-4

Moretto, A., Ronchi, S., & Patrucco, A. S. (2017). Increasing the effectiveness of procurement decisions: The value of big data in the procurement process. *International Journal of RF Technologies: Research & Applications, 8*(3), 79–103.https://doi.org/10.3233/RFT-171670

O'Dair, M. (2016). The networked record industry: How blockchain technology could transform the consumption and monetisation of recorded music. Strategic Change, *26*(5), 471–480.

Panday, A. (2021). Virus outbreak drives down automobile sales in March. *Livemint*. Retrieved from https://www.livemint.com/companies/news/automakers-hit-hard-bycovid-19%-march-sales-decline-over-50-11585749547879.html

Paul, J., Lim, W. M., O'Cass, A., Hao, A. W., & Bresciani, S. (2021). Scientific procedures and rationales for systematic literature reviews (SPAR-4-SLR). *International Journal of Consumer Studies, 45*(4), O1–O16.

Pettit, T. J., Croxton, K., & Fiksel, J. (2013). Ensuring supply chain resilience: Development and implementation of an assessment tool. *Journal of Business Logistics, 34*, 46–76.

Piotrowicz, W., & Cuthbertson, R. (2009). Sustainability – A new dimension in information systems evaluation. *Journal of Enterprise Information Management, 22*(5), 492–503.

Ranney, M. L., Griffeth, V., & Jha, A. K. (2020). Critical supply shortages – The need for ventilators and personal protective equipment during the COVID-19 pandemic. The New England Journal of Medicine, *382*, e41.

Saberi, S., Kouhizadeh, M., & Sarkis, J. (2019). Blockchains and the supply chain: Findings from a broad study of practitioners. *IEEE Engineering Management Review, 47*(3), 95–103. https://doi.org/10.1109/EMR.2019.2928264

Sanjeev, H. R. (2019). Quantum computing: The next big thing in digital supply chain disruption, TATA Consultancy Services. Retrieved from https://www.tcs.com/blogs/quantum-computing-digital-supply-chain-disruption

Sarkis, J. (2019). Sustainable transitions: Technology, resources, and society. *One Earth, 1*(1), 48–50.

Schiller, B. (2012). Transport's cleaner future. *Financial Management*, 26–30. CIMA magazine.

Sharma, A., Adhikary, A., & Borah, S. B. (2020). COVID-19's impact on supply chain decisions: Strategic insights for NASDAQ 100 firms using Twitter data. *Journal of Business Research, 117*, 443–449.

Sourirajan, K., Centonze, P., Helander, M. E., Katircioglu, K. M., Ben-Hamida, K., & Boucher, C. (2009). Carbon management in assembly manufacturing logistics. *IBM Journal of Research and Development, 53*(3), 433–448. doi:10.1147/JRD.2009.5429021

Srivastava, S. K. (2007). Green supply-chain management: A state-of-the-art literature review. *International Journal of Management Reviews, 9*(1), 53–80. doi:10.1111/j.1468-2370.2007.00202.x

Suh, K., Smith, T., & Linhoff, M. (2012). Leveraging socially networked mobile ICT platforms for the last-mile delivery problem. *Environmental Science & Technology, 46*(17), 9481–9490.

Szmerekovsky, J., & Zhang, J. (2008). Coordination and adoption of item-level RFID with vendor managed inventory. *International Journal of Production Economics, 114*(1), 388e398.

Tseng, M.-L., Zhu, Q., Sarkis, J., & Chiu, A. S. (2018). Responsible consumption and production (RCP) in corporate decision-making models using soft computation. *Industrial Management and Data Systems*, *118*(2), 322–329.

Umar, M., Khan, S. A. R., Zia-ul-haq, H. M., Yusliza, M. Y., & Farooq, K. (2021). The role of emerging technologies in implementing green practices to achieve sustainable operations. *The TQM Journal*. doi:10.1108/TQM-06-2021-0172

Verma, S., & Chaudhuri, R. (2008). Creating customer satisfaction and profitable value chain with e-commerce in rural India: A case based approach. *International Journal of Business Insights & Transformation*, *2*(1), 51–63.

Villena, V. H., & Gioia, D. A. (2021). A more sustainable supply chain. *Harvard Business Review*. Retrieved from https://hbr.org/2020/03/a-more-sustainable-supply-chain

Zhang, X., & Zhu, W. (2019). Application framework of digital twin-driven product smart manufacturing system: A case study of aeroengine blade manufacturing. *International Journal of Advanced Robotics Systems*, *5*, 16. https://doi.org/10.1177/1729881419880663

CHAPTER 26

DETECTING AND PREVENTING FRAUD IN FINANCIAL TRANSACTIONS: A CASE STUDY ON BIG DATA ANALYSIS AT KAREEM EXCHANGE COMPANY

Shafeeq Ahmed Ali[a], Mohammad H. Allaymoun[a], Ahmad Yahia Mustafa Al Astal[b] and Rehab Saleh[b]

[a]*Administrative Science Department, College of Administrative and Financial Science, Gulf University, Sanad, Kingdom of Bahrain*
[b]*Accounting and Financial Science Department, College of Administrative and Financial Science, Gulf University, Sanad, Kingdom of Bahrain*

ABSTRACT

This chapter focuses on a case study of Kareem Exchange Company and its use of big data analysis to detect and prevent fraud and suspicious financial transactions. The chapter describes the various phases of the big data analysis cycle, including discovery, data preparation, model planning, model building, operationalization, and communicating results, and how the Kareem Exchange Company team implemented each phase. This chapter emphasizes the importance of identifying the business problem, understanding the resources and stakeholders involved, and developing an initial hypothesis to guide the analysis. The case study results demonstrate the potential of big

Digital Technology and Changing Roles in Managerial and Financial Accounting: Theoretical Knowledge and Practical Application
Studies in Managerial and Financial Accounting, Volume 36, 305–317

Published under exclusive licence by Emerald Publishing Limited
ISSN: 1479-3512/doi:10.1108/S1479-351220240000036028

data analysis to improve fraud detection capabilities in financial institutions, leading to informed decision making and action.

Keywords: Fraud; detection; big data analysis lifecycle; decision making; financial transactions; forensic accounting

I. INTRODUCTION

Fraud is a significant issue for financial institutions, costing them billions of dollars yearly (Ritika, 2022). Fraudulent activities in financial transactions can take various forms, such as identity theft, credit card fraud, money laundering, and embezzlement. The increasing volume, velocity, and variety of financial data generated daily pose a significant challenge for traditional fraud detection techniques (Hummer & Byrne, 2023). Financial institutions need to be able to identify fraudulent activities quickly and accurately to prevent financial loss and maintain their reputation. Fraud detection is a critical area of research for financial institutions and has gained significant attention recently (Chhabra Roy & Prabhakaran, 2022).

Fraud detection in financial transactions is critical for financial institutions, as the cost of fraudulent activities can be high (Ogwiji & Lasisi, 2022). The impact of fraud is not only limited to financial loss, but it can also damage the financial institution's reputation, leading to a loss of customer trust and loyalty. Traditional fraud detection techniques, such as rule-based systems and anomaly detection, are no longer effective in detecting sophisticated fraud (Fernández, 2019). This has led to adopting big data analytics techniques to handle the large volume of data generated in financial transactions and identify patterns that may indicate fraudulent activities. Big data analytics can provide a more comprehensive understanding of fraud patterns and reduce the number of false positives, which can help financial institutions make informed decisions and take timely actions to prevent fraudulent activities (Wright, Robin, Stone, & Aravopoulou, 2019).

The main objective of this chapter is to explore the use of big data analytics in detecting fraud in financial transactions. Specifically, this chapter aims to provide an overview of the big data analysis life cycle, its stages, and its importance in fraud detection. This chapter will also examine the limitations of traditional fraud detection techniques and how big data analytics can overcome these limitations. This chapter will provide a case study to demonstrate the application of big data analytics in fraud detection in financial transactions. Finally, the chapter will discuss the implications of the results of the case study and identify future research directions.

This chapter will be organized into seven sections. The Section 1 will introduce the topic of fraud detection in financial transactions and its significance. The Section 2 will review the existing literature on fraud detection in financial transactions, including the limitations of traditional fraud detection techniques and the advantages of big data analytics. Section 3 will explain the big data analysis life cycle concept and its stages. Section 4 will discuss the limitations of traditional fraud detection techniques and how big data analytics can overcome these limitations. Section 5 will present a case study to demonstrate the application of big data analytics in fraud detection in financial transactions. Section 6 will discuss the implications of the results of the case study and identify future research directions. Finally, Section 7 will conclude by summarizing the key points from this chapter.

2. LITERATURE REVIEW

Financial fraud is the illegal act of gaining financial benefits, and it is prevalent in several areas, such as insurance, banking, taxation, and corporate sectors. Traditional methods to detect fraudulent activities are manual and impractical, and more efficient approaches are needed (Al-Hashedi & Magalingam, 2021).

Fraud detection in financial transactions has been a hot area of research in recent years. Various techniques have been proposed and developed for fraud detection, including rule-based systems, anomaly detection, and machine learning algorithms (Arfeen & Khan, 2022). However, traditional fraud detection techniques have limitations in detecting sophisticated fraud cases. According to Gandomi and Haider (2015), traditional techniques are often based on predefined rules and cannot detect previously unknown fraud patterns. Moreover, traditional techniques can generate many false positives, wasting resources and time (Pandey, Peddoju, & Deshpande, 2018).

Several researchers have proposed the use of machine learning techniques for fraud detection. For example, Dornadula and Geetha (2019) presented a machine learning approach for fraud detection that combines unsupervised and supervised learning algorithms. The authors reported that their approach could achieve higher fraud detection accuracy than traditional techniques. Another study by Christian, Basri, and Arafah (2019) proposed a deep learning-based approach for fraud detection. The authors reported that their approach could achieve high accuracy in detecting fraudulent activities in credit card transactions.

Traditional fraud detection techniques have several limitations. As mentioned earlier, traditional techniques are often based on predefined rules and cannot detect previously unknown fraud patterns, Traditional techniques also rely on small samples of data, which can limit their ability to see subtle patterns and relationships in the data (Abbassi, El Alaoui, & Gahi, 2022).

The big data analysis life cycle can overcome the limitations of traditional fraud detection techniques. According to Malik, Khaw, and Chew (2022) big data analysis can provide a more comprehensive understanding of fraud patterns and reduce the number of false positives, leading to more effective fraud detection. The big data analysis life cycle is a set of stages involved in the processing and analysis of big data, including data acquisition, data storage, data processing, data analysis, and data visualization (Rahul & Banyal, 2020). The big data analysis life cycle allows for the processing and analysis of large volumes of data, enabling the detection of subtle patterns and relationships in the data (Pramanik & Bandyopadhyay, 2023). Moreover, the big data analysis life cycle can handle various data types, including structured, semi-structured, and unstructured data. The big data analysis life cycle also allows for integrating multiple data sources, which can enhance the accuracy and completeness of fraud detection (Abd Elhady, Ghali, Abo-Elfetoh, & Idrees, 2023).

Elastal et al. (2023) presented a simplified model using the six phases of the big data analytics lifecycle, including data preparation, model planning, and operationalization, to detect money laundering. Elastal et al. (2023) model is supposed to help exchange companies detect money laundering and reduce suspicious financial operations, enabling decision makers to make prompt and appropriate decisions. Moreover, the big data analysis lifecycle's importance extends beyond detecting money laundering to applying laws and building a comprehensive model that provides financial institutions with an integrated solution to address suspicious operations promptly and early Elastal et al. (2023).

The article by Allaymoun, Al Saad, Majed, and Hashem (2022) describes how the big data analytics lifecycle can be used to obtain charts and graphs for decision making. The chapter emphasizes the importance of following the methodology and stages of the lifecycle and suggests using Google Data Studio to create graphs based on problem framing and hypotheses proposed in the discovery phase. The author applies the lifecycle steps to a set of data on Islamic banks to monitor their performance in 2019 and 2020 and assess the impact of the COVID-19 pandemic.

Allaymoun, Al Saad et al. (2022) demonstrate how the big data analytics lifecycle can be used to generate graphs and charts to aid decision making for Mega Start Company (virtual). The author emphasizes the importance of the discovery stage to frame the problem, proposes appropriate hypotheses to solve it, and then applies the rest of the steps in the lifecycle to reach results that inform decision making. The chapter also illustrates how the big data analytics lifecycle can be used to take advantage of the results of big data analytics, build predictive models, track sales operations, and predict the future Allaymoun, Al Saad et al. (2022).

3. BIG DATA ANALYSIS LIFE CYCLE

The big data analysis life cycle is a set of stages involved in the processing and analysis of big data. It is a comprehensive approach that enables the efficient and effective handling of large volumes of data (Sivaranjani, 2023). The big data analysis life cycle involves discovery, data preparation, model planning, model building, communicating results, and operationalization. The big data analysis life cycle aims to extract insights from data and turn them into actionable knowledge. It is a powerful tool that can give organizations a competitive advantage in various domains, including fraud detection in financial transactions (Allaymoun, Qaradh, Salman, & Hasan, 2022; Education, 2023).

The six stages of the big data analysis cycle are described in the paragraphs. The first stage is discovery, where the business problem or question is identified, and the scope of the analysis is determined. The second stage is data preparation, which involves cleaning, preprocessing, and transforming data to prepare it for analysis. The third stage is model planning, where the data scientist selects the best approach to solving the problem by choosing the proper modeling technique and algorithm. In the fourth stage, model building, the chosen modeling technique is applied to the data to create a predictive model. In the fifth stage, communicating results, the data scientist presents the insights and findings to stakeholders using visualizations and reports. The final stage is operationalization, where the insights and findings are implemented into the business operations by integrating predictive models into decision-making processes and automating the data analysis process (Allaymoun, Qaradh et al., 2022; Koo, Kang, & Kim, 2020).

Big data analysis life cycle can be used in fraud detection in financial transactions by enabling the analysis of large volumes of financial data from various sources. The data can be acquired from multiple sources, such as transaction logs, credit reports, and financial statements (Lee, 2020). The data can then be processed to clean and transform into a suitable format for analysis. Statistical and machine learning techniques can be applied to data to extract patterns and anomalies indicative of fraudulent activities. The insights obtained from the data analysis can then be represented in a visual format that fraud analysts can easily interpret. The big data analysis life cycle can thus enhance the accuracy and efficiency of fraud detection in financial transactions (Dhingra & Ashok, 2021).

4. FRAUD DETECTION TECHNIQUES

Traditional fraud detection techniques include rule-based systems, anomaly detection, and predictive modeling. Rule-based systems involve the creation of a set of rules that are used to detect fraudulent activities. Anomaly detection involves identifying activities outside the expected behavior of an individual or group. Also, the predictive modeling consists of statistical and machine learning techniques to predict the likelihood of fraudulent activities (Pawar, Kalavadekar, & Tambe, 2014).

The big data analysis life cycle can be used to overcome the limitations of traditional fraud detection techniques by enabling the analysis of large volumes of data from various sources. Using machine learning techniques in big data analysis can help identify patterns and anomalies indicative of fraudulent activities. By processing and analyzing large volumes of data, big data analysis can also help reduce the number of false positives and false negatives in fraud detection.

Examples of fraud detection techniques used in the big data analysis life cycle include the similarity tree, which uses decision tree logic to label nodes with attribute names and edges with attribute values that satisfy certain conditions. Another technique is using algorithms, such as genetic algorithms and neighborhood-based and probabilistic algorithms, to predict suspect behavior (Kagan, 2019). Clustering techniques, such as peer group analysis and breakpoint analysis, are also suggested for detecting suspicious accounts or behavior (Kumar et al., 2022).

5. CASE STUDY

The first phase of the big data analysis cycle is discovery, which involves understanding the business problem that needs to be solved. Identifying the issue at hand is crucial before solving it, as it helps frame the problem and develop a hypothesis. In the case of Kareem Exchange Company (virtual), the problem is detecting and preventing fraud and suspicious financial transactions. Through research and analysis, it was discovered that there were numerous fraud and money laundering attempts, and it became apparent that the company could enhance its financial procedures, put laws into place, and keep a close eye on operations to decrease suspicious transactions.

Technology, systems, people, and information must be available to solve the problem. Learning on the job is an essential aspect of the discovery phase. It enables the company to develop the necessary skills and knowledge to improve its financial performance, implement legislation, and monitor financial operations to prevent fraud. It is essential to identify the key stakeholders involved in the project, such as the business users, project sponsors, and project managers, to ensure that goals are being met and the project is being completed on time and within the budget drawn up.

Developing an initial hypothesis is a crucial step in the discovery phase, as it helps to guide the analysis and identify potential solutions to the problem. In the case of Kareem Exchange Company, the hypothesis is that specific patterns in financial transactions, such as customers using the same account to conduct transactions at various physical locations or providing non-civic addresses to conceal their actual residence, may indicate fraudulent activity. By analyzing these patterns and identifying outliers, the company can develop effective strategies to prevent fraud and safeguard its financial operations.

The discovery phase of the big data analysis cycle is crucial for identifying the business problem, understanding the resources and stakeholders involved, and developing an initial hypothesis to guide the analysis. For Kareem Exchange Company, the problem at hand is detecting and preventing fraud and suspicious financial transactions. By analyzing patterns and outliers in financial transactions, the company can enhance its financial procedures and implement laws to decrease suspicious transactions.

In the data preparation phase, Kareem Exchange Company gathers and prepares data from various departments for analysis. This involves tasks related to information planning, such as exploring, preprocessing, and conditioning the data. The company must ensure the information is logically sandboxed before modifying, stacking, and executing it in groups. Additionally, they must collect data and information on fraud, money laundering, and suspicious financial transactions from various sources, such as websites and internal records.

Organizations focus on how data can reveal connections between factors and underlying data in the model planning phase. Information indexes are highly desired for planning, testing, and construction. For the Kareem Exchange Company, the team decided to track the database's income growth over time by conducting a longitudinal study. They will use the customer's phone number, name, amount, date, country of the transaction, and country of residence to test the first hypothesis through data collection. By creating and testing different models, the company can gain insights into patterns and relationships in the data that can help them make better decisions and improve its financial procedures.

Fig. 26.1 shows the decision tree resulting from the first hypothesis: customers using the same account to conduct transactions at various physical locations.

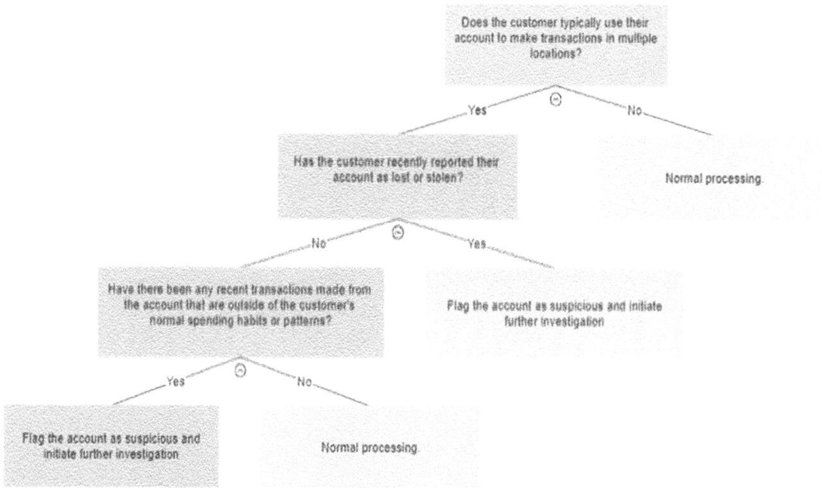

Fig. 26.1. Decision Tree for the First Hypothesis.

A decision tree for fraud detection in the case of a customer using the same account to conduct transactions at various physical locations would involve creating a tree structure that uses decision tree logic to determine whether a transaction is legitimate or suspicious. The tree would be constructed recursively, with nodes labeled with attribute names and edges labeled with values of attributes that satisfy certain conditions.

Fig. 26.2 shows the decision tree resulting from the second hypothesis providing non-civic addresses to conceal their residence.

The Kareem Exchange Company defined the business objectives of the fraud detection model and selected the appropriate statistical and machine learning techniques for analysis. The team decided to use a supervised machine learning algorithm to identify fraudulent transactions.

In the fourth phase of the big data analysis cycle, model building, the Kareem Exchange Company team will create a predictive model to detect potentially fraudulent transactions. The team will first identify the relevant variables and features that can be used to train the model, such as customer transaction history, location, and other relevant data. Then, the team will use machine learning algorithms and statistical models to develop a predictive model that can identify potentially fraudulent transactions.

The team will continue to refine the model until it achieves the desired level of accuracy and can effectively detect potentially fraudulent transactions in real time. Once the model is complete, it can be integrated into the Kareem Exchange Company's financial system to continuously monitor and flag any suspicious transactions, helping to prevent fraud and protect the company's financial integrity.

The operationalization phase integrates the insights and models developed during the analysis phase into the organization's operations. This phase involves

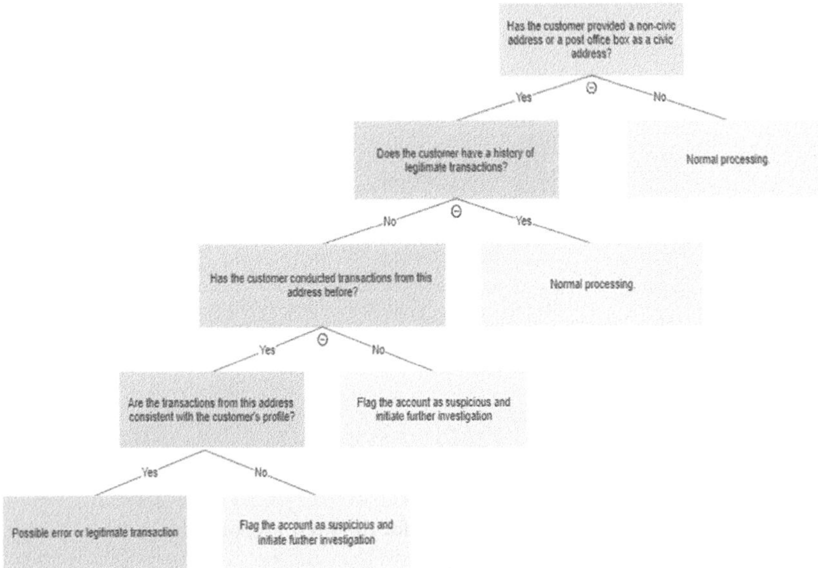

Fig. 26.2. Decision Tree for the Second Hypothesis.

implementing the model into the organization's existing systems, such as transaction processing systems, and monitoring the system's performance. This phase also involves training employees on the new system and ensuring that the system meets regulatory and legal requirements. In the case of the Kareem Exchange Company, the fraud detection model was integrated into their transaction processing systems to monitor and flag potential fraud cases in real time. The system was continuously monitored and refined to ensure that it remained effective in detecting new types of fraud.

In the communicating results phase, the focus is on presenting the analysis results to key organizational stakeholders. This phase involves creating reports, visualizations, and dashboards to communicate the insights and findings from the analysis. In the case of the Kareem Exchange Company case, the team presented the study results to key stakeholders, including fraud investigators and senior management. The results included a list of high-risk transactions identified as potential fraud cases. This phase also involves obtaining feedback from stakeholders and incorporating that feedback into the analysis and model development. The goal of this phase is to ensure that the insights and findings are effectively communicated to stakeholders, leading to informed decision making and action.

6. DISCUSSION

The results from this case study have important implications for financial institutions in terms of improving their fraud detection capabilities. By leveraging big data analytics, organizations can gain valuable insights into customer behavior and transaction patterns, allowing them to identify potential fraud cases and take proactive measures to prevent financial losses. This will not only help protect customers and the institution's assets but also help build trust and confidence among customers, which is crucial for the success of any financial institution.

Moreover, the successful implementation of the big data analytics lifecycle in this case study demonstrates the importance of a structured and systematic approach to data analysis. It highlights the need for organizations to invest in the necessary technology and expertise to collect, store, and analyze large volumes of data effectively. It also emphasizes the importance of involving key stakeholders, including fraud investigators and senior management, throughout the process to ensure that the insights gained from data analysis are effectively communicated and integrated into the organization's decision-making processes. Overall, this case study is a compelling example of the transformative power of big data analytics in the financial sector and underscores the need for continued investment in this area to stay ahead of the evolving fraud landscape.

The analysis results will be discussed by the supervisory learning algorithm/ decision tree to detect fraud in financial transactions involving training a model on historical data to identify patterns and characteristics of fraudulent transactions. The decision tree algorithm is a machine learning technique that can classify new transactions as either fraudulent or legitimate based on their features, such as transaction amount, time, location, and source.

The decision tree works by recursively partitioning the data into subsets based on the values of the features and then assigning a class label to each subgroup based on the majority class of the examples in that subset. The algorithm seeks optimal splits that maximize the separation between fraudulent and legitimate transactions while minimizing the misclassification error. Fig. 26.3 shows the decision tree from Weka for the First Hypothesis.

Using the decision tree algorithm allows us to detect fraud with high accuracy and efficiency and adapt to new types of fraud as they emerge. Once the decision tree model is trained, it can classify new transactions in real time and alert the appropriate personnel if a transaction is potentially fraudulent. However, it is

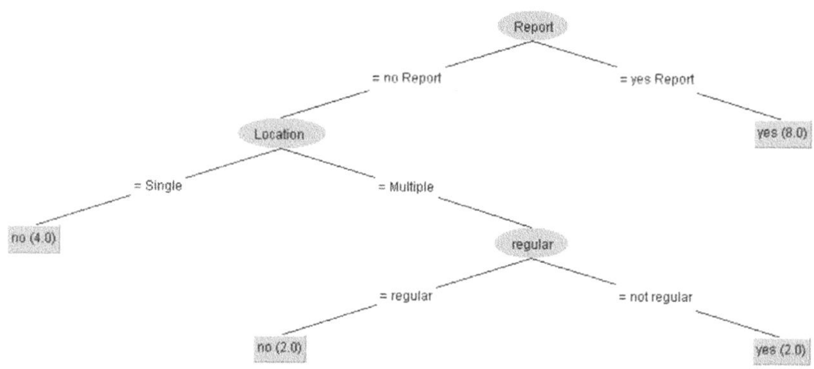

Fig. 26.3. Decision Tree From Weka for the First Hypothesis.

essential to continuously monitor and update the model to ensure its effectiveness and reliability over time.

Table 26.1 shows the performance of the classification model for two classes, "yes (fraud)" and "no (no fraud)," in terms of various performance measures such as TP rate, FP rate, precision, recall, F-measure, MCC, ROC area, and PRC area. The performance measures help evaluate the model's effectiveness in predicting the class labels of the instances. The weighted average of the measures for both classes indicates that the model correctly classified 75% of the cases with a moderate level of agreement (MCC = 0.467).

The output is from Weka, a widely used open-source machine learning and data mining software tool. Weka provides a user-friendly interface to apply various machine learning algorithms and evaluate their performance on datasets. The output shows detailed accuracy by class, which is one of the many evaluation methods provided by Weka. Fig. 26.4 shows the Decision Tree from Weka for the Second Hypothesis.

Fig. 26.5 shows the performance of the classification model for two classes, "yes (fraud)" and "no (no fraud)." The model correctly classified 60% of the instances with the moderate agreement (Kappa statistic = 0.2857). Table 26.1 also shows various performance measures, such as TP rate, FP rate, precision, recall, *F*-measure, MCC, ROC area, and PRC area, for each class and the weighted average of these measures for both classes.

Table 26.1. The Performance of the Classification Model for the First Hypothesis.

	TP Rate	FP Rate	Precision	Recall	*F*-Measure	MCC	ROC Area	PRC Area	Class
	0.667	0.2	0.667	0.667	0.667	0.467	0.9	0.806	No
	0.8	0.333	0.8	0.8	0.8	0.467	0.9	0.943	Yes
Weighted Avg.	0.75	0.283	0.75	0.75	0.75	0.467	0.9	0.891	

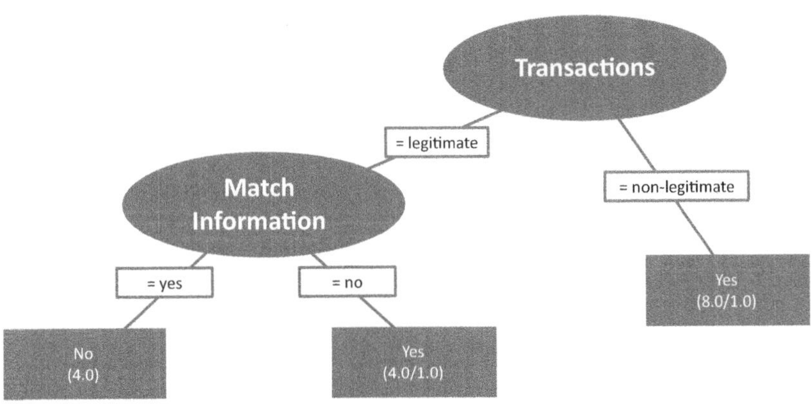

Fig. 26.4. Decision Tree From Weka for the Second Hypothesis.

```
Correctly Classified Instances           3               60      %
Incorrectly Classified Instances         2               40      %
Kappa statistic                          0.2857
Mean absolute error                      0.4286
Root mean squared error                  0.5041
Relative absolute error                 89.8618 %
Root relative squared error            102.8412 %
Total Number of Instances                5

=== Detailed Accuracy By Class ===
```

	TP Rate	FP Rate	Precision	Recall	F-Measure	MCC	ROC Area	PRC Area	Class
	1.000	0.667	0.500	1.000	0.667	0.408	0.667	0.500	no
	0.333	0.000	1.000	0.333	0.500	0.408	0.667	0.733	yes
Weighted Avg.	0.600	0.267	0.800	0.600	0.567	0.408	0.667	0.640	

Fig. 26.5. The Performance of the Classification Model for the Second Hypothesis.

For the "no" class, the TP rate is 1.000, indicating that all actual positive instances were correctly classified. However, the FP rate is 0.667, meaning that two out of three negative instances were incorrectly classified as positive. For the "yes" class, the TP rate is 0.333, indicating that only one out of three actual positive instances were correctly classified. However, the precision is 1.000, meaning that all positive predictions for this class were correct. The weighted average of the performance measures for both classes suggests that the model correctly classified 60% of the instances, with an *F*-measure of 0.567.

One strength of using the big data analysis life cycle in fraud detection in financial transactions is that it identifies potential fraud cases that might be missed using traditional methods. By analyzing large volumes of data, anomalies, which indicate fraudulent behavior, can be detected. Additionally, big data analytics can be used in real time to monitor transactions as they occur, providing an early warning system for potential fraud cases.

Another strength of using big data analysis in fraud detection is that it can be applied to various financial transactions, including credit card transactions, wire transfers, and online purchases. This makes it a versatile tool for fraud detection across different industries and sectors. Moreover, the insights gained from big data analysis can be used to improve fraud prevention strategies, leading to more effective and efficient detection and prevention of fraud.

One weakness of using big data analysis in fraud detection is that it requires a significant investment in data infrastructure, technology, and skilled personnel. This can be a barrier for smaller organizations or those with limited resources. Additionally, the reliance on algorithms and automation in big data analysis can lead to false positives and negatives, potentially causing unnecessary harm to innocent customers or missing actual cases of fraud. Therefore, it is essential to consider the trade-offs and risks of using big data analytics in fraud detection and ensure that appropriate safeguards and monitoring mechanisms are in place.

Future research directions in big data analysis for fraud detection could include exploring new and innovative machine learning algorithms to improve the accuracy and efficiency of fraud detection models. Additionally, future research could focus on developing more comprehensive data sources and integrating data from various sources to provide a complete picture of fraudulent activity. Another area of research could be the application of blockchain technology to enhance the security and transparency of financial transactions and prevent fraud. Moreover, future research could investigate the ethical implications of big data analysis in fraud detection and establish best practices for handling sensitive data. Finally, future research could also examine the potential use of big data analysis in detecting other types of financial crimes, such as money laundering and terrorist financing.

7. CONCLUSION

The chapter discusses using big data analytics in fraud detection in financial transactions. It highlights the importance of using a comprehensive big data analysis lifecycle involving several stages, including data collection, exploration, model building, communicating results, and operationalization.

The chapter implemented the big data analysis lifecycle to detect and prevent fraud in Kareem Exchange Company. The results showed that implementing big data analytics helped the company significantly reduce credit card fraud, leading to increased customer trust and cost savings. The chapter also discusses the strengths and weaknesses of using big data analytics in fraud detection and identifies future research directions. The strengths include analyzing large volumes of data, identifying patterns and anomalies, and improving fraud detection accuracy. The weaknesses include data quality issues, data privacy concerns, and the need for specialized skills and expertise. Future research directions include improving fraud detection accuracy, addressing data quality issues, and exploring new data sources and technologies.

REFERENCES

Abbassi, H., El Alaoui, I., & Gahi, Y. (2022). Fraud detection techniques in the big data era. In *Proceedings of the 2nd international conference on big data, modelling and machine learning* (Vol. 1, pp. 161–170). doi: 10.5220/0010730300003101

Abd Elhady, S. Z., Ghali, N. I., Abo-Elfetoh, A., & Idrees, A. M. (2023). Comparison of four ml predictive models predictive analysis of big data. *Journal of Theoretical and Applied Information Technology*, *101*(1), 282–292.

Al-Hashedi, K. G., & Magalingam, P. (2021). Financial fraud detection applying data mining techniques: A comprehensive review from 2009 to 2019. *Computer Science Review*, *40*, 100402.

Allaymoun, M. H., Al Saad, L. H., Majed, Z. M., & Hashem, S. M. A. (2022). Big data analysis and data visualization to facilitate decision-making-mega start case study. In *Explore business, technology opportunities and challenges after the Covid-19 pandemic* (pp. 370–379). Berlin: Springer.

Allaymoun, M. H., Qaradh, S., Salman, M., & Hasan, M. (2022). Big data analysis and data visualization to help make a decision-Islamic banks case study. In *Explore business, technology opportunities and challenges after the Covid-19 pandemic* (pp. 54–63). Berlin: Springer.

Arfeen, A. A., & Khan, B. M. A. (2022). Empirical analysis of machine learning algorithms on detection of fraudulent electronic fund transfer transactions. *IETE Journal of Research*, 1–13.

Christian, N., Basri, Y., & Arafah, W. (2019). Analysis of fraud triangle, fraud diamond and fraud pentagon theory to detecting corporate fraud in Indonesia. *The International Journal of Business Management and Technology*, *3*(4), 73–78.

Dhingra, D., & Ashok, S. (2021). The emerging role of big data in financial services. In *Industry 4.0 technologies for business excellence* (pp. 175–189). Boca Raton, FL: CRC Press.

Dornadula, V. N., & Geetha, S. (2019). Credit card fraud detection using machine learning algorithms. *Procedia Computer Science*, *165*, 631–641.

Education, C. (2023). *Data science*. Noida: Certybox Education.

Elastal, M., Allaymoun, M. H., Jasim, Z. A., & Elbastawisy, T. K. (2023 February). Employing big data analytics' lifecycle in money laundering detection. In *International congress on information and communication technology* (pp. 757–769). Singapore: Springer Nature Singapore..

Fernández, A. (2019). Artificial intelligence in financial services. *Banco de Espana Article*, *3*, 19.

Gandomi, A., & Haider, M. (2015). Beyond the hype: Big data concepts, methods, and analytics. *International Journal of Information Management*, *35*(2), 137–144.

Hummer, D., & Byrne, J. M. (2023). Techno-crime cause, prevention, and control: Issues to consider. *Handbook on Crime and Technology*, *1*.

Kagan, P. (2019). Big data sets in construction. In Paper presented at the E3S web of conferences.

Koo, J., Kang, G., & Kim, Y.-G. (2020). Security and privacy in big data life cycle: A survey and open challenges. *Sustainability*, *12*(24), 10571.

Kumar, S., Ahmed, R., Bharany, S., Shuaib, M., Ahmad, T., Tag Eldin, E., … Shafiq, M. (2022). Exploitation of machine learning algorithms for detecting financial crimes based on customers' behavior. *Sustainability*, *14*(21), 13875.

Lee, J. W. (2020). Big data strategies for government, society and policy-making. *Journal of Asian Finance Economics and Business*, *7*(7), 475–487.

Malik, E. F., Khaw, K. W., & Chew, X. (2022). Fraud detection by machine learning techniques.

Ogwiji, J., & Lasisi, I. O. (2022). Internal control system and fraud prevention of quoted financial services firms in Nigeria: A smart PLS-SEM approach. *European Journal of Accounting, Auditing and Finance Research*, *10*(4), 1–13.

Pandey, V. C., Peddoju, S. K., & Deshpande, P. S. (2018). A statistical and distributed packet filter against DDoS attacks in Cloud environment. *Sādhanā*, *43*, 1–9.

Pawar, A. D., Kalavadekar, P. N., & Tambe, S. N. (2014). A survey on outlier detection techniques for credit card fraud detection. *IOSR Journal of Computer Engineering*, *16*(2), 44–48.

Pramanik, S., & Bandyopadhyay, S. K. (2023). Analysis of big data. In *Encyclopedia of data science and machine learning* (pp. 97–115). Hershey, PA: IGI Global.

Rahul, K., & Banyal, R. K. (2020). Data life cycle management in big data analytics. *Procedia Computer Science*, *173*, 364–371.

Ritika, H. (2022). Fraud detection and management for telecommunication systems using artificial intelligence (AI). In Paper presented at the 3rd international conference on smart electronics and communication (ICOSEC).

Roy, N. C., & Prabhakaran, S. (2022). Internal-led cyber frauds in Indian banks: An effective machine learning-based defense system to fraud detection, prioritization and prevention. *ASLIB Journal of Information Management*.

Sivaranjani, R. (2023). An overview of the big data technology for computer-assisted learning. In *Computer-assisted learning for engaging varying aptitudes: From theory to practice* (pp. 66–74). Hershey, PA: IGI Global.

Wright, L. T., Robin, R., Stone, M., & Aravopoulou, D. E. (2019). Adoption of big data technology for innovation in B2B marketing. *Journal of Business-to-Business Marketing*, *26*(3–4), 281–293.

CHAPTER 27

FINANCIAL HEALTH ANALYSIS OF SELECTED PUBLIC AND PRIVATE-SECTOR BANKS IN INDIA – AN ALTMAN Z-SCORE APPROACH

Ibha Rani

0000-0003-2081-7934, Kristu Jayanti College (Autonomous), Bengaluru, India

ABSTRACT

The study aims to evaluate the financial distress position of selected sample banks in India. The top 10 banks with the highest levels of gross non-performing assets (NPA) under both public and private sector ownerships have been chosen for the study. Application of the Altman Z-score model has been used to compare both ownership banks' financial distress for five years from 2017 to 2021. Based on the study's findings, it was found that private sector banks demonstrated better financial stability than their public sector counterparts. Specifically, the average Z-score of the selected sample banks was higher than the safe zone threshold of 2.9 during the study period.

Keywords: Financial health; Altman *Z*-score; public bank; private banks; financial distress and non-performing assets

Digital Technology and Changing Roles in Managerial and Financial Accounting: Theoretical Knowledge and Practical Application
Studies in Managerial and Financial Accounting, Volume 36, 319–328

ISSN: 1479-3512/doi:10.1108/S1479-351220240000036029

1. INTRODUCTION

The banking sector is considered as the financial heart of the country. In this turbulent global business climate, a strong banking system is critical for any economy attempting to achieve good growth. The banking industry must be trouble-free and capable of meeting new difficulties that may arise either from internal or external sources. Altman Z-score has been used to check selected banks' credibility and financial distress. This chapter emphasizes the usage of the Z-score for the comparison between the public and private sector banks of India. The total banks are 20 in number; among the sample banks, 10 banks are from public sector banks and the other 10 are from private sector banks. The selection of the sample is based on the level of NPA of the bank; nowadays Indian banking sector is struggling with the rising level of NPA in their asset structure. NPA means that a loan or asset isn't being paid on time either in terms of interest or principal and it adversely impacts banks' ability to generate adequate income and profitability.

This chapter is segmented into distinct parts, comprising research questions, a survey of existing literature, an objective, and methodology followed by a conclusion.

2. LITERATURE SURVEY

Nishi Sharma and Mayanka (2013) analyzed the financial distress situation of 20 Indian public and 16 private banks for the period of five years from 2008 to 2012. As per findings, two banks in distress situations are Canara Bank (Publicly Owned) and Kotak Mahindra Bank (Private ownership, according to the findings, despite the fact that both the banks' capital adequacy ratio was sound when compared to those of other sample banks.

Roli Pradhan (2014) used the Altman Z-score model for the prediction of bankruptcy for three Indian public sector banks namely Oriental Bank of Commerce, Punjab National Bank, and SBI for 10 years from 2000 to 2009. As per her findings, OBC is having highest Z-score among all three banks while the State Bank of India has improved from 2011 onward.

Abdullah (2015) has made an empirical analysis of the Solvency, liquidity, and profitability of 29 Bangladeshis banks from the year 2009 to 2014. As per findings, there are seven banks that are financially sound while 22 banks are in financial distress situation during the study period.

Parvin, Rahman, and Nitu (2016) have made a comparison between private banks and state-owned banks in Bangladesh with the Altman Z-score model. The results indicate that, in terms of financial distress, state-owned commercial banks are in a more favorable position compared to private commercial banks. The study also determined that there was a significant difference in the Z-scores of state-owned banks when compared to those of private banks.

Khaddafi et al. (2017) conducted a study to assess the ability of the Altman Z-score to predict the likelihood of bankruptcy among 29 banks listed on the Indonesia Stock Exchange between 2011 and 2013. Their analysis revealed that in 2011, 13 banks had a Z-score of more than 2.99 and were considered to be in a healthy financial situation, while 14 were in distress and 2 were in a gray area.

In 2012, 10 banks were deemed healthy, 14 were in bankruptcy, and 5 were in the gray area. In 2013, the number of healthy banks increased to 11, with 4 in the gray area and 14 in bankruptcy.

Soumya Agarwal (2018) has analyzed the health of five Indian public sector banks (BOB, SBI, PNB, CBI, and IDBI) for the period of five years from 2012 to 2016 and these banks have been selected based on the market capitalization. As per the analysis, IDBI secured first rank in terms of Z-score with an average value of 4.478.

Joshi (2020) has applied the Altman Z-score for selected 10 public banks in India for a period of 10 years. As per findings, the Z-score of all the selected banks is higher than 2.9 which is a safe zone as per the Altman Z-score statics. He has also employed linear regression to examine the relationship between NPA and the Z-score. Their findings revealed that a 1% increase in gross NPA was associated with a decrease of approximately 3.1% in the Z-score.

Sharma and Kumar (2021) assess the financial health of selected public and private sector banks in India using the Altman Z-score approach. The findings suggest that while some banks are in good financial health, others are at risk of bankruptcy. The study also identified several factors that contribute to the financial stability of banks such as profitability, asset quality, and liquidity.

Nagendra and Nimbalkar (2022) aimed to predict bankruptcy for the cement industry in India using the Altman Z-score model. The findings suggest that some companies in the cement industry in India are at a higher risk of bankruptcy than others. The study also identified several factors that contribute to the financial stability of the companies such as profitability, liquidity, and leverage.

Based on the literature review, it appears that researchers have not utilized the Altman Z-model extensively for forecasting the bank's bankruptcy. Most papers analyzed the financial health of a bank either by the traditional approach of ratio analysis or the CAMELS model. This chapter will focus on the comparative analysis of the top 10 public and private sector banks by using the tool Altman Z-score.

2.1. Research Questions

For this study, the major three following research questions have been derived:

> *RQ1*. How is the financial distress position of chosen public and private banks of India?
>
> *RQ2*. Are there any significant distinctions between the selected public and private banks in India?
>
> *RQ3*. Is there any relationship exist between GNPA and Altman Z-score?

2.2. Research Objectives

- To predict the financial distress position of chosen sample banks during the study period.
- To conduct a comparison of banks in public and private banks ownership.
- To establish the relationship between the GNPA and Altman Z-score.

2.3. Hypotheses

Hypotheses have been formulated based on research questions and objectives, which are as:

H1. There is a significant difference in the financial health of sample banks during the study period.

H2. The public sector banks are less financially sound than the private banks.

H3. A significant negative correlation exists between GNPA and Altman *Z*-score.

3. RESEARCH METHODOLOGY

This study has a descriptive research design aimed at predicting the probability of bankruptcy for the sample bank that has been chosen, followed by a comparison of public and private sector banks over the study period.

3.1. Sample Banks

For the study, 20 banks are chosen for the study period of five financial years from 2017 to 2021 based on the highest level of gross NPA. The sample included 10 banks from the public and other 10 banks from the private sector reflects in Table 27.1.

3.2. Research Period

The researcher has considered five consecutive financial years from March 2017 to March 2021.

3.2.1. Data Sources

The data used in this study is obtained from secondary sources such as the annual reports of sample banks as well as the websites moneycontrol.com, economic-times.com, and indiatimes.com websites.

Table 27.1. List of Sample Banks.

Type	Bank Name	Type	Bank Name
Pub	Bank of Baroda (BOB)	Pvt	Axis Bank Limited (AXIS)
Pub	Bank of India (BOI)	Pvt	Federal Bank Ltd (FED)
Pub	Canara Bank (CAN)	Pvt	HDFC Bank Ltd. (HDFC)
Pub	Central Bank of India (CBI)	Pvt	ICICI Bank Limited (ICICI)
Pub	Indian Bank (IND)	Pvt	INDUSIND Bank Ltd (INDUS)
Pub	Indian Overseas Bank (IOB)	Pvt	Jammu & Kashmir Bank Ltd (J&K)
Pub	Punjab National Bank (PNB)	Pvt	Karur Vysya Bank Ltd (KARUR)
Pub	State Bank of India (SBI)	Pvt	Kotak Mahindra Bank Ltd. (KMB)
Pub	UCO Bank (UCO)	Pvt	Lakshmi Vilas Bank Ltd (LVB)
Pub	Union Bank of India (UBI)	Pvt	YES Bank Ltd. (YES)

3.3. Tools and Techniques

The researcher has selected the Altman *Z*-score model as a statistical tool and average, independent sample *t*-test, correlation matrix, and ranking as drawing the conclusion for the research.

3.3.1. Altman Z-Score Model

This model was created by American Finance professor, "Edward Altman" in 1968 to assess the financial distress situation of companies. This is a useful method of predicting the chances of companies going bankrupt in the next two years by using some balance sheet values and their income. As per the study, this model was 72% accurate at forecasting bankruptcy two years prior to its occurrence. The original model was evolved for public manufacturing companies and later in 1983 two other models have been designed for private manufacturing companies and non-publicly traded companies.

The original five-variable models of manufacturing companies have been modified to a four-variable model for the companies functioning in the non-manufacturing sector. The following equation has been used for the calculation of the *Z*-score:

$$\text{Z-score} = 6.56\ \text{A1} + 3.26\ \text{Abull2} + 6.72\ \text{A3} + 1.05\ \text{A4}$$

In the above equation, "*Z*" is known as the Altman Zeta score.

- *A1 is the ratio of working capital divided by total assets*
  The value of working capital indicates its short-term financial condition and it is the gap between current assets and current liabilities. This ratio determines the bank's liquidity and it identifies the bank's ability to cover its short-term financial obligation.
- *A2 is the ratio of retained earnings and total assets*
  This ratio indicates the accumulated profitability over a period of time. A high ratio exhibits that the company uses its retained earnings to fund its capital expenditure rather than rely on borrowings.
- *A3 is the ratio of earnings before interest and tax (EBIT) and total assets*
  EBIT is the operating profit and this ratio measures earning capabilities of a firm's assets before the influence of taxes and interests.
- *A4 is the ratio of the market value of equity and total liabilities*
  The market value of equity is calculated by multiplying the market price of the company's share by the total number of outstanding shares, resulting in total market capitalization. Investors' trust in the company's financial stability is high when this ratio has a high value.

3.3.2. Altman Z-Score Implications

This *Z*-score is helped to predict the likelihood that a bank will go bankrupt in the next two years (Altman, 2000).

A bank having greater than 2.99 indicated that the banks are in a safe position for the next two years. A *Z*-score having less than 1.88 indicates that the banks are at considerable risk of going into bankruptcy and it will consider in a "Grey Zone." Banks having less than 1.8 indicates the "Financial Distress" condition having a high probability of bankruptcy.

Altman Z-Score Implications
Safe zone $Z > 2.99$
Gray zone $1.88 < Z > 2.99$
Distress zone $Z < 1.88$

4. DATA ANALYSIS

Table 27.2 indicates the value of the Altman Z-score of 20 sample banks for the period of 2017–2021.

As per the findings, all banks considered for the study have a higher score than 2.99 which indicates all the banks are in the safe zone. It shows that the banks will maintain sound financial positions without any serious financial difficulties, which are classified in the category of a "Safe Zone."

In particular, Kotak Mahindra Bank has the highest average score followed by IndusInd and HDFC Bank with a Z-score of 6.7597, 6.4052, and 6.2375, respectively.

4.1. Comparative Analysis Between Public and Private -Sector Banks

Table 27.3 indicates the comparative analysis of public and private sector banks through the average Z-score for the years 2017–2021.

Table 27.2. Altman Z-Score of Sample Banks.

Type	Bank Name	2017	2018	2019	2020	2021	Mean
Pub	BOB	5.8772	5.6085	5.5599	5.5359	5.6068	5.6377
Pub	BOI	5.4938	5.2561	5.1879	5.1598	5.1093	5.2414
Pub	CAN	5.3639	5.4591	5.5455	5.4158	5.4811	5.4531
Pub	CBI	5.2423	4.9858	4.5312	4.2715	4.2454	4.6552
Pub	IND	5.0660	5.1970	5.4874	5.3630	4.9960	5.2219
Pub	IOB	5.1415	5.2037	5.3104	4.8471	4.6791	5.0364
Pub	PNB	5.4087	5.3067	5.3781	5.2317	5.0403	5.2731
Pub	SBI	5.1517	5.0185	5.3212	5.2984	5.0514	5.1682
Pub	UCO	4.8956	4.7369	4.5588	4.4255	4.4697	4.6173
Pub	UBI	5.5087	5.4315	5.4029	5.2511	4.9992	5.3187
Pvt	AXIS	5.8093	5.7161	5.7906	6.0839	5.7150	5.8230
Pvt	FED	5.7395	5.8896	6.0143	5.9979	6.0705	5.9424
Pvt	HDFC	6.2810	6.3907	6.3989	6.0884	6.0284	6.2375
Pvt	ICICI	6.2713	6.0381	6.1165	5.9583	5.9942	6.0757
Pvt	INDUS	6.5273	6.2971	6.2932	6.4829	6.4258	6.4052
Pvt	J&K	5.5415	5.3611	5.6748	5.5223	5.5174	5.5234
Pvt	KARUR	5.8267	5.8333	5.9486	5.8770	5.8607	5.8693
Pvt	KMB	6.8468	6.7253	6.8797	6.8936	6.4532	6.7597
Pvt	LBK	5.6667	5.5479	5.3203	5.3701	5.5508	5.4912
Pvt	YES	5.8901	5.8743	5.7157	6.3343	6.3000	6.0229

Table 27.3. Comparative Analysis of Public and Private Banks Based on *Z*-Score.

Type	Bank	2017	2018	2019	2020	2021
Pub	BOB	5.8772	5.6085	5.5599	5.5359	5.6068
Pub	BOI	5.4938	5.2561	5.1879	5.1598	5.1093
Pub	CAN	5.3639	5.4591	5.5455	5.4158	5.4811
Pub	CBI	5.2423	4.9858	4.5312	4.2715	4.2454
Pub	IND	5.0660	5.1970	5.4874	5.3630	4.9960
Pub	IOB	5.1415	5.2037	5.3104	4.8471	4.6791
Pub	PNB	5.4087	5.3067	5.3781	5.2317	5.0403
Pub	SBI	5.1517	5.0185	5.3212	5.2984	5.0514
Pub	UCO	4.8956	4.7369	4.5588	4.4255	4.4697
Pub	UBI	5.5087	5.4315	5.4029	5.2511	4.9992
Average *Z*-score of public sector banks		5.3149	5.2204	5.2283	5.0800	4.9678
Pvt	AXIS	5.8093	5.7161	5.7906	6.0839	5.7150
Pvt	FED	5.7395	5.8896	6.0143	5.9979	6.0705
Pvt	HDFC	6.2810	6.3907	6.3989	6.0884	6.0284
Pvt	ICICI	6.2713	6.0381	6.1165	5.9583	5.9942
Pvt	INDUS	6.5273	6.2971	6.2932	6.4829	6.4258
Pvt	J & K	5.5415	5.3611	5.6748	5.5223	5.5174
Pvt	KARUR	5.8267	5.8333	5.9486	5.8770	5.8607
Pvt	KMB	6.8468	6.7253	6.8797	6.8936	6.4532
Pvt	LVB	5.6667	5.5479	5.3203	5.3701	5.5508
Pvt	YES	5.8901	5.8743	5.7157	6.3343	6.3000
Average *Z*-score of private sector banks		6.0400	5.9673	6.0153	6.0609	5.9916

As per Table 27.3, the public sector banks show a decreasing trend from 5.31 to 4.96 for the study periods from 2017 to 2021, while private banks do not reflect any particular trend either increasing or decreasing trend. All the five years private sector's average *Z*-score is better than public sector banks. Less value of the *Z*-score exhibits a higher probability of banks going into financial distress situation. So, the private banks show a better financial position than the public sector banks for the study period in terms of the Altman *Z*-score.

4.1.1. Hypotheses Testing

H1. There is significant difference financial health of selected banks changed during the study period.

To check this, one-sample *t*-test has been conducted.

As per Tables 27.4 and 27.5, the value of significance is less than 0.05, which means we have rejected the null hypothesis and accepted that there are changes in the financial health of sample banks during the study period.

H2. The public sector banks are less financially sound than the private banks.

An independent sample *t*-test has been conducted.

Table 27.4. One-sample Statistics Based on *Z*-Score.

Measure of Financial Health	*N*	Mean	Standard Deviation	Standard Error Mean
Z-score	20	5.59	0.557	0.124

Table 27.5. One-sample *t*-Test.

	Test Value = 0					
Measures of Financial Health	*t*	df	Sig. at (Two-tailed)	Mean Difference	95% Confidence Interval of the Difference: Lower	95% Confidence Interval of the Difference: Upper
Z-score	44.842	19	0.000	5.589	5.32	5.84

The data from Tables 27.6 and 27.7 does not assume equal variances, if the significance or the *p*-value is less than 0.05 then the data. The *p*-values are less than 0.05, indicating rejection of null hypotheses and acceptance of alternate hypotheses. So, the public sector banks are less financially sound as compared to private sector banks.

H3. There is a significant negative correlation between GNPA and Altman *Z*-score.

As per Table 27.9, there is negative correlation exists between GNPA and Altman *Z*-score, and also the correlation is significant as the significance value is less than 0.05.

Table 27.6. Group Statistics for Independent Sample *t*-Test.

Type		*N*	Mean	Standard Deviation	Std. Error Mean
Z-score	Pub	10	5.16	0.321	0.101
	Pvt	10	6.015	0.385	0.122

Table 27.7. Independent Sample *t*-Test.

		Levene's Test for Equality of Variances		*t*-Test for Equality of Means						
		F	Sig.	*t*	df	Sig. (Two-tailed)	Mean Difference	Std. Error Difference	95% Confidence Interval of the Difference: Lower	95% Confidence Interval of the Difference: Upper
Z-score	Equalvariances assumes	0.246	0.03	5.48	18	0.00	−0.857	0.158	−0.44	−0.20
	Equal variances not assumes			5.18	17.42	0.00	−0.852	0.158	−0.44	−0.19

Table 27.8. Descriptive Statistics of NPA and *Z*-Score.

	Mean	Standard Deviation	*N*
NPA	32,399.3827	37,718.91826	20
Z-score	5.5887	0.55736	20

Table 27.9. Correlations Matrix.

		NPA	*Z*-Score
NPA	Pearson correlation	1	−0.394*
	Sig. (one-tailed)		0.043
	N	20	20
Z-score	Pearson correlation	−0.394*	1
	Sig. (one-tailed)	0.023	
	N	20	20

*Correlation is significant at the 0.05 level (one-tailed).

5. CONCLUSION

In this competitive environment, competition in banks getting increasing, and handling their NPAs is a more concerning issue. Hence soundness of banks is of utmost importance for the financial and economic development of a country. This study focuses to analyze the financial health of selected banks operating in India. As per the data analysis based on Altman *Z*-score, all the selected banks belong to the safe zone having a *Z*-score of more than 2.99 over the period of 2017–2021. According to findings, the *Z*-score is slowly decreasing over the study period while Kotak Mahindra ranked first followed by IndusInd and HDFC bank. Between public and private sector banks, private banks have scored better than public over the study periods.

REFERENCES

Abdullah, M. (2015). An empirical analysis of liquidity, profitability and solvency of Bangladeshi banks. *Journal of Business & Financial Affairs*, *5*, 157.

Agarwal, S., & Singh, G. (2018). Altman Z score with reference to public sector banks in India. *International Journal of Research and Analytical Reviews*, *5*(4), 955–963.

Altman, E. I. (2000). *Predicting financial distress of companies: Revisiting the Z-score and zeta models*. New York, NY: New York University.

Joshi, M. K. (2020). Financial performance analysis of select Indian public sector banks using Altman's Z-score model. *SMART Journal of Business Management Studies*, 16(2), 74–87.

Khaddafi, M., Heikal, M., & Nandari, A. (2017). Analysis Z-score to predict bankruptcy in banks listed in Indonesia stock exchange. *International Journal of Economics and Financial Issues*, *7*(3), 326–330.

Liang, D., Lu, C.-C., Tsai, C.-F., & Shih, G.-A. (2016). Financial ratios and corporate governance indicators in bankruptcy prediction: A comprehensive study. *European Journal of Operational Research*, *252*, 561–572.

Malik, M., Muzammal, B., & Amin, A. (2017). Evaluating financial distress in developing economies: A case study of Pakistani and Indian public sector banks using Altman's Z score. *South Asian Journal of Banking and Social Sciences*, *3*(1), 119–116.

Nagendra, M., & Nimbalkar, P. (2022). Bankruptcy prediction for cement industry in India using Altman Z score model. *Asian Journal of Economics, Business and Accounting*, *22*(24), 77–85.

Niresh, J., & Pratheepan, T. (2015). The application of Altman's z-score model in predicting bankruptcy: Evidence from the trading sector in Srilanka. *International Journal of Business and Management*, *10*(12), 269–275.

Parvin, A., Rahman, B., & Nitu, A. A. (2013). Prediction of financial health of banking industry in Bangladesh using Altman's Z score: A comparison between state-owned commercial banks and private commercial banks. In *Proceeding of the international conference for bankers and academics* (pp. 335–344). Researchgate.net

Pradhan, R. (2014). Z score estimation for Indian banking sector. *International Journal of Trade, Economics and Finance*, *5*(6), 516.

Sharma, N. (2013). Altman model and financial soundness of Indian banks. *International Journal of Accounting and Finance*, *3*(2), 55–60.

Sharma, S., & Kumar, A. (2021). Financial health analysis of selected public and private sector banks in India – An Altman Z-score approach. *Journal of Banking and Financial Services*, *15*(2), 14–6. https://doi.org/10.1177/0022109021102002

Sreekala, S., Santhi, D. V., & Kumar, V. M. (2016). Evaluating the Financial Health of selected commercial banks in Indian Banking Sector. *Asian Journal of Research in Social Sciences and Humanities*, *6*(3), 121–27.

CHAPTER 28

IMPACT OF REMUNERATION COMMITTEE'S CHARACTERISTICS ON FIRM PERFORMANCE

Mujeeb Saif Mohsen Al-Absy and Husain Isa Merza

Accounting and Financial Science Department, College of Administrative and Financial Science, Gulf University, Sanad 26489, Kingdom of Bahrain

ABSTRACT

The aim of the study is to examine the influence of remuneration committee (RC) characteristics, namely separation, size, independence, meetings, and female directors, on firm performance (FP) by using return on assets (ROA), return on equity (ROE) and earnings per shares (EPS). The study covers all firms being listed in Bahrain Bourse for two years which are 2020 and 2021. The results of the study show that having more directors in RC would significantly increase firm performance "ROE and EPS." Further, having more females in RC would significantly increase firm performance "ROA." In addition, having separate RC would significantly decrease firm performance "ROA and EPS." Moreover, the independence of directors in RC and its frequent meetings has no significant impact on the firm's performance. The results show that there is a need to re-evaluate the role of the RC and strengthen its effectiveness, as some of the variables examined by this study have an insignificant impact on a firm's performance. Further, there is a need to allocate additional efforts and policies in developing corporate governance and RCs as well.

Keywords: Corporate governance; Board of Directors; Remuneration Committee; Independence; gender equality; firm performance

Digital Technology and Changing Roles in Managerial and Financial Accounting: Theoretical Knowledge and Practical Application
Studies in Managerial and Financial Accounting, Volume 36, 329–345

ISSN: 1479-3512/doi:10.1108/S1479-351220240000036030

1. INTRODUCTION

The term firm performance (FP) is very significant for business as it is viewed as an objective for any business to reach their ultimate performance which leads them to get through the experience of improvement. According to Taouab and Issor (2019), FP as the efficiency and effectiveness of the firm along with the ability to hold and make value to their clients and shareholders. The global financial scandals and fraud have had a huge impact on economies throughout the world (Al-Absy, 2020, 2022a) and caused large businesses to fail (Al-Absy, 2022b; Al-Absy, Ismail, & Chandren, 2017), where the management's stance on manipulating earnings is still a problem (Ai-Absy, Ismail, & Chandren, 2021). Further, the financial crisis has shown strong weaknesses in the corporate governance (CG) practices which cause the standards to fail to offer checks and balances for the purpose of having better practices in business.

Thus, there was an urgent need to create new and strong CG (Al-Absy & Hasan, 2023; Al-Absy, Almaamari, Alkadash, & Habtoor, 2020; Al-Absy, Ismail, Chandren, & Al-Dubai, 2020) which has involved several committees that each one is specialized for a certain role, for example, audit committee (AC), risk management committee (RMC), remuneration committee (RC), and nomination committee (NC) (Harymawan, Agustia, Nasih, Inayati, & Nowland, 2020). Having efficient CG is a very vital factor for organizations since it is in charge of monitoring businesses' operations and has the authority to influence how businesses make decisions (Mahdi, Al-Absy, & Alastal, 2023). To expand, the structure of CG includes controls, policies, and guidelines that push the organization to meet its objectives along with fulfilling the needs of their stakeholders where the company's ultimate objective is to maximize the wealth of its stakeholders (Gharaibeh & Qader, 2017).

An important committee of the board of directors (BOD) is the RC, which RC which plays a crucial role in matters pertaining to the firm's senior management and directors' compensation policies (Al-Absy, Ismail, & Chandren, 2018). The purpose of having a RC is to reduce disputes between shareholders and managers and to decide on the optimum compensation plan for directors in order to increase FP (Borlea, Achim, & Mare, 2017). Further, the members of the RC should review the company's compensation policies, which should be approved by the shareholders. They should then make recommendations to the full board regarding the remuneration policies and amounts for specific individuals, considering total remuneration, which includes salaries, fees, expenses, and employee benefits. Additionally, members of the RC should pay board members according to their performance and attendance (CBB, 2010).

Hence, the role played by RC members will affect the performance of directors and hence the FP. Directors and officers should get the compensation that is adequate to entice, keep, and inspire individuals with the qualifications essential to successfully operate the business, but the company should avoid spending more than is necessary to achieve that goal (Aslam, Haron, & Tahir, 2019). An effective RC will reduce the agency problem arising from the conflict between managers and shareholders (Chua & Ab Razak, 2018; Harymawan et al., 2020). Countries, for example, Bahrain, request all companies to have a RC with at least three members and meet twice a year.

Scholars have always been interested in evaluating the FP. However, there is a gap in the literature and ongoing discussion in this area (Taouab & Issor, 2019). In terms of CG, previous studies have extensively examined the effect of BOD on FP. However, research in the role of RC and its effect on FP is limited and all of them are done in developed countries. Further, the results of this few research that investigate the relationship between RC and FP is a mix bag (Aslam et al., 2019).

Further, the few previous studies conducted shown inconsistent results. As study done in among firms in Pakistan shows that there is a weak relationship between the remuneration characteristics and the FP (Aslam et al., 2019). Another study was conducted in Indonesia among 847 firms that are being listed on Indonesia Stock Exchange to examine the relationship between RC and FP, which revealed that there is a positive relationship between them (Harymawan et al., 2020). Hence, there is a need for further studies to investigate the influence of RC characteristics on FP.

The efficiency of the RC's monitoring function in ensuring that directors' compensation is commensurate with FP was not guaranteed by a company's adherence to the CG guideline (Lokman & Mohd Tareh, 2020). Hence, this study specifically covers the role and effect of RC characteristics on the FP. Based on the knowledge of the researcher, there was no study conducted on the effect of RC characteristics on FP in Gulf Cooperation Council (GCC).

This research will contain deep literature review of studies to investigate the relationship of RC on FP. Also, the literature review will involve detailed explanation of the variables included in the research. Furthermore, this study will be the first in Bahrain context in which it will involve examining the influence over all companies listed on Bahrain Bourse. In addition, the study and its results will be beneficial to the industry and more specifically to Bahraini context in which the results will be related. This would allow firms to adjust and benefit from accordingly. Moreover, the study will be beneficial to future researchers who could refer to the information and results offered by this study.

2. LITERATURE REVIEW

2.1. Effects of Board of Directors Characteristics on Firm Performance

Previous studies have extensively examined the effect of BOD' characteristics on FP. However, the results of these studies were inconsistent. These previous studies are presented in Table 28.1.

2.2. Effects of Remuneration Committee Characteristics on Firm Performance

Calvin (2017) defines the RC as a payment of reward in exchange to work done by an individual. Moreover, the author identifies some indicators such as basic salary, wages, allowances like for transportation, and pension schemes. Also, the

Table 28.1. Previous Empirical Studies on BOD and FP.

	DV	IV	Results
Abdulsamad, Yusoff, and Lasyoud (2018)	ROA and EPS	CEO duality	⁻Sig
		Independent directors	⁺Sig
		Board size	⁻Insig
		Board meeting	⁻Sig
Freihat, Farhan, and Shanikat (2019)	Tobin's *Q*	Ownership concentration	⁺Sig
		Board meetings	⁺Sig
		CEO duality	⁺Sig
		Board size	⁺Insig
		Board independence	⁺Insig
Atty, Moustafasoliman, and Youssef (2018)	ROA, ROE, and Q ratio	CEO duality	⁻Insig
		Board size	⁻Insig
		Board meetings	⁺Insig
		Independence board members	⁻Insig in ROA, ROE, and ⁺Insig in Q ratio
		Gender diversity	⁺Insig in ROA, ROE, and ⁻Insig in Q ratio
Saleh, Shurafa, Shukeri, Nour, and Maigosh (2020)	ROA and ROE	Multiple directorships	⁺Insig in ROA and ⁺Sig in ROE
		Multiple independent directorships	⁺Insig in ROA and ⁺Sig in ROE
		Multiple executive directorships	⁺Insig
		CEO busyness	⁺Sig
		CEO tenure	⁺Sig
		CEO's financial experience	⁺Sig
		COE's political connections	⁺Sig in ROA and ⁺Insig in ROE
Mishra and Kapil (2018)	Tobin's *Q* and ROA	Board size	⁺Sig
		Board independence	⁻Insig in Tobin's *Q* and ⁺Sig in ROA
		Number of meetings	⁺Sig in Tobin's *Q* and ⁺Insig in ROA
		CEO duality	⁺Sig
Makhlouf, Laili, Ramli, and Basah (2017)	ROA and Tobin's *Q*	BOD independence	⁺Sig
		Board size	⁻Sig in ROA and ⁺Insig in Tobin's *Q*
		BODs' meetings	⁺Insig
		Leadership structure	⁻Insig
		BODs' ownership	⁺Insig in ROA and ⁺Sig in Tobin's *Q*
Hezabr, Qeshta, and Alsoud (2020)	ROA, ROE, and EPS	Board size	⁺Insig in ROA, ROE, and EPS using fixed effect and ⁺Sig using random effects
		Board independence	⁻Insig
		Board meeting frequency	⁺Sig using fixed effect and ⁺Insig using random effects
		Board meeting attendance	⁺Insig

(Continued)

Table 28.1. *(Continued).*

	DV	IV	Results
Ganesan, Kanthan, Mushtaq, and Yeap (2018)	ROA	Bord size	$^{-}$Insig
		Gender diversity	$^{-}$Insig
		CEO duality	$^{+}$Insig
		Independent director	$^{+}$Insig
		Multiple directorship	$^{-}$Sig
Roffia, Simón-Moya, and Sendra García (2022)	ROA, ROS, and EVA	Board size	$^{-}$Insig
		Board composition (NEID)	$^{-}$Insig
		Skill level of board directors	$^{+}$Sig
		Existence AC, RC and RC	$^{-}$Sig
		Board Meeting	$^{+}$Insig
		Directors' ownership	$^{+}$Sig
		Family firms	$^{-}$Sig in ROS and $^{-}$Insig in ROA, and EVA
Khan and Abdul Subhan (2019)	ROA and ROE	Quality audit	$^{+}$Insig in ROE and $^{-}$sig in ROA
		Audit cost	$^{+}$Sig in ROE and $^{+}$Insig in ROA
		Present of Female directors	$^{+}$Sig
		No of female members	$^{-}$Insig
		Nationality diversity	$^{-}$Sig in ROE and $^{+}$Insig in ROA
Sobhan (2021)	ROA	Board size	$^{+}$Sig
		Board independence	$^{-}$Insig
		Board meeting	$^{-}$Insig
		Female directorship	$^{+}$Sig
		Director's ownership	$^{-}$Insig
Saleh and Islam (2020)	ROE	Women on the board %	$^{-}$Insig
		Board size	$^{+}$Sig
		Board meeting	$^{+}$Sig
		Board financial knowledge	$^{+}$Sig
Saleh (2016)	ROA	Board size	$^{+}$Insig
		Non-executive directors%	$^{-}$Insig
		Board experience "banking"	$^{+}$Sig
		Firm size	$^{+}$Sig
Yasser, Al Mamun, and Rodrigs (2017)	EVA, ROA and Tobin's *Q*, and.	Non-executive directors%	$^{+}$Insig in RVA and Tobin's *Q* and $^{-}$Insig in ROA
		Family directors	$^{-}$Insig in ROA $^{+}$Insig in Tobin's *Q* and EVA
		Family ownership	$^{+}$Insig in RVA, $^{-}$Insig in ROA $^{+}$Sig in Tobin's *Q*
		Independent director	$^{-}$Sig in ROA and Insig in EVA and Tobin's *Q*
		Board size	$^{+}$Sig
		Gender diversity	$^{+}$Insig in ROA and EVA and $^{+}$Sig in Tobin's *Q*
		Minority representation	$^{+}$Sig in ROA and EVA and $^{+}$Insig in Tobin's *Q*
Riyadh, Al Mamun, and Rodrigs (2017)	ROA	Board independence	$^{+}$Insig
		Board size	$^{+}$Sig
		Board diversity	$^{-}$Sig

(Continued)

Table 28.1. (*Continued*).

	DV	IV	Results
Al-Matari (2019)	Tobin's *Q*	Board size	$^{+}$Insig
		Non-executive directors%	$^{+}$Insig
		Board meeting	$^{-}$Insig
		Top Executive size	$^{-}$Insig
		Professional top executive	$^{-}$Insig
		Experience top executive	$^{+}$Insig
		Top executives' accounting experience	$^{+}$Sig
Bin Khidmat, Ayub Khan, and Ullah (2020)	ROA, ROE, EPS, Tobin's *Q*, and ER.	Board size	$^{+}$Sig in ROA and $^{-}$Sig in Tobin's *Q*. $^{+}$Insig in ROE and EPS
		Female directors	$^{+}$Sig
		Foreign national directors	$^{+}$Sig in ROA, Tobin's *Q*, EPS and $^{+}$Insig in ROE
		Age of directors	$^{-}$Insig in ROA, Tobin's *Q*, ROE, and $^{+}$Sig in EPS
		Independence directors	$^{-}$Insig in ROA, Tobin's *Q*, ROE, and $^{+}$Sig in EPS
		Education directors	$^{-}$Insig in ROA and ROE, and Insig ROA and Tobin's *Q*
Pavić Kramarić, Aleksic, and Pejic-Bach (2018)	ROE and ROA.	Board chair gender	$^{+}$Insig
		Share of women directors	$^{-}$Sig in ROA and $^{-}$Insig in ROE
		Size of the BODs	$^{-}$Sig
		supervisory board chair gender	$^{-}$Sig in ROA and $^{-}$Insig in ROE
Scholtz and Kieviet (2018)	ROA and Tobin's *Q*.	Female directors%	$^{+}$Sig
		Directors of ethnic%	$^{-}$Sig in Tobin's *Q* and $^{-}$Insig in ROA
		Business qualified directors%	$^{+}$Sig
		Board size	$^{+}$Sig
Chua and Ab Razak (2018)	ROA and Tobin's *Q*	Board size	$^{-}$Insig in ROA and $^{+}$Insig in Robin's *Q*
		Board independence	$^{+}$Sig
		CEO duality	$^{-}$Insig in ROA and $^{+}$Insig in Robin's *Q*.
		Board gender diversity	$^{-}$Sig in ROA and $^{-}$Insig in Tobin's *Q*.
Borlea et al. (2017)	ROA and Tobin's *Q*	Equilibrium between executive and non-executive members.	$^{-}$Insig
		board Independence	$^{+}$Sig in ROA and Insig Tobin's *Q*
		Training of board	$^{+}$Insig
Akter, Ali, Abedin, and Hossain (2020)	ROA and ROE.	Independent directors%	$^{+}$Insig in ROA and $^{-}$Insig in ROE

Note: $^{+}$ is positive; $^{-}$ is negative; Sig is significant; Insig is insignificant.

remuneration is viewed as both monetary the financial benefits being given such as salaries and other forms like incentives and bonuses. Executive managers' and directors' involvement in the operations of the company is influenced by their compensation practices (Borlea et al., 2017). One of the crucial tools to address the agency problem is board compensation. Hence, the RC play an important role in the CG to align the interest of managers with shareholders (Chua & Ab Razak, 2018; Harymawan et al., 2020).

According to the results revealed by Chua and Ab Razak, the directors' remunerations including salary, bonuses, fees, and benefit-in-kind have a significant positive impact the FP. The findings supported the idea that board compensation serves as efficient governance methods to reduce agency costs. With these findings, businesses must carefully plan director compensation and choose the right amount of independent and female directors for the board because they have an impact on the FP.

Further, according to Aslam et al. (2019), the FP, measured by Tobin's *Q* (TQ) and earnings per share (EPS), has a significant positive relationship with cash base remuneration of CEOs. However, it is insignificant with non-cash base remuneration of CEOs. Regarding the remuneration of BODs, all performance measures are not significantly associated with cash base remuneration but positive and significant relationship with the non-cash base remuneration. Further, they found that CG variables (board size, CEO duality, non-BODs) had no substantial impact on CEO and BODs' salary. Further, Akter, Ali, Abedin, and Hossain (2020) reveal that there is a negative association between board remuneration and FP. They claimed that increased board compensation does not encourage improved FP, which leaves shareholders with little in return. As a result, they said, this raises serious concerns for them.

Makhlouf, Laili, and Bash theorize a connection between the "presence of RC" and the FP of industrial enterprises listed on the Amman Stock Exchange in Jordan as one of the boards of director's features. However, an empirical study has been contacted by Borlea et al. (2017) to examine the relationship between the existence of RC and FP. They found that existence of RC has insignificant negative with FP, either by using the measurement of ROA or Tobin's *Q*.

According to Lokman and Mohd Tareh (2020), the size of the company has a positive and significant relationship with directors' compensation. On the other hand, the relationship between a FP and the compensation of its directors is favorable but tenuous. According to Harymawan et al. (2020), the existence of a RC is positive and significant associated with the level of remuneration of executives. It means that the presence of the RC is associated with higher remuneration for executives. On the other hand, the study found no relationship between the presence of RCs and BOD remuneration. In terms of independent boards of directors, Harymawan et al. (2020) found some evidence that bigger and more independent boards of directors are associated with higher BOD remuneration.

Harymawan et al. (2020) found that a significant positive relationship between the presence of RCs and FP using the measurement of Tobin's *Q* and ROA. They claimed that by creating an RC, the committee would be able to oversee and counsel top management on pay decisions that might lower agency expenditures and eventually improve FP. However, they did not find a significant relationship between the presence of RCs and FP using the measurement of ROE. According to Agyemang-Mintah (2016) and Ahmed (2010), once the RCs are in place, the committee will oversee and counsel executive management on pay decisions that can lower agency expenses and eventually improve FP.

According to Khan, Shinwari, Ahmed, and Sulaiman (2021), the RC characteristics have a significant positive impact on the FP measured by ROA. For example, RC size has a significant positive relationship with ROA. In terms of independence of RC, it was found to be significant positive associated with ROA. Concerning the RC chairman independence, it found to be significant positive associated with ROA. Similarly, RC meetings were found to have a significant positive with ROA. However, the study failed to provide evidence of significant impact of RC size, independence of chairman and directors, and meetings on the measurement of ROE.

According to the theories of agency and resource dependence and previous study who claim that RC has positive impact on the FP, the following hypothesis is built:

H1. Separate RC is positively related to FP.

H2. RC size is positively related to FP.

H3. RC independence is positively related to FP.

H4. RC meeting is positively related to FP.

H5. RC female director is positively related to FP.

3. RESEARCH DESIGN

3.1. Population and Sample Selection Procedures

The study will cover all firms being listed in Bahrain Bourse and for two years which are 2020 and 2021. The companies listed in Bahrain Bourse are 42 firms. Therefore, the study will use list numbers of firms as a sample to the research. This means that the study will cover 84 firms' observation for two years. This research is quantitative research using secondary data. The collected data will mainly be taken from the annual repost the firms that are listed on Bahrain Bourse. As for the variables of CG, the data taken from the annual report of CG that are being published by the firms on their websites.

3.2. Variable Measurement

FP is measured by using return on assets (ROA), return on equity (ROE), and earnings per share (EPS). In terms of RC characteristics, the study sues the RC separation, size, independence, meeting, and female directors.

Further, the study involves some of the control variables which are related to the characteristics of BOD, like size and meeting and AC, like size and meeting.

Table 28.2. Summary of the Variable's Measurements and Definitions.

Variable	Acronym	Measurement
Return on assets	ROA	"Net income divided by total assets"
Return on equity	ROE	"Net income divided by total Equity"
Earnings per share	EPS	"Ratio of net profit after deducting all the taxes divided by the outstanding equity shares"
Separate RC	SRC	1 if separate RC, and 0 otherwise
RC size	RCSIZE	"Total Directors' Remuneration"
RC independence	RCIND	"Number of non-executive directors in the RC"
RC meeting	RCMEET	"Number of meetings that carried out by RC in the year"
RC female directors	RCGEN	Number of females in the RC
Board size	BSIZE	"The number of directors on the board"
Board meeting	BMEET	"Total number of BODs meetings over the year"
AC size	ACSIZE	The presence of members in AC
AC meeting	ACMEET	"Number of meetings carried out by AC members in the year"
Total assets	TA	"Total assets"
Leverage	LEV	"The ratio of total debt to total assets"
Industry	INDU	"The value of 1 if the firm belongs to a particular industry, otherwise 0"
Firm age	FA	"The number of years since the establishment"
Audit firm	Big4	"1 if the firm's auditor is a Big-4 audit firm and 0 otherwise"
Cash from operation	NCFOD	"1 if the firm's has positive cash flow from operation and 0 otherwise"

Moreover, some others control variables related to firm's specific characteristics such as total assets, leverage, industry, firm age, and audit firm have been included in the study. The details of variables are presented in Table 28.2.

3.3. Regression Models

The study will use OLS regression to investigate the influence of RC characteristics, namely, separate RC, RC size, RC independence, RC meeting, RC female directors on FP, namely, ROA, ROE, and EPS. Also, the regression will be controlled by different control variables which are related to BOD, AC, and firm-specific characteristics. The following Moodle will be used:

$$\begin{aligned}\text{ROA} = {} & \beta_1\,\text{SRC} + \beta_2\,\text{RCSIZE} + \beta_3\,\text{RCIND} + \beta_4\,\text{RCMEET} + \beta_5\,\text{RCGEN} \\ & + \beta_6\,\text{BSIZE} + \beta_7\,\text{BMEET} + \beta_8\,\text{ACSIZE} + \beta_9\,\text{ACMEET} + \beta_{10}\,\text{TA} \\ & + \beta_{11}\,\text{LEV} + \beta_{12}\,\text{INDU} + \beta_{13}\,\text{FA} + \beta_{14}\,\text{Big4} + \beta_{15}\,\text{NCFOD} + \varepsilon_i\end{aligned}$$

$$\begin{aligned}\text{ROE} = {} & \beta_1\,\text{SRC} + \beta_2\,\text{RCSIZE} + \beta_3\,\text{RCIND} + \beta_4\,\text{RCMEET} + \beta_5\,\text{RCGEN} \\ & + \beta_6\,\text{BSIZE} + \beta_7\,\text{BMEET} + \beta_8\,\text{ACSIZE} + \beta_9\,\text{ACMEET} + \beta_{10}\,\text{TA} \\ & + \beta_{11}\,\text{LEV} + \beta_{12}\,\text{INDU} + \beta_{13}\,\text{FA} + \beta_{14}\,\text{Big4} + \beta_{15}\,\text{NCFOD} + \varepsilon_i\end{aligned}$$

$$\begin{aligned}\text{EPS} = {} & \beta_1\,\text{SRC} + \beta_2\,\text{RCSIZE} + \beta_3\,\text{RCIND} + \beta_4\,\text{RCMEET} + \beta_5\,\text{RCGEN} \\ & + \beta_6\,\text{BSIZE} + \beta_7\,\text{BMEET} + \beta_8\,\text{ACSIZE} + \beta_9\,\text{ACMEET} + \beta_{10}\,\text{TA} \\ & + \beta_{11}\,\text{LEV} + \beta_{12}\,\text{INDU} + \beta_{13}\,\text{FA} + \beta_{14}\,\text{Big4} + \beta_{15}\,\text{NCFOD} + \varepsilon_i\end{aligned}$$

4. RESULTS AND DISCUSSION

4.1. Descriptive Statistics

Table 28.3 shows the mean value of the FP, the dependent variable of the study. Regarding ROA, the mean value is 1.96% with a minimum of −22.97% and a maximum of 25.79. Concerning ROE, the mean value is 3.46% with a minimum of −60% and a maximum of 53.76% for EPS, the mean value is 0.020% with a minimum of −0.179% and a maximum of 0.319%.

The mean value of RC size is 3.631 members. This means that in average listed firm in Bahrain has around four members in the RC. Further, the minimum value is two directors in the RC as it reflects that there is no RC include less than two members. Regarding the maximum value, Table 28.3 shows that the biggest remuneration size includes six members. This means that in average listed firm in Bahrain has around four members in the RC. Further, the minimum value is two directors in the RC as it reflects that there is no RC include less than two members. Regarding the maximum value, Table 28.3 shows that the biggest remuneration size includes six members.

In terms of RC independence, the mean is 2.071 members, and it indicates that in average listed firm in Bahrain has around two independent members in the RC. Moreover, the maximum value in remuneration independence is four members while the minimum is 0. This indicates that there could be 0 number of independent members within RC. Also, the average listed firm in Bahrain got around four independent members. To expand, the minimum value is 0 indicating that there could be no independent members in the RC. As for the maximum, Table 28.3 presents that the biggest number of independent members involves four members.

As for the RC meetings, Table 28.3 shows the mean at 3.369 which indicates that the average number of meetings for firms listed in Bahrain Bourse is three meetings with respect to RC. Furthermore, the minimum number of meetings is 1 while the maximum number of meetings is 8. This means that there could be 1 meeting only for the RC, and the maximum number of meetings for RC could

Table 28.3. Descriptive Statistics for Dependent Variable Measurements.

Variable	Mean	Min.	Max.
ROA	1.96	−22.97	25.79
ROE	3.46	−60	53.76
EPS	0.020	−0.179	0.319
RCSIZE	3.631	2	6
RCIND	2.071	0	4
RCMEET	3.369	1	8
RCGEN	0.167	0	1
BSIZE	9.464	6	13
BMEET	5.821	3	15
ACSIZE	3.738	3	7
ACMEET	4.917	1	13
TA	2,133,867	3,298	21,800,000
LEV	18.122	0	59.41
FA	36.738	3	138

reach 8 meetings. To illustrate, the maximum number for RC meetings is 8 while 1 meeting is the minimum.

Moving to the number of females in the RC, Table 28.3 shows the mean at 0.167 indicating that the average number of females in RC for companies listed on Bahrain Bourse is 0 mainly. Added to that, the maximum number of females in RC is 1. As for the minimum number of females in RC is 0. This means that there could be no females in RC. Also, the maximum number of females in the RC could be 1. As presented in the table the maximum number of females in RC is 1 and the minimum is 0.

Table 28.4 shows there are only five firm observations that have separate RC with the percentage of 5.95%. However, most of the firm's observations did not separate the RC. Regarding the Big four audit firms, 69 firm observations audit their financial statement in these Big four audit firms, which are the majority. However, 15 companies did not audit their financial statements in the big four audit firms which. Most of the companies are considered non-industrious firms, which are 74, while 10 are considered industrial specialized in manufacturing. As for the net cash value from operating, most firms' observation 62 (73.81%) have positive value while 22 firms' observation (26.19%) have a negative value.

4.2. Diagnostic Tests

The study investigated the sample data fitness with statistical assumption. The study employs the winsorization strategy to decrease the influence of the outliers(Al-Absy, 2023; Al-Absy, Ismail, & Chandren, 2019). This study is viewed as the most extreme with respect to variables observation with connection to outliers (Yoon, Miller, & Jiraporn, 2006), such as EPS and Firm age, by converting the value of observations from their original value to the normal value.

Regarding the normality, Table 28.5 shows that the dataset of every variable has no violation that is serious with respect to the assumption of normality, with the Skewness not surpassing the ±3 threshold and Kurtosis is not surpassing the ±10 threshold Kline (2015).

Concerning multicollinearity, the Correlations Matrix test shows different statistically significant relationships over the variables. The significant correlation over the variables does not exceed the threshold of ±0.80 (Table will provide upon request). As a result, there is no indication of serious multicollinearity issues because the correlations do not reach the threshold of ±0.80.

Table 28.4. Descriptive Statistics for Dummy Control Variables.

	Yes		No	
	No	%	No	%
SRC	5	5.95	79	94.05
Big4	69	82.14	15	17.86
INDU	10	11.90	74	88.10
NCFOD	62	73.81	22	26.19

Table 28.5. Descriptive Statistics of Skewness and Kurtosis.

Variable	Skewness	Kurtosis
ROA	−0.516	8.991
ROE	−1.317	8.818
EPS	−0.527	8.403
RCSIZE	0.811	3.439
RCIND	−0.304	2.483
RCMEET	0.836	3.286
RCGEN	1.789	4.200
BSIZE	0.146	2.548
BMEET	1.798	8.075
ACSIZE	1.319	4.519
ACMEET	1.673	7.215
TA	0.353	2.137
LEV	0.937	2.777
FA	−0.183	1.924
NCFOD	−1.083	2.173

Concerning the heteroscedasticity, the Breusch-Pagan\Cook-Weisberg test was implemented to identify the presence of the heteroscedasticity to the present study models, ROA, ROE, and EPS (Baum, Schaffer, & Stillman, 2003). Table 28.6 shows that the *p*-value of ROA and EPS Models is higher than the level of 0.05. So, this lead that the data of the model not suffering from the problem of heteroscedasticity. Regarding model of ROE, *p*-value of the model is lower than the level of 0.05, and therefore, the data are suffering from heteroscedasticity in this model.

4.3. Regression Results

Table 28.7 shows the results of OLS regression. The models of ROA, ROE, and EPS are fit and significant. Regarding the *R*-squared, the percentage for ROA, ROE, and EPS Models are more than 30%. This means that the study covered most of variables that affect the FP.

Table 28.7 shows that SRC has significant negative with ROA and EPS. This means that separating the RC from other committee would result in decrease FP. In terms of ROE, the separation of RC does not have a significant impact on the FP. The results of the study are inconsistent with the agency and resource dependence theory where it is assumed that separate the RC could enhance the FP.

Table 28.6. Heteroscedasticity Tests.

Test	Model	Chi^2	Prob > Chi^2	*H*0 (Null)
Pagan/ Cook-Weisberg	ROA	1.69	0.1938	Accepted
	ROE	4.20	0.0405	Rejected
	EPS	0.07	0.7954	Accepted

Note: H0. No heteroscedasticity problem.

Table 28.7. Regression Results Using OLS.

Variables	ROA			ROE			EPS		
	Coef.	*T*	*P*>*t*	Coef.	*t*	*P*>*t*	Coef.	*t*	*P*>*t*
SRC	−7.044	−2.210	0.031**	−11.38	−1.300	0.198	−0.061	−2.820	0.006***
RCSIZE	0.742	0.780	0.436	4.381	2.050	0.044**	0.011	1.710	0.091*
RCIND	−0.956	−1.320	0.192	−3.005	−1.470	0.146	−0.005	−1.070	0.288
RCMEET	−0.582	−1.040	0.302	0.851	0.590	0.557	−0.002	−0.470	0.638
RCGEN	3.854	1.940	0.057*	−1.261	−0.300	0.761	0.015	1.140	0.258
BSIZE	−0.841	−1.820	0.073*	−0.914	−0.930	0.358	−0.003	−0.930	0.355
BMEET	0.220	0.470	0.643	0.498	0.490	0.627	0.004	1.180	0.242
ACSIZE	1.464	1.660	0.102	4.377	1.790	0.078*	0.015	2.550	0.013**
ACMEET	0.357	0.770	0.442	−1.105	−0.880	0.385	0.004	1.230	0.221
TA	0.351	0.870	0.387	−0.857	−0.630	0.529	0.000	0.140	0.888
LEV	−0.010	−0.200	0.838	0.163	1.470	0.146	−0.001	−1.640	0.106
FA	−0.031	−0.600	0.553	−0.218	−1.990	0.051*	−0.001	−1.990	0.050
Big4	0.324	0.170	0.868	9.332	1.400	0.167	−0.002	−0.160	0.871
INDU	4.079	1.620	0.110	9.799	1.370	0.176	0.046	2.720	0.008***
NCFOD	4.897	2.960	0.004***	3.747	0.910	0.368	0.018	1.620	0.109
_cons	−5.097	−0.950	0.348	−9.622	−0.730	0.465	−0.064	−1.760	0.084
F-value		2.28			1.48			2.20	
Sig		0.0110			0.0304			0.0144	
R^2		0.3351			0.3032			0.3270	
Observe		84			84			84	
Firms		42			42			42	

Regarding the RC size, Table 28.7 shows a significant positive relationship between the size and FP measured by ROE and EPS. It means that a high number of RC members will increase the FP. This is in line with the theories as they will spend more time monitoring and advising the managers. Apart from these results, the study found no relationship between the RC size and ROA.

In terms of RC independent, the study found no relationship between the independent members in the committee and FP which is against the agency and resource dependence theories. The results of the study suggest for the ineffectiveness of independent directors for monitoring and supervisor the managers.

For the RC meeting, the study found no relationship between the numbers of the committee meeting and the FP. This result seems to be inconsistent with the agency and resource dependence theories that suggest more meetings will lead to more concern with firms' activities and hence increase the FP. The results of the study indicate that meeting is not effectively helping in achieving the firm's strategy and hence increases the FP.

Regarding the gender diversity, female directors in the RC have a significant positive relationship with FP measured by ROA. This is in line with agency and resource dependence theories. In against this result, the study finds that female directors in the RC have no significant relationship with other measurement of FP, for example, ROE and EPS.

5. CONCLUSION

This chapter examines the influence of RC characteristics on FP. The study finds that having more directors in RC would significantly increase FP, ROE, and EPS. Having more females in RC would significantly increase FP, namely ROA. Having separate RC would significantly decrease FP, ROA, and EPS. Independence of directors in RC and its frequent meeting has no significant impact on FP.

This study would help in the explorations of the influence of some specific characteristics of RC on the FP that are listed on the Bahrain Bourse. It has some implication for different parties such as policy makers, regulators, chiefs, financial backers, and analysts. The evidence on the relationship between the CG, namely RC characteristics, and FP came to support the policy makers and the regulators with the new emerging arrangements to create serious legitimate and administrative framework to enhance the quality of CG the lead to strengthen and enhance the FP. In addition, the new guidelines help in keeping on advance CG for the companies that are recorded.

The study has covered a sample of firms in Bahrain only which are for two years only. In accordance with the limitations, it is suggested for future research to examine the relationship in between additional years and varied time frame. In addition, the study could be implemented for all GCC countries leading to make the results more accurate since the sample will be larger along with considering that GCC counties have more resemblances in their business.

REFERENCES

Abdulsamad, A. O.,. Yusoff, W. F. W., & Lasyoud, A. A. (2018). The influence of the Board Of Directors' characteristics on firm performance: Evidence from Malaysian public listed companies. *Corporate Governance and Sustainability Review*, *2*(1), 6–13.

Agyemang-Mintah, P. (2016). Remuneration Committee Governance and firm performance in UK financial firms. *Investment Management and Financial Innovations*, *13*(1), 176–190.

Ahmed, H. J. A. (2010). Impact of Independent Directors and Remuneration Committee on firm performance? Evidence from Malaysian capital market. *Corporate Ownership Control*, *8*(1), 202–243.

Akter, S., Ali, H., Abedin, T., & Hossain, B. (2020). Directors' remuneration and performance: Evidence from the textile sector of Bangladesh. *Journal of Asian Finance, Economics and Business*, *7*(6), 265–275.

Al-Absy, M. S. M. (2020). The Board Chairman's characteristics and financial stability of Malaysian-listed firms. *Cogent Business & Management*, *7*(1), 1823586.

Al-Absy, M. S. M. (2022a). Impactful women directors and earnings management. *Cogent Business & Management*, *9*(1), 2148873.

Al-Absy, M. S. M. (2022b). Board Chairman characteristics and real earnings management. *Sustainability*, *14*(22), 15025.

Al-Absy, M. S. M. (2023). Impactful female directors and earnings management: The moderating effect of ownership concentration. *Administrative Sciences*, *13*(5), 129.

Al-Absy, M. S. M., Almaamari, Q., Alkadash, T., & Habtoor, A. (2020). Gender diversity and financial stability: Evidence from Malaysian listed firms. *The Journal of Asian Finance, Economics and Business*, *7*(12), 181–193.

Al-Absy, M., & Hasan, M. (2023). Impact of the Board of Directors'characteristics on firm performance: A case of Bahraini listed firms. *Problems and Perspectives in Management*, *21*(1), 291–301.

Al-Absy, M. S. M., Ismail, K. N. I. K., & Chandren, S. (2017, November 2). Board Chairmen's involvement in Audit Committees and earnings management practices. Retrieved from https://ssrn.com/abstract=3063845.

Al-Absy, M. S. M., Ismail, K. N. I. K., & Chandren, S. (2018). Board Chairmen's involvement in the nomination and Remuneration Committees and earnings management. *Australasian Accounting, Business and Finance Journal*, *12*(4), 60–76.

Al-Absy, M. S. M., Ismail, K. N. I. K., & Chandren, S. (2019). Audit Committee Chairman characteristics and earnings management: The influence of family Chairman. *Asia-Pacific Journal of Business Administration*, *11*(4), 339–370.

Al-Absy, M. S. M., Ismail, K. N. I. K., & Chandren, S. (2021). The association between real activities and accruals earnings management in Malaysian listed companies. *Contaduría Y Administración*, *66*(3), 1–31.

Al-Absy, M. S. M., Ismail, K. N. I. K., Chandren, S., & Al-Dubai, S. A. A. (2020). Involvement of Board Chairmen in Audit Committees and earnings management: Evidence from Malaysia. *The Journal of Asian Finance, Economics and Business*, *7*(8), 233–246.

Al-Matari, E. M. (2019). Do characteristics of the Board of Directors and top executives have an effect on corporate performance among the financial sector? Evidence using stock. *Corporate Governance: The International Journal of Business in Society*, *20*(1), 16–43.

Aslam, E., Haron, R., & Tahir, M. N. (2019). How Director Remuneration impacts firm performance: An empirical analysis of Executive Director Remuneration in Pakistan. *Borsa Istanbul Review*, *19*(2), 186–196.

Atty, A. M. A., Moustafasoliman, M., & Youssef, A. E. (2018). The effect of Board of Directors characteristics on firm's financial performance: An empirical study on the most active firms in the Egyptian Stock Exchange. *Open Access Library Journal*, *5*(11), 1–19.

Bin Khidmat, W., Ayub Khan, M., & Ullah, H. (2020). The effect of Board Diversity on firm performance: Evidence from Chinese listed companies. *Indian Journal of Corporate Governance*, *13*(1), 9–33.

Borlea, S. N., Achim, M. V., & Mare, C. (2017). Board characteristics and firm performances in emerging economies. Lessons from Romania. *Economic Research-Ekonomska Istraživanja*, *30*(1), 55–75.

Calvin, O. Y. (2017). The impact of remuneration on employees' performance (a study of Abdul Gusau Polytechnic, Talata-Mafara and State College of Education Maru, Zamfara State). *Arabian Journal of Business and Management Review (Nigerian Chapter)*, *4*(2), 34–43.

CBB, Central Bank of Bahrain (2010). Corporate Governance Code Kingdom of Bahrain. Retrieved from https://www.moic.gov.bh/en/FAQ/Documents/Corporate%20Governance%20Code%20Bahrain%20-%20English.pdf

Chua, M. S., & Ab Razak, N. H. (2018). The impact of Board of Directors' characteristics and remuneration on companies' performance in Malaysia. *Indian Journal of Public Health Research And Development*, *9*(11), 1220.

Freihat, A. F., Farhan, A., & Shanikat, M. (2019). Do Board of Directors characteristics influence firm performance? Evidence from the emerging market. *Journal of Management Information and Decision Sciences*, *22*(2), 148–166.

Ganesan, Y., Kanthan, G., Mushtaq, M., & Yeap, J. A. (2018). The moderating role of internal audit function on the relationship between Board of Director characteristics and business performance in Malaysia. *Global Business and Management Research: An International Journal*, *10*(1), 356–378.

Gharaibeh, A. M. O., & Qader, A. (2017). Factors influencing firm value as measured by the Tobin's Q: Empirical evidence from the Saudi Stock Exchange (TADAWUL). *International Journal of Applied Business and Economic Research*, *15*(6), 333–358.

Harymawan, I., Agustia, D., Nasih, M., Inayati, A., & Nowland, J. (2020). Remuneration Committees, Executive Remuneration, and firm performance in Indonesia. *Heliyon*, *6*(2), E03452.

Hezabr, A. A., Qeshta, M. H., & Alsoud, G. F. A. (2020). Board of Directors characteristics and firm performance: Evidence from the Insurance sector in Bahrain. *Truy Cập Ngày*, *10*(1), 2022.

Khan, A. W., & Abdul Subhan, Q. (2019). Impact of Board Diversity and Audit on firm performance. *Cogent Business & Management*, *6*(1), 1611719.

Khan, M. W. J., Shinwari, M. I., Ahmed, Z., & Sulaiman, G. (2021). Impact of Audit and Remuneration Committee attributes on firm performance: Evidence from non-financial firms of PSX. *Pakistan Business Review*, *22*(4), 525–550.

Kline, R. B. (2015). *Principles and practice of structural equation modeling* (4thd ed.). New York, NY: Guilford Publications.

Lokman, N., & Mohd Tareh, F. (2020). How are company size, financial performance and corporate governance related to Directors' Remuneration? *Research in World Economy*, *11*(6). Retrieved from https://ssrn.com/abstract=3712770

Mahdi, S. M. A., Al-Absy, M. S. M., & Alastal, A. Y. (2023). Corporate social responsibility and firm's performance: Evidence from Bahrain. In B. Alareeni & A. Hamdan (Eds.), *International conference on business and technology* (pp. 957–967), Berlin.

Makhlouf, M. H., Laili, N. H. B., & Basah, M. Y. A. (2008). Board of Directors characteristics and firms performance among Jordanian firms, proposing conceptual framework. *International Journal Of Technical Research And Applications*, *2*(4), 18–23.

Makhlouf, M. H., Laili, N. H., Ramli, N. A., & Basah, M. (2017). Board of Directors' effectiveness and firm performance: Evidence from Jordan. *Research Journal of Finance and Accounting*, *8*(18), 23–34.

Mishra, R. K., & Kapil, S. (2018). Effect of Board characteristics on firm value: Evidence from India. *South Asian Journal of Business Studies*, *47*(1), 41–72.

Pavić Kramarić, T., Aleksic, A., & Pejic-Bach, M. (2018). Measuring the impact of Board characteristics on the performance of Croatian Insurance Companies. *International Journal of Engineering Business Management*. https://doi.org/10.1177/1847979018765864

Riyadh, H. A., Sukoharsono, E. G., & Alfaiza, S. A. (2019). The impact of corporate social responsibility disclosure and board characteristics on corporate performance. *Cogent Business & Management*, *6*(1), 1647917.

Roffia, P., Simón-Moya, V., & Sendra García, J. (2022). Board of Director attributes: Effects on financial performance in SMEs. *International Entrepreneurship and Management Journal*, *18*(3), 1141–1172.

Saleh, M. (2016). Effect of Board of Directors' attributes on the financial performance of listed deposit money banks in Nigeria. *Governance*, *2*(10), 1–15.

Saleh, M. W., & Islam, M. A. (2020). Does Board characteristics enhance firm performance? Evidence from Palestinian listed companies. *International Journal of Multidisciplinary Sciences and Advanced Technology*, *1*(4), 84–95.

Saleh, M. W., Shurafa, R., Shukeri, S. N., Nour, A. I., & Maigosh, Z. S. (2020). The effect of Board Multiple Directorships and CEO characteristics on firm performance: Evidence from Palestine. *Journal of Accounting In Emerging Economies*, *10*(4), 637–654.

Scholtz, H., & Kieviet, S. (2018). The influence of Board Diversity on company performance of South African Companies. *Journal of African Business*, *19*(1), 105–123.

Sobhan, R. (2021). Board characteristics and firm performance: Evidence from the listed non-banking financial institutions of Bangladesh. *International Journal of Management, Accounting & Economics*, *8*(1), 25–41.

Taouab, O., & Issor, Z. (2019). Firm performance: Definition and measurement models. *European Scientific Journal*, *15*(1), 93–106.

Yasser, Q. R., Al Mamun, A., & Rodrigs, M. (2017). Impact of board structure on firm performance: Evidence from an emerging economy. *Journal of Asia Business Studies*, *11*(2), 210–228.

Yoon, S. S., Miller, G., & Jiraporn, P. (2006). Earnings management vehicles for Korean firms. *Journal of International Financial Management & Accounting*, *17*(2), 85–109.

CHAPTER 29

THE IMPACT OF ARTIFICIAL INTELLIGENCE ON SMALL AND MEDIUM ENTERPRISES IN YOGYAKARTA

April Lia Dina Mariyana, Ariq Idris Annaufal and Ratna Roostika

Universitas Islam Indonesia, Daerah Istimewa, Yogyakarta, Indonesia

ABSTRACT

The contemporary business environment has been revolutionized by artificial intelligence (AI), which has undoubtedly impacted the operational and competitive strategies of small and medium-sized enterprises (SMEs). In this write-up, we delve into AI's influence on SMEs by delving into the advantages, obstacles, and prospects associated with adopting AI technology. Based on an exhaustive analysis of current literature, this essay contends that SMEs can optimize their functions, enhance decision-making processes, and deliver superior customer experiences with the adoption of AI. However, SMEs face several challenges in embracing AI technology, including the high cost of implementation, lack of technical expertise, and concerns about data confidentiality and security. This chapter also illuminates prospective opportunities that SMEs can leverage through AI, such as establishing a foothold in new markets and competing effectively with larger enterprises. Overall, this chapter concludes that SMEs must carefully evaluate the costs and benefits of adopting

Digital Technology and Changing Roles in Managerial and Financial Accounting: Theoretical Knowledge and Practical Application
Studies in Managerial and Financial Accounting, Volume 36, 347–354

Published under exclusive licence by Emerald Publishing Limited
ISSN: 1479-3512/doi:10.1108/S1479-351220240000036031

AI, and develop a strategic plan for implementation that aligns with their business goals and resources.

Keywords: Artificial intelligence; small and medium enterprises; productivity; decision-making processes; customer experiences; Indonesia; SMEs; business environment

1. INTRODUCTION

SMEs stand to reap significant benefits from AI integration in their operations. AI can streamline processes, save costs, and enhance decision making. For instance, it can automate repetitive tasks, parse data to uncover patterns, and optimize supply chain management. SMEs can also leverage AI to personalize customer interactions and improve support services. Nonetheless, SMEs may grapple with challenges such as expertise shortages and financial constraints in the deployment of AI solutions. These concerns may relate to employee job security, reskilling, and upskilling. In Yogyakarta, the local business environment, government policies, and labor availability could influence AI adoption in SMEs. To comprehend the adoption of AI in Yogyakarta's SMEs, a detailed study is necessary.

SMEs in Yogyakarta and beyond must urgently embrace AI in their operations to remain competitive and sustainable in the long run. There are numerous benefits to incorporating AI for SMEs, including better decision making, improved customer experience, increased efficiency, and reduced costs. If SMEs fail to integrate AI, they risk falling behind their competitors who have embraced it, putting them at a disadvantage in responding to changes in the market and customer needs. As AI technology progresses, it will become more affordable and accessible to SMEs, meaning those who adopt it early on can establish themselves as leaders in their industries. In recognition of AI's economic potential, the Indonesian Government has launched initiatives to promote its adoption among SMEs. For example, the Ministry of Industry has developed a roadmap for Industry 4.0, which includes the integration of AI, and the government has established the National AI Strategy to support the development and adoption of AI. In conclusion, there is an urgent need for SMEs in Yogyakarta to adopt AI in order to remain competitive and sustainable and to take advantage of the opportunities presented by the advancing AI technology and government support.

The significance of AI in modern-day business cannot be overstated. With its potential benefits being vast, businesses of all sizes are exploring ways to incorporate AI technology into their operations. SMEs are no exception; they too are looking to AI as a means of attaining a competitive edge and enhancing profitability. This report will delve into the impact of AI on SMEs by exploring the benefits, challenges, and opportunities presented by its adoption. By examining case studies and existing literature, we will highlight how AI is transforming the way SMEs operate and compete in today's business landscape.

This chapter will begin with an overview of AI technology and its potential applications for SMEs. We will then explore the benefits of AI, including improved productivity, enhanced decision-making processes, and better customer experiences. We will also examine the challenges associated with the adoption of AI by SMEs, including the high cost of implementation, the lack of technical expertise, and concerns around data privacy and security. AI can help businesses improve efficiency and productivity by performing routine tasks automatically and faster than humans. This allows employees to focus on more complex and creative tasks, increasing the quality and added value of their work (Lee, 2018). AI can help businesses make more accurate and faster decisions by analyzing data and providing recommendations based on relevant information. This can help businesses make better decisions and produce better results. AI can help businesses improve customer service by providing faster and more accurate responses to customer inquiries and requests through chatbots and virtual assistants. It also allows businesses to provide 24/7 service without the need for additional employees.

In addition to exploring the benefits and challenges of AI adoption by SMEs, this chapter will also highlight the potential opportunities for SMEs to leverage AI technology. This may include new market opportunities, increased efficiency and cost savings, and the ability to compete with larger businesses. The use of AI can help businesses improve business prediction and analysis by processing large and complex data quickly and accurately. This enables businesses to make better decisions and take more effective actions as well as identify new business opportunities and optimize overall business performance. Moreover, AI can help businesses increase innovation by driving new ideas and creativity. AI can assist businesses in the research and development process as well as in identifying new market trends and opportunities. This allows businesses to continue to innovate and compete in an increasingly competitive marketplace. How does the adoption of AI impact the performance and competitiveness of SMEs?

This study has three main sub-sections, firstly Introduction, which explains the theoretical issues and business phenomena related to the impact of AI on businesses. Next is Literature Review and Methods, which includes theories on AI and business performance. Lastly, Results, Discussion, and Limitations of the study.

1.1. Research Objectives

The research objective of studying the impact of AI on businesses is to explore the various ways in which AI is being used in businesses across different industries and sectors and to evaluate its impact on their performance and productivity. By examining the use cases of AI in businesses, we can gain insights into how it is transforming business models and disrupting traditional industries, as well as the challenges and opportunities that arise from this transformation. Furthermore, by analyzing the ethical and social implications of AI adoption in businesses, we can develop strategies for promoting responsible AI adoption and mitigating the risks associated with it. Ultimately, the research objective of studying the impact of AI on businesses is to help businesses harness the full potential of AI and maximize its benefits, while ensuring that it is implemented in a responsible and ethical manner.

2. RESEARCH METHODOLOGY

Research on the impact of AI on SME can be carried out through a quantitative approach by mini review to prove propositions or hypotheses previously built. The topic of AI will be very relevant if it is carried out within the scope of SME that operate based on individual owner decision (refer Fig. 29.1). This aims to determine the impact of AI in businesses productivity, decision-making process, and better customer experience. Furthermore, research in the context of AI will be more appropriate if conducted through the survey method, namely by conducting direct interviews with managers or owners of the SME to obtain accurate and credible data in proving propositions or research hypotheses.

3. PROPOSITIONAL FRAMEWORK

3.1. AI Can Increase the Business Productivity

The integration of AI in business operations has the potential to revolutionize productivity. By automating monotonous tasks, providing real-time insights and predictions, and facilitating efficient decision making, AI-powered solutions can process vast amounts of data in mere seconds. This translates to a significant reduction in operational costs and time, allowing employees to focus on more value-added endeavors. The adoption of AI can improve accuracy and speed in

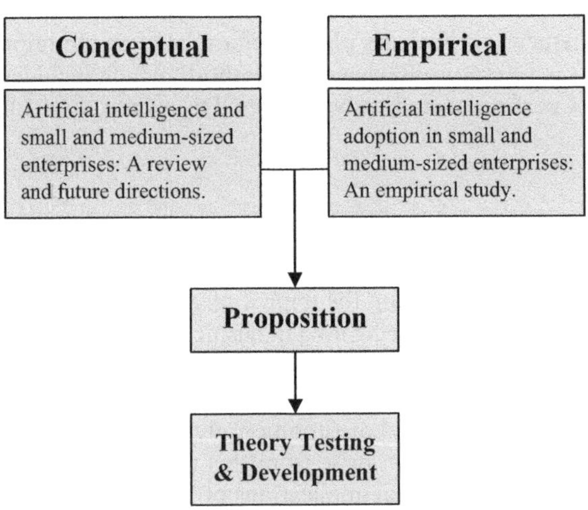

Fig. 29.1. The Conceptual Framework.

decision making, empowering businesses to respond swiftly to market changes and customer demands. As a result, AI can provide a competitive advantage, boosting productivity, profitability, and overall performance.

Many experts have stated that AI can increase business productivity. However, because AI is a fast-evolving field, views and research on this topic vary. AI-patenting firms, with smaller and more agile structures, have had the flexibility to adapt and swiftly implement AI-powered applications in their production processes. This has enabled them to achieve significant gains in productivity, outpacing larger companies (Damioli, Van Roy, & Vertesy, 2021). Moving from automating labor to automating "cognitive labor" marks a considerable breakthrough. With machines capable of learning and mastering new skills far quicker than humans, technological progress won't be limited by the availability of human capital. As a result, technological evolution could occur at an unprecedented speed (Ernst, 2022). AI technologies have made significant breakthroughs in the last 10 years, and their impact is anticipated to be profound for companies, particularly in terms of productivity and labor demand (Yang, 2022). Many articles and studies have shown that the use of AI can increase business productivity by assisting in time-consuming tasks and increasing efficiency.

3.2. AI Can Increase the Business Decision-making Process

Integrating AI can revolutionize the business decision-making process by providing real-time insights and predictions based on data analytics. By analyzing vast amounts of data, AI-powered solutions can identify patterns and trends, ultimately providing actionable insights that can help businesses make informed and improved decisions. For instance, AI can identify potential risks and opportunities, forecast future trends, and optimize resource allocation. Additionally, AI can eliminate human subjectivity, reduce bias, and errors in decision making, ensuring consistency in the process. Thus, AI can help businesses achieve their goals, stay ahead of their competition, and respond quickly to market changes, leading to better outcomes and increased profitability.

Many experts in technology and business have discussed how the use of AI can improve the decision-making process within an organization. It is revealed that there is a positive relationship between AI and improved decision making (Alasmri & Basahel, 2022). There are ample opportunities to enhance decision-making processes, especially when dealing with intricate issues that surpass our capacity to understand and establish correlations between various factors within the environment (Phillips-Wren & Jain, 2006). The emergence of superhuman AI heralded a profound shift in decision making for human beings. As AI could identify optimal decisions objectively, unencumbered by human biases, there was a marked improvement in human decision making, particularly in relation to innovative solutions. Self-play training allowed AI to uncover superior solutions previously overlooked by human decision makers, who may have been limited by their tendencies to focus on more familiar avenues (Shin, Kim, Opheusden, & Griffiths (2023). The use of AI can provide significant benefits in increasing the effectiveness and efficiency of decision making. In some cases, AI can even provide views that are more accurate and faster than humans. However, it is important to consider the ethical and responsible use of these technologies in the decision-making process.

3.3. AI Can Increase the Customer Experience

Incorporating AI into customer experience management can undoubtedly revolutionize the way businesses interact with their customers. AI-powered solutions can efficiently analyze customer data, behavior, and preferences to offer personalized recommendations and promotions. Furthermore, businesses can leverage AI's capabilities to automate customer service inquiries, enabling real-time assistance and improved response times. Besides, AI can also be used to evaluate customer feedback and sentiments, allowing businesses to identify areas of improvement and optimize the customer experience. By providing personalized and efficient interactions, AI can help foster stronger relationships with customers, enhance satisfaction, increase loyalty, and drive business growth. Embracing AI in customer experience management can indeed be a game-changer for businesses navigating today's fiercely competitive market.

The dependability and safety of AI-backed assistance along with timely aid, well-received by consumers, was a key takeaway from the study. The study also built upon previous research that pointed out potential challenges when implementing AI-based services (Ameen, Tarhini, Reppel, & Anand, 2021). The authors demonstrate that the integration of AI technology in call centers and after-sales support services can significantly improve customer experience. Furthermore, using descriptive analysis, they establish a direct correlation between personalized customer service throughout the customer's buying journey and after-sale customer support, with AI. Reducing waiting times using AI results in enhanced customer experiences (Daqar & Smoudy, 2019). Assessments given by customers regarding service quality, customer satisfaction, and customer loyalty using Virtual Assistant services get good expectations from customers (Alam, 2020). The adoption of digital technology provides businesses with increased flexibility and efficiency, allowing them to respond more quickly to customer requests and market demands with shorter turnaround times (Parashar, Sharma, Rana, & Balaji, 2023).

4. DISCUSSION

The far-reaching potential of AI cannot be overstated when it comes to its impact on businesses. Its benefits are multifold, encompassing increased productivity, optimized decision-making processes, and enriched customer experiences.

By automating mundane and time-consuming tasks, AI can enhance productivity, enabling workers to tackle more complex and strategic duties. With advanced chatbots and virtual assistants handling customer inquiries and support, human agents can now devote more time to intricate workloads. Moreover, AI can meticulously scrutinize large datasets and furnish valuable insights essential for informed business decisions, thereby reducing expenses and boosting efficiency.

In addition, AI has the ability to enhance decision making by furnishing data-based perspectives and prognoses. With machine learning algorithms, businesses can scrutinize enormous quantities of information and uncover patterns and trends that would have otherwise escaped human attention. Such insights can help companies gain a competitive edge. AI can also facilitate faster decision making, as it can analyze data in real-time and provide insights that can inform immediate action.

Lastly, AI can enhance customer experience by providing personalized and responsive support. AI-powered chatbots can provide instant and accurate responses to customer inquiries, while recommendation engines can provide personalized product and service recommendations based on individual customer preferences and behavior. This can lead to increased customer satisfaction and loyalty.

However, it is important to note that there are also potential drawbacks to the use of AI in businesses. One concern is the potential loss of jobs as tasks are automated, which can have negative economic impacts. Additionally, there are ethical considerations around the use of AI, such as ensuring fairness and avoiding bias in decision-making processes. Overall, AI has the potential to significantly impact businesses by increasing productivity, improving decision-making processes, and enhancing customer experience. However, it is important for businesses to carefully consider the potential benefits and risks of AI and implement it responsibly to ensure the best outcomes for both the business and its stakeholders.

5. CONCLUSION AND IMPLICATIONS

AI's effect on SMEs is not straightforward. It is intricate and diverse. On the one hand, AI technology can empower SMEs by increasing efficiency, refining judgment, and enriching customer experiences. For instance, chatbots powered by AI can provide customer support 24/7, while predictive analysis can enable SMEs to recognize market trends and seize opportunities.

Despite the advancements brought on by AI, SMEs face some challenges and limitations. Some SMEs may find the costs associated with implementing AI technologies too high, while others struggle with hiring the specialized expertise required for adoption. Ethical and legal considerations tied to data collection, storage, and customer usage further complicate the matter.

In conclusion, while the impact of AI on SMEs can be significant, it is important for SMEs to carefully consider the potential benefits and risks associated with the use of AI technologies. SMEs should seek to identify areas where AI can provide the greatest value and prioritize investment in those areas. Additionally, SMEs should ensure that their use of AI technologies aligns with their overall business strategy and is conducted in a transparent, ethical, and responsible manner.

By providing a theoretical basis for exploring the impact of AI on businesses, this chapter serves as a launching pad for further research. AI systems are rapidly expanding, and understanding their effects is critical for stakeholders in the business world. Additionally, this chapter aims to address the specific impact of AI on SME.

Employing AI technology can revolutionize the decision-making process within organizations. By examining vast data sets, AI can supply immediate predictions and insights, facilitating more informed and data-backed choices. Furthermore, AI's potential is not confined to internal operations; it can revamp how businesses reach out to their customers. With AI, marketing messages can be tailored to cater to individual customer preferences and behaviors, enhancing customer satisfaction and loyalty.

REFERENCES

Alam, S. (2020). Artificial intelligent service quality to increase customer satisfaction and customer loyalty (survey of PT. Telkomsel customers). In *Proceedings of the first ASEAN business, environment, and technology symposium (ABEATS 2019)*, Bogor. doi:10.2991/aebmr.k.200514.023

Alasmri, N., & Basahel, S. (2022). Linking artificial intelligence use to improved decision-making, individual and organizational outcomes. *International Business Research*, *15*(10), 1. doi:10.5539/ibr.v15n10p1

Ameen, N., Tarhini, A., Reppel, A., & Anand, A. (2021). Customer experiences in the age of artificial intelligence. *Computers in Human Behavior*, *114*, 106548. doi:10.1016/j.chb.2020.106548

Damioli, G., Van Roy, V., & Vertesy, D. (2021, March). The impact of artificial intelligence on labor productivity. *Eurasian Business Review*, *11*(1), 1–25. doi:10.1007/s40821-020-00172-8

Daqar, M. A. M. A., & Smoudy, A. K. A. (2019). The role of artificial intelligence on enhancing customer experience. *International Review of Management and Marketing*, *9*(4), 22–31. doi:10.32479/irmm.8166

Ernst, E. (2022). Artificial intelligence: Productivity growth and the transformation of capitalism. In A. Bounfour (Ed.), *Platforms and artificial intelligence* (pp. 149–181). Cham: Springer International Publishing. doi:10.1007/978-3-030-90192-9_7

Lee, K.-F. (2018). *AI superpowers*. New York: Houghton Mifflin Harcourt.

Parashar, B., Sharma, R., Rana, G., & Balaji, R. D. (2023). Foundation concepts for industry 4.0. In A. Nayyar, M. Naved, & R. Rameshwar (Eds.), *New horizons for industry 4.0 in modern business. Contributions to environmental sciences & innovative business technology*. Cham: Springer. doi:10.1007/978-3-031-20443-2_3

Phillips-Wren, G., & Jain, L. (2006). Artificial intelligence for decision making. In B. Gabrys, R. J. Howlett, & L. C. Jain (Eds.), *Knowledge-based intelligent information and engineering systems*, In *Lecture notes in computer science* (Vol. 4252, pp. 531–536). Berlin: Springer. doi:10.1007/11893004_69

Shin, M., Kim, J. Opheusden, B. V., & Griffiths, T. L. (2023). Superhuman artificial intelligence can improve human decision making. *Proceedings of National Academy of Sciences*, *120*(12), e2214840120. doi:10.1073/pnas.2214840120

Yang, C.-H. (2022). AI can help businesses improve customer service by providing faster and more accurate responses to customer inquiries and requests through chatbots and virtual assistants. It also allows businesses to provide 24/7 service without the need for additional employees (Satya Nadella, 2019). *Research Policy*, *51*(6). doi:10.1016/j.respol.2022.104536

CHAPTER 30

STRENGTHENING WORK ENGAGEMENT THROUGH DIGITAL HUMAN RESOURCES MANAGEMENT

Fereshti Nurdiana Dihan, Alldila Nadhira Ayu Setyaning and Ferdyan Ilhaam Saputro

Universitas Islam Indonesia, Yogyakarta, Indonesia

ABSTRACT

The relationship between employees, co-workers, and the company is crucial because it determines its success in achieving its goals. This engagement is strongly influenced by job demands and work resources at the company, affecting how employees feel about their workplace's physical, psychological, and mental conditions. High job demands with supportive work resources can increase employee motivation and create an employee's high commitment to the company. Digitalizing all human resources information systems will make it easier for employees to achieve their work targets, so digitalization has a role in strengthening or weakening the influence of work demands and resources on employee engagement. The concept is that existing job demands should be balanced with the availability of appropriate job resources to minimize or even eliminate psychological disturbances and improve employee health. This physically and psychologically healthy condition greatly supports the ability

Digital Technology and Changing Roles in Managerial and Financial Accounting: Theoretical Knowledge and Practical Application
Studies in Managerial and Financial Accounting, Volume 36, 355–363

Published under exclusive licence by Emerald Publishing Limited
ISSN: 1479-3512/doi:10.1108/S1479-351220240000036032

of employees to use digital technology in the human resources management (HRM) process.

Keywords: Job demand; job resources; employee engagement; digital human resources management; employee physical conditions; employee mental conditions

1. INTRODUCTION

The development of today's technology undeniably has entered all aspects of human life. The business world cannot be separated from technology if companies want to maintain their life cycle and increase their competitive advantage. The internet is alleged to be the primary driver of change in the company because it is considered a new way of exchanging information efficiently and can reach a broader range of communication objects (Tripathi & Kushwaha, 2017). In the marketing field, it is known as "experiential marketing," which means a new method where customers get a comfortable shopping experience in digital marketing (More, 2023). Also, the digital process has examined the writing of the *Qur'an* in processing, text tagging, and phylogenetics. It is shown that digital manuscript editing impacts methodological implications (Fedeli, 2020).

In addition, various companies operating systems have carried out the digitization process, including in the human resources sector. The concept of digital human resources, which will be related to multiple related variables such as digitization, transformation, and digital disruption of human resources, is increasingly attractive and has become the subject of scientific discussions (Strohmeier, 2020). Therefore, HR professionals must respond to increase competition for global digital transformation and pay more attention to rapid advances in human resources technology.

Recently, technical skills and abilities will be urgently needed by HR practitioners. People nowadays are demanded to be more flexible and be able to deal with the unpredictable pace of change in the workplace. The digitalization of human resources allows work to be done easier, faster and simpler so that work can be completed more efficiently.

Employees in the company require physical and psychological efforts that are continuously related to certain costs (Han, Yin, Wang, & Zhang, 2019). These job demands can be a stressor when an enormous continuous effort is necessary to achieve job demands. These efforts can be in the form of high pressure at work, a less supportive physical environment, and emotional needs through social interaction (Skaalvik, 2020).

To avoid the occurrence of work stress, support from the company is needed through job resources. These job resources can include physical, psychological, social and organizational aspects that can balance work demands or sacrifices that employees must make regarding their physical and psychological elements. Job resources at this corporate level include salary, career opportunities, and job security. The interpersonal level has support from colleagues, superiors, and the work environment. Meanwhile, at the job level, it includes clearly defined roles and participation in decision making, giving feedback, autonomy, and the importance of a job. Job resources can also stimulate personal growth, learning, and development (van Rensburg, Rothmann, & Diedericks, 2018) through company support in the form of existing facilities and infrastructure, specifically the system and its equipment which greatly assist employees in meeting job demands. The work environment comprising job demands and resources is the job demands-job resources model. Job demands and resources are directly or indirectly related to work engagement (Huck-Fries, Prommegger, Wiesche, & Krcmar, 2019). In several works of literature, there needs to be more consistency in mentioning work engagement, employee engagement, and personal engagement. Employee engagement is defined as a positive and satisfying mental state related to work characterized by three dimensions: vigour, dedication and absorption (Schaufeli, Salanova, Gonzales-Roma, & Bakker, 2002). This employee engagement shows the level at which employees feel satisfied with their work, feel valuable, and feel togetherness and trust.

Employees who think they have this attachment will remain in the company long. Also, they will continuously get more competent at work and have effective ways of adding value to the company (Bhuvanaiah & Raya, 2014). Employee engagement must be a severe concern for the company. If not, employees will lose motivation and commitment, leading to low attendance and increasing the tendency to leave the company. Digitization, most of the work in a company has been digitized using technology. The work process that was initially routine and manual has changed by implementing a digital revolution which will undoubtedly make it easier for employees to complete their work.

The digitalization of human resources means a digital transformation in managing human resources using electronic media, "mobile" devices, analytical processes, and information technology, making HRM more efficient. In other words, the digitalization of human resources is essentially managing all work related to the HR field using software technology, applications and the internet (Halid, Yusoff, & Somu, 2020).

This study aims to review the critical role of HRM digitization in bridging the influence of job demands and job resources on employee engagement. In several kinds of literature, there has been much research on the effect of the digitalization of human resources on employee performance. At the same time, in this paper, the author wants to find out how the role of digitization in the HRM process explicitly affects the sense of employee engagement, which is more related to the psychological and mental side. There are three sub-sections in this study: the introduction consisting of the gap and concept of the study; the literature review presenting the relationship of each variable; lastly, the discussion and conclusion, which explain the propositions and limitations of the paper. The result proposes the effect of job demands on employee engagement, job resources on employee engagement, and the moderating role of digital HRM that can strengthen or weaken the impact of job demands and job resources on employee engagement. The relationship between these variables will be briefly presented in a framework. The following section will explain the paper's methodology, which forms the basis for proposing a discussion of the literature and conclusions. Limitations and suggestions for further studies the authors present at the end.

2. LITERATURE REVIEW

2.1. Job Demand on Employee Engagement

The clarity of a task given by the company will impact what is thought, felt, said, and most importantly, what employees will do regarding work. This will significantly affect employee commitment, positively influencing employee engagement (Armstrong & Taylor, 2014). Work-related matters, such as employee-job fit, mastery of work, small-scale teams, and available free time, are essential components that will affect the increase in employee engagement (Bersin, 2020). Other research mentions factors that influence job characteristics and resources (Crawford, LePine, & Rich, 2010).

Providing job challenges, variety, developing creativity, and clarity of work will give employees a sense of usefulness and worth. The researcher also stated that when there is a certainty of the relationship between employees and their social environment, it will build a higher sense of attachment within employees. Still, the opposite will occur when feelings of insecurity arise, and no positive psychological feelings arise because employees are sceptical of the company (Kahn, 1990).

There are two kinds of psychological conditions: psychological meaningfulness and psychological availability. They positively relate to employee engagement, where work role suitability is the best predictor of both (Rothmann & Rothmann, 2010). Other findings state that job demands and resources moderate the effect of downsizing on health and employee engagement. It was further explained that the relationship with employee health is through the job demands factor, namely job overload and job insecurity. On the other hand, it relates to employee engagement through job resources factors, namely superior support and opportunities for growth (Dlouhy & Casper, 2021).

P1. Job demand effects on employee engagement.

2.2. Job Resources on Employee Engagement

Lack of attention to job resources will make it easier to achieve job targets, leading to errors and frustration, further reducing motivation and increasing absenteeism. If employees do not get enough job resources in their work environment, the adverse effects of job demands cannot be avoided, resulting in difficulties in achieving targets (Bakker & Demerouti, 2007).

Employees who work for a company that implements a corporate volunteering program will have a higher level of job resources than those who work for a company that does not implement a similar program. In other words, implementing the volunteering program within the company is positively related to perceptions of job resources and is also positively associated with work engagement (Bostjancic & Antolovic, 2018).

Job design that applies autonomy to employees is also critical. Employees feel they understand the conditions better than others, so their work perspectives must be heard and considered. The trust given by this company will arouse the desire of employees to give their best performance and increase their engagement (Nguyen, Nguyen, Ngo, & Nguyen, 2019). Job design is positively related to employee engagement because personal growth, which appears consistent with why employees stay and contribute, can be achieved by learning by doing. This is associated with the process by which employees gain knowledge, develop skills, and change behavior and other characteristics due to daily practice with direct experience in their work (Nguyen & Pham, 2020).

Some conditions that are part of job resources and are a driving force for the emergence of engagement in other employees are positive work culture, inspiring leadership, meaningful work, professional development programs, and recognition (Shahid, 2019). All the job resource factors positively related to employee engagement, with organizational support and development opportunities being the best predictors of vigour, dedication, and absorption (Rothmann & Rothmann, 2010). Other studies have found that engagement mediates the relationship between job resources and turnover intention, while burnout mediates the relationship between job demands and health problems (Schaufeli & Bakker, 2004).

P2. Job resources effects on employee engagement.

2.3. Effect Moderation of Digital HRM on Employee Engagement

HR digitalization is an aspect of the basic needs of every company, which will help maintain strong relationships between the company and its employees (Varadaraj & Al Wadi, 2021). Job resources are a "tool" to eliminate the adverse effects of job demands. Digitalization in human resources with the application of technology allows work to be carried out in a more straightforward, accessible, faster, integrated and cost-effective way. This can minimize errors in completing work and reduce employee stress levels, thereby increasing employee motivation and commitment and employee engagement in work (Sharon & Aggarwal, 2017).

HR digitalization can increase employee productivity, employee morale, decision making, and knowledge sharing to improve innovation and product marketing processes from companies. Furthermore, fundamentally digitizing HR can change how employees relate to one another and the company (Bektas, 2021). Digitizing human resources is crucial in improving emotional and behavioral aspects that will direct employees to maximize all their energy to achieve the company's strategic goals (Hunitie et al., 2023).

Digitalizing the HR field and using mobile devices at work will enable employees to do their jobs more efficiently. Through HR digitization, employees will be more informed, involved and concerned because they can handle and carry out their duties from anywhere and at any time, thus enabling feedback to management to be carried out in real-time (Saini, 2018). High HRM digital capabilities can support employees in strategic business planning. The various conveniences that arise from digitalization will help minimize the adverse effects of job demands and increase the positive impact of job resources, which will ultimately be related to employee engagement. When digital HRM capabilities are high, digital HRM practices make it easier to provide more efficient services, which will better meet managers' needs, enhancing social networking between HR and line managers. Such conditions will help realize complementary HR function practices (Sangaji, Setyaning, Alldila, & Marsasi, 2023). Thus, the research model is presented in Fig. 30.1.

P3. Digital HRM moderates job demand and job resources in employee engagement.

2.4. Methodology

This study is designed with a quantitative approach. The objects are workers in Yogyakarta, Indonesia. Data are collected through Google Forms with 7-Likert scale questionnaires, observations, and documentation. Later, the hypothesis will be carried out by Regression Analysis with the help of SPSS. The researcher determines 100 workers as the sample. Besides, this paper is a literature study by managing several references from research journals examining job demands, job resources, employee engagement, and HRM digitization. From this literature study, the authors analyzed the various relationships formed between variables from multiple research results, which later became the basis for determining the results of this study.

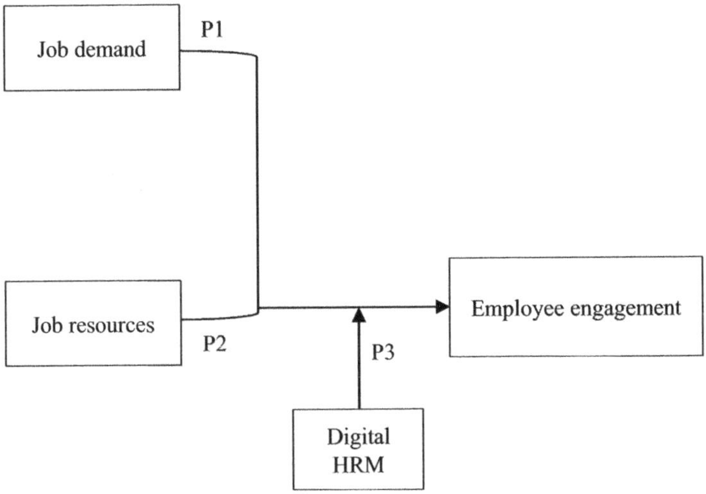

Fig. 30.1. Proposed Research Model.

3. DISCUSSION

In carrying out a job, an employee will be related to two things: job demands and job resources, which will significantly affect the physical, psychological and mental conditions of employees at work. Various job demands that are not balanced with the availability of company resources will cause an imbalance in employment, leading to different unfavorable conditions.

High job demands, both in terms of quantity and quality, tend to put pressure on employees. This condition can be physical disturbances such as fatigue, weakness, dizziness, inability to concentrate, etc. It can also impact psychological disorders such as anxiety, low personal accomplishment, and depersonalization. This needs to be considered by the managerial level to avoid the negative impacts of job demands, for example, by person-job fit policies and appropriate job designs. By determining the right job demands, employees' physical, psychological and mental conditions will be favorable so that positive feelings will appear in the workplace, including increased attachment to work and the company.

Fulfilment of job resources is urgently needed considering the complex negative impact that can arise from job demands. Job resources are required to minimize these negative impacts by taking various actions at the company level, the level of interpersonal relations, and the level of the job itself. When job demands are accompanied by proper management of job resources, employees will feel that job demands are balanced with what employees receive for carrying out their duties in terms of infrastructure and recognition. Such conditions can positively maintain employees' psychological and mental health, increasing work motivation and commitment and strengthening employee engagement. Also, digitalization in human resources by digitizing human resources information systems has changed many things, namely helping work to be completed in a more straightforward, more accessible, faster, more efficient, cost-effective way, and so on. The process of recruitment, selection, training, compensation, attendance, and others has been implemented digitally by most companies. Job demands that are supported by adequate job resources and made more accessible with digital technology will make it easier to achieve each employee's work targets. This will further increase work motivation and organizational commitment so that employees will be more engaged with each other and the company.

In many cases, job demands will be closely related to health problems because the burden of job demands significantly affects the psychological condition of employees, which does not rule out the possibility of continuing to work stress and can disrupt physical conditions. Meanwhile, job resources will be more in touch with employee engagement or turnover intention. The concept is that existing job demands should be balanced with the availability of appropriate job resources to minimize or even eliminate psychological disturbances and improve employee health. This physically and psychologically healthy condition greatly supports the ability of employees to use digital technology in the HRM process. Adequate job resources supported by digital technology will make all jobs more accessible and faster (maintaining physical conditions); cost-effective, and comfortable; raising employee motivation; and attachment to work.

4. CONCLUSION

Digital transformation into all aspects of company operations has changed the work behavior of employees in it. All work can be completed more efficiently so that work demands can be met more easily and quickly. This fact will improve employees' physical, psychological, and mental conditions because it can reduce work stress, absenteeism, and turnover intention.

Companies must pay more attention to maintaining digital human resources systems because digitalization can play an essential role in strengthening or weakening the effect of job demands and resources on employee engagement. The system is continuously updated and upgraded to keep up with the latest developments. Human resources are also constantly improving their skills to keep up with rapid technological developments, increasing the allocation of financing in the technology development sector and other related matters.

The limitation of this study is that the researcher needs to include training variables which play a critical role in supporting the ease of employees implementing HRM digitization, thereby minimizing resistance to this change. In addition, the age and years of service of employees are not considered, which significantly affects individual motivation in accepting digitization changes in all aspects of the organization.

Future studies are expected to be able to answer the limitations of this literature study by considering the existence of training programs in digitalized work systems, as well as focusing more on determining the types of respondents related to age and years of service.

REFERENCES

Armstrong, M., & Taylor, S. (2014). *Armstrong's handbook of human resource management practise*. London: Kogan.

Bakker, A. B., & Demerouti, E. (2007). The job demands-resources model: State of the art. *Journal Management and Psychology*, *22*, 309–328.

Bektas, C. (2021). Digital human resource management and its effects on the hospitality industry. In *Astana 1st international symposium on law and social sciences*, Kemer (pp. 311–324).

Bersin, J. (2020). Becoming irresistible: A new model for employee engagement. *Deloitte Review*, *1*(16), 146–163.

Bhuvanaiah, T., & Raya, R. P. (2014). Employee engagement: Key to organizational success. *SCMS Journal of Indian Management*, *11*(4), 61–71.

Bostjancic, E., & Antolovic, S. (2018). VanjaErculj: Corporate volunteering: Relationship to job resources and work engagement. *Journal Frontiers in Psychology*, *9*, 1–10.

Crawford, E. R., LePine, J. A., & Rich, B. L. (2010). Linking job demands and resources to employee engagement and burnout: A theoretical extension and meta-analytic test. *Journal of Applied Psychology*, *95*(5), 834–848.

Dlouhy, K., & Casper, A. (2021). Downsizing and surviving employee's engagement and strain: The role of job resources and job demands. *Human Resource Management*, *60*(3), 435–454.

Fedeli, A. (2020). Digital humanities and Qur'anic manuscript studies: New perspective and challenges for collaborative spaces and plural views. *Journal of College of Sharia & Islamic Studies*, *38*(1), 147–158.

Halid, H., Yusoff, Y. M., & Somu, H. (2020). The relationship between digital human resource management and organizational performance. *Advances in Economics, Business and Management Research*, *141*, 96–99.

Han, J., Yin, H., Wang, J., & Zhang, J. (2019). Job demands and resources as antecedent of university teacher's exhaustion, engagement, and job satisfaction. *Educational Psychology*, *40*(3), 318–335.

Huck-Fries, V., Prommegger, B., Wiesche, M., & Krcmar, H. (2019). The role of engagement in agile software development: Investigating job demands and job resources. *Proceedings of the annual Hawaii international conference on system science* (Vol. 2, pp. 7048–7056).

Hunitie, M. F. A., Hamadneh, S., Al-Kharabsheh, S. A., Alzoubi, A. B., Abufares, M. O. M., & Al-Hawary, S. I. S. (2023). The mediating role of employee engagement on the relationship between electronic human resource management and organizational effectiveness. *Information Science Letters*, *12*(3), 1307–1318.

Kahn, W. (1990). Psychological conditions of personal engagement and disengagement at work. *Academy of Management Journal*, *33*(4), 692–724.

More, A. B. (2023). Implementing digital age experience marketing to make customer relations more sustainable. In A. Nayyar, M. Naved & R. Rameshwa (Eds.), New horizons for industry 4.0 in modern business (pp. 99–119). Berlin: Springer.

Nguyen, H. M., Nguyen, C., Ngo, T. T., & Nguyen, L. V. (2019). The effects of job crafting on work engagement and work performance: A study of Vietnamese commercial banks. *Journal of Asian Finance, Economics and Business*, *6*(2), 189–201.

Nguyen, L. G. T., & Pham, H. T. (2020). Factor affecting employee engagement at not-for-profit organizations: A case in Vietnam. *Journal of Asian Finance, Economics and Business*, *7*(8), 495–507.

Rothmann, S., & Rothmann, S. (2010). Factors associated with employee engagement in South Africa. *SA Journal of Industrial Psychology*, *36*(2), 12.

Saini, S. (2018). Digital HRM and its effective implementation: An empirical study. *International Journal Management Study*, *2*(7), 62–66.

Sangaji, R., Setyaning, C., Alldila, N. A., & Marsasi, E. G. (2023). A literature review on digital human resource management toward digital skills and employee performance. *Lecture Notes in Networks and Systems*, *1*, 743–750.

Schaufeli, B. W., & Bakker, A. B. (2004). Job demands, job resources, and their relationship with burnout and engagement: A multi-sample study. *Journal of Organizational Behavior*, *25*, 293–315.

Schaufeli, W. B., Salanova, M., Gonzales-Roma, V., & Bakker, A. B. (2002). The measurement of engagement and burnout: A two sample confirmatory factor analytic approach. *Journal of Happiness Studies*, *3*, 71–92.

Shahid, A. (2019). The employee engagement framework: High impact drivers and outcomes. *Journal of Management Research*, *11*(2), 45–54.

Sharon, D., & Aggarwal, V. (2017). Digital human resource management. *Gyan Management*, *11*(2), 23–27.

Skaalvik, C. (2020). Emotional exhaustion and job satisfaction among Norwegian School Principals: Relation with perceived job demands and job resources. *International Journal of Leadership in Education*, *26*, 1–25.

Strohmeier, S. (2020). Digital human resource management: A conceptual clarification. *German Journal of Human Resource Management*, *34*(3), 345–365.

Tripathi, R., & Kushwaha, P. (2017, March 24–25). A study on innovative practices in digital human resource management. In *National seminar on digital transformation of business in India: Opportunities and challenges*, IMS Unison University, Dehradun (pp. 1–14).

van Rensburg, C. J., Rothmann, S., & Diedericks, E. (2018). Job demands and resources: Flourishing and job performance in South African Universities of Technology settings. *Journal of Psychology in Africa*, *28*(4), 291–297.

Varadaraj, A., & Al Wadi, B. M. (2021). A study on contribution of human resource management toward organizational performance. *International Journal of Management Science and Business Administration*, *7*(5), 43–51.

CHAPTER 31

ORCHESTRATING PARTICIPANTS OF ECOSYSTEM WITH THE USE OF DIGITAL TECHNOLOGIES: ANALYSIS IN THE HOSPITALITY INDUSTRY

Dwi Asih Anggetha, Suhartini, Anjar Priyono and Galuh Candya Callista

Universitas Islam Indonesia, Yogyakarta, Indonesia

ABSTRACT

This research aims to analyze how companies in the industry act as orchestrators and manage participants in their networks. The service industry has received little attention from scholars in this field, and this research gap was investigated in this study. Qualitative case study research with an exploratory approach is applied in this research so that in-depth insights can be obtained. Mamikos.com, a platform for room rent in Indonesia, was used as the research subject. Mamikos does not only facilitate tenants to find rooms to live in but also manages how landlords can serve tenants better and help tenants understand what the landlords want. In other words, Mamikos seeks to smoothen the value stream from landlords to tenants and vice versa. This research has implications that the value orchestrator must be able to facilitate the parties in the ecosystem to obtain the fundamental values needed

Digital Technology and Changing Roles in Managerial and Financial Accounting: Theoretical Knowledge and Practical Application
Studies in Managerial and Financial Accounting, Volume 36, 365–374

Published under exclusive licence by Emerald Publishing Limited
ISSN: 1479-3512/doi:10.1108/S1479-351220240000036033

and other side values so that they are loyal to the ecosystem managed by the orchestrator.

Keywords: Digital business ecosystem; business model innovation; ecosystem orchestration; digital technologies; open innovation; collaborative innovation

1. INTRODUCTION

Digital technology includes a variety of digital-based technologies, such as the Internet, cloud computing, big data, analytics, artificial intelligence (AI), Internet of things, blockchain, and other technologies that enable organizations to operate digitally, manage data digitally, efficiently, interact with customers online, and optimize business processes (Warner & Wäger, 2019).

In a broader context, digital technology also includes the cultural and organizational transformations required to adopt digital technologies, including changes in organizational structures, policies, work processes, employee skills, and relationships with customers and business partners (Priyono, Darmawan, & Witjaksono, 2021). In organizational transformation, digital technology is used to update organizational or corporate strategies to deal with rapid and complex changes in the business environment (Warner & Wäger, 2019).

Digital technology facilitates interaction between ecosystem participants so that they can communicate efficiently. Through digital platforms, participants can interact, share information, collaborate, and communicate in real time. In addition, digital technology facilitates knowledge exchange, data integration, and decision-making acceleration (Addo, 2022).

In addition, digital technology can automate business processes and operational activities within ecosystems so that interactions between ecosystem members can run efficiently (Lingens, Böger, & Gassmann, 2021). Within the ecosystem, innovators do not just share knowledge but also seek to create knowledge collectively. Participants in the ecosystem can contribute to each other to provide solutions and create value among themselves. Even though some actors in the network dominate, it cannot be denied that they need each other (Schepis, Purchase, & Butler, 2021).

Orchestration can be defined as an act designed from the start by a focal actor to develop a network of innovation and collaboration (Hurmelinna-Laukkanen, Möller, & Nätti, 2022). Implicitly, this means that network orchestration is about how actors can influence other actors in the network they manage. This influence implies that the orchestrator must have the power to make the other actors behave as the orchestrator expects. With digital technology, ecosystem orchestration can be carried out more efficiently and reach broader geographical coverage (Addo, 2022).

However, no research has observed how the focal firm influences the actors in the network to synergize. Most of the previous research was conducted in the manufacturing industry. Based on this background, the suitable formulation of the proposed problem is: *How does a focal firm manage network orchestration in the hospitality industry?*

This chapter is organized into six sections. The next section will present a Literature Review, which summarizes the existing research on the topic of business model and digital technologies. Section 3 is the Research Method, which describes the case study design, data collection methods, and analysis techniques used in the study. The Findings and Analysis section follows, where the empirical findings from the fields are presented and analyzed. Section 5 presents Discussion, where the results are interpreted and compared to the existing literature. Finally, the Conclusion section summarizes the main findings and offers recommendations for future research.

2. LITERATURE REVIEW

2.1. Basics Elements of Business Models

There has been a diverse definition of business model configurations. One of the definitions accepted in the literature is "a stripped-down characterization that captures the essence of the cause–effect relationships between customers, the organization, and money" (Baden-Fuller & Haefliger, 2013). Due to the wide variety of business model configurations, researchers categorize business models into several groups based on their characteristics. Although several attempts have been made, the resulting categorization of the business models is still quite diverse; for example, Timmers (1998) categorizes business models into 11 groups, while other scholars classify the concept into 45 groups (Lüdeke-Freund, Carroux, Joyce, Massa, & Breuer, 2018). More recent works attempt to develop business model taxonomy with the use of empirical data (Taran, Nielsen, Montemari, Thomsen, & Paolone, 2016). The taxonomy is considered better in providing an understanding of the concept of business models, thus supporting the development of knowledge in this field (Perelygina, Kucukusta, & Law, 2022).

One of the existing taxonomies was developed based on the drivers of business models (Taran et al., 2016). In their taxonomy, they group five main drivers: value proposition, value segment, value configuration, value network, and value capture. From the results of their analysis of empirical data, they concluded that the value proposition has been considered the most critical element, indicated by its dominance of all objects under observation. Regardless of existing taxonomies and classifications, all business models must consist of at least three elements: value proposition, value delivery, and value capture (Teece, 2018), and this opinion is widely accepted among scholars.

2.2. Digital Technologies and Business Model

Digital technologies can reduce the capability gap between small and large-sized firms so that the two groups nearly have equal capabilities (Li, 2020). Digital technologies have enabled equality of access among employees to stock ownership (Li et al., 2023). However, limited financial conditions can hinder the adoption of digital technology; firms must spend a certain amount of funds to acquire the technologies. In addition, firms must also train their employees, make structural adjustments, and redesign their business processes (Li et al., 2023).

Furthermore, digital technologies play a significant role in business model innovation. The technologies have supported small-sized firms so that they have capabilities that are almost on par with those of large-sized ones (Rachinger, Rauter, Müller, Vorraber, & Schirgi, 2019). In addition, digital technologies can be categorized as multi-purpose technologies which can be combined easily with other technologies. In the manufacturing industry, digital technologies have enabled firms to serve customers beyond what we have imagined in the past (Björkdahl, 2020).

Due to the proliferated use of digital technologies, customers are increasingly expecting personalized and immersive experiences from businesses. These expectations create challenges to firms. Furthermore, firms are required to develop sustainable customer relations through appropriate channels, develop measurements, and analyze the results (More, 2023). However, not firms are interested to implement personalized experiences to customers because these are considered as costly activities. To cope with this issue, AI-powered automation offers solutions because the technology can lead to increased efficiency, productivity, and profitability, and it has been demonstrated suitable in in various industries (Mathew, Brintha, & Jappes, 2023).

Value proposition determines how the business model should be designed with the support of digitalization. Organizational capabilities and employee competencies can be major challenges when firms should continuously renew their business model; existing competitive position could lose their relevance because new opportunities will always emerge due to rapid changes caused by digital technologies (Rachinger et al., 2019). With the use of the technologies, firms can offer after-sale services so that the firms are not only offering physical products but also services. This strategy offers many advantages, which are only possible with the support of digital technologies (Björkdahl, 2020). However, how digital technologies are utilized to support business model innovation in the service industry needs more attention, particularly in the hospitality industry. This is the research gap which this study aims to address.

3. RESEARCH METHOD

3.1. Case Study Design: Single Case Study

This study employs case study research with a single case design. Mamikos was selected as the subject due to its success in orchestrating its ecosystem with the support of digital technologies. Case studies offer the advantage of in-depth analysis of specific details often overlooked by other methods, focusing on relationships and interconnected processes (Yin, 2018). They allow for understanding linkages between factors rather than just outcomes and provide opportunities to explain why specific results occur. Additionally, case studies are conducted in the natural setting of the organization, avoiding artificial environments (Volmar & Eisenhardt, 2020).

However, the method has been criticized since it may create an observer effect. The method is carried out in various ways and with multiple data sources, but this flexibility may result in "soft" data that is difficult to analyze. To overcome this issue, this study employs triangulation to ensure data reliability and validity (Jick, 1979).

3.2. Data Analysis

Research questions determine the data that should be collected and data analysis techniques (Miles, Huberman, & Saldana, 2018). Most of the data in the research were obtained from interviews, observations and field observations, field notes, and field documentation serving as the primary source of evidence. The collected data was then reduced to look for the emerging main themes and compared among analyses (Gehman et al., 2018). Significant patterns were found from the comparison among the unit analysis, which later became the basis for theory development (Gioia, Corley, & Hamilton, 2013).

4. FINDINGS AND ANALYSIS

4.1. The Case Company

Mamikos is a startup providing property management and information technology-based boarding house search services. It was established on November 11, 2015, by Maria Regina Anggit Tut Pinilih, with two of her colleagues. The main office is in Yogyakarta and Jakarta. Mamikos operates under the legal entity name of PT. Mama Technology Property has the tagline "the first boarding house searching engine in Indonesia." It is equipped with filters to make it easier for tenants to find boarding houses according to gender, price, facilities, places, etc.

This research analyzes how companies based on digital technology can align interests between parties who are members of innovation networks. Effective orchestration between parties who are partnership members will work if they benefit from the formed network. Meanwhile, the role of the orchestrator is to ensure that each party receives benefits.

Mamikos is an online boarding house rental platform with an easy and fast search feature. From the point of view of landlords and tenants, the digital innovation business models offered by Mamikos are as follows:

- The boarding house search feature is complete and integrated with the map so that users can see the house's location.
- An online booking system integrated with online payments so that users can order boarding houses quickly and safely.
- An effective and efficient boarding house management system allows the owners to manage their properties more easily and regularly.
- The affiliate program allows users to earn commissions from every boarding house order generated through their referrals.

4.2. Products Offered to the Landlord

Mamikos offers two categories of services for boarding houses fully managed by the company: Apik and Singgahsini. Although both packages provide accommodation services, there are differences in the characteristics of the services offered by each of these services. The following are the different characteristics of the services offered by Apik and Singgahsini.

4.2.1. Apik

Apik is an affordable accommodation service. The facilities offered include shared bat rooms, clean and comfortable bedrooms, and a standard room to gather and relax. This service is suitable for those who need temporary housing at a low price.

4.2.2. Singgahsini

Singgahsini is an accommodation service offering more complete and more comfortable facilities than Apik. The facilities offered include a bathroom inside, a larger bedroom, access to a kitchen, air conditioning, and TV facilities. This service is suitable for those who need a place to live with better and more comfortable facilities.

Landlords who are not interested in handing over the management of their assets to Mamikos can choose partnerships in marketing activities only. In this partnership, Mamikos is a search engine for boarding house seekers. Mamikos offers free services (Regular), GoldPlus 1, and GoldPlus 2 so that the clients can advertise their offerings on the firm's website. A comparison of the three packages offered is presented in Table 31.1.

Table 31.1. Comparison of the Package from Mamikos.

Comparison Table	Without GoldPlus	GoldPlus 1	GoldPlus 2
Ranking in listing search*	×	Prioritized	
MamiAds Balance Cashback	–	Rp 25,000	Rp 100,000
MamiAds balance top-up bonus (for every balance purchase)	×	10%	15%
See the condition of the boarding house business near your location (with the check nearby property feature)	×	√	√
Create Ad promotions	×	√	√
MamiPoint	×	Got points	Got more points
Opportunity to join the exclusive price promo	×	×	√
Broadcast chat	×	×	√
Package price	Free	IDR 59,000	IDR 145,000

Source: Firm's official website.

5. DISCUSSION: ORCHESTRATING THE PARTNERS

The orchestration mechanism carried out by Mamikos as the focal firm is presented in Fig. 31.1. From the orchestration, ecosystem participants receive benefits according to the expected value.

5.1. Benefits for the Landlords

Mamikos as an orchestrator often conducts training for boarding house tenants or landlords. As a result, landlords motivated to join the Mamikos network and want to benefit from rental fees and access knowledge. This knowledge will have a multiplier effect on the landlord's income. Some of the knowledge transfers carried out by Mamikos to landlords include how to save energy, deal with problematic customers, and address security issues. This knowledge transfer is done by consulting or providing articles displayed on the platform.

Landlords that provide conventional rent rooms only offer physical facilities for residents. However, for the Mamikos business model, all tenants obtain additional services to support careers and studies. In other words, tenants obtain the value not offered by conventional rent rooms. All the values the landlord provides are offered with information technology support. Meanwhile, from the tenants' perspective, Mamikos has succeeded in increasing operational efficiency and providing a better customer experience.

5.2. Digital Technology Support

With the help of data analytics, Mamikos can increase sales volume. In addition, with the help of Amazon web services, the occupancy rate increased from 20% to 100% within one month. With data analytics, it can also be seen that room offers for female tenants are oversupplied, while those for male tenants are far below the demand.

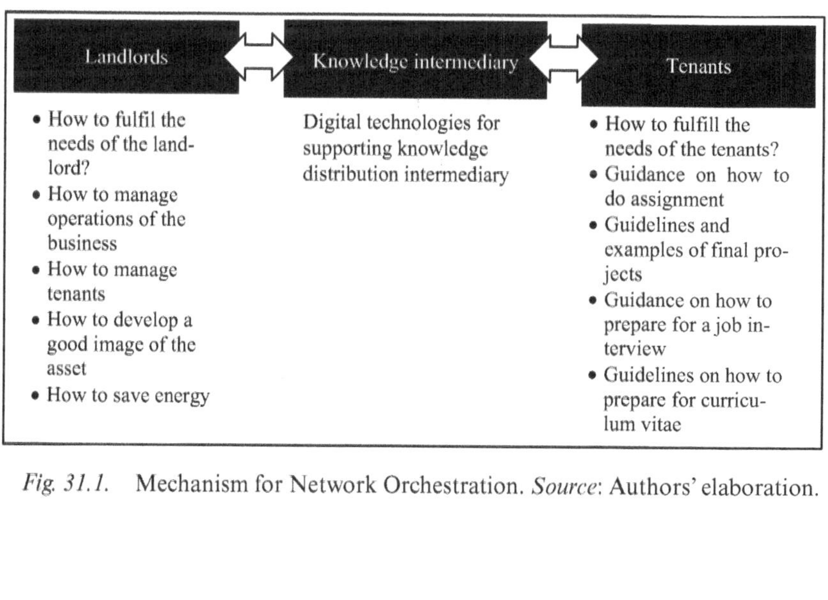

Fig. 31.1. Mechanism for Network Orchestration. *Source*: Authors' elaboration.

Mamikos uses AI technology and machine learning to optimize users' search for boarding houses. The algorithm used by Mamikos can learn user preferences from time to time and provide increasingly accurate boarding house recommendations. As a platform providing information for searching for rooms to rent or boarding houses, Mamikos offers more than 50,000 properties in Indonesia. Mamikos offers the convenience of searching for boarding houses with various search criteria such as location, price, facilities, and type of boarding house. For those who want to rent by sharing, Mamikos also provides a feature to find roommates. All these are possible due to the support of digital technologies.

5.3. Orchestrating Mechanism

They initially did not realize the knowledge that Mamikos distributed to the landlords and tenants. For this reason, many landlords and tenants feel that the network formed is unintentional and serendipity. Knowledge distributed by Mamikos can also be accessed by outsiders who are not members of Mamikos. From Mamikos' point of view, as a hub of innovation networks, this knowledge is also positioned as a means of promotion to encourage prospective tenants and landlords to join.

Business networks usually have the character of mutual dependence between actors (Schepis et al., 2021). However, this research found that network leaders try to make partners feel dependent on Mamikos. The partners are deliberately designed to continue to get value from Mamikos' offers. As a result, landlords and tenants are also made to feel interdependent after receiving education from Mamikos. Furthermore, with the various values offered by Mamikos to tenants, tenants increasingly understand "do's and don'ts" when using facilities from landlords. On the other hand, landlords also understand what value the tenants expect.

The success of Mamikos in conducting this orchestration is reflected in the sales value, which continues to increase yearly. In fact, during the COVID-19 pandemic, when most of the hospitality industry experienced a decline in performance, Mamikos continued to experience growth. Various promotions are offered to maintain sales, including a 10% discount, the opportunity to reschedule three times the check-in date, discount of up to 1.5 million. Mamikos also provides the opportunity to check-in for up to six months in the future. To prevent virus transmission, Mamikos provides disinfectant spraying services every week.

6. CONCLUSION

This research found that Mamikos only acts as a knowledge supplier to partners. Mamikos acts as a hub where tenants and landlords understand each other and what they need. In addition, Mamikos supplies knowledge to landlords so that they can provide services to tenants and vice versa. Mamikos educates tenants to understand better the "do's and don'ts" while they stay in the accommodation. Mamikos also provides facilities to tenants to support their careers or studies. For example, Mamikos provides tips for writing a final project or job interview. This research implies that landlords and tenants do not only need basic needs when renting or staying in accommodation. Therefore, the orchestrator company must be willing to identify the needs of the ecosystem's members beyond their basic needs.

This study uses case study method with a single design. The research design has enabled researchers to conduct depth analysis but lack of generalizability. Future studies can analyze the framework developed in this study using surveys so that generalizations can be improved. If the findings confirm the proposed framework, the studies affirm the concept we develop in this study. However, if the results of the analysis demonstrate different results, a new concept will emerge so that the knowledge development cycle continues.

REFERENCES

Addo, A. (2022). Orchestrating a digital platform ecosystem to address societal challenges: A robust action perspective. *Journal of Information Technology*, *37*(4), 359–386.

Baden-Fuller, C., & Haefliger, S. (2013). Business models and technological innovation. *Long Range Planning*, *46*(6), 419–426.

Björkdahl, J. (2020). Strategies for digitalization in manufacturing firms. *California Management Review*, *62*(4). https://doi.org/10.1177/0008125620920349

Gehman, J., Glaser, V. L., Eisenhardt, K. M., Gioia, D., Langley, A., & Corley, K. G. (2018). Finding theory–method fit: A comparison of three qualitative approaches to theory building. *Journal of Management Inquiry*, *27*(3), 284–300.

Gioia, D. A., Corley, K. G., & Hamilton, A. L. (2013). Seeking qualitative rigor in inductive research: Notes on the Gioia methodology. *Organizational Research Methods*, *16*(1), 15–31.

Hurmelinna-Laukkanen, P., Möller, K., & Nätti, S. (2022). Orchestrating innovation networks: Alignment and orchestration profile approach. *Journal of Business Research*, *140*, 170–188.

Jick, T. (1979). Mixing qualitative and quantitative methods: Triangulation in action. *Administrative Science Quarterly*, *24*, 602–611.

Li, C., Huo, P., Wang, Z., Zhang, W., Liang, F., & Mardani, A. (2023). Digitalization generates equality? Enterprises' digital transformation, financing constraints, and labor share in China. *Journal of Business Research*, *163*, 113924.

Li, F. (2020). Leading digital transformation: Three emerging approaches for managing the transition. *International Journal of Operations & Production Management*, *40*(6), 809–817.

Lingens, B., Böger, M., & Gassmann, O. (2021). Even a small conductor can lead a large orchestra: How startups orchestrate ecosystems. *California Management Review*, *63*(3), 118–143.

Lüdeke-Freund, F., Carroux, S., Joyce, A., Massa, L., & Breuer, H. (2018). The sustainable business model pattern taxonomy – 45 Patterns to support sustainability-oriented business model innovation. *Sustainable Production and Consumption*, *15*, 145–62.

Mathew, D., Brintha, N. C., & Jappes, J. T. W. (2023). Artificial intelligence powered automation for industry 4.0. In A. Nayyar, M. Naved, & R. Rameshwar (Eds.), *New horizons for industry 40 in modern business contributions to environmental sciences & innovative business technology* (pp. 1–28). Cham: Springer.

Miles, M. B., Huberman, A. M., & Saldana, J. (2018). *Qualitative data analysis: A methods sourcebook (4th ed.)*. Tempe, AZ: Arizona State University.

More, A. B. (2023). Implementing digital age experience marketing to make customer relations more sustainable. In A. Nayyar, M. Naved, & R. Rameshwar (Eds.), *New horizons for industry 40 in modern business contributions to environmental sciences & innovative business technology*. Berlin, Germany: Springer.

Perelygina, M., Kucukusta, D., & Law, R. (2022). Digital business model configurations in the travel industry. *Tour Manager*, *88*, 104408.

Priyono, A., Darmawan, B. A., & Witjaksono, G. (2021). How to harnesses digital technologies for pursuing business model innovation: A longitudinal study in creative industries. *Journal of Systems and Informational Technology*, *23*(3/4), 266–289.

Rachinger, M., Rauter, R., Müller, C., Vorraber, W., & Schirgi, E. (2019). Digitalization and its influence on business model innovation. *Journal of Manufacturing Technology Management*, *30*(8), 1143–1160.

Schepis, D., Purchase, S., & Butler, B. (2021). Facilitating open innovation processes through network orchestration mechanisms. *Industrial Marketing Management*, *93*, 270–280.

Taran, Y., Nielsen, C., Montemari, M., Thomsen, P., & Paolone, F. (2016). Business model configurations: A five-V framework to map out potential innovation routes. *European Journal of Innovation Management*, *19*(4), 492–527. https://doi.org/10.1108/EJIM-10-2015-0099.

Teece, D. J. (2018). Business models and dynamic capabilities. *Long Range Planning*, *51*(1), 40–49.

Timmers, P. (1998). Business models for electronic markets. *Electron Markets*, *8*(2), 3–8.

Volmar, E., & Eisenhardt, K. M. (2020). Case study research: A state-of-the-art perspective. In *Oxford research encyclopedia of business and management*. Oxford: Oxford University Press.

Warner, K. S., & Wäger, M. (2019). Building dynamic capabilities for digital transformation: An ongoing process of strategic renewal. *Long Range Planning*, *52*(3), 326–349.

Yin, R. K. (2018). *Case study research and application* (6th ed). London: Sage Publications, Inc.

CHAPTER 32

A REVIEW OF INTERNET OF THINGS (IOT) SMART OFFICE DATA SECURITY THREATS

Elizabeth Frieda Ndamono Shipena and Attlee M. Gamundani

Faculty of Computing and Informatics, Department of Computer Science, Namibia University of Science and Technology, Windhoek, Namibia

ABSTRACT

Internet of things (IoT) involves the connection of various devices. IoT's application ranges from wearables: Smart Home Application, Health Care, Smart Offices, Smart Cities, Agriculture, and Industrial Automation. While the number of connected devices grows by the day, so does the number of security risks and vulnerabilities that these devices face. Billions of the connected devices collect and transmit huge volumes of data making Data Security one of the most pressing technical concerns in IoT. Smart Office is one of the increasing IoT applications and Data Security has become today one of the most challenging areas in its application. It is important to identify data security threats. This chapter therefore presents a review of IoT Smart Office Data Security Threats based on existing research done.

Keywords: Data security; threats; IoT; Smart Office; architecture; Literature Review; systematic review

Digital Technology and Changing Roles in Managerial and Financial Accounting: Theoretical Knowledge and Practical Application
Studies in Managerial and Financial Accounting, Volume 36, 375–381

ISSN: 1479-3512/doi:10.1108/S1479-351220240000036034

1. INTRODUCTION

The chapter aims to explore the IoT Smart Office applications and its continued growth. This chapter also seeks to reflect upon the threats these advancements of IoT pose on Data Security in Smart Office applications. Informed by Literature Review on IoT Smart Office Data Security threats, this chapter will draw some key trends and features on such threats. The review will include an overview of IoT in general, Smart Office IoT applications overview, and an outline of the systematic review approach used. To give a broad scope on IoT, the section on IoT will cover from IoT security challenges to security threats in IoT systems with particular focus on the IoT architecture. As a contextual focus on the smart office domain, the IoT threats and some possible solutions to those threats will be discussed as the core section of this chapter.

The main contribution of this chapter is a collated set of data on the various threats specific to smart office applications. By zooming into the data security threats we offer a clear outline of the possible solution space to be focused on, in research aligned to Smart Office IoT applications. With the IoT field being dynamic and heterogeneous, selecting a specific application domain gives a more nuanced approach in improving quality of discussions, propose secure designs and a pool of potential threats to isolate for the specific domain.

The rest of this chapter is organized in chorological order, with Section 2 covering the systematic review approach used for populating this chapter. Section 3 looks at IoT from the overview, security challenges to security threats. Section 4 then zooms into smart office overview, security threats peculiar to smart office applications, and possible solutions to such threats. A conclusion of the main discussion points in this chapter is given in Section 5.

2. SYSTEMATIC REVIEW APPROACH

To classify and analyze computer protection risks in IoT Smart Offices, systematic qualitative and quantitative literature review was conducted. This method is capable of identifying areas covered by recent research as well as revealing discrepancies. It approaches literature from a variety of perspectives and promotes the spread of new ideas.

To carry out the study, several guidelines were implemented. The following digital sources: Google Scholar, Science Direct, IEEE, and Springer were combed through for the terms IoT, cyber security threats, and Smart Office. Several documents had been gathered. To decide which of them to closely analyze, the reviewer performed two exclusion measures, one based on published dates and the other on abstracts. The selected literature was in the age range 2017–2021, this was on the basis of maintaining the recency of the works and keeping up with the trends in the domain of focus. From the four selected databases, the number of articles found were 390 and after screening the articles found based on the abstracts and conclusion from those articles, the final selection ended up having a total of 21 articles.

The following systematic literature review was adopted as summarized in Fig. 32.1 to classify and analyze IoT Smart Offices security threats, systematic qualitative, and quantitative literature review.

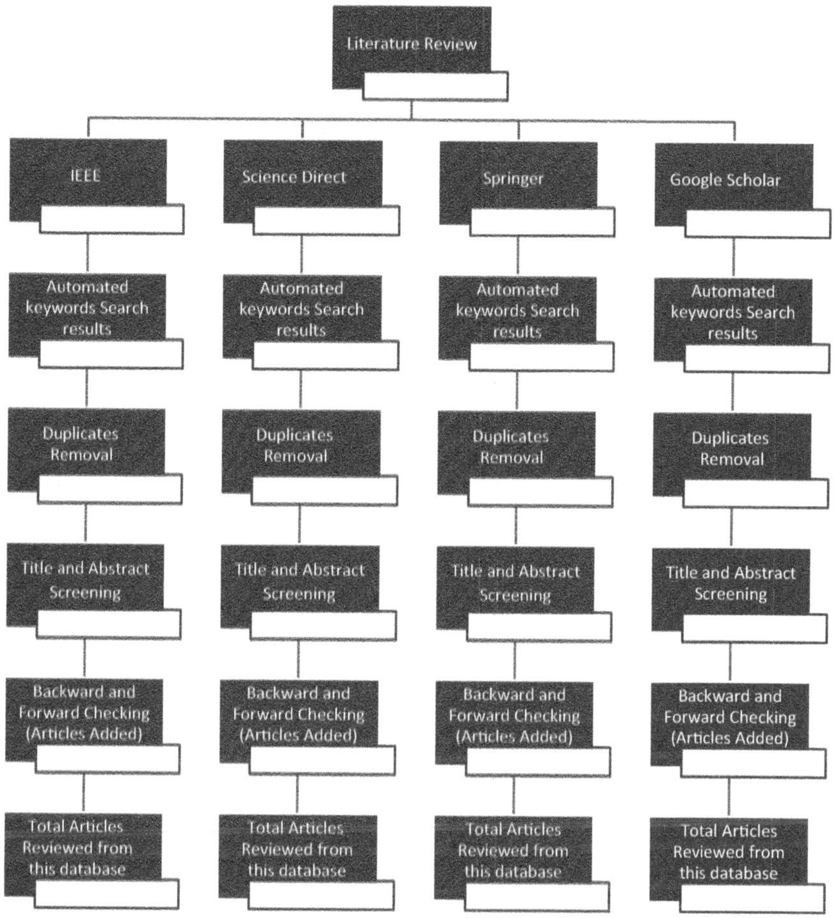

Fig. 32.1. Systematic Review Approach.

3. IOT: OVERVIEW

The definition of the IoT has evolved due to the convergence of multiple technologies, real-time analytics, machine learning, commodity sensors, and embedded systems. Smart Office is one of IoTs applications. Data Security threats are some of the contributing factors to the delay in growth of the IoT application in Smart Offices.

The demand for Internet application development continues to rise with the increase in the use of Internet. IoT is one of the main technologies, which are useful in the production of different Internet applications. An increase in the usage of the IoT devices has proven its importance in our daily lives. Smart Homes, Wearables, Autonomous vehicles, Smart Cities, and Smart Retails are some of the common applications for IoT devices. According to Al-sharekh and Al-shqeerat (2019), IoT applications have become popular in many different areas including Smart Offices.

4. IOT SECURITY CHALLENGES

Helode et al. (2017) identified huge data volumes and privacy protection as some of the concerns in IoT applications. Different IoT architectures and systems are hosted on different servers, resulting in the occupation of huge amounts of data and making security a huge concern. In addition to the abovementioned constrains, scalability and automatic control are also some of the challenges identified. The competition of developing the latest products in the market by manufacturers is very high that even the manufactures often forget to incorporate or think about some of the security issues associated with IoT devices. This is further echoed by a study done by Helode et al. (2017), which highlighted interoperability as one of the security challenges associated with IoT.

Resource constraints are also one of the security challenges in an IoT environment. Different security measures, which could be used to secure IoT device communication such as the public key encryption algorithms and frequency hopping communication cannot be utilized due to the inability of the different IoT devices storage, capacity, bandwidth, and CPU shortcomings making securing an IoT network complicated.

5. SECURITY THREATS IN IOT SYSTEMS

Alshohoumi et al. (2019) conducted a study on the consideration of protection and privacy aspects in IoT architectures, which provides a broad overview of the security threats at different IoT architectural levels. The results revealed that current IoT architectures lack protection and privacy features. Data, as in other technologies, is the most important component of IoT. A review done by Alshohoumi et al. (2019) regarding the consideration of security and privacy aspects in IoT architectures gives a broad overview on the security threats at various IoT architectural levels. The findings showed that the existing IoT architectures lack security and privacy aspects. Similar to other technologies, data is the main component of IoT. The data gathered by sensors is saved, analyzed, and finally displayed to users. As a result, data security is an unavoidable requirement at each IoT layer.

The IoT architecture comprises the perception layer, the network layer, and the application layer (Aydos et al., 2019). The perception layer is responsible for the production of and collection data through the direct connection of the various devices. Network layer allows communication between IoT objects and IoT application servers. Application layer is responsible for the provision of user-specific application services. It defines a variety of IoT applications, such as Smart Homes, Smart Cities, and Smart Health, among others. There are various threats at each layer.

Findings identified Sniffer/Loggers and Injection as some application layer threats. Session Hijacking, Social Engineering, and Distributed Denial of Service are also application layer security threats. Network Layer threats include selective forwarding, Sybil attack, and the Blackhole Attack (Sinkhole). Other Network Layer threats include the Wormhole attack, which is a type of DoS attack, Man-in-the-Middle Attack that is a form of eavesdropping attack, the Hello-flood Attack, and the Acknowledgment Flooding attack.

Spoofing, Signal/Radio Jamming, and Node-capturing/Device-tampering as some of the Perception Layer attacks. Other Perception Layer security threats are Path-based DoS Attack, Node Outage, and Eavesdropping. Node Interruption attack is applied to the network in a logical or physical way.

6. SMART OFFICE DOMAIN

Smart Office, which is one of the IoT applications, have become a hotshot term. More and more companies are adopting solutions to transform their work environment into smart, interconnected, and hi-tech domain. Smart Office systems include office monitoring among other things and allows real-time communication within the various employees. Smart Office concept involves biometric, door-access, lighting, enlightening, and office heating.

Implementation of Smart Office does not only bring advantages but also comes with concerns regarding its convenience, controlling, security, and privacy. With the increase in the use of IoT Smart Office concept, various measures need to be established to ensure that the IoT Smart Office technology is secure.

Data security refers to the process of protecting data from unauthorized access and data corruption throughout its lifecycle. It is important to protect data from security threats. Cyber criminals, who usually make money through fraud or the sale of valuable information, are some of the threats to data security. Industrial rivals and foreign intelligence agencies seeking to gain economic benefit, hacktivists targeting companies for social or political purposes and staff, and those with legal access, either deliberately or unintentionally misused, are the purposes because the Smart Office data protection idea should be seriously addressed.

IoT data security threats have various impacts on the office applications. Data security is of supreme importance for Smart Office concept and so is the identification of the data security issues associated with the IoT devices and analyzing security weaknesses in existing Smart Office IoT devices and challenges. The identification of security threats will be beneficial in searching for solutions to the security problems troubling the implementation of the IoT in the Smart Office concept and work as a guideline for current and future developers designing devices for the Smart Office IoT.

7. THREAT FOCUS IN SMART OFFICE APPLICATIONS

According to Aleisa and Renaud (2017) most identified threats centered on personal details such as individuals' names, ages, and locations, which are commonly used by intruders to carry out attacks. Most of the current proposed data security threats identification models are mostly used for smart devices used in households or for health tracking, with only few being used for smart devices used in smart workplaces thus the need to design threat identification model for smart offices.

There are many more IoT constraints, features, and threats, which have not been covered, and could affect the security as stated in a study done by Zhou et al. (n.d.). To fill the gap, more research which will provide a more detailed analysis on the data security issues associated with the IoT devices and security in existing IoT devices with specific focus on Smart Office IoT devices is needed.

7.1. Possible Solutions to Security Threats in Smart Office Threats

There are many proposed solutions to IoT data security threats. These proposed methods include cryptographic techniques and information manipulation, or data minimization, to prevent data from being sniffed in the process of data exchange. A research confirms that penetration testing is vital in confirming the effectiveness or ineffectiveness of the security measures that have been implemented. Penetration testing technique is split into three stages: test preparation, test, and test analysis. Ensuring the security of IoT hardware is also important. This involves rigorous testing of the range, capacity, and latency of the IoT system. The importance in the usage of Intrusion Detection Systems and Intrusion prevention system was also highlighted.

8. CONCLUSION

Under the themes mentioned beforehand, it is clear from the literature reviewed that there are various security challenges in the application of IoT. Along with this, it is also clear that with the current architecture of IoT, there are several threats at each layer making the identification of the data security threats hard. There are several more IoT drawbacks, features, and risks which have not been discussed and may influence security and adaptation of IoT. While there are existing studies on IoT security threats in general, there are currently fewer Studies on the detection of security threats specifically for the IoT Smart Office.

REFERENCES

Aleisa, N., & Renaud, K. (2017, January 4–7). Privacy of the Internet of things: A systematic literature review. In *Proceedings of the 50th Hawaii international conference on system sciences* (pp. 5947–5956). https://doi.org/10.24251/hicss.2017.717

Al-sharekh, S. I., & Al-shqeerat, K. H. A. (2019). Security challenges and limitations in IoT environments. *International Journal of Computer Science and Network Security*, *19*(2), 193–199.

Alshohoumi, F., Sarrab, M., AlHamadani, A., & Al-Abri, D. (2019). Systematic review of existing IoT architectures security and privacy issues and concerns. *International Journal of Advanced Computer Science and Applications*, *10*(7), 232–251. https://doi.org/10.14569/ijacsa.2019.0100733

Aydos, M., Vural, Y., & Tekerek, A. (2019). Assessing risks and threats with layered approach to Internet of Things security. *Measurement and Control (United Kingdom)*, *52*(5–6), 338–353. https://doi.org/10.1177/0020294019837991

Helode, P. S., Walse, K. H., & Karande, M. U. (2017). An online secure social networking with friend discovery system. *International Journal of Innovative Research in Computer and Communication Engineering*, *5*(4), 8198–8205. https://doi.org/10.15680/IJIRCCE.2017

Zhou, W., Zhang, Y., & Liu, P. (n.d.). *The effect of IoT new features on security and privacy: New threats, existing solutions, and challenges yet to be solved*, Piscataway, NJ (pp. 1–11).

INDEX

Printed and bound by CPI Group (UK) Ltd, Croydon, CR0 4YY
15/09/2026
14962484-0006